Cross-Examination Skills for Law Students

Larry Pozner
Reilly Pozner LLP
A Litigation Practice
511 16th St., Suite 700
Denver, Colorado 80202
(303) 893-6100
lpozner@rplaw.com
www.rplaw.com

Roger J. Dodd
Spohrer & Dodd P.L.
701 W. Adams Street
Jacksonville, Florida 32204
(904) 309-6500
rdodd@sdlitigation.com
http://sdlitigation.com/

Dodd & Burnham P.C
P.O. Box 1066
Valdosta, Georgia 31603-1066
(229) 242-4470
rdodd@doddlaw.com
http://www.doddlaw.com/

First Edition

LexisNexis®

QUESTIONS ABOUT THIS PUBLICATION?

For CUSTOMER SERVICE ASSISTANCE concerning replacement pages, shipments, billing, reprint permission, or other matters,

please call Customer Service Department at 800-833-9844
email *customer.support@lexisnexis.com*
or visit our interactive customer service website at *www.lexisnexis.com/printcdsc*

For QUESTIONS or FEEDBACK concerning this publication,

please call: 800-446-3410 ext. 7522
or email: *lncps@lexisnexis.com*

For **information on other LEXISNEXIS MATTHEW BENDER publications**,

please call us at 800-223-1940
or visit our online bookstore at *www.lexisnexis.com/bookstore*

ISBN: 978-1-4224-5546-3

LexisNexis®

Matthew Bender & Company, Inc.
Editorial Offices
P.O. Box 7587
Charlottesville, VA 22906-7587
800-446-3410
www.lexisnexis.com

Product Number 6599510

(Pub. 65995)

ABOUT THE AUTHORS

LARRY POZNER began his career as a State Public Defender. He is Past President of the more than 10,000-member National Association of Criminal Defense Lawyers. He is a partner in the 21-lawyer Reilly Pozner LLP where he handles both criminal cases and protracted commercial cases. His practice includes consultation on the preparation and delivery of difficult or complex cross-examinations. Mr. Pozner is also litigation counsel to the Denver Broncos football franchise. He is co-author (with Roger J. Dodd) of America's best selling book on cross-examination, Cross-Examination: Science and Techniques, Second Edition (Lexis Nexis).

Mr. Pozner was the NBC News legal analyst for the Oklahoma City Bombing trials and the JonBenet Ramsey case. He is a nationally recognized legal commentator and is frequently seen on such shows as the NBC Nightly News, the Today Show, Fox News, CNN, and Court TV. Mr. Pozner has been listed in The Best Lawyers in America for 20 consecutive years and has been named a Colorado Super Lawyer every year since the inception of that list. He served many years on the faculty of the University of Denver College of Law, where he was voted Best Professor.

Reilly Pozner is a full-service trial firm, with experience in a broad range of litigation arenas from complex civil and commercial litigation and appellate work, to class actions, personal injury and mass tort litigation to criminal and white collar criminal defense.

Across the country, RP lawyers represent both plaintiffs and defendants, focusing primarily on matters that involve significant liability exposure, public visibility, and a high likelihood of going to trial. The firm's success on behalf of its clients stems from its fundamental orientation toward achieving victory at trial. RP's lawyers are regularly in court presenting cases and arguments to judges and jurors, and the firm approaches each case as if it will go to trial. That litigation posture pays dividends to clients, whether the ultimate resolution of their case is by settlement or verdict.

ROGER J. DODD: Spohrer & Dodd is a firm of trial attorneys singularly focused on representing clients' interests in challenging cases in Florida, nationally and internationally. We have a record of taking and successfully concluding complex cases against formidable opponents, often cases which other firms are unwilling to handle. Many cases come to us through law firms who partner with us to achieve the best possible outcome for the client. We undertake each case with a talented team of attorneys and staff, the firm's intellectual and financial resources, and our network of specialized experts.

As a partner in Spohrer and Dodd, a ten-lawyer firm, of Jacksonville, Florida, Roger J. Dodd and his partners are available to co-counsel cases throughout the United States in aviation accidents, trucking cases, medical malpractice and catastrophic personal injury and wrongful death cases.

Mr. Dodd is a frequent guest and commentator on Court TV and other legally-oriented programs. He has recently provided trial commentary on such programs as Good Morning America and Geraldo At Large. Mr. Dodd is co-author of the best-selling legal title ever published by LexisNexis, entitled: Cross-Examination: Science and Techniques. Listed among the nation's most elite lawyers in The Best Lawyers in America since 1991, Mr. Dodd has also been named a Georgia "Super Lawyer" every year since the program's inception in 2004.

Roger J. Dodd also maintains a practice in Georgia, Dodd & Burnham located in Valdosta, Georgia.

DEDICATION

To James W. Barley, for the person that he was, and to Matthew A. Dodd and Andrew J. Dodd, for the persons that they will become.

Roger J. Dodd
Spohrer & Dodd
Jacksonville, Florida

This law school edition of our book is dedicated to the trial lawyers in the making.

We too were students searching for a way to make ourselves into trial lawyers.

We too were full of questions and doubts.

We too struggled to find the techniques that would enable us to take on the momentous responsibility of protecting the rights of people and entities involved in litigation.

With those struggles firmly in mind I make special mention of a few people to whom I owe a special debt.

To Alan Dressler, San Francisco, California, my best friend and gambling partner in law school. Thank you for continually reminding me that what trial lawyers need to know is only rarely taught in the classroom. As a result we both graduated summa cum barely and we have both made a career as trial lawyers.

To the memory of Frank Simons, head of Colorado Springs office of the Colorado public defender system. Here was a kind and gentle person who displayed great patience with me at a time in my career when I mistakenly thought that strong advocacy meant loud advocacy.

To Steve Rench, former Training Director of the Colorado public defender system. You, were the one who first showed me how trial work is a completely interlocking set of skills rather than a hodgepodge of tricks performed in only vaguely related phases of a case. While I have had many fine teachers since, they all built upon the foundation you first provided.

To Dan Reilly, my partner, my friend. Thank you for convincing me to undertake the frightening breadth and complexity of civil cases. The creation and growth of our law firm stands for the proposition that members of a law firm, and their support staff, can and should enjoy their careers and their relationships with each other.

Larry Pozner
Reilly Pozner LLP
Denver, Colorado

FOREWORD

(Foreword to *Cross-Examination: Science and Techniques, Second Edition*)

This is simply the best book on the art and science of cross-examination ever written. Before I contemplate a major cross-examination in a criminal case or a deposition of a significant witness in a civil case, I literally go back to this book to stimulate my thinking. I give this book to all my law students, lawyers who work with me, and even my own children who have used it to great effect during their mock trial competitions during high school and college. Looping (on cross and direct), using trilogies, pyramiding trilogies upon trilogies, repeating a question to the witness who won't answer and other control techniques for the runaway witness, organizing by the chapter method, sequencing, and sliding off objections have all become indispensable concepts for teachers of trial practice.

Larry and Roger are wonderful teachers and terrific lawyers. But better still, they were smart enough to steal and refine all the good techniques employed by colleagues at the NACDL's National College of Criminal Defense Lawyers. We are all indebted for this marvelous piece of larceny because it takes real talent to organize and communicate the accumulated wisdom of your betters in an effective way.

When I began practicing law and teaching in law school more than 30 years ago, it was conventional wisdom that good cross-examination was the product of talent—it couldn't really be taught. The best one could do, following Irving Younger's Ten Commandments of Cross-Examination (which were really eight commandments), was to minimize one's losses. Larry Pozner and Roger Dodd have fundamentally changed the pedagogy. Good cross-examination, even great cross-examination, can be taught. Just follow the rules outlined in this seminal book and you can do better than just avoid disaster—you can win your case.

Barry Scheck
New York City, New York
October 28, 2004

ACKNOWLEDGMENTS

What seems like many years ago, my friend, Larry Pozner, came to me with the request that we should write a book about cross-examination. I laughed and told him that we knew how to talk not how to write. He insisted there was a need for the book.

After many long hours of discussion and persuasion, and many gallons of Dewar's White Label, it turned out that we were both right. We are better speakers than we are writers and there was a need for the book.

Roger J. Dodd

TABLE OF CONTENTS

Chapter 1

PHILOSOPHY AND OVERVIEW OF THE SCIENCE OF CROSS-EXAMINATION

§ 1.01 "Great" Cross-Examination: A Misleading Term

Success in cross-examination is an imprecise determination, but it can be judged by the accomplishment of the factual goals set out by the cross-examiner. Few cross-examinations accomplish every goal, but with the sound application of techniques, the advocate can expect to accomplish far more of her goals than would have been possible without the application of the science and techniques of cross-examination.

The science and techniques are not designed to make cross-examination into breathtaking adventures, but to simplify the difficult task of cross-examination. The cross-examiner must strive for the consistency of success that comes from preparation advanced by sound technique. There is an element of risk-taking in every cross-examination. Sound application of techniques can reduce but never extinguish the risks of cross-examination. A hallmark of great cross-examination is the systematic application of techniques to establish the greatest amount of helpful information while minimizing the risks inherent in cross-examination.

The primary object of cross-examination is to provide evidence that supports one's theory of the case. The secondary but closely related goal is to provide evidence that undermines the opponent's theory of the case. The advocate seeks to accomplish these goals while minimizing the ability of the witness to provide additional evidence that works against the dual goals of the cross-examiner. Note the word "additional." A repetition of harmful testimony does relatively little to harm the cross-examiner. It may be painful to listen to, and it may momentarily divert attention from our goals, but the true price of bad evidence is almost always fully paid on the first telling. The lawyer applies techniques to minimize a witness's opportunity to retell his story, as she does not need to hear it again and it interferes with her storytelling.

§ 1.02 Attaining Basic Competency in an Era of Fewer Trials

In the past, the popular conception was that trial skills, especially cross-examination, could be learned only in trial. Years of trial work were required before competency could be reached in the skill of cross-examination. The implication was that an indeterminate number of clients would suffer as the cross-examiner learned her trade.

This book flatly rejects that view as unrealistic and pessimistic. Maybe it was true in a different time. If so, this advice was probably based on a legal system that had room for an enormous number of short trials, built around relatively simple disputes, where comparatively little money was at stake.

There was a time when the courts were open to the small commercial or personal injury trial. With the advent of what is termed "tort reform" and the creation of tort thresholds that require a minimum amount of damage in order to bring a personal injury action, opportunities for small civil trials dried up.

The proliferation of professional mediation and arbitration services has led to the non-trial resolution of a substantial percentage of the cases that might well have ended up in a conventional jury trial. Yes, arbitration is akin to trial, but there is great disparity in how arbitration hearings are run. The rules of evidence can range from formal, to relaxed, to almost unrecognizable. The availability of discovery in most arbitrations is ordinarily far less than in a trial setting, which in turn affects the material available for the scripting of cross-examinations. In addition, there are the problems created by the lack of instructions of law in an arbitration setting. The instructions of law provide firm structure to jury deliberations and, to a lesser extent, to a judge who is sensitive to the important interplay between law and fact. Instructions of law are absent in most arbitrations. If we add the possibility that one or more of the arbitrators may not even be schooled in law, as for instance in arbitrations in the securities industry, it is fair to say that the common arbitration exercise is but a faint replica of a trial to a judge or jury. Overall, arbitrations are an inadequate arena in which to learn the skills of trial cross-examination, though arbitration is a suitable place to practice those learned trial skills.

In the criminal arena, the creation of public defender systems has had a profound but unintended consequence on the overall quality of a community's trial bar. Before the widespread creation of public defender systems, large numbers of lawyers in private practice were appointed to defend criminal cases. The advent of public defender systems in the 1970s meant that the vast majority of criminal cases were funneled into a much smaller pool of full-time criminal defense attorneys. While public defender systems greatly serve the interests of criminal justice, lawyers in private practice now have far fewer opportunities to establish or practice their trial skills in criminal cases.

Happily, trial is not the exclusive venue in which to learn the techniques of cross-examination. Trial work and cross-examination, in particular, call upon specific skills. And those skills can be acquired without sacrificing clients — or decades — to the task.

First, we can and must accept the premise that there are methods for the preparation and delivery of predictably successful cross-examinations. Cross-examination skills — indeed all trial skills, — are not the creations of nature but of nurture. Individuals are not born great cross-examiners, though they can certainly acquire the skills of great cross-examiners. The techniques upon which solid cross-examination results are built can be identified, explained and learned. Thus, trial lawyers willing to study and practice the science and techniques of modern cross-examination can dramatically improve their abilities as cross-examiners through methods that are not exclusively or even predominantly learned in the courtroom.

§ 1.03 Cross-Examination Is Designed to Teach, Not to Argue

Our role in the trial is much more teacher than persuader. We are dependent upon facts to win our case. As a result, our best strategy is to concentrate on the facts. The teaching of facts is the critical component of strong cross-examination. It is helpful to view the trial as a seminar on a particular event and the judge or jury as a class we seek to educate.

We dare not think that the jury is voting on who has the best lawyer. Jurors and judges are adept at separating that decision from who has the best case. The advocate calls upon the jury to vote on how well she has done in supporting her theory of the case. When the advocate accepts the burden to teach the facts that support her theory of the case, it reduces the self-imposed pressure to be the best lawyer in the courtroom. That mythical honor can go to someone else. She will have to be satisfied with just winning the case. The focus shifts from supporting one's ego to the ability to convey to listeners the facts that build the logical formation for one's theory of the case. Once the focus shifts from cross-examiner as lawyer to cross-examiner as teacher, the aim becomes conveying understandable information that guides the fact finder in real time.

§ 1.04 Re-thinking the Goals of Cross-Examination

Cross-examination has historically been viewed as an effort in damage control. The message many repeatedly receive is that cross-examination is a dangerous thing to be sharply limited, even forgone if possible. A corollary line of thinking has been that cross-examination is a form of legal combat. Cross-examination techniques were built around the largely false notion that cross-examination is a series of battles with the witness. For many decades cross-examination skills have been premised on the notion that a witness called by the opponent is only to be beaten down or minimized, and seldom to be gainfully employed as a provider of constructive information for the cross-examiner's theory of the case. It has been drummed into all trial lawyers that every witness called by the opponent is predisposed to obstruct the cross-examination by interruption, denial, and confusion. As a result of such advice, too many lawyers have come to believe that developing one's case through cross-examination is too emotionally arduous, too time consuming, and too risky to be attempted. The flip side of such a limited and negative view is the belief that it is easier, quicker, safer, and more effective to establish as many facts as possible through one's own witnesses. In short, the conventional wisdom has been that the trial lawyer ought to limit the goals of cross-examination and wait to establish the facts through a friendly witness who can be guided through a direct examination. The conventional wisdom is outmoded. It is counterproductive. It is wrong.

Fundamentally, cross-examination is a superb and often the superior opportunity to elicit favorable facts within their context so as to prove one's theory of the case. Once cross-examination is seen in this light, the goals of cross-examination are greatly expanded, as are the techniques necessary and available to accomplish them.

§ 1.05 Cross-Examination Is the Primary Method of Proving the Case

Why not use direct examination to teach the case? After all, the advocate can work with her own witnesses and certainly expect them to cooperate rather than resist her during direct examination. There are several answers. On the defense side of the case, the advocate cannot afford to wait until she can put her case on through direct examination. If she is on the plaintiff side of the case, she may well be calling for cross-examination of the opponent's witness to prove her case. There is the added problem that the more she saves for her own witnesses, the more they are burdened with the obligation to carry that side of the case. They are not the advocate's best witnesses. The advocate is. She knows the case best, and she is in the best position to carry the ball.

You are the best witness you can call. Cross-examination is the best time to take control of the courtroom dialogue. The leading question is the most reliable method to place your facts before the jury.

§ 1.06 Learning How to Get to the Goal

Somebody, in fact just about everybody, is going to tell an advocate that she should always keep control of the witness in cross-examination. You will not need this book in order to recognize when you lose control of a witness. So, while this advice is completely valid, it falls far short of providing a series of techniques that demonstrate *how* to control the witness, how to encourage short answers while discouraging long explanations or evasions, and most important, how to affirmatively use the opponent's witness to support one's theory of the case.

Similarly, we are instructed never to ask one question too many. But how will we recognize one question too many? Not to worry. At the exact moment we ask the witness that one question too many, we all recognize that we have done so.

And so you now see the issue: having cross-examination goals is not the same as learning how to reach those goals. Learning to recognize a problem is not equivalent to learning how to solve that problem. It is a decidedly inefficient form of instruction to educate lawyers to recognize when things have gone wrong unless we simultaneously teach methods to diminish the chances that things will go wrong. It is impossible to learn how to cross-examine by learning only what the lawyer must not do. It is equally impossible to become a better cross-examiner by being repeatedly told that control is essential, without being schooled in the techniques needed to establish and maintain witness control.

The good news: There exists a body of cross-examination techniques that greatly facilitate the lawyer's goal of controlling the witness during cross-examination. There are recognized techniques of cross-examination that will further the search for the truth more than the search for the opportunity to one-up the witness. There are techniques of preparation, sequencing questions, minimizing risk, and maximizing the impact of the best facts. These techniques are not built around personality or showmanship. We are not believers in and will not teach acting for lawyers. We do not conceive of trials as a contest of egos or showmanship. Trials are supposed to be about decision making based on the facts. Verdicts are to represent a decision on the evidence, not a referendum on the personalities of the opposing lawyers. If it were otherwise, we no longer have a system of justice, and our profession is reduced to fodder for reality shows.

Successful cross-examination is and ought to be the product of preparation and delivery of fact-based questioning, using techniques that are designed to encourage the witness to tell the truth and to allow the fact finder to understand the facts and their significance in this setting.

However, often the best techniques of cross-examination have been ignored or used only sporadically and inconsistently. Often cross-examination has been transformed into a demonstration of the ego of the cross-examiner, or as an opportunity to "beat" or "one-up" the witness. For too many lawyers, cross-examination has been viewed as a battle between two people rather than an avenue to prove one's case. These are neither the goals nor the necessary byproducts of good cross-examination.

§ 1.07 Identifying the Building Blocks of Successful Cross-Examinations

Of course, control is critical to the success of any cross-examination. The lawyer needs to control the topics upon which she will cross-examine. One can do so through the chapter method of cross-examination. (See chapter 5, *The Chapter Method of Cross-Examination*.)

The advocate needs to control the flow of facts she adduces from the witness. By understanding and following three rules of cross-examination, the advocate discovers that there are simple techniques that govern the formation of the questions in a modern cross-examination. (See chapter 4, *The Only Three Rules of Cross-Examination*).

The advocate needs to control herself. She needs to come to court equipped with easy, repeatable cross-examination techniques prepared properly for the hearing. The lawyer who organizes cross-examinations around a theory of the case (see chapter 2, *Developing a Theory of the Case*), through the use of the chapter method (see chapter 5, *The Chapter Method of Cross-Examination*), will become not merely a competent cross-examiner but a truly formidable cross-examiner.

The science and techniques of cross-examination do not operate on hunches. Valid techniques of witness control and factual exposition do not depend on oratorical tricks or showmanship. The move that causes a juror to love an advocate may be the move that causes another juror to view her as phony or as a trickster. Quite simply, when one resorts to trickery or showmanship, when one relies on a loud and angry voice to make a point, when one behaves aggressively in the hope that one will be thought of as an aggressive trial lawyer, it is very risky trial behavior. This alone is a problem. But the worse problem is that a lawyer engages in these risks without any way of gauging the rewards. If the advocate believes that her showmanship and force of personality can win one juror, then she must accept that the identical behavior can lose another juror. And one cannot know which result will be obtained. The advocate needs to develop a more dependable trial style. Clients deserve a well reasoned approach to trial advocacy. They hired lawyers more for their minds than their guts. If they didn't, they should have.

The science of cross-examination relies on the marshaling of facts in support of a series of clearly identified goals. One must initially recognize the importance of the formation of the questions that comprise a cross-examination. Cross-examination is made much easier and more effective simply by recognizing and acting on the understanding that good cross-examination questions are designed to efficiently introduce facts necessary to prove or support those goals. These techniques are aimed at bolstering a defined theory of the case or undermining the opponent's theory of the case.

The science of cross-examination equips the cross-examiner with the ability to predict where and how a witness will seek to evade and with techniques to limit those evasions and their effectiveness. This is not to say that the unknown or unexpected will be eliminated from the trial. The infinite variations of human behavior mean that the unpredictable will sometimes occur in cross-examination. But with solid cross-examination techniques, advocates can sharply reduce the likelihood that the witness will respond in an unpredictable or harmful fashion. Lawyers can prepare with techniques designed to take advantage of the unexpected answer, or to discourage the witness from volunteering unsolicited information.

§ 1.08 Constructive vs. Destructive Cross-Examination

Building one's theory of the case through cross-examination can be thought of as "constructive cross-examination." The more conventional, more frequently taught approach to cross-examination is as an attack on the opponent's theory of the case, frequently in the form of an attack on unfavorable testimony by that witness. This destructive approach we will term "confrontational cross-examination."

There is room for, and often the necessity for, both constructive and confrontational material within the cross-examination of any particular witness. Nothing in this book should be read to the contrary. However, the modern approach to cross-examination calls upon the lawyer to use the opponent's witnesses — at least in part — as if they were one's own witness.

When focusing solely on the destructive or confrontational aspects of cross-examination, advocates channel their preparation into areas of conflict with the witness. How can she impeach an answer, how can she demonstrate the bias of a witness, how can she show disbelief in their harmful assertions? This type of cross-examination is most often featured in the movies. It is dramatic. Scorn and ridicule almost drip from the cross-examiner's mouth. The phrases "Do you expect us to believe . . ." or "Are you telling this jury that . . ." are voiced or implied. And in the movies it works. Then these exaggerated mannerisms and insulting or argumentative tones and phrases are copied in a courtroom. In a real trial. By a real lawyer. And there such tactics do not work nearly so well.

Naturally, having been repeatedly exposed to such dramatic images advocates mistakenly think that this is the stuff of hard-core cross-examination. Lawyers come to believe that cross-examination is measured by one's domination of the witness. They may come to believe that the domination of the witness is rooted in a highly emotional and confrontational presentation. Then they go into court and find that, for so many reasons, this style does not work or, worse, is counterproductive. And they find that often they are not proving their case with their witnesses but setting up additional battles they must now win through their witnesses or — worse — setting themselves up for battles they do not need or cannot win.

Certainly, there are elements of an attack within some cross-examinations. Certainly, cross-examination can show that a witness's direct testimony is out of context, exaggerated, or simply false. Yes, cross-examination can offer an excellent opportunity to discredit the credibility of the witness. Yes, within a particular cross-examination there can be elements of high drama. But these are not the goals of cross-examination. They are merely byproducts of limited portions of a cross-examination.

So if domination of the witness by the lawyer is not the goal, what is? The primary goal of modern cross-examination is to provide evidence in an appropriate context that assists in establishing the cross-examiner's theory of the case. The secondary goal of cross-examination is to provide evidence to the fact finder that in its context undermines the opponent's theory of the case. While pursuing these fact-based objectives, the cross-examiner may simultaneously influence the fact finder's judgment concerning the credibility of a witness as to the facts testified to by the witness in both direct and cross-examination.

Setting emotions aside, cross-examination is a unique opportunity to build a theory of the case and insert helpful facts into the story. This relieves the cross-examiner of the burden of building a case solely through her witnesses and client.

The modern advocate must be prepared to expose and develop the truth of the case through witnesses called by the opponent. For reasons which we will discuss, cross-examination offers a superior opportunity to establish facts that will be accepted by the fact finder. It offers better tools to control the flow of facts. And, frequently, it offers an earlier opportunity to introduce the advocate's most favorable facts.

§ 1.09 No Damage = No Cross: An Outmoded Rule

The conventional wisdom of a generation ago was that if a witness had done no damage to the cross-examiner's case on direct examination, the lawyer should elect to ask no questions. That rule was completely defensive in nature. It viewed cross-examination under the premise that the cross-examiner would run unacceptable risks by the very asking of questions.

If no questions are asked, certainly the witness cannot repeat or add to the material provided in direct examination. However, even in circumstances where no damage has been done, it may be that the witness could testify to several additional facts that aid the cross-examiner's case. Thus, even the witness who has done no damage may need to be cross-examined. It is far better to view every witness as an opportunity to introduce testimony that supports the advocate's theory of the case. Simultaneously lawyers need to employ techniques designed to minimize opportunities for the witness to enhance his previous testimony or open new areas that will damage the cross-examiner's positions.

§ 1.10 When to Say "No Questions on Cross, Your Honor"

What then should the cross-examiner be asking if the opponent's witness on direct has neither hurt the cross-examiner nor given much support to the opponent's theory of the case? Cross-examination is always available in two areas. First and foremost, any fact that the witness can give on cross-examination that would support the cross-examiner's theory of the case should be considered. Second, any fact that hurts the opponent's theory of the case should be raised on cross-examination.

Cross-examination offers an excellent opportunity to affect the fact finders' judgment of the credibility of a witness, including the credibility of a witness who is not currently on the stand. It may be that in direct examination, the witness has said nothing that particularly hurts the cross-examiner's case. However, the witness may be able to testify to some fact that harms the credibility of another witness called by the opponent or that enhances the credibility of a witness a lawyer may call. All of this is to say that there may be areas of cross-examination that should be exploited even when the witness has done no damage on direct examination. Consequently, the times when the cross-examiner will utter the words, "No questions on cross-examination, Your Honor," will be few and very far between.

§ 1.11 Facts Established in Cross-Examination Are Likely to Be More Credible than Facts Adduced Through Your Own Witnesses

Assume that a fact could be established through the cross-examiner's own witness on direct examination or through the opponent's witness on cross-examination. We are not discussing facts that are in dispute, but facts that a witness on either side of the case is likely to admit. Most lawyers learned to reserve the question for the direct examination of one of their own witnesses. Following this guidance, the cross-examiner declines to elicit the information on cross-examination and must now prove a fact of significance through direct examination of her own witnesses. During that direct examination the jury will certainly understand that the witness is asserting a fact that helps the lawyer who called him. If the witness is a party, or closely aligned with a party to a lawsuit, the jury will see that the witness is, in essence, helping himself through the testimony. As a natural consequence, before the testimony is accepted the jury must first assess the credibility of the witness as to this factual point. However, if the cross-examiner elicits from the opponent's witness that same fact, it is likely that the jury will understand that the testimony is coming from a witness not aligned with the cross-examiner. Moreover, the more the witness is perceived as being aligned with the opponent, i.e. the side that originally called him, the jury will likely give the information greater credibility and weight. The jury's logic is that the witness would not give up that fact if it were untrue. This assumption is both correct and enormously helpful. As we can see, the same fact, introduced through cross-examination, will likely be more convincing with less danger of being doubted due to credibility issues.

There is additional value in establishing a fact through cross-examination rather than direct examination. Once a fact is admitted by the opponent's witness, the opponent is far less able to argue against belief in that testimony. As proof of this, think of what the opponent can say in closing argument should the cross-examiner prove a fact of importance through the direct examination of her own witness. The opponent would clearly be positioned to argue: "Witness X testified that the fact is Y. What would you expect that witness to say when called by the cross-examiner? That is just what she needed to say to help her case." Now let us reverse the scenario by using cross-examination to introduce that fact from the opponent's witness. If the opponent's own witness testified that the fact was Y, the opponent is not in a position to credibly argue: "My witness testified that the fact was Y. What would you expect my witness to say? Let me point out why my witness is not to be believed." By introducing facts through an opponent's witness we deprive the opponent of arguments against those facts.

Many questions on cross-examination are verbal requests for admissions. Once admitted by the other side, these requests are largely beyond dispute.

§ 1.12 Relationship of Cross-Examination to Anxiety and Confidence

We perform better when our confidence is high. When a cross-examiner is confident, words come easier. The thoughts come quicker. When a cross-examiner is confident, the goal appears attainable and thereby becomes more attainable.

For most of us, anxiety is part of the trial experience. This book cannot eliminate anxiety. But mastery of the techniques of cross-examination can substantially diminish a lawyer's anxiety during cross-examination. Advocates need to be mindful of anxiety not because of what it does to their bodies, but because of what it does to their minds.

Anxiety impedes the processing of information. This is its major debilitating effect. Anxiety interferes with thought processes and, in trial, this is an effect the advocate cannot afford. Especially during cross-examination, the lawyer needs to be completely focused on the complex job. She is forming questions, weighing the answers, and evaluating the witness's word choices, hesitations, and moods. She is simultaneously judging the value of the information she is receiving while progressing toward goals and options for her next question. She is doing all this while responding to objections, watching the jury, and searching for the right transcript or exhibit. The lawyer is busy. And each of these activities requires complex thinking. Cross-examination demands that one performs multiple mental tasks simultaneously. Anxiety interferes with the brain's ability to process the many abstractions, judgments, and facts that are the components of cross-examination.

The goal-oriented advocate simply cannot afford added anxiety. In fact, she needs techniques that lower anxiety. If she can use cross-examination techniques that lower her anxiety, she is mentally positioned to raise the level of her cross-examination.

§ 1.13 Effect of Anxiety on the Witness

Anxiety destroys confidence. Anxiety undermines confidence. Anxiety leads to frustration. Above all, anxiety impedes the processing of information.

This goes for witnesses, too.

Why do we care about this? Truthful testimony takes relatively little mental processing. The advocate asks a question. The witness gives a complete and truthful response. The lawyer should not hold her breath. This is not the cynic's view of trial, but the Anglo Saxon view. The right of cross-examination exists because our search for justice requires that it exist. We believe that lawyers for one side of the case will not willingly ask questions designed to reveal or explore facts that will be of assistance to the opponent's theory of the case. We also accept the reality that witnesses called by one side may well attempt to hide, distort, or fail to completely reveal all the facts if those facts might hurt their perceived side of the case.

Any deception on the part of a witness requires far more mental processing than is occasioned by fully and fairly answering the question. The witness needs to consider his prior answers, the facts he may have provided pretrial, whether in depositions, interviews, reports, emails. A witness calculating how to give less than the whole truth must consider what he believes other witnesses will say. And the witness will try to think through how any deceptive answer will change the answers he may have to give to succeeding questions. Which means the witness must also try to think of what the following questions will be.

This is a great deal of information to process, especially when we consider that the witness is on the stand, being questioned at this very moment. And anxiety impedes the processing of information. As a consequence, cross-examination techniques that ethically introduce anxiety in an opposing witness will interfere with the witness's ability to engage in the advanced processing required of people who are attempting to evade telling the truth, the whole truth, and nothing but the truth.

There may be opposing witnesses whom the advocate treats kindly and gently. There may be witnesses who will tell the truth if only the lawyer poses them the appropriate questions. For such witnesses, one need not induce any anxiety. There are no special or different techniques of cross-examination for such witnesses. The techniques of cross-examination that produce anxiety in the deceptive witness produce no such effect in the honest witness, who does not need extra time to process the myriad factors in deceptive responses. As the cooperative witness does not need additional time to consider his answers, the valid techniques of cross-examination for the hostile witness remain valid for the cooperative witness. It is only the effect of the techniques that changes, only because the mind-set of the witness changes.

There is an inverse ratio between the cross-examiner's anxiety level and that of the witness. When the cross-examiner's confidence is high, the witness's confidence tends to be low. When the cross-examiner's anxiety is high, the witness's anxiety is low. When a witness's anxiety is high and his confidence is low, he is more likely to blurt out the truth and less likely to engage in the careful word selection that masks the truth. The anxious witness unable to buy the time needed to process complex thoughts of deception is less likely to offer additional information to explain his position. He is less likely to volunteer new testimony. Ultimately the witness is less likely to tailor his testimony, whether in the obvious form of "lying" or in the less obvious form of carefully orchestrating his testimony to fit into the theory of the opponent's case.

With the three rules of cross-examination and other techniques in this text, the cross-examiner's confidence can remain at a high point while the witness's confidence may erode, replaced with anxiety. The three rules are designed to keep the lawyer's confidence high while keeping the anxiety level of the witness at a high level. Said a different way, the rules are designed to keep the lawyer's confidence high and her anxiety low, while keeping the anxiety of the witness high and his confidence low.

§ 1.14 Advantage of Cross-Examination-Centered Trial Preparation

When the major cross-examinations are thoroughly understood and prepared, the theory of the case becomes readily apparent to the jury. When the lawyer knows how she will cross-examine, the theme phrases of her case inevitably emerge. Preparation of the major cross-examinations of the case reveals the indisputable facts that the trial lawyer must address. The lawyer preparing for trial must also evaluate what facts will realistically be available to the other side through the direct testimony of her own witnesses. From this preparation of the major cross-examinations and analysis of the cross-examination of her witnesses, a stronger closing argument will develop.

As the advocate works backward from the planned cross-examinations, it will become easy to develop the powerful theory-driven, fact-intensive opening statement. From the opening statement flow the issues to be discussed with a jury in voir dire. A powerful closing argument flows naturally from the planned cross-examinations.

The direct examinations are then developed as enhancements and supplementation of the facts admitted through the cross-examinations. Instead of relying solely on the cross-examiner's own witnesses to support a theory of the case, the trial attorney views the opponent's witnesses as equal opportunities to develop her theory. (It must be noted that only prosecutors are saddled with the task of relying primarily on direct examinations to build their case. However, every technique discussed in this book is equally useful to a prosecutor faced with the important and difficult task of cross-examining the defendant or the witnesses called in support of the defendant, while armed with little or no discovery.)

§ 1.15 Preparation Enhances All Techniques

Preparation is still the single best trial technique. This book embraces this philosophy and therefore spends considerable time discussing methods and techniques for the preparation of cross-examinations. The chapter method of cross-examination builds upon the materials created through cross-examination preparation systems. This very focused approach to the drafting of cross-examination chapters translates to a dramatic reduction in the time required to find and catalogue useful facts, and a correspondingly dramatic reduction in the amount of time lost through haphazard searches through disorganized discovery and investigation materials. In addition, once we identify the areas in which cross-examination might be fruitful, we gain a focus that allows us to bypass large groupings of facts that are of relatively little or no significance to the competing theories of the case.

The techniques of cross-examination can both reduce associated risks from cross-examination and produce greater opportunities to establish favorable facts for the cross-examiner's theory of the case. A detailed analysis of impeachment techniques (see chapter 8, *Seven Steps of Impeachment by Inconsistent Statement*) and multiple techniques to control the runaway witness is presented in depth (see chapter 9, *Controlling the Runaway Witness*).

Having established and developed these building blocks of cross-examination, the book will then discuss techniques useful in the delivery of cross-examination (see chapter 10, *Loops, Double Loops, and Spontaneous Loops*).

§ 1.16 Maximizing the Value of Preparation

It must be emphasized that the preparation to perform a technique allows a lawyer to incorporate that technique into her trial skill set long before the technique is practiced in the courtroom. Once we learn these techniques, we own them. Instead of thinking of trial as the only place to learn how to do trial work, this book advocates that techniques be practiced before trial so that they will feel natural when used in trial. The preparation systems and cross-examination techniques discussed throughout this book can be practiced and learned outside of trial so that they can be employed easily in a trial. Like all other skills, cross-examination preparation and delivery systems are best mastered by repetition. The cross-examiner acquires the skills more quickly by practicing the techniques in non-trial hearings where witnesses must be examined through cross-examination. The more a lawyer practices these techniques outside of trial, the easier the lawyer will find it to use these techniques in trial.

§ 1.17 Time-Saving Aspects of Cross-Examination-Centered Preparation

Every lawyer wishes she had more time to prepare. In fact, the motion for a continuance becomes a critical motion in her arsenal. Preparation time is a commodity ordinarily in short supply. As a result, time, like the client's money, must be profitably spent. Less time wasted in the preparation of cross-examinations, direct examinations, opening statements, and closing arguments, is the equivalent of having more time. Using the chapter method of cross-examination-centered preparation greatly decreases the amount of time needed since areas not related to the opposing theories of the case are not explored. Whatever preparation time available is devoted to identifying and preparing for goals obtainable through cross-examination. Even in circumstances in which preparation time is severely limited, with understanding of the competing theories of the case, one can devote attention to the preparation of the chapters most likely to have the greatest effect on those theories. Using the three rules of cross-examination allows us to frame our cross-examination questions in a simple form which in turn reduces considerations about how to phrase our questions or in what order to place questions within a chapter.

§ 1.18 Preparation Leads to Greater Creativity

The systematic approach to cross-examination advanced throughout this book frees the cross-examiner to devote more time and creative energy to the presentation of cross-examination. A lawyer at the podium who is searching for the next area, trying to frame the next question, or who is trying to remember other facts that could be of use, is ill-equipped to rise to her greatest level of proficiency. A lawyer who approaches the cross-examination with facts organized in the chapter method is far more confident and therefore far more able to listen to answers and make spontaneous judgments concerning strategy, voice, pace, and movement.

The scientific approach to cross-examination frees the cross-examiner in a way that permits the cross-examiner to have the time and creative energy to utilize the more sophisticated techniques of cross-examination.

§ 1.19 Shorter Questions = Better Control, More Efficient Trials

When experienced cross-examiners are presented with the only three rules of cross-examination (see chapter 4, *The Only Three Rules of Cross-Examination*), and particularly the one fact per question rule, they often ask: "How do judges react to what appears to be a slow method of questioning?"

The answer is that judges increasingly embrace this form of presentation because the method actually speeds the flow of a trial. An organized cross-examination designed to accomplish a series of specific goals moves more quickly. There is purpose. There is rhythm. When questions are phrased in the concise, one-fact-per-question manner, the cross-examination actually moves faster. Each question isolates a particular fact to be answered. Where the open-ended question automatically invites a narrative answer, the short leading question isolates the fact to be discussed and invites a short answer. By forming groups of questions in the chapter method (see chapter 5, *The Chapter Method of Cross-Examination*), the advocate avoids skipping from one area to another and then skipping back to a partially developed topic requiring additional questions in order to be fully developed.

The rule of one new fact per question means that there are no compound questions, and therefore no objections to compound questions. The use of leading questions means that there is no real confusion on the part of the witness as to what was asked. Experienced trial judges recognize the difference in a trial conducted by a lawyer employing modern techniques of examining witnesses. Judges recognize that the cross-examination portion of the case moves with precision toward identifiable goals of importance.

By developing the witness examinations around an articulable theory of the case, the lawyer can establish clear-cut goals. She can develop those goals by a fact-by-fact method, so that the judge is not in the position of having to guess where the cross-examination is going, whether a goal has been reached, or whether certain facts have been developed that would support a conclusion to be argued in closing.

More often than not in non-jury settings, judges will advise cross-examiners to "break down the question into smaller parts" when a witness seems to have trouble answering a longer question. This is the same philosophy that gave birth to the one fact per question rule. Judges have praised this scientific approach, inasmuch as it eliminates rambling.

§ 1.20 Scientific Methods of Cross-Examination Interlock to Create a System of Cross-Examination

An important goal of this book is to provide an integrated, scientific method of cross-examination. The chapter method of cross-examination explains how the logical development of one chapter supports and interconnects with other chapters of cross-examination. The progress of each chapter makes it more likely that the subsequent chapters will produce favorable answers that are immediately understood and appreciated by the fact finder. The basic rules of cross-examination provide all the structure needed to employ the more advanced techniques of cross-examination. The scientific preparation of cross-examination supports the ability to control the field of cross-examination and thereby use the hostile witness to establish important facts.

The techniques of leading question formation support the cross-examiner's control of the witness. Each technique has a purpose and a place in the trial plan. The employment of a particular technique of cross-examination often provides the foundation for more advanced techniques.

In order to be usable and therefore valid, any trial technique must be both easy to learn and easy to replicate under the pressures of trial work. Any complicated technique is, by virtue of its difficulty, an invalid technique. Trial work is tough enough without introducing hyper-technical, rarely usable, or highly risky methods of cross-examination. Advanced cross-examination is often nothing more than the consistent recognition and use of cross-examination techniques appropriate to the situation. Because the problems of cross-examination repeat throughout the career of a lawyer, it only makes sense that the solutions to the problems should repeat. As a result, the techniques that allow a law student to engage in goal-directed, tightly controlled questioning of a witness are the same techniques used by veteran lawyers at the peak of their career. Undoubtedly, the comfort level of the cross-examiner may be different, but for that very reason it is critical that we all practice our trial techniques in non-trial situations, including depositions, motions hearing in which evidence is taken, and even silently in our heads as we think about cross-examinations we will need to do. Similarly, the fundamental principles of the chapter method of cross-examination do not change with experience or situation. While there is enormous room for customization of the science and techniques of cross-examination, and while the personality and style of individual lawyers will vary greatly, there remain a core of techniques that can serve us throughout an entire career.

§ 1.21 The Science of Cross-Examination Leads to More Success in Each Cross-Examination

Trial lawyers who rely on the basic building blocks of cross-examination can dramatically elevate the effectiveness of their cross-examinations. The goal of this book is not to help the advocate create a single beautiful cross-examination or develop the ability to occasionally devastate a witness on cross-examination but to raise the advocate's success rate in every cross-examination. By that we do not mean that more cross-examinations will be successful. We aim far higher. We mean that each cross-examination will be more successful in accomplishing the preselected goals that caused the lawyer to cross-examine that witness.

The overriding purpose of these techniques is to make the best use of the available facts, including facts that may become available only through a hostile witness. Consistent and confident execution of the basic techniques of cross-examination creates the aura of a devastating cross-examiner. But it is the facts that devastate, not the lawyer. And the devastation is to the case, not to the person. To make witness devastation a goal is to place the ego needs of a cross-examiner over the factual needs of the case. Cross-examination is not a contest between the witness and the lawyer. Cross-examination is simply another opportunity to build or teach a case.

Once we understand the techniques of modern cross-examination, including the science of cross-examination preparation, we are far better positioned to listen to the witness's answers, including their verbal and nonverbal cues. We can concentrate on the word selections of the witness rather than being consumed by the need to figure out where we are in our own examination, where should we go next in our questioning, what is our goal. When we are prepared with our chapters of cross-examination we are better positioned to take advantage of unexpected opportunities. Less time is spent considering what to ask and how to ask it, as those questions have been settled on by cross-examination preparation techniques (See chapter 3, *Cross-Examination Preparation: Topic Charts*, chapter 5, *The Chapter Method of Cross-Examination*, and chapter 6, *Page Preparation of Cross-Examination.*). Mastery of the techniques permits the cross-examiner to work with such confidence that the cross-examiner is now free to consider additional factors such as voice, movement and phraseology. Trial lawyers free the talent within by applying the scientific approach to cross-examination preparation and delivery.

§ 1.22 Adding Technique to Technique to Build Cross-Examination

We hesitate to use the phrase "advanced techniques." The truth is that the most advanced thing we can do in trial is to consistently use the appropriate techniques of cross-examination. Having said that, we can agree that certain techniques are used in every cross-examination and some techniques are used far less frequently. An example of the first is the consistent use of leading questions. An example of the latter is impeachment by omission. Both should be part of the trial lawyer's arsenal. What is important to recognize is that most cross-examination techniques make use of other previously learned techniques. Each technique builds in part on the others. A simple technique, once learned and mastered, supports other techniques. Once we can perform the techniques consistently, we raise the level of our cross examinations, we practice control of the witness, we learn to set the agenda for the cross-examination.

§ 1.23 Techniques Are Not Used to Accomplish Style Points

We speak much of the value of employing scientifically based techniques of cross-examination. A word of warning, however. It is the effect of the techniques that is sought, not recognition of the techniques themselves. The solid cross-examiner seeks results, not merely style points. Few of these techniques will be recognized for the skills that they are. The reward is that the lawyers, judges, witnesses, juries, and clients will recognize the products of good cross-examination.

The thought needed to assemble a group of cross-examination chapters will be lost on everyone else in the courtroom, save the cross-examiner. Observers should recognize that the cross-examination seemed to have order and matters of importance were developed in a logical method. The techniques of the chapter method may not be recognized, but the effect will not be lost on the jury. But we should not care if anyone notices or remarks on our use of a particular technique. It is not in the least necessary that others recognize the specific techniques. The greatest tribute to any cross-examiner is the verdict in favor of her client. The science and techniques set forth in this book assist in attaining that goal.

§ 1.24 Acknowledging the Difficulty of Cross-Examination

A final admission: Nothing in this book is meant to imply that cross-examination is easy. But it can be made easier. The preparation of cross-examination will always be time consuming, but preparation times can be shortened. Cross-examination can never be made perfect, but it can be made more productive. These things can be accomplished through systems of preparation and techniques of delivery. If, after considering the material in this book, these techniques remain unclear, the fault is with the authors, not the readers.

§ 1.25 Summary

Cross-examination is much more science and application of technique than it is art. The ability to cross-examine superbly (not just competently) can be taught, learned and practiced. This book is devoted to that task.

Chapter 2

DEVELOPING A THEORY OF THE CASE

§ 2.01 A Definition of a Theory of the Case

A theory of the case is a cogent statement of an advocate's position that justifies the verdict she is seeking. A theory of the case is not necessarily cast in the words that will be used with the jury, but words that are heard in the lawyer's mind as the case is prepared. The goal of the trial plan is to create factual support for the advocate's theory of the case. A secondary but important goal of the trial plan is to create factual attacks on the opponent's theory of the case.

Just as an artist paints a realistic picture from a fixed perspective, so must the lawyer prepare the case from the perspective of her theory of the case. If the advocate has no theory of the case, she has no unifying focal point to the various portions of the case, from voir dire through instructions. The theory of the case is not a strategy — it is a philosophy. It is the reasoning by which the advocate is entitled to the verdict she is seeking. The theory of the case is advanced through the trial strategy. That is, to say, all phases of the trial, from jury selection through closing argument, are executed in a manner designed to assist the fact finder in understanding and accepting the advocate's theory of the case.

The different phases of the trial interlock to advance the theory of the case. Jury selection is designed to acquaint the possible jurors with the theory of the case (to the real but limited extent that jury questioning can do so), to allow the possible jurors to discuss events in their lives that resonate with the advocate's theory of the case, and eventually to select as jurors those individuals who appear most inclined to accept the advocate's theory of the case. The opening statement must unambiguously communicate the advocate's theory of the case, outlining the facts that will support the theory. It is only a secondary goal of the opening statement to communicate facts that hurt the opponent's theory. The factual support for a lawyer's theory of the case comes through the examination of witnesses, whether on direct examination or cross-examination, and the introduction of exhibits. Closing argument allows the lawyer to again clearly articulate the theory of the case and to package for the fact finder the facts that support that theory of the case. In closing argument the lawyer is now positioned to discuss how the critical facts interact with the court's instructions of law to justify the verdict sought by the advocate.

The desired special instructions and the compulsory stock instructions of law are also a component of theory of the case. The instruction conference, although out of view of the jurors, is an important battleground over the theory of the case. Counsel seeks instructions of law that make the proven facts legally relevant to the verdict sought.

§ 2.02 A Theory of the Case Must Be Adopted Long Before Trial

Only by adopting a theory of the case can a lawyer prepare for trial. Only by following a theory of the case can a lawyer meaningfully conduct the component phases of a trial. Only by understanding a theory of the case can a fact finder appreciate the significance of the facts produced by an advocate and apply those facts to the instructions of law given by the court.

Trial advocacy begins well before the parties announce they are ready for trial. The lawyer has come to court to advocate a position, a view of what the facts mean. The lawyer needs to have settled on that position long before trial. The lawyer's position on the meaning of the facts, coupled with her position on how the law interprets the significance of those facts, may be thought of as the lawyer's theory of the case. For most of the trial, the lawyer will discuss the facts, leaving the interplay between fact and law largely for closing argument.

The law permits a lawyer to try a lawsuit even if the lawyer has failed to adopt a well-defined theory of the case. The law cannot require good advocacy, but the legal system certainly encourages and rewards good advocacy. Any lawyer is permitted to pick a jury, give an opening statement, examine and cross-examine witnesses, and give a closing argument. When a theory of the case is lacking, voir dire, opening statement, witness examinations, and closing argument are all seemingly unrelated elements of a trial. A lawyer may be technically proficient in the various aspects of trial but, lacking a unifying theory of the case, such a lawyer can win only style points, not the verdict. The verdict is more likely to favor the advocate who has provided the fact finder with a theory of the case and has armed the fact finder with the facts necessary to support that theory.

§ 2.03 The Best Theories of the Case Reflect Common Life Experiences

The best theories of the case are consistent with the ordinary life experiences of the jurors. By selectively refreshing those memories and emotions generated by ordinary experiences of the prospective jurors, we remind the fact finders that the dominant emotion of the case is one they too have felt under parallel (not necessarily similar) circumstances.

For instance, assume the case involves an allegation of breach of fiduciary duty. Few jurors can be counted on to understand the term and to have experience with it. However, many jurors have been in matters of importance felt let down by someone they counted on to guide them with superior knowledge. Given the opportunity to talk about that life experience, a prospective juror will recall the feeling of counting on somebody and the feeling of helplessness and even betrayal when their reliance on that person proved to be misplaced. An open-ended question in voir dire that allows a juror to talk about any such type of life experience may promote within that juror the dominant emotion of the plaintiff's case.

Assume an investment company is charged with intentionally failing to get its clients out of a failing investment. The defense is that the failure of the investment is obvious only in hindsight. A voir dire question might be: "Have you ever been second-guessed about a decision you made?" The lawyer is attempting to selectively refresh a memory of an episode in which the person did the best he could with the information he had, but through no fault of his own made an erroneous judgment. Worse, the person suffered criticism by people who were not fair and who did not have to make the judgments on the spot. Now, after the situation is all too clear, those parties perceive that the solution was obvious and clues were missed.

Any prospective juror who has endured such an unpleasant experience and who recalls that episode will immediately be put into the frame of mind that understands the defendant's theory of the case permeated with the dominant emotion of that theory.

§ 2.04 The Theory of the Case Guides the Trial Strategy

Only after the theory of the case is chosen can the lawyer craft a strategy that advances that theory. For this reason, a lawyer must adopt a theory of the case long in advance of trial, since both investigation and formal discovery, motion practice, pleadings, and virtually every other facet of pre-trial work should be designed to advance that specific theory.

Just as a lawyer may go to trial without a theory of the case, a lawyer could have a theory of the case but lack a strategy. Lawyers with a theory but with no strategy engage in questioning that is not goal oriented, or in a voir dire that deals with issues that have nothing to do with the issues to be tried. Such lawyers use closing argument to attack the testimony of witnesses as if the attack alone was the goal of the case. They fail to marshal the evidence in support of their particular theory of the case.

A theory of the case is the dominant concept that links all other aspects of the trial. By developing a theory of the case, counsel is able to define the field of battle. The theory tells the lawyer what battles must be fought and what issues are immaterial to the outcome. This overall philosophy guides the strategy of the trial. Its support is the goal of all trial tactics the trial lawyer adopts.

§ 2.05 Developing a First Draft Theory of the Case

It is very difficult to successfully try a case unguided by a theory of the case. It is not at all difficult to craft a theory. While an advocate's theory of the case may go through several refinements, in most situations, an advocate will begin developing a useful theory of the case upon first hearing the client's recitation of facts. Of course, this first client meeting can acquaint the lawyer with only a tiny fraction of the facts of the case, but the viewpoint of the client will likely lead to a rough formulation of the theory of the case. Whether it is, "I acted in self-defense," or "If they had told me the truth I never would have invested," or "He stole from Peter to pay Paul," or "We caught him cheating us so we fired him," the client can often articulate the starting point for the theory.. While the lawyer will refine the theory of the case over time, refinement is based on an analysis of the available facts integrated into the working theory of the case.

The first draft of the theory of the case may be stated as broadly as, "The doctor did not do the tests necessary to diagnose my client's illness" or "The doctor was in a hurry, and that is how the bowel got perforated during surgery." In commercial litigation, the initial attempt at a theory might be, "The landlord is hiding all kinds of unrelated expenses under the guise of common area maintenance fees, and thereby jacking up my client's rent." In criminal defense work, a review of the facts may lead to a theory such as, "The snitch was about to go to prison until he made up a story about the defendant confessing" or "It was the deceased who kept advancing, forcing my client to shoot in self-defense."

How can we draft the working theory of the case before most of the facts are known? Facts are best understood in relation to a proposed theory of the case. Without a theory, a fact may be understood but its significance may not be appreciated. It is the goal of the lawyer to package the facts in groupings that support a theory of the case and the points the lawyer wishes to make. Without a working theory, the lawyer may well recognize packages of facts that prove a conclusion. But that conclusion may be of no value in relationship to what will eventually be the theory of the case.

By way of example, assume a civil case in which the plaintiff real estate development company alleges that it was fraudulently induced to enter into a partnership with the defendant's real estate company based on repeated assertions by representatives of the defendant that the defendant company had great plans for the proposed development and should be trusted with the responsibility of managing it. Pretrial discovery reveals that the plaintiff's witnesses are vulnerable on their description of promises that were allegedly made to them, and by which of the defendant's representatives. One might think that a cross-examination demonstrating a lack of specific representations would be a profitable line of inquiry for the defense. However, if the defendant's theory of the case is that such representations were made, but circumstances led to the failure of the project, there is relatively little or no value to a series of cross-examinations designed to expose plaintiff's inability to cite specifics. Few lawyers have the resources to study every fact as if it is of equal importance. No lawyers have the time. By adopting a first draft theory of the case, the lawyer can review facts with a critical eye, better able to recognize the facts that are important and worth further development.

§ 2.06 A Theory of the Case Is Always Fact Dependent

Every theory of the case is factually driven. The vitality of a theory of the case is judged by the strength of the facts that support that particular theory coupled with the law that recognizes the consequences of the fact finder's belief in those facts. When lawyers say that they have a cold winner on the law, what they really mean is that they have facts of such high quality that a fair application of the law (the instructions) must inevitably lead to a successful verdict. (A lawyer claiming this has usually misjudged the strength of her case, but that is another matter.)

Although a theory of the case may begin its development based only upon a client interview, it must remain fluid in the face of changing facts. Developing facts may strengthen a theory, modify it, or extinguish its vitality. The process is a bit like the chicken and the egg riddle. What comes first? Does the advocate develop a theory of the case and then search for facts that support it, or does the advocate develop the facts and then fashion a theory to fit those facts? The answer is that the theory of the case is responsive to the facts, but it must be developed long before all or even most facts are known.

The case begins with a client with a problem. The problem must be understood before the trial lawyer can adopt a theory of the case. The trial lawyer must know the client's position before designing a trial plan to support that position. In most cases the client is able to articulate his position. For example:

- "I shot in self-defense."
- "I intended to pay for it but hadn't gotten to the checkout counter yet."
- "We fired him because he did bad work, not because of his age."
- "If he used the product the way it was intended this never would have happened."

So it goes from shoplifting cases to corporate antitrust actions, from drunk driving prosecutions to insurance premium class actions. The first interview is sufficient to arm the advocate with a working theory of the case. Trial counsel begins work based on that theory. The next step is to develop the facts that most aid that theory. The advocate also envisions the opponent's theory of the case. From this point forward, the lawyer's first priority is to gather facts that support that preferred theory and then to develop the facts that weaken the opponent's theory of the case. Inevitably, the facts that are gathered strengthen or weaken the combating theories. Theories respond to the facts available. The facts should not be forced into fitting a pre-selected theory. The theory may be tailored or discarded as factual development informs us that our initial theory is not well supported. Simultaneously, we must envision the opponent's theory of the case. In order to develop the destructive aspect of cross-examinations, we develop facts that will undermine the opponent's theory.

In analyzing facts, the lawyer needs to judge them for the inferences that can fairly be drawn from them. If more than one inference can be drawn from an anticipated fact, the lawyer is given greater leeway in developing her theory. If, on the other hand, only one clear inference can reasonably be drawn from a set of facts, the advocate must utilize that one inference as much as if the inference were itself a fact. The reality of trial work is that many facts can be viewed as helping both sides. It can be useful to adopt seemingly bad facts and incorporate them into the theory of the case. A good theory does not evade or ignore seemingly bad facts but accommodates them so that they can be seen as supporting the lawyer's theory of the case.

Once a theory is postulated, trial counsel will discover that many facts of the case are neutral, neither conflicting with nor supporting that theory. Such facts may provide context, but by themselves they are of no great importance. So long as the theory remains the same, the lawyer need not fight these facts or their inferences. However, if the theory is changed, the advocate must reanalyze facts first thought to be neutral to determine if they have now become negatives or positives to the new theory. Conversely, trial counsel must constantly scrutinize supposedly neutral facts to see if there is a way of utilizing those facts and the inferences to be drawn from them into the chosen theory. Throughout this process, the lawyer is often seeking to convert "neutral" facts into facts that support the theory. While the incorporation of neutral facts into the theory is a helpful goal, such facts are not the limiting or driving forces in theory development. The facts that most limit the lawyer in the development of a theory of the case are "facts beyond change." (See § 2.15 *et seq.*, below.)

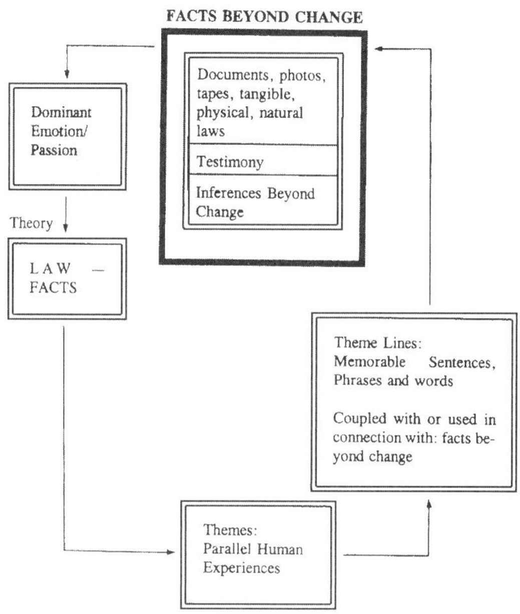

§ 2.07 Using a Mock Closing Argument as a Method to Shape a First Draft Theory

In order to develop a first draft theory of the case, it is helpful to think backward from the lawyer's conception of her closing argument. Upon first hearing the client's version of the facts, the advocate might ask, "If I had to argue the case right now, what would I say to a jury?" Undoubtedly the answer will lack the fine detail provided by discovery and trial, but the broad outline of the argument is apparent soon after meeting with the client.

As soon as the lawyer can begin making closing arguments in her head, the lawyer is on the way to developing a theory of the case. Others may find it easier to think in terms of cross-examinations to be made and to be defended against. It may be that the theory first developed is later modified or discarded. As she modifies the theory, the lawyer hears herself giving slightly different closing arguments. The case may not have dramatically changed, only the realization that other facts have taken on greater importance, and some facts believed to be very important are now less important or even unimportant. As the facts are developed before trial the lawyer better gauges her ability to successfully argue the proposed theory of the case. As facts that support the theory are developed, the advocate's case becomes stronger. As the advocate realizes there are insufficient facts to support her theory, or when she realizes that the facts available could be recast into a modified theory, the theory evolves and is strengthened. This is a natural process in pre-trial evolution of the case. Once trial commences it is extraordinarily difficult to change one's theory of the case. Certain facts may take on greater or lesser importance but once in trial the theory will remain the same.

§ 2.08 The Theory of the Case as a Guide to Discovery and Investigation

In civil litigation the two sides frequently have the right and the ability to engage in formal discovery processes including depositions, interrogatories, and requests of documents and items. A draft theory of the case is necessary to engage in a meaningful discovery process. The discovery process yields the most useful information for the smallest investment of time and money. Even if a lawyer has all the time and money necessary (a nonexistent state of affairs), the lawyer would not ordinarily choose to ask an opponent to produce all documents on every conceivable issue. The result would be thousands of computer files and emails. Instead, the advocate first formulates a theory of the case before envisioning what types of documents might exist to support that theory, and which witnesses need to be deposed to prepare for the likely cross-examinations on that theory of the case and on the opponent's theory. It is the contrasting theories of the case that drive pre-trial preparation, including the conceptualization of the cross-examinations necessary and available.

§ 2.09 Civil Theories Must Encompass Liability, Proximate Causation, and Damages

Civil cases have theories that encompass liability, proximate causation, and damages, though sometimes one or more of these issues may not be disputed. It is critical that the lawyer spend time on the area of the case that represents the greatest chance of success. In a commercial case, the plaintiff's theory of the case may be stated as: "The defendant stole my software program and cost me millions of dollars." The defense might counter with an initial theory of the case: "We did not steal your software program (denial of liability) coupled with "Your software was of very little value" (an attack on damages). There are two theories at work, and both may deserve complete development. But there are those cases where the lawyer's honest appraisal is that a jury is likely to conclude that there was a misappropriation of the software, though the software may have had little value. In such a case, the lawyer may well go to trial contesting both liability and damages, but the lawyer would be well advised to devote the majority of discovery and investigation effort to the development of facts that support the lawyer's theory of the case that damages are minimal to nonexistent.

§ 2.10 Relationship of Theory to the Likely Standard or Uniform Instructions of Law

When adopting a theory of the case, counsel must be cognizant of the applicable law. A successful theory of the case must be consistent with both the law and the facts. In fact, a theory of the case describes counsel's position on how the facts and law come together to justify the outcome sought.

A successful theory of the case incorporates the likely instructions of law likely to be given. In every case there are predictable standards or uniform instructions of law that the lawyer can anticipate in her first moments of work on the case. A review of the judge's standard or uniform charge book will make obvious certain instructions that will be given. In developing a theory of the case, the lawyer must be mindful of these stock instructions, as they guide the conceptualization of the law of the lawyer's case theory.

A theory of the case that has great emotional appeal but lacks support in the instructions is destined to fail. The advocate cannot adopt a theory simply because it can be argued with great emotion or even because it incorporates the best facts available. Those facts must be made relevant by the applicable law. The power of a fact stems primarily from its legal significance as defined by the instructions, its logical ability to support the advocate's theory or, alternatively, its logic that might undermine the opponent's theory of the case. If the fact is otherwise significant in the context of both the instructions of law and the theory of the case, then its emotional impact will enhance the value of that fact. But, lacking legal relevance and a tie to the theory, a highly emotional fact may bother a fact finder but not compel the decision.

For instance, there are uniform instructions on the credibility of witnesses, the burden of proof, and the elements of every tort. It is useful for the advocate to gather the uniform instructions that are likely to apply to the case. This task is not too time-consuming but helps enormously in developing a theory of the case. The earlier it is done, the better. In both criminal and civil actions, uniform instructions tell the lawyer what the party must prove. A failure to prove any one of the elements of the crime or the cause of action must result in a defense verdict on that claim. Thus the prosecution or the plaintiff must adopt a theory of the case that incorporates these legal requirements.

§ 2.11 Instructions That Are the Basis of Certain Theories

Uniform or stock instructions alone are the bedrock of some theories, especially in criminal cases, where the burden of proof is upon the government to prove guilt beyond a reasonable doubt. The credibility of prosecution witnesses is often the chief issue in contention. In these cases, the instruction on the credibility of witnesses is a required instruction. A sample of that instruction:

Credibility of Witnesses

> You may have to decide what testimony to believe. You should carefully consider all of the testimony given and the circumstances under which each witness has testified.
>
> Consider each witness's knowledge, motive, state of mind, demeanor, and manner while on the stand. Consider the witness's means of knowledge, ability to observe, and strength of memory. Consider also any relationship each witness may have to either side of the case; the manner in which each witness might be affected by the verdict; and the extent to which, if at all, each witness is either supported or contradicted by other evidence in the case. You should consider all facts and circumstances shown by the evidence which affects the credibility of the witness' testimony.
>
> You may believe all the testimony of a witness, or part of it, or none of it.

Colo. JI: Crim. 3:06.

In a case in which the theory of the case is, in its most general terms, "misidentification," this credibility of witness instruction is of tremendous assistance. It instructs the jury that inconsistencies in a witness's testimony can themselves produce a reasonable doubt. Although the lawyer must do a great deal more work to flesh out the theory of the case by making it more precise and descriptive of facts than "misidentification," the ultimate theory is greatly assisted by this uniform instruction.

Similarly, if it is to be argued that a witness has intentionally lied about a material fact, many states have an instruction that warns jurors that a witness who was found to be lying in one aspect of his testimony can be disregarded in all other aspects of his testimony. This instruction applies to all types of cases.

The elements of the cause of action are essential building blocks in both the plaintiff and defense sides of civil litigation. If the plaintiff's theory of the case involves fraud by the omission to disclose critical facts to an investor, the stock instruction on that issue might read as follows:

Elements of Fraud

> 1. Elements. The plaintiff must prove by the greater weight of the evidence each of the following elements:
>
> (A)(1) A false representation of fact was made with knowledge of its falsity or with utter disregard and recklessness about its falsity that knowledge may be (concluded) (found).
>
> (or)
>
> (A)(2) A knowing concealment of fact which was done (when) (where) there was a duty to disclose.

(and)

(B) The (representation) (concealment) was material to the transaction.

(C) The (representation) (concealment) was made with the intent of misleading plaintiff into relying upon it.

(D) The plaintiff was justified in relying on the (representation) (concealment), and did, in fact, so rely.

(E) The plaintiff was injured and the injury was (proximately) (directly) caused by his reliance on the (representation) (concealment).

3 Ohio JI 307.03.

Having settled on fraudulent omission as the centerpiece of the theory of the case, and armed with the stock instruction given on that issue, it is apparent that the cross-examinations will almost certainly have to focus on the material known to the defendant, and the defendant's recognition of its importance and failure to disclose the material information.

Again, the lesson is that we need to develop our theory of the case and then research the instructions that apply to that theory. Legal research, like factual investigation, is driven by theory, not by curiosity.

§ 2.12 Vague Theories: A Roadmap to Disaster

While the theory of the case cannot be an elaborate position on all facts, it is more than a conclusory statement such as, "There exists reasonable doubt" or "Plaintiff has proved her case by a preponderance of the evidence." Or even, "The plaintiff has proved the defendant drove negligently, which caused the accident and thereby injured the plaintiff." Such theories are too vague to serve as a focusing mechanism for winning trial strategies. As will be later discussed (see chapter 4, *The Only Three Rules of Cross-Examination* and chapter 5, *The Chapter Method of Cross-Examination*), conclusory statements create no pictures. People remember cases by their mental images. The powerful theory of the case should be stated in such a way as to create a mental image that is favorable to the proponent of that theory.

Conclusory statements cannot be used as a substitute for a theory of the case. We cannot build a theory around words like "injury" or "bad driving conditions." Similarly, a theory of the case should not be stated in legalisms, such as "negligence" or "breach of fiduciary duty." There is nothing remotely memorable about such a "theory" because it conveys only an abstract idea. Such statements do not conjure up an image of the facts — any image that jurors create for themselves is not under the control of the lawyer. Legalisms do not compel a juror to any emotion or passion nor do they remind the jurors of any parallel human experience. The successful theory must be case specific. Jurors need some handle on how the facts of this particular case compel a particular decision. In the absence of such specificity, there truly is no theory of the case. Therefore, the lawyer is incapable of identifying what facts will underscore the chosen theory.

In criminal cases, the ultimate non-theory is: "The defendant is not guilty." This is no theory at all, but a purely conclusory statement. Theories such as "The evidence does not prove guilt beyond a reasonable doubt" offer no guidance as to the critical facts to be produced in cross-examination. Such a conclusory statement creates no mental image. It does not assist the jurors in recalling any particular facts of the case. Neither does this naked conclusion assist the lawyer in excluding facts or areas that are irrelevant to the theory.

The theory of the case must be factually specific enough to narrow the scope of the cross-examinations the lawyer needs to deliver and to provide a sense of direction for each of the components of the cross-examination (see chapter 5, *The Chapter Method of Cross-Examination*). The theory of the case must also be vivid enough to allow jurors to integrate the facts they are going to hear in the cross-examination into a theory of the case that they understand. In other words, the fact finder must understand the theory of the case so that an answer (fact) can be immediately appreciated in the context of that theory of the case. It is the goal of the trial lawyer to place a theory of the case before the fact finder with sufficient detail so that the answers elicited on cross-examination can immediately be appreciated for their effect on the advocate's theory of the case.

When a vague theory is created, the case is adrift. If vague theories are bad, having no theory is far worse. We cannot be deluded into thinking that by adopting or advancing no theory, we have created ultimate trial flexibility. By leaving open any course of action, the lawyer compels herself to follow no particular course of action. Cross-examinations without goals wander. Cross-examination becomes a series of unrelated attacks on the witness or an unfocused discovery device.

When a theory drifts, cross-examinations lack focus and jurors become confused about what the lawyer is trying to prove. Since the jurors do not comprehend the goal, they cannot tell whether the goal has been achieved. Juries do not vote for what they do not understand. Juries do not vote in favor of confusion. The advocate's lack of clarity in advancing a theory is likely to be penalized by the jury's verdict. The theory of the case must be understood so that the fact finder can choose to adopt it. It is inappropriate and unrealistic to ask the fact finder to assemble the facts into their own theory of the case.

§ 2.13 Using Words and Voice That Fit Theory

Too often cross-examination is pictured as a chance for the lawyer to rip into the witness. TV and movies distort the trial process and overly dramatize the courtroom scenes. It is best to conceptualize cross-examination as a conversation with the witness rather than as a confrontation. The power of the cross-examination lies in the information conveyed, not the style of the lawyer. Trial work is and should be about the facts. One of the most interesting aspects of trial work is that everything in a courtroom is magnified. The fact finder is interested in the case, and there are no alternative forms of entertainment in the room. A juror's mind may wander, but not for long and not very far.

As a result, by far the safest voice in a courtroom is a normal voice. Emphasis can more safely be added by speaking in a softer voice rather than a louder voice. That being said, there is room for appropriate methods of voice or mood modulation. Every theory of the case has its own emotional level. The cross-examination of the lying witness has an entirely separate emotion from the cross-examination of the mistaken witness. Entrapment in a drug case involving a young defendant allows more of a self-righteous indignation than does self-defense that leads to the death of another. On the civil side, defense of an auto accident case resulting in fatalities must be keyed at a lower emotional level than a defense in which no one is hurt.

In determining the appropriate voice or emotion, the cross-examiner must factor in the jury's perceptions of the witness, the mood the lawyer wishes to create within the courtroom, and the emotional content of the theory of the case. When in doubt, the cross-examiner is better served by less emotion. The jurors' perceptions of a witness are important and, to a great extent, predictable. A witness who is indeed the victim of a crime will arouse the jury's sympathy. While that witness might be proven to be mistaken, the method of proof must be gentler because the witness has already been victimized. The jury will not tolerate a second victimization. Children and the elderly are psychologically protected by the jurors. While they may be discredited, it must be done with subtlety and gentleness. The witness must be left with self-respect.

On the other hand, the witness who would lie is perceived by the jurors as fair game for far more punishing cross-examination. The mood can be more aggressive, though the words and voice tone must still be within the bounds of courtroom decorum. The cross-examinations may be more abrupt, the pace of questions can be quicker, and control in general can appear to be tighter.

While the jurors will not protect an expert witness, they expect experts to be treated with a degree of professional respect. Conversely, because the expert is expected to be able to fend for herself, questioning can be vigorous, and control can be tight (and appear to be tight). In general, a more intense emotional level of cross-examination can be tolerated than with that of a sympathetic lay witness.

§ 2.14 Cross-Examination Is a Critical Opportunity to Advance a Theory of the Case

Cross-examination is not performed to earn style points or to prove that the lawyer can control the witness. And cross-examination does not occur simply because a direct examination has been concluded. The lawyer does not cross-examine because she has the right to do so but because she needs to do so. She cross-examines not simply to disprove a point. Cross-examination offers her superb opportunities to advance her theory of the case. The lawyer needs to advance her theory of the case throughout trial. Cross-examination is not simply another opportunity to establish facts that support her theory of the case. It is ordinarily the best opportunity to establish one's theory.

§ 2.15 Facts Beyond Change — A Definition

Facts beyond change are the givens of a lawsuit — facts that will be believed by the jury to be fair, accurate, and relevant regardless of a lawyer's best efforts to dispute or modify them. In a positive sense, facts beyond change are the structure that supports and channels the theory. The negative aspect of facts beyond change is that they limit the possible theories of the case.

Any successful theory of the case must either incorporate all facts beyond change, or be neutral to them. That is, a theory must either build upon the facts beyond change, or stand in harmony with them. A successful theory of the case can never contradict a fact beyond change because, if the fact finder is confronted with a theory and an actuality (a fact beyond change), and the two cannot exist simultaneously — the fact finder must decide the case in accordance with the actuality (the fact beyond change).

Remember, a fact beyond change is one that will not be diminished by an effective cross-examination. If cross-examination can affect the fact finder's perception that the fact is fair or accurate or relevant, the fact is capable of dispute and is no longer a fact beyond change.

§ 2.16 Theories Must Accommodate Facts Beyond Change

It is the theory of the case that accommodates the facts beyond change, not vice versa. Facts create, support, limit and extinguish theories. The facts come first, and the theory follows. But once a theory is postulated, it must make use of facts. A theory of the case can make a fact important, but a theory cannot create facts. Of course, discovery and investigation are designed to uncover the facts that breathe life into a theory. Once a theory has been adopted, some facts become more important than others. The facts are not changing, only their value relative to the theory. The theory of the case allows the fact finder a framework in which to understand the facts. Without a theory of the case the fact finder might hear the answer but not understand its significance. With the aid of a theory, the fact finder can immediately integrate an answer into the decision-making process. As a result while the facts do not change, their impact upon a jury is changed depending on the theory advanced by the advocate. In order to gain the value of a theory, the fact finder must understand the theory before cross-examinations begin. Explanations in closing argument of the importance of facts come too late to achieve full advantage of the facts.

While a theory of the case may make a fact beyond change less relevant, or perhaps even irrelevant, its relevance is revitalized as soon as the theory contradicts the fact. A theory that contradicts a fact beyond change is fatally wounded. A successful theory of the case cannot beg the fact finder to ignore believable facts. Advocates may show the fact finder why the facts either support the theory (positive), or do not harm the theory (neutral). An advocate can never successfully argue against facts beyond change.

The advocate is reminded that a fact beyond change that is productive of alternative inferences, one of which supports the advocate's theory, is a fact not at odds with the theory of the case. It is for the advocate to establish the likelihood that the favorable inference is more accurate. In order to win the battle of alternative inferences, cross-examination is used to bring out additional facts that relate to the fact beyond change.

§ 2.17 A Quick Guide to Finding Facts Beyond Change

One of the most important aspects of developing a theory of the case is the recognition of the relevant facts beyond change. Once these facts beyond change are found, the vitality of a proposed theory quickly advances or recedes. As a starting place to find facts beyond change, we should scrutinize documents, photographs, videotapes, audiotapes, and other exhibits or tangible items. What do the exhibits undisputably say? For instance, in a contract case, the contract itself is likely to be a fact beyond change. Its meaning may be debated, but the document itself is likely to be the starting point for many theories and the destruction or limitation of other theories. Tangible items are not the only place facts beyond change can be found, but they are a good starting place.

Historical facts are also facts beyond change. When history records that an event occurred, it is a fact beyond change, though the significance of that event may still be argued. While the interpretations of such items may be argued, often the existence of the item itself enormously influences the available theories.

Historical events may be facts beyond change of great relevance to a theory of the case. For instance, the price of natural gas ballooned up in the early 1980s, and then, from 1984 to 1988 it fell to a fraction of its highest price. In the face of these dramatically declining prices, the federal government repealed several gas pricing regulations. In the face of these unprecedented events, many purchasers of gas declined to live up to their purchase contracts, which contained imbedded high gas prices. Lawsuits abounded. In defense of their actions, the purchasers made great use of these historical events which were facts beyond change.

§ 2.18 The Initial Search for Facts Beyond Change

Sources of facts beyond change include, but are certainly not limited to, documents, photographs, scientific tests, other tangible items, and the laws of nature. These facts are less disputable than witness testimony, which is subject to human frailties. That is not to say that test results must be accepted as infallible; they are not. Once verified, they are more likely to be accepted by a jury as a fact beyond change. In a civil case, if appropriate investigation determines that the client's car left 96 feet of skid marks before impact, the fact is indeed 96 feet. There may be room to interpret the meaning of the skids, but a theory of the case that relies on the client never applying her brakes is simply not viable. The client obviously saw, heard, or perceived something, hit her brakes for some reason, and left the 96 feet of skid marks. That is a fact beyond change. It will not go away. The theory must incorporate or accommodate it.

In a contract case, assume that all agree that the document that represents the contract is not fraudulent. Consequently, the words of the document become facts beyond change. One may seek different interpretations of the words, but there will be no room to assert that the document does not exist, or that the parties did not sign it. The existence of the contract becomes a given of the case — a fact beyond change. It serves to limit possible theories of the case for the advocate who seeks to dispute it. A successful theory must incorporate this fact as positive to the theory or make that fact neutral by accommodation.

§ 2.19 Neutral Facts Beyond Change

In any lawsuit, there are literally thousands of facts beyond change, but most have no particular relevance to the case. For instance, in a certain case, it may be completely indisputable, yet wholly irrelevant, that an event happened at night, or that it happened in the city, or that it happened on a Tuesday. On the other hand, these same facts may be critical if the day, date, or time is important to either you or your opponent's theory of the case. While these may be facts beyond change, if they have no consequence to the case, they neither compel nor prohibit a particular theory.

§ 2.20 How Facts Beyond Change Affect a Theory

A relevant fact beyond change limits the available theories of the case only to the extent that the fact beyond change impacts a particular theory. A fact may be a bad fact, but it may leave open inferences necessary to support a theory of the case. For example, take the case of a blood alcohol test of the defendant taken shortly after a car accident. The relevance of that fact may be judged only in comparison to a particular theory of the case. The initial hypothesis of the defense case might be based on the assumption that the lab work quantifying the defendant's blood alcohol level can be successfully challenged. If this is true, the blood alcohol level is no longer a fact beyond change. If, however, after diligent research and preparation, the criminal defense or civil lawyer comes to the conclusion that the blood work will indeed be accepted as that of the defendant, and that the test was correctly performed, then the blood alcohol level becomes a fact beyond change. The cross-examiner may have available a series of questions concerning other, better tests that could have been done, or chain of custody issues, but such questions are not useful. To ignore this while developing the theory is self-deceptive and case-destructive.

This same fact beyond change, the blood alcohol level of the defendant, is of far less importance if the defense is that this defendant was not the driver.

Alternatively, if the defense is that the driving conduct of the defendant did not cause the accident, acceptance of the BAC as a fact beyond change still leaves the lawyer with room to argue the chosen theory of the case. Thus, even the acceptance of a fact beyond change may leave ample room to craft a successful theory of the case.

§ 2.21 Incorporating Facts Beyond Change into a Theory of the Case

The best theories, meaning theories of the case most likely to succeed, are built upon facts beyond change. Facts beyond change capable of admission that clearly support the advocate's theory are the safest facts upon which to build a theory of the case. Note that the opponent also must seek to accommodate these facts beyond change into her theory or face the inevitable failure when facts beyond change contradict theory.

In developing a theory of the case, it is vital that all information be searched for facts beyond change that could possibly bolster the proposed theory. To the extent that a theory rests on facts beyond change, an advocate puts an opponent in the position of having to respond to her theory of the case. The opponent must now either craft a theory of the case that is dependent upon the disbelief of the advocate's facts beyond change (and in so doing, the opponent must fail if the facts beyond change are truly facts beyond change), or the opponent must craft a theory of her case that accommodates the facts beyond change developed by the advocate. An adversary who fails to face up to an opponent's facts beyond change in adopting her own theory is doomed. The adversary will be forced to argue a theory that can succeed only if a jury does not believe a fact beyond change. In other words, she must ask a jury to be illogical or ignore facts that will be perceived as both accurate and relevant. This is too much to ask of the jury.

As an example in a civil case, assume that there is an automobile accident. The defendant struck the plaintiff's slower truck from behind. The defendant admits the truck was slower, admits that she saw it, and admits it was properly in the right-hand lane. It would appear that liability is clear based on these facts beyond change. But the defendant also shows that another car, going much faster, forced her back into the right lane after she began to pass the truck. Now those same facts beyond change might be inconsistent with the plaintiff's theory of the case.

Every case contains both positive and negative facts beyond change. Facts that initially appear positive or negative should be studied to see how they can be integrated into the advocate's theory and how they will likely be employed by the opponent.

Assume the search of a defendant yields drugs. Assume that the entire issue is whether the defendant consented to a search of her suitcase. In addition, assume the following facts beyond change: When the defendant was first stopped, she protested. She refused to sign a "Miranda" form. The officers never advised her of her right to leave without being searched. She offered some minimal physical resistance. She pulled her suitcase towards her. At no time did she manifest an attitude of cooperation.

While the officers will always testify that they had consent (itself a conclusion), these additional facts beyond change can create an unmistakable picture of a lack of cooperation. These detailed facts make the officers' assertion of her cooperation less credible. As this example shows, starting with facts beyond change, the lawyer may craft a motion to suppress and argue favorable inferences from what first appeared to be negative facts beyond change.

Assume, in a domestic relations case, the wife alleges that the husband had a chronic drinking problem for the last six years of their marriage. This may first be viewed as a negative fact beyond change in the case. However, this fact may be coupled with the additional facts beyond change, such as the husband was passed over for promotion just prior to the time his drinking problem began, and that the husband continued to do poorly financially for the remaining six years of the marriage until the filing of the divorce decree. While some would argue that the drinking problem is a negative fact, it may be viewed favorably in the context of being able to show the fact finder that this husband has not and cannot produce sufficient income to pay the alimony requested by the wife.

In a homicide case in which the defendant is accused of second-degree murder, the coroner's report showing five bullet wounds to the deceased is a negative fact beyond change to a self-defense theory. The same coroner report shows that all of the wounds are contact or near contact. This may at first appear to be a very negative fact beyond change. However, in comparing the bullet wounds to the defendant's statement to the police that the victim had jumped on him and was on top of him when the defendant fired upward into him, the coroner's report is in accordance with the statement. The facts beyond change, while not pleasing, are consistent with the defendant's statement. The defense can accept the coroner's findings and still maintain the chosen defense theory.

In this sense, the angle of the wounds and the distance from which the bullets were fired are not now negative facts beyond change, but positive facts beyond change. It is dependent upon the manner, perspective, or context in which the facts are viewed. A slightly different manner, perspective, or context changes the same "fact" from negative to positive. This view of the facts permits the lawyer to argue to the jury that the defendant, if he made up this story, could not have come up with a version that would fit a coroner's report created weeks later. The coroner's report, initially thought to contain numerous bad facts beyond change, in essence now verifies the truthfulness of the defendant's version.

§ 2.22 Facts Beyond Change Are Proven in Cross-Examinations

It is in cross-examination rather than direct examination that the facts beyond change are best proven. A fact finder expects that a witness in direct examination will support the side of the case responsible for calling that witness. This expectation of a bias in favor of the side calling the witness does not hold true for witnesses taken on cross-examination, or witnesses called for purposes of cross-examination. Here the expectation is that the witness will admit a fact helpful to the cross-examining lawyer only if that testimony is factually accurate. As a result, it is better to establish facts beyond change through the mouth of a witness perceived by the fact finder to be aligned with the opponent.

Assume in a copyright infringement case the plaintiff alleges that the defendant wrongfully made use of the copyrighted name of plaintiff's product. Assume the plaintiff testifies that the name of his product was widely known in the industry and that he had displayed his product at trade shows also attended by sales executives of the defendant corporation. At this point there is a disputable inference whether the defendant was aware of the product name used by the plaintiff.

However, if plaintiff's attorney cross-examines one or more sales executives of the defendant corporation, either by calling that witness in their case in chief or by cross-examining that witness after they have been called by the defendant, and establishes that indeed the defendant sales executive was aware that plaintiff was marketing that product under that name, the defendant no longer has the option of arguing that it was unaware of the fact. Knowledge on the part of the defendant of the existence of the product and the name under which it was being marketed are now facts beyond change.

The defendant is not foreclosed from other defenses, including that the product name was generic, or that the plaintiff's copyright was improperly obtained, or that the manner in which the defendant used the name did not amount to a copyright infringement. However, the fact beyond change established in cross-examination has limited the available theories of the case. That limitation may be small, but it is real. Attorneys on both sides must now consider that limitation in building their opposing theories of the case.

§ 2.23 Positioning a Witness with Regard to a Fact Beyond Change

When a lawyer adopts a theory of the case that is contradicted by a fact beyond change, the credibility of the lawyer is greatly diminished. Similarly, and for the same reasons, when a lawyer places a witness in a position where the witness testifies in opposition to a fact beyond change, the witness damages his own credibility. The cross-examiner may wish to set up cross-examinations where the impeachment of a witness occurs not through the testimony of another witness, but through a document, photograph or other exhibit that will be judged by the jury to be a fact beyond change. In this way, while the witness may leave the stand feeling secure that he has testified forcefully and accurately, the jury perceives his testimony to contradict a fact beyond change. Credibility is thereby diminished.

By way of example, let us examine the testimony of a defendant concerning how he allegedly killed a person in self defense. Assume the witness/defendant testified that he was involved in a face-to-face struggle with the victim and shot him twice at very close range during a fight. Further assume the coroner's report shows an absence of powder burns on the skin or clothing of the victim and the police crime lab testing of the weapon shows that if it were fired in a range closer than four feet, gunpowder residue would be found on the clothing of the victim. Defense counsel might contest the accuracy of the coroner's report and lab tests. But lacking some solid basis to cast doubt on test accuracy, a fact beyond change will be that the barrel of the gun was at least four feet from the victim at the time it was fired. Even though the witness may testify to the contrary, to the extent that the testimony contradicts the lab tests and coroner's report, his testimony cannot and will not be believed. The witness loses credibility.

We must be careful not to confuse the opportunity to impeach with the opportunity to advance one's theory of the case. In fact, there may be opportunities to impeach that must be disregarded as to impeach would harm our theory of the case.

Assume a criminal charge with identification as the defense. The sole witness claims the attacker was very tall, approximately 6'4". The defendant is 5'7". This gigantic discrepancy may well be the very heart of the defense, and therefore deserving of substantial time in cross-examination. However, if the lawyer's theory is self-defense and identification of the defendant is conceded, it is not enormously productive to impeach the witness on his description of an assailant who was supposedly man 6'4" even though the defendant is 5'7". The height issue by itself is largely irrelevant in the face of an admission of identity. However, if the witness is going to testify to his perceptions of other parts of the fight, and those perceptions hurt the theory of self-defense, then the cross-examiner may wish to cross-examine on the height discrepancy not for the purpose of showing misidentification, but for showing the general inability of the witness to correctly perceive other facts.

§ 2.24 Changing Facts Beyond Change: The Use of Motions in Limine — Civil Applications

To review: A fact beyond change is a fact that will be believed by the jury as accurate regardless of the best efforts to dispute or modify it. But in order for the fact finder to form that judgment, the fact must be introduced at the trial or hearing. As discussed, the consequence of a fact beyond change limits or channels the available theories of the case. If the lawyer removes a harmful fact beyond change, the lawyer simultaneously opens up available theories of the case. The motion in limine is a method of potentially removing harmful facts beyond change.

In civil cases, the motion in limine remains an entirely appropriate vehicle to employ in shaping the theory of the case. Though often based on evidentiary rules rather than constitutional grounds, the motion in limine's application is identical to a motion to suppress in criminal law; it limits the evidence available to an opponent or expands the evidence for the lawyer's theory of the case. The consequence of winning a motion in limine is to either weaken the foundation of an opponent's theory of the case or to remove an impediment to the theory proposed by the proponent of the motion. Just as discovery provides additional facts with which to fashion theories and block the opponent's theories, the motion in limine seeks to withdraw or add facts useful to the opponent or harmful to your theory of the case. Thus, counsel should use the motion in limine to preclude the admission of harmful evidence. Simultaneously counsel should explore methods of incorporating that evidence into their theory of the case, or neutralizing that evidence.

§ 2.25 Using the Motion in Limine to Add Evidence in Support of a Theory

A motion in limine is not always designed to limit evidence; it can be designed to seek a pre-trial ruling permitting the admission of evidence. When finding evidence that supports the lawyer's theory of the case, but that may be ruled inadmissible, it is necessary to create ways of verifying its admissibility. The motion in limine seeking the admission of evidence needs to be heard as far before trial as possible. In overall trial tactics, the ruling will have consequences on the theory of the case, including the definition of the scope of the cross-examinations.

Many judges put off such rulings until shortly before trial and at times even until trial has commenced. This makes for a great uncertainty, but such is life in the courtroom. A theory of the case cannot safely be predicated on the belief that counsel will prevail in the motion in limine. In other words, the theory of the case must be able to rest on other facts whose admissibility is not in question. By winning the right to admit the evidence subject to the motion, counsel expands the available theories of the case, or creates additional facts in support of that theory or obtains additional facts useful in undermining the opponent's theory. By admitting additional evidence, a good theory of the case can be dramatically strengthened, or a non-viable theory may be restored.

§ 2.26 Changing Facts Beyond Change — The Role of Criminal Motion Practice

If a fact beyond change is a fact that, if testified to, will be believed by the jury in spite of efforts by opposing counsel, how then can a fact beyond change be changed? In criminal cases, the goal can be achieved through motion practice. A motion to suppress evidence is a motion to delete certain facts beyond change.

The worst part of a drug case is normally the defendant's possession of the drug. In many cases, it would be a fact beyond change. That is to say, after the agents testify, a jury will believe that the defendant did possess the illegal drug. However, that will only be a fact beyond change if the opponent is permitted to get in the evidence of the defendant's possession of the substance.

In many cases, the defendant's confession is a fact beyond change. This narrows the available theories. Even if the confession is explainable, that a confession was made is itself a fact beyond change.

To the extent that a motion to suppress evidence succeeds in whole or in part, these facts beyond change disappear from the trial. Since the suppressed facts are never available to the fact finder, they cannot be facts in dispute. They cannot be facts beyond change.

The absence of drugs in a drug case is almost always fatal to the prosecution. The absence of a confession in other cases may open wide the available theories of the case. For this reason, in a criminal case, defense counsel must zealously search out facts subject to a motion practice, such as suppression of an identification, an item of evidence, a confession, or similar evidence. The motions are the greatest method of broadening the available theories of the case, while simultaneously eliminating the opponent's best facts beyond change.

Prosecutors also have access to a motion practice that can alter the facts heard by the fact finder. For instance, prosecutors have increasingly sought to admit evidence of similar transactions. This is fertile ground for both the prosecution and defense motion practice. When a prosecutor seeks the admission of similar transactions, the effect is to compound harmful facts with which the defense must now contend. The motion, if granted, has added support for the prosecution's case.

A prosecution motion to admit evidence may impact defendant's available theories of the case or it may simply make the current theory of the case more difficult for the opponent to establish. For instance, by admitting a series of similar transactions to prove identification, the government seeks to deprive the defense of the ability to argue identity successfully. Showing that the defendant committed an earlier crime, and showing the similarities to the present crime, the government hopes to establish the identity of the defendant as the perpetrator of both crimes. While a misidentification theory of the case may still remain arguable, it is greatly injured by the similar transactions evidence. A successful motion in limine, defeating the use of a similar transaction, may revitalize a theory of the case based on mistaken identification by eliminating certain facts beyond change.

When the prosecution seeks the admission of statements of a codefendant, or the right to call an expert to interpret the meaning of supposedly code words the defendant has said over the telephone, the prosecution is asking to add facts, and in some instances moving to add facts and inferences that can become so strong that they become facts beyond change.

§ 2.27 Prioritizing Motion Practice and Pre-trial Discovery by Effect on the Theory

In a perfect world, infinite time and resources would be available to explore every theory, litigate every motion, and fully investigate every fact. The world of the trial lawyer will never be one of infinite time and resources. Both time and money must be focused, and that focus is dependent on recognition of the competing theories of the case.

In developing a theory for a civil or a criminal trial, time and effort must be directed to those areas most likely to advance the theory of the case. Translating this to pre-trial discovery and motion practice, the following can be said: If the best theory of the case is blocked by the existence of a fact, or can be made substantially better by the introduction of a fact, it is worth all the time to develop a motion or request for admission that precludes the introduction of the undesired fact, or to develop a motion or request for admission that permits the inclusion of that fact. By prevailing in this single endeavor, the lawyer more favorably alters the course of trial than through use of the same time in an attempt to prepare a theory that is blocked by a fact beyond change or that fatally lacks supporting facts.

It may take 25 hours of preparation to try a drug possession case and an additional 25 hours to prepare fully and try the motion to suppress the drugs. Assuming counsel truly does not have available time to do both, and assuming that the drug case is solid and easily proven, counsel would be better off fully preparing and litigating the motion to suppress evidence, as its success erases the need to spend any hours in trial preparation. Conversely, its failure dramatically limits the theories available to the defense. Viewed another way: The same hours devoted to the motion practice could potentially produce a dead certain winner while (assuming admission of the drugs) the hours spent in trial preparation produce, at best, a skillful loss.

In order to prioritize many pre-trial endeavors that deserve the lawyer's time, the lawyer must look at which motion has the greatest effect on the theory of the case. In theory, the advocate may file an endless array of discovery motions or litigate all motions that may be conceived. But in a world of finite resources, the lawyer must allocate her resources to those motions whose success most profoundly affects the theory of the case. By doing so, the lawyer spends her efforts in areas most likely to affect the outcome.

In a personal injury case based on an automobile accident case where the insurance defense attorney's theory rests upon the fact that the plaintiff's injuries suffered in his collision are more minor than are being portrayed, less time should be spent as to the "fault" or liability concerning the collision. Much time and precise investigation will be committed to the diagnosis and proximate cause of the alleged injuries and to the medical condition of the plaintiff before the collision.

Chapter 3

CROSS-EXAMINATION PREPARATION: TOPIC CHARTS

§ 3.01 The Value of Organization by Topic

A cross-examination is a series of goal-oriented exercises, each designed to make a particular point. This method is referred to throughout the book as the chapter method of cross-examination. Each chapter of cross-examination is built around logically related facts established through leading questions or the grouping of questions pursuing a goal. The goal is not so limited as to be thought of as the last question of the chapter; it can better be described as the entire picture painted by the blending and accumulation of facts within the chapter.

In order to move efficiently from undigested facts found throughout discovery or informal investigation to the prepared cross-examination chapters, it is necessary to envision the case in very small increments. The scope of an increment depends on the relationship of that item to the theory of the case. Some topical increments can be rather large when they bear little relationship to the theory of the case or are not in dispute. Some topics need to be broken down minutely because they are critical to the theory of the case or are very much in dispute. The more important the topic is to the theory of the case, the greater the detail must be devoted to it. As a result, the more important the topic, the more likely it needs to be subdivided into even smaller parts so that each part may be separately proved as fully as possible. The cross-examiner cannot afford to leave out facts in those areas of greatest importance.

In order to efficiently undertake a topic method of preparation, it is necessary that the cross-examiner devise a first-draft theory of the case. It is also necessary for the cross-examiner to recognize the opponent's theory of the case. Having done so, the advocate is now in a position to recognize the topics of likely importance, and begin to sort the available facts into those topics. Simultaneously, the advocate is equipped to recognize topics of no importance and therefore skip any preparation in these areas.

This later step of discarding facts of little or no importance is important. We lack the time to digest all facts and we waste the time we have by dwelling on the inconsequential facts. For instance, let us assume we are trying a medical malpractice case where the critical event occurred on Wednesday, December 12. Let us further assume that day and date have no impact on the competing theories of the case. Once we recognize that there is no importance to the day and date, we should discontinue efforts to catalogue facts verifying those dates. However, if we find an evidentiary significance to the day or date, we need to gather facts that can prove that day or date.

Similarly, it may not be significant that there was a lightning storm and the lights flickered off and on at one point during the surgery. On the other hand, if part of the theory of the case is that the surgeon attempted to do something very intricate and important during the time the lights were flickering, then the proponent of that theory would want to know many details about that episode, and would undoubtedly write several chapters dealing with the flickering lights, the lack of vision, the necessity for vision at that moment, exactly what part of the surgical procedure was occurring at that moment, as well as other related facts. What information is important is dependent on what the lawyer wishes to prove, and what the opponent wishes to prove. We need to understand both competing theories of the case in order to judge what facts are of importance. Then we can appreciate the dual goals of building our theory of the case and undermining the opponent's theory. Until a factual goal is set, it is difficult, if not impossible, to recognize the chapters that advance the case toward that factual goal.

Whether the advocate uses a computer program to compile related facts, note pads, index cards, or some other method, the process is the same. The available facts are taken from their source material and placed into a topical organization so that the advocate might see available facts organized by topic.

When doing this by hand, the cross-examiner begins with a lot of blank legal pads. When working on a computer, the best way to begin is in an outline program. Regardless of the medium we use to catalogue our facts, it is not necessary to begin the process of fact cataloguing by writing out the names of the topics we are looking for within the facts. A general understanding of the topics comes from our recognition of the competing theories of the case. What is important is that we be able to spot facts that need to be saved within the preparation system. Of course, once we recognize the contrasting theories of the case, we will envision many of the most important topics before beginning our review of the formal or informal discovery. However, while reading the facts, the advocate is likely to see a finer breakdown of topics in the most important areas. In addition, as we identify facts of importance we may identify additional topics of interest which can be prepared as potential areas of cross-examination.

The process of fact identification and cataloguing is not difficult. However, even the most perceptive lawyer will find it difficult to conceive of all the chapters of cross-examination weeks or months in advance of trial. Happily, it is unnecessary. The most efficient method of digesting large quantities of facts is not to pre-conceive of topics in any more than a general sense. It is important that the cross-examiner be able to spot the chapters as they are encountered in discovery. In other words, knowing the general theory of the case allows the cross-examiner to review discovery and recognize facts of significance. The object of this preparation technique is to extract those useful facts from discovery and bring them together in the creation of the chapters of cross-examination.

§ 3.02 Definition of "Discovery"

"Discovery," as used here, includes the material made available by the opponent and to the opponent in either criminal or civil cases. Discovery in most civil cases is formalized: interrogatories, depositions, requests to produce documents, requests for admissions, and the right of inspection are the customary forms of civil discovery. This is augmented by independent investigation. The lawyer's independent investigation often includes private interviews with potential witnesses and searches of electronic databases. In discussing the creation of topic chapters, the term "discovery" includes both the facts gained through the formal discovery process as well as any facts gained through an independent investigation.

In criminal cases, where discovery is generally more restrictive than in civil cases, defense counsel must push for as much discovery as possible and then turn toward motion practice to generate additional discovery. All results, regardless of their origins, are sources for the topic organizational system.

We must survey the material we provide as thoroughly as the material we receive from the opponent. We are preparing two forms of cross-examination: the cross-examination topics that establish our theory of the case, and the cross-examination that attacks the opponent's theory. The documents and depositions we provide are instructive in both areas.

§ 3.03 Topic Pages Make Facts Accessible, Comprehensible, and Usable

Knowing that somebody said some fact is not the equivalent of having a fact trial-ready. We need to build our chapters on facts we can prove. We need to know who or what document said what and where that fact can instantly be found. Memory is not the solution. Once a case has generated more than even a few pages of discovery, no lawyer can hope to remember all the facts in detail *and* remember where that fact was found. A fact becomes accessible when the advocate can immediately identify the page where the fact appears. But even more is required to make a fact accessible. What the advocate needs is the ability to see the relationships among facts. The creation of topic pages begins that process. By entering onto a topic page all facts that relate to that discrete topic, we can see how those facts support or fail to support the topic. The grouping of facts on a topic page allows the lawyer to quickly judge the strength of the evidence currently available to prove a particular point. That is the turning point in the process of transforming data into presentable evidence or facts. The facts are now comprehensible. Because the facts on a particular point can be found on the appropriate topic page, and because that topic page carries the source of the fact, the cross-examiner can move quickly into the cross-examination drafting process.

§ 3.04 The Contents of a Topic Page

A topic page is a single page devoted to cataloguing all relevant facts on a particular small facet of a case. If an event has importance, it is itself too large to be treated as a single topic. For instance, assume a plaintiff sues for injuries sustained in an accident on an all-terrain vehicle. Assume that the defense centers on the plaintiff's failure to obey various warnings relating to the operation of the vehicle. A topic page devoted to "the Accident" would be impossibly large and would inevitably mix many subordinate topics that warrant their own chapters. If the plaintiff started the machine in gear in spite of a written warning that the machine should not be started in gear, that alone requires its own topic page. The warning deserves at least one topic page as well. If there is a special warning light that shows that the machine is in gear, that very specific topic with its supporting facts would receive its own topic page. And so we would break down the many aspects of the accident that we see might assist us in our theory that the plaintiff ignored many warnings and otherwise operated the vehicle in a manner that was itself negligent.

A topic page must contain facts in a form capable of immediate insertion into a cross-examination chapter. This does not mean that every topic page will be converted into a chapter; after review, the cross-examiner will undoubtedly find many topics unworthy of cross-examination. In addition, some topics may have such minor value that a single question will suffice. However, we must keep in mind that anything worth a chapter cannot be adequately covered in a single question. When we see a single fact in isolation, it is almost certainly part of some other chapter. In other words, the fact is important only to the extent that it supports some other, larger goal.

Other topics may be combined as we realize that there is only one point to be made and that the topics we have gathered support that one goal. More often we recognize that what we first believed to be one topic is actually more than one goal of importance. Once we recognize that we are forming multiple chapters of cross-examination on closely related materials, we can continue putting all those related facts on a single large topic page only if we realize that the pages will yield several distinct chapters.

Our mixing of several chapters of material on one or more pages will require that we later separate those facts into their finished chapters. As a result, once we recognize that we are cataloguing facts belonging to two or more chapters on several sheets of paper, we may be better off stopping the mix of facts by dividing the facts into their component chapters and continuing the topic breakdown process by putting all these related facts on a single topic page. In this way we correctly divide the facts into their smaller components or goals in a form more easily converted into trial-ready chapters.

What is important is that the topic page conveys all the information a cross-examiner would find necessary if she chose to use that material inside any single chapter of cross-examination. It is this minute division of facts into their separate topic pages that leaves us in a position to take our next step; the efficient and easy creation of our trial-ready chapters. The process is raw discovery broken into topic pages reformatted as finished chapters of cross-examination.

§ 3.05 A Topic May Generate Facts Sufficient to Fill More than One Page

The creation of a topic page is the intermediate step between undigested data and completed cross-examination chapters. The creation of chapters is discussed at length in chapter 5, *The Chapter Method of Cross-Examination* and chapter 6, *Page Preparation of Cross-Examination*. The finished chapters of cross-examination should be prepared one chapter per page. However, in the preparation of a topic page it may well be that the useful facts under a single topic require more than one page. Although the facts that relate to a single topic require more than one page of preparation materials, throughout this chapter, those pages of facts will still be referred to as a single topic page.

It is acceptable at this stage of the development of a proposed cross-examination chapter for the facts to consume more than one page. However, we should recognize that a single topic requiring multiple pages of facts will likely support more than one chapter at trial. This is simply a recognition that the material may be best handled by a finer breakdown of topics at trial. As always, that breakdown will only occur if the facts, when presented in greater detail, create additional support for the theory of the case. It is quite possible to have multiple pages of facts on a topic at the preparation stage but decide later that there are relatively few facts of significance deserving proof at trial. If an individual topic requires several pages of facts, and those facts break into separate sections or chapters, each supporting the theory of the case, the result at trial will be a chapter bundle. The creation of a chapter bundle is the result of our recognition is that the material is so voluminous that it is necessary to break the material into several related trial cross-examination chapters.

For instance, assume plaintiff sues on the basis that defendant interfered in plaintiff's business relationships. In preparing the pictured cross-examination of one of defendant's executives, we might begin the breakdown with a topic page titled: "Interference with Plaintiff's sale of furniture to the Horton Co." The single sale is not the heart of the matter but solely one example of problems the plaintiff encountered in selling their goods. That one topic, the interference with that one company, may generate two or three pages of facts. That multi-page conglomeration of facts is sufficient for cross-examination preparation purposes. However, when it comes time to draft the cross-examination chapters, counsel must study the multiple pages of facts under this topic in order to determine whether the facts should be broken down further into separate topics. The answer is wholly dependent on the theory of the case, the opposing theory of the case, and the value of the facts in relation to one's theory of the case.

The question may arise: Why not cross-examine at trial from this several-page conglomeration of facts and save the time and effort of creating several individual chapters of cross-examination? There are several related answers. One answer is that we gain control of the flow of the material only after we group the facts into their individual stories. The several pages of facts all vaguely relate to the defendant's alleged interference with plaintiff's attempts to sell furniture to The Horton Company, but they almost certainly tell different stories. The facts may break into disparaging of plaintiff's line of goods, urges to cancel certain contracts with Plaintiff, and false calls made to the Horton Company using the name of Plaintiff's company. Each deserves its own chapter. In fact, if plaintiff can prove more than one attempt to disparage its goods, that alone may deserve two closely related but separately developed chapters. When we mix many facts relating to more than one chapter, we often fail to realize that this long list of facts is deficient in some areas. Once we separate the facts into their appropriate chapters, we can more easily see where we have factual gaps. In turn, this will equip us to better review discovery for facts that might fill in our gaps. Spotting our weak areas also helps us develop a discovery and an investigation plan tailored to yield the most useful results. When we know the competing theories, rough-draft the chapters we would like to use to reinforce or question those theories, and identify the weaknesses of those chapters, we can use our always scarce resources — time and money — to search out the facts that will strengthen those chapters.

A second answer is that when we try to cross-examine from a mass of loosely related facts on several pages, we end up drawing arrows and circling facts in sending ourselves coded messages we have developed. But in trial, all of the codes and arrows are a distraction — not a benefit. We are better off dividing the facts into their separate pictures so that each chapter of cross-examination stands alone and can be performed without our trying to decipher what we meant before trial and where we are supposed to go next.

Finally, when cross-examining from a mass of facts that actually represents several chapters, we lose our ability to easily manipulate the order of our presentation. A grocery list of facts locks us into its own order. We tend to follow the list even when it is taking us into areas we are better off avoiding. We end up cross-examining this witness on whatever facts are on the sheets of paper.

We deserve better from ourselves. It can easily happen that we start with too global a grouping of facts; we look down and discover that the facts are best divided into several chapters. Do so. It is no big deal to rearrange the facts into the chapter method. It is a big deal, and a bad one at that, to attempt the always difficult act of cross-examining an opposing witness using a factual buffet.

§ 3.06 The Contents of a Discrete Topic Page

We need to note again that there are many facts and episodes that do not deserve a topic page. Items we recognize to be of no consequence to the cross-examinations to come, or even important facts that each side concedes to be true, do not deserve a topic workup.

We want to create our topic pages in a form that eases their transition to chapters. It only makes sense then that our topic pages share a format with our completed chapter pages. The minimal contents of a discrete topic page should include:

1. The name of witness whose testimony is under scrutiny on this page.
2. The title or brief description of the topic discussed on this page.
3. Each potentially useful statement of the witness or fact on that particular topic.
4. The source of the fact.
5. The date the fact was asserted.

Each of these entries deserves discussion:

1. The name of the witness.

Each topic page carries the name of the witness because that same topic may need to be replicated for additional witnesses. There may be five people at the key meeting, three at the fight, six witnesses to the accident. The topics and their chapters may well repeat, but the cross-examination of one may not be the cross-examination available to all. Working on the assumption that things get mixed up, the advocate is advised that something as simple as entering the name of the witness at the top of a topic page can save time and aggravation later. In fact, the moment at which the information is needed is likely the moment the advocate is least in the mood to cope with missing, misfiled, or ambiguous information.

2. The title or brief description of the topic.

The value of this topic page method is in breaking facts into their logical groupings. A topic such as "the fraud" is not a chapter. It's a case. Each topic page must be small enough to be useful. The cross-examiner needs to be able to find very specific information useful in creating a single chapter. Each topic page carries the name of the topic on that page. That name or topic may well often become the name of the chapter that is built on that material.

3. The facts relating to that topic.

The value of the topic page is that it contains the facts or testimony relating to that particular topic as related by any one identified witness. This is truly the process of cross-examination preparation, as gathering closely related facts is critical to building each individual chapter to prove one central goal, or to create one picture of importance. Moved out of voluminous discovery and onto a single topic page, these closely related facts immediately become accessible, comprehensible, and usable. These are three critical attributes of any cross-examination preparation system.

4. The source of the fact.

A fact whose source cannot be found may be a fact wasted. If the advocate drafts a leading question designed to use that fact and the witness denies that fact, the cross-examiner needs the ability to immediately find the source of that fact for purposes of impeachment. Moreover, a fact asserted by an opposing party in a prior inconsistent statement may now come in as substantive evidence. In other words, if the cross-examiner cannot find the source of a disputed fact, she loses not only the opportunity to impeach, but also the evidentiary value of that prior statement and a piece of her credibility. There is a great deal of witness control to be gained by noting the source of a fact. Trial work is based on the utilization of available facts. Because the value of sourcing those facts is so high, we need to add detail to the process.

5. The date the fact was asserted.

The date of a hearing is ordinarily more important than the title of the hearing. The date a statement was made is part of the foundation for impeachment by inconsistent statement. For that reason alone we should add the date to our coding of the source of a fact. We note the date the deposition was given, the date the police interviewed the witness, the date the surgical note was dictated. Of course, if there is special significance to the title of a hearing, or its date in a chronology of statements, it is appropriate that we note that in the source code.

Example: Let us assume a plaintiff brings a legal malpractice claim based on her representation that her patent lawyer mishandled an application for a patent and thereby caused the plaintiff to lose rights to an extremely valuable patent. We may well have the plaintiff's deposition statements on that precise issue of value, and of course these statements will make their way onto an appropriate topic page that is devoted to **Value of the Patent.** We would also enter the date plaintiff took that position on value. But let us now add that in the year before bringing the malpractice action, plaintiff went through a divorce and that within the divorce the plaintiff asserted, by way of testimony or document, that the patent had a negligible value. We will certainly note the dates each statement was made. But in addition, it is significant that when the plaintiff testified that the patent had no value, it was to plaintiff's advantage to take that position, and that later, when a contrary position on value was helpful, plaintiff's testimony changed. This change in positions, standing alone, is certainly worth noting and will be the subject of a cross-examination chapter on the plaintiff's shifting valuation of the patent.

Now let us reverse the sequence of events. Plaintiff brings the malpractice suit and, while the suit is pending, plaintiff files the divorce affidavit or testimony taking the position that the patent has no value. We have the same two statements on value, but the later sequence is far more harmful to plaintiff's current position. The cross-examination on the change is significant. We would also cross-examine on the fact that plaintiff's position on value is in accordance with plaintiff's needs at the time. But what may be of the greatest significance is that after saying the patent had great value, plaintiff's most recent position is that the patent lacks value. Of course, we may anticipate that plaintiff will testify in direct examination that the value has great value. The result is that there is not a single change of positions, but two changes of position, and a sequence of changes that makes no sense, absent an involved explanation. The lesson is that we not only note the date a statement is made for purposes of laying a foundation, but we also value the date as a fact in and of itself. We study the date of a statement in its context or sequence to see if there is an independent or additional relevance to that date. This may lead us to a cross-examination on dates of statements that goes far beyond the mere recitation of the date as part of a foundation for a prior inconsistent statement.

§ 3.07 Special Systems in Documenting Depositions as Sources

By this point in our discussion of the chapter method the necessity of repeatedly and accurately noting the source of a fact should become apparent. This sourcing process is easy so long as we stick to a single system and realize that in times of great stress (like the rest of the lawyer's career) we must be able to instantly and correctly rely on and interpret our source codes.

By way of example, let us begin with a single witness and a single deposition. Assume the witness has testified in deposition at page 106 to a fact that we wish to track on a topic page. The fact is at page 106 line 12. The code for that testimony can be shown on our topic page as Dep 106:12, or D 106:12, or simply 106:12. This later designation works only if the witness has testified in a single transcript. If their are multiple sources of facts from the same witness — say depositions, emails, documents, and police interviews — we need to show our code for **deposition** as the source of the testimony. As the depositions pile up and other forms of source material are added, something more elaborate is required. Here are a few suggestions for a system with the firm understanding that every lawyer can create her own set of codes as long as that code makes sense and is used consistently.

If a fact is found within a deposition, note on the topic sheet the page and line of the statement of importance as found in that deposition. If there are multiple days of depositions from a single witness it is imperative that the court reporter be instructed in advance to number the pages sequentially beginning with 1. There is nothing as prone to confusion as multiple volumes of a witness's deposition, each beginning with page one. If we chose to keep each day as a separate volume, we can mark each day of the depositions as its own volume number. Each volume number should be followed by page number and line number. The resulting source code would be: Bob Borden (witness name) v4 (volume number), 863:9 (page and line) **has substantial experience as an auditor** (the fact that we are documenting). The meaning of this code is that the witness Borden will admit that he has substantial experience as an auditor. That fact is found in the Borden deposition, volume 4, page 863, line 9.

An advantage of the volume method is that we can more easily track the day of the statement. Deposition day two may well be separated from day one by days or even months. The fact that a volume number appears in our source code reminds us that our foundation for an inconsistent statement will need to include the appropriate date and that the date for a statement on page 223 may not be the date for a statement on page 224.

More commonly we have only one day of a deposition or we have pages numbered in order day to day. We may then decide that we will put all the pages in a single binder with one cover showing the name of the witness. So far, so good. But again, if there are two days of deposition, we need some indication in our source code that tells us which day the statement was made.

From a transcript other than a deposition, such as the transcript of a preliminary hearing, a code needs to show the source — i.e., "P.H." for preliminary hearing. Some hearings have names that should not be used in front of a jury. For instance, a transcript that results from a motion to suppress evidence should not be referred to as "the hearing on the defense motion to suppress evidence." Similarly, referring to a "*Daubert* hearing" or a 'motion in limine hearing" may make sense in a brief, in arguing a motion, or in a trial to the court, but such legal slang is a poor method of referring to a transcript in front of the jury. Even if we are trying the case to a judge or to lawyer-arbitrators, an impeachment of a witness by the slang name of a hearing may well result in confusion. Witnesses do not usually think of hearings by their legal tag line.

§ 3.08 Special Systems in Documenting Exhibits as Sources

Depositions and reports, while rich in facts, are hardly the only sources of facts useful for possible cross-examination chapters. The exhibits in a case are all possible sources of facts as well. Virtually everything that can be marked as an exhibit would be marked only if it had evidentiary value. Items have evidentiary value only when they provide a fact or an inference. The facts of importance in any item of evidence should be keyed in to the appropriate topic page.

Start with the most obvious example: documents. Lawyers engage in great discovery battles in order to obtain documents. Prosecutors send law enforcement agents out with subpoenas and search warrants to obtain documents. Criminal defense lawyers file discovery motions with the goal of obtaining additional documents. The value of these documents is measured by the recorded facts. As much as transcript testimony, the facts contained in documents must be made accessible, comprehensible, and useful. The important facts in the document need to be sifted into the appropriate topic page. In some instances, the topic page may be filled with a series of facts obtained from a particular document.

Assume a party suggests as part of her theory of the case that the opponent was desperately in need of money. Further assume that part of the proof on this issue is a bank loan with a heavy payment schedule. The topic page might well be titled "the American Big Bank loan" or "owing $18 million." Whatever the name of the chapter, if there are facts of importance that counsel wishes to prove, the lawyer needs to establish the source of those facts. It is insufficient to merely note on the page "see Exhibit 473." Any fact of importance concerning that loan needs its own specific source. Set out below is a topic page "owing $18 million."

January 2005. Owing $18 million

Ex 473 (21) B	Loan taken out January 16, 2005
Ex 473 (1) § 7	From American Big Bank
Ex 473 (5)	Loan amount $18,453,095
Ex 473 (3) § 4	plus interest of 9% on declining balance
Ex 473 (3) § 4	Payments beginning April 16, 2008

In this way even complex documents can be broken down into their component facts and placed on the appropriate topic page. It may occur that something in Exhibit 473, the bank loan document, could touch upon another topic. For instance, if the bank loan had been secured by a cosigner, that fact may well appear on this topic page dealing with the loan, and again on a topic page discussing the relationship of the witness with the person who was the cosigner of the loan.

Complex cases frequently require many exhibits with multiple pages. The resulting source codes will reflect the complexity of the source document but are still easily understood. For instance, in the above example, Ex 473 means trial exhibit 473. Some exhibits are documents containing a great many pages. In such cases we need a source code that directs us to the exact page. We note the second set of numbers (21) meaning page 21 of Ex 473. Alternatively, we might write the source code as Ex 473 p21 or Ex 473:21. The designation § 7 translates to paragraph 7 on page 21 of Ex. 473. In addition, if we can refer to an exact paragraph by its number, we should do so.

Many business documents lack paragraph numbers. In such instances, it is very helpful to at least create a code so that the lawyer knows approximately where on the page that fact can be found. In this example the lawyer has adopted "T" for the top one third of the page, "M" for the middle one third of the page, and "B" for the bottom one third of the page.

The most important features of any source code are that it be in a form we understand and that we use the same codes consistently so that we do not have to ask ourselves what we meant when we wrote the code. The system is crucial. Each of us needs to create a source code system used repetitively (no matter the type of the case) so that in trial we can move immediately to the desired document and page, and even line where possible.

§ 3.09 Creating Topic Pages on a Computer

The topic pages can be created directly on the computer with little effort. The computer is used as equivalent to an endless pad of paper. Once again, it is unnecessary and counterproductive to envision the chapters we will find or develop out of our source materials. We create and title the topic pages as we come upon the material within the source documents. As we recognize a topic we wish to track we note the title on the computer. We put that fact and its source code under that topic heading and move to the next fact we wish to track. We do not search our documents a page at a time to finish any topic card. To do so would require that we read our source documents innumerable times. Instead we read each page and digest it. We move the facts of importance on any particular page into its topic pages, whatever they may be, and then we move to the next page of material. We read and digest discovery a page at a time for the information on that page. We fill each topic page as we read each page of source material. The facts we need seldom appear in a coherent group. As a result, we cannot be sure our topic pages are completed until we have digested the last page of our source material.

A simple method:

1. Open the computer program to any outline function.
2. Search the first page of discovery for the first fact that deserves to be on a topic page.
3. Figure out a name of the topic page that makes sense.
4. Go into the outline function and type the title of the topic page.
5. On that titled topic page enter the fact and the appropriate source code.
6. Find the next fact deserving of entry into any topic page.
7. In the outline function type the title of a new topic page.
8. On that titled topic page enter the fact and the appropriate source code.

The process from here on is to proceed a page at a time through the discovery, moving potentially relevant facts to their appropriate topic pages. In other words, we cannot afford to create topic page and then search through the entire discovery to finish the page. Instead we review each page of discovery, and as we see that a fact belongs under a new topic, we create a topic page for that fact. By this method we digest the facts and create new topic pages while reviewing the pages of discovery in sequence, until the facts of value are digested into their appropriate topics. In the outline function, every time a new topic is spotted a new topic page is created in the outline. The advocate is invited to temporarily number the topics and create a chart of the numbers, or to rearrange the topics into chronological order or other groupings. The important technique is to separate the facts into their appropriate topics for use in creating chapters of cross-examination.

It is possible to move information or answers directly from transcripts to the topic pages. The transcripts need to be on disk. The process of reviewing the transcript pages remains the same. When the lawyer finds a fact in the transcript that should be placed on a topic page, the lawyer can select the transcript material needed, copy it with the copy function under the edit menu, then place the cursor on the fact column of the topic page, and use the paste function. Be sure to source each entry.

§ 3.10 Coping with Document-Intense Litigation

Truly massive discovery creates massive document review efforts. It is beyond the scope of this book to discuss the various systems available to cope with extreme discovery. Suffice it to say the documents will need to be read and the team of people reading will need to be working toward the same topic pages. This can only be accomplished once the trial team has identified the issues it believes to be important for the two opposing theories of the case. Once this is done, the trial team can create issues and the document review team and code documents to show what issues are contained within any one document or page. While multiple people can review documents and place the facts in a topic page system, it is critical that there be coordination concerning what facts are important and the names of the topics being searched. The most important topics must be identified in advance but as document readers spot new topics, the new topic must be disseminated to all document readers and issue coders. This process invariably involves computer tracking of topics and documents.

§ 3.11 A Sample of Some of the Chapters in a Multi-Topic Breakdown

The entire cross-examination of a critical witness may well require a breakdown of a very large number of topics. The following example provides a picture of what a partial topic breakdown might look like. These particular topics come from a hypothetical copyright infringement case and all deal with the potential cross-examination of a single witness. The witness is the marketing director of the plaintiff corporation. He is expected to testify that the plaintiff developed a very valuable software program that was pirated by the defendant corporation. The purpose of the software was to demonstrate the tax advantages of using a certain insurance product to pass large estates to family members. The software generated hypothetical illustrations designed to show prospective purchasers of life insurance the tax advantages they might enjoy by binding a particular insurance product. It is plaintiff's allegation that when the defendant corporation copied the critical aspects of the plaintiff's software program, the defendant destroyed the market for plaintiff's software.

The defense contests both liability and damages. On the damages issue the defense theory is that the software was very poorly received in the marketplace, and was defective in several critical respects. As part of that theory, the defense wishes to make substantial use of the fact that the National Association of Securities Dealers (NASD) reviewed the hypothetical illustrations produced by the software, and instructed one insurance company that they could not use the illustrations produced by the software. The NASD calls this action a "Do Not Use" letter. Here is a partial listing of the topics that relate solely to the issue of the NASD issuance of a "Do Not Use" letter.

NASD warned American Amalgamated Insurance "Do Not Use."

American Amalgamated complained to you.

American Amalgamated canceled its licensing agreement.

American Amalgamated required to tell its brokers not to use the illustrations.

You continued to market the software to other companies.

You did not tell the other companies about the "Do Not Use" letter.

Thereafter you made no changes in the software illustrations.

As this partial listing demonstrates, our sorting of material into the possible chapters of cross examination allows us to move very efficiently from our review of discovery into our draft cross examination chapters. Let us look at another partial breakdown, this from a self-defense case. The defendant is charged with a vicious assault. The complaining witness has alleged that the defendant hit him over the head with a piece of wood, knocking him down, and then began kicking him repeatedly. The defendant, when interviewed by the police, said that the alleged victim was drunk and stumbled and hit his head on a railing, causing only a small cut; thereafter, the complaining witness advanced on the defendant and began to swing at him. According to the defendant, he kneed complaining witness one time in the stomach but never kicked him. Below is a partial list of the cross-examination of the emergency room physician designed to show that the injuries found were inconsistent with the complaining witness's story of the beating and kicking.

You were aware of complaining witness's story of being clubbed in the head.

Found "tiny scalp injury."

No stitches needed.

Were aware of complaining witness's story of being repeatedly kicked.

Substantial bruising would be consistent with the repeated kicking described.

Conducted complete physical exam.

Found no bruising anywhere.

Again, this is but a partial listing of the possible areas or topics we need to examine in preparing for cross-examination chapters. However, our early recognition of the fertile areas of cross-examination leads to greater efficiency in the task of creating our chapters of cross-examination. Having begun the process of identifying our chapters, we can fluidly move facts from our source materials into our topic pages and then from the topic pages into our draft chapters of cross-examination.

§ 3.12 Examples of Topic Pages Filled Out with Facts and Sources

Witness: Dr. Letz

Topic: Head Injury

Source	Facts	Notes
Taped interview pg 6 of transcript	I took a history of the incident as reported by the patient. He told me he had walked into the house when he was hit from behind by some kind of club. He explained that the force of the blow knocked him down and then he covered himself up and rolled into the fetal position as the assailant began repeatedly kicking him in the abdomen.	Show full history is required and was done
Med records 0013 History and physical	"tiny scalp laceration found."	Show inconsistent with victim's story
Med records 0011	"Patient is seen in the emergency room complaining of attack by roommate. Oriented by three, in some distress, no bleeding noted.	Use this to show that the head injury described by victim would have bled, so story of being clubbed is probably not true
Med records 0027 para 5	"Betadine solution applied to scalp laceration."	No stitches or other repair required

§ 3.13 Using the Competing Theories of the Case to Identify and Create Topic Pages

Facts of importance can only be identified once we formulate our theory of the case and recognize our opponent's theory of the case. Topic pages are built around facts of importance. We do not recognize the importance of a fact until we examine it in relationship to the two opposing theories of the case. Topic pages are not simply a device to take all of discovery and rearrange them into a giant number of topics — some useful, some completely unimportant. Our job is to sift through the facts in order to cull the smaller number of useful facts from the very large number of available facts. We profitably read discovery only after we have a sense of where we want to go with the case. This is not particularly difficult, as any first interview with the client will almost certainly aim us toward our theory of the case. While we may refine our theory as the case progresses, for the most part facts we are interested in will remain the same.

§ 3.14 Using Topic Pages to Identify Impeachment Materials

Most cross-examinations are both constructive and destructive in nature. As we have discussed, we use cross-examination chapters to bring out facts that the direct examination ignored or touched upon too briefly. This is the constructive of use of cross-examination. We are of course gathering facts on topic pages to help us prepare to guide an opposing witness through facts that assist us in building our theory of the case. The other aspect of cross-examination is destructive in nature. In destructive cross-examination we are challenging the credibility of a witness in a particular area, often by challenging a statement by the witness. Sometimes our challenge is indirect, as when we try to show that the witness lacked an opportunity to observe. More often challenges are direct, in that we attempt to show that the witness's testimony is inconsistent with that of another witness, or most frequently that the witness has been inconsistent with his own earlier recitation of an event.

The topic page system of cross-examination preparation is an excellent method to prepare for the chapters of cross-examination needed to attack the credibility of a witness or attack the credibility of a story told by multiple witnesses. The customary credibility cross-examination places a great emphasis on finding and exploiting internal inconsistencies (that is, inconsistencies in various versions of an event as related by a single witness), external inconsistencies (that is inconsistencies that occur when multiple witnesses describe a single event in differing ways), inconsistencies with physical facts, impeachment by omission, and other ways in which the testimony of the key witnesses can be shown to be contradictory. The topic method of cross-examination preparation is well suited to this task. In addition, the credibility of a witness may be attacked by showing the bias, interest, or motive of the witness. The gathering of facts along these topics allows the advocate to move the facts very efficiently from the topic pages into prepared chapters of cross-examination.

Presume an issue of eyewitness identification. Identification issues are often thought of as occurring in the criminal context, and are ordinarily thought of as relating to the identity of the defendant. This is too limited a view. "Identification" really means "perception." Perception issues occur often in civil cases on identification of things or events rather than persons. For instance, in a car accident case, the description of how a collision occurred may be the critical aspect of the suit. In a product defect case, eyewitness testimony concerning what the plaintiff was doing with the product at the time of the allegedly damage-producing event may be the critical issue.

In a variety of civil contexts it may be necessary to cross-examine the witness concerning his perceptions. This type of cross-examination is based on chapters relating to credibility issues. A cross-examiner seeking to establish a lack of credibility as to the eyewitness testimony will need to study and digest the facts along topics designed to challenge the credibility of certain aspects of the witness's story. This form of cross-examination will be based on such things as internal inconsistencies, lack of opportunity to observe, vagaries in descriptions, and other factors leading a jury to the conclusion that the information given by the witness cannot be trusted. In any case in which eyewitness testimony may need to be discredited, the cross-examiner must first analyze what the witness claims to have observed. Finally, the lawyer will need to analyze the witness's opportunity to observe. In addition we will need to take into account the witness's version of each part of the event as compared to the observations of other witnesses, the laws of nature, any available documentary or physical evidence, and common sense.

Example: In this criminal case example, the prosecution's case is based upon an eyewitness's identification testimony. This identification in turn is based upon the physical description of the perpetrator, as related by the eyewitness. For ease of explanation, this chapter will focus on a criminal identification case. The initial set of topic pages will focus on possible identification issues: height, weight, body hair, head hair, pants, shirt, jewelry, scars, etc. See Chart 1, below.

Below is a listing of a few possible identifying factors requiring factual research prior to cross-examination in the misidentification defense. However, before studying the list the advocate should bear in mind that it is not necessary to have such a list in advance of the construction of the topic pages. The cross-examiner has no way of knowing which of these topics may be mentioned within the discovery or the investigation. It often proves more efficient for the lawyer to simply begin the process of cataloguing the facts by topic by studying a single page of discovery and sorting onto a topic page any facts relating to the description of the alleged perpetrator.

Chart 1

Potential topics relating to identification

Height	Tattoos
Weight	Scars
Clothing	Nose
Age	Eyes
Facial Hair	Teeth
Head Hair	Voice
Glasses	Accent
Glasses Frame	Shoes
Contact Lenses	Socks
Skin Color	Hat
Gun Color	Gun Size
Gun Style	Body Build

As can be seen from this list, the number of possible topics in an identification case is quite large. Furthermore, any one of these items could have enormous significance as to guilt or innocence of the person identified. For instance, if the defendant has a gold front tooth and, after a face-to-face robbery, the sole victim/witness fails to describe a robber with a gold front tooth, that omission alone could produce a reasonable doubt as to guilt. Alternatively, if the witness describes a robber with a gold front tooth, and the defendant has no gold front tooth, the entire prosecution case may fail on that issue alone. However, a topic card concerning the gold front tooth of the assailant would not alone prepare us for a cross-examination on that identifying feature. The witness might testify that the lighting was poor, or that the robbery occurred very quickly, or that the robber spoke with his hand over his mouth. In order for the topic of the gold front tooth to have significance, defense counsel would need to show that the witness had an opportunity to observe the identifying feature. This would lead us to create topic page which we might call **Watched robber talk,** or **Saw robber's face** or **Opportunity to see his teeth.**

In the above example, where we wished to show that the defendant has a very significant identifying characteristic but that the witness has never identified that characteristic, topic pages designed to show that the witness had an excellent opportunity to observe are useful to our theory of the case. However, as we go through discovery including police reports, interviews, preliminary hearing transcripts, scene photographs, and any other documents that help us understand the physical and mental barriers to the ability to perceive identifying characteristics, we would note those as well. We may also need topic pages on the issues of lighting, how long the robbery took, or the way the robber was standing, to help us prepare for cross-examination of the eyewitness on issues of identification. If the witness has stated to a police officer that the robbery took mere seconds, that the lighting was very dim, and that the victim/witness did her best not to look at the robber, we would want topic pages for the topics **Lighting Conditions, Short time to view,** and **Tried not to look at robber.**

Topic pages have the name we give them. We use whatever description reminds us of the aspect of the case we are tracking on that page. There is no magic, no right or wrong description — as long as the description sufficiently orients us to put facts on that page that are assignable to that topic. One thing we must guard against is a topic page that is overly inclusive. A lawyer preparing an identification defense might well be very interested in many circumstances of the robbery scene. However, a single topic page entitled **Place of the robbery** or **Circumstances surrounding the identification** would be far too broad and will result in our mixing on one page many facts that will belong eventually in their own chapters.

How is the lawyer to decide on the topics that merit topic pages? The topics of importance are derived from her theory of the case and the opposing theory of the case. If the theory is that the defendant was indeed present but was only attempting to take back something that belonged to him, the failure of a witness to see the defendant's gold tooth is of little or no importance. It may still be a topic of some value in that the failure of the eyewitness to detect the gold tooth might assist in showing that the witness did not have a good opportunity to observe the entire transaction, or that the witness is wrong on a myriad of details and cannot be trusted as to any portion of his story that hurts the cross-examiner's theory of the case.

Obviously, the topic pages required will differ from one type of case to another, as the theories of the cases differ. Although some duplication of topics can be expected in most identification cases, a standard list of topics will not be efficient. The proper way to employ the topic system is to work directly from the discovery itself, not from the universe of possibilities of topics. That universe of possible topics is far too broad to be of use. The lawyer must begin her preparation with what is described by the witnesses in this case.

Any topic on an identification factor that has come up anywhere in discovery or investigation needs to have its own topic page. Each topic index page must be limited to those pieces of information dealing with that single factual category. For example, "What did the robber look like?" is far too broad a topic. A physical description must be broken down into all of its components, including height, weight, eyes, hair, scars, marks, or other identifying topics.

Additional topic pages should be made for every descriptive topic recounted by a victim/witness. For instance, if an identification witness describes a weapon, a getaway car, or even a peculiar odor about the perpetrator, a topic page must be prepared containing all descriptions given by the witness of these topics. Internal or external inconsistencies on these issues can accumulate to undermine the credibility of the witness just as much as inconsistencies on issues of description of the suspect.

§ 3.15 Building Topic Pages for a Case May Increase Efficiency in Other Cases

The object of our efforts is to create a system that allows us to read discovery materials a single time while building the necessary topic pages. In a case that generates only a small amount of discovery or documents it may be possible (but inefficient) for the lawyer to review the entirety of discovery a single time before beginning the process of creating the topic pages. Even if the discovery is voluminous, counsel certainly has a draft theory of the case in mind. Working from that draft theory of the case, the lawyer is ready to begin filling out the topic pages.

Every case develops its own set of topics, so the topics used in one identification case will vary from the topic pages of a prior identification case. However, there are some types of cases that are heavily repetitive such as the defense of driving under the influence cases. In these cases there will ordinarily be roadside tests, and those tests will repeat from case to case. While the individual circumstances of the tests will vary, lawyers practicing in a particular area of law may well find that the general topic pages they will need to prepare their cross-examinations frequently repeat from case to case.

For instance, a lawyer might well become familiar with the many possible field sobriety (roadside) tests, including the field sobriety test in which the driver suspected of driving under the influence is asked to walk along a straight line. In the first case the lawyer may have created a topic page showing that the police manual directs that the straight line be marked or that it otherwise exist. The lawyer might then develop a second topic page showing that the officer failed in this instance to create or use a marked line. While those topic pages have been created for this first case, those very topics and the chapters of cross-examination they would lead to might be used for years to come with little or no change.

In preparing for a particular case, that lawyer might well develop a topic page relating to how a particular test was performed and whether that test was administered in accordance with the appropriate law enforcement manual. Undoubtedly that lawyer will have many more cases in which he or she can use chapters of cross-examination on how that particular field sobriety test was performed. Those chapters may have to be customized for the circumstances of an individual case. But, having created a topic page on how that particular matter should be accomplished, and a topic page showing how that matter was in fact accomplished, the lawyer becomes accustomed to the process of looking for facts on these often repeating subjects and reducing those facts to the topic cards or pages necessary to create those chapters of cross-examination.

§ 3.16 Transfer Information, Do Not Translate Information

Topic pages are built by moving facts out of case discovery and onto appropriate topic pages while neither losing nor adding anything to the information. Remember, the lawyer's job is **transferring** — *not* **translating**. Complete accuracy is ordinarily attainable as we are reading from some source document. We should correctly quote that source document, even if the witness might later say that the source document is incorrect. It is critical that in our process of moving the information out of discovery and onto the appropriate topic page that we do not change the testimony. Our complete accuracy is final because the words that we place on the topic page become our leading questions of cross-examination.

The danger of translation is that in response to our leading question the witness may deny that he said a particular thing. The cross-examiner, working from the written chapter of cross-examination, would believe that she had quoted the witness directly from the discovery, only to find during the act of impeachment that the cross-examiner has in some way changed the wording from the discovery to the topic page. Because the facts were translated, the question has become inaccurate for the prepared chapter of cross-examination. By translating the facts, the cross-examiner risks losing credibility with the jury and will undoubtedly lose confidence in her own system. The facts that are pulled out of discovery must not be altered in the process.

Example: assume the witness statement or deposition reads "I noticed my purse was missing that night or the next morning." Let us further assume that what is most helpful to our theory of the case is that the witness discovered her purse was missing that night. We may well have created a topic page on **losing the purse** or **Discovering the purse was missing**. On that topic page we should enter the completely accurate recitation of the event, per the document. We dare not ignore or unfairly summarize the position of the witness as found in the source document. To do so could lead to the following interchange at trial:

Question: You noticed your purse was missing that night?

Answer: No. (or) I'm not sure.

Question: Let me take you to your statement, page121, line 12. (At which time cross-examining counsel reads back the witness's full answer, "I noticed my purse was missing that night or the next morning."

The net effect of this is that the lawyer's inaccuracy has the appearance of either sloppiness or outright deception. The witness didn't say what the lawyer recited in her leading question and what should have been a simple point well may now becomes a chink in the credibility of the lawyer.

Now let us change this example only slightly.

Question: You noticed your purse was missing that night?

Answer: That night or the next morning.

The witness's response is a less direct confrontation with the lawyer's leading question, and as a result the lawyer should not go to the transcript to impeach. But if the lawyer has written this leading question in just the way she asked it, and has shown a source for that answer in her prepared page of cross-examination, the lawyer might erroneously commence an impeachment.

Question: Let me take you to your statement, page 121, line 12. (At which time cross-examining counsel discovers to her embarrassment that the answer that the witness has just given was indeed in conformity with the transcript and not in conformity with what the lawyer implied in her leading question.)

Once again the net effect is that we lose credibility with the jury. We have asked leading questions and have thereby asserted that we know a fact when in reality our leading question is erroneous.

§ 3.17 Building Topic Pages

While the example that follows is drawn from a criminal case, the system works equally well in civil cases. Simply substitute the civil discovery; i.e., deposition, answers to interrogatories, etc., for the criminal items discussed.

Step One: Work from Source Documents to the Creation of Topic pages

Take the first page of discovery in a criminal case, often a police report detailing the offense, begin at the top and look for every piece of information that touches upon the broad issue of identification if that is the theory of the case, or upon any other issue in which the lawyer may be interested.

Assume there is a single victim/witness who will testify to identification. There may be other witnesses, including police officers and lay people who will testify to surrounding issues, but only one witness will testify to identification. The number of topic pages built for this identification witness is unknown until we end the process of digesting the available information on the issue of identification. If there is more than one identification witness, a separate set of identification topic pages is required for each.

Each index page should show the witness's name and the topic of the page.

Bennett: HEIGHT	Bennett: AGE	Bennett: HAIR COLOR
Chart 2	*Chart 3*	*Chart 4*

Assuming there is only one identification witness (Scott Bennett), the cross-examiner needs to create individual topic pages dealing with identification issues showing every item of identification as related by Mr. Bennett. Here, for instance, Chart 2 deals with witness Bennett, and the limited topic of Height"; Chart 3 deals with the same witness, but the different topic of "Age." This system continues for each additional topic perceived by this witness. Inconsistencies will ordinarily form the basis of the successful cross-examination of the identification witness. Various forms of inconsistencies may appear on our topic pages including internal inconsistencies (inconsistent statements by the same witness), inconsistencies between the description given and the physical characteristics of the accused, and inconsistencies between this witness and other eyewitnesses but other facts described by the identification witness are equally useful. For instance, the witness may have described the weapon, the getaway car, and the door from which entry was made. All are particularly useful topics for cross-examination, and therefore require their own topic index pages.

In reviewing the first page of discovery in this example, the offense report (see Chart 5 below), we begin the process of transferring information into the topic page system. We are looking for any information in the first page of discovery information that deals with any issue in which the lawyer might be interested. For example, page one of our discovery may disclose that the victim/eyewitness had been drinking. As this is a fact that can be of value to our theory of the case and hurt the opponent's theory, it is therefore a fact that must be placed onto its appropriate topic page.

In this first page of discovery, or source document, the lawyer finds a block of information in which the officer has apparently asked the witness for a description of the robber (see Chart 6). These answers are in categories and can be easily placed onto the index page, and thus the page system begins.

Chart 5

First Source

DENVER POLICE DEPARTMENT GENERAL INCIDENT REPORT

☐ Domestic Violence ☐ Suspect Arrested ☐ Gang Involved ☐ Gang Motivated ☐ Graffiti

Sheet 1 of 5

☒ Original ☐ Additional ☐ Completed by Victim ☐ For Record Only

OFFENSE

Location of Offense	Apt #	Precinct
66514 W Hilfax St.		

Date/Time Offense	On or Between	Date	24 hour time	Day
		7/20/08	23:05	
		Date	24 hour time	Day
Date and Time Reported		7/20/08	23:15	

Offenses	Susp	Atmpt/Comp		Hate Crime
1. Robbery - Business		☐	☐	☐
2.		☐	☐	☐
3.		☐	☐	☐

VICTIM

#1 TOTAL NUMBER OF VICTIMS — VICTIM CONNECTED TO OFFENSE # ABOVE 1 ☐ 2 ☐ 3 ☐

VICTIM NAME (Last, First, MI) or COMPANY: Speedy Burrito #512 — Written Statement Yes ☐ No ☐ — Ordered to Appear on: / /

Residence Address — City — County — State — Zip Code — Residence Phone

Business Name and Address	City	State	Zip Code	Business Phone
Speedy Burrito, 66514 W. Halifax St.	Denver	CO	80219	321-1234

TYPE OF VICTIM - CHECK ONE: I ☐ Individual; B ☒ Business; F ☐ Financial; G ☐ Government; R ☐ Religious; S ☐ Society/Public; O ☐ Other; U ☐ Unknown

RACE: ☐ White ☐ Black ☐ Asian ☐ Native American ☐ East Indian ☐ Unknown

DENVER RESIDENT: ☐ Yes ☐ No ☐ Unknown

SEX: ☐ Male ☐ Female ☐ Unknown

AGE — DOB — HGT — WGT — ☐ SBI

AMB # — Trip # — Hospital/Physician

Assault/Homicide Circumstances (Check up to Two): 01 ☐ Argument; 02 ☐ Assault on Law Officer; 03 ☐ Drug Dealing; 04 ☐ Organized Crime; 05 ☐ Gang Related; 06 ☐ Domestic Violence; 07 ☐ Doctor Assisted; 08 ☐ Other Felony Involved; 09 ☐ Other Circumstances; 10 ☐ Unk Circumstances

Injury Type (Check up to Five): N ☐ None; B ☐ Broken Bones; I ☐ Possible Internal Injuries; L ☐ Severe Laceration; G ☐ Gun Shot; M ☐ Other Minor Injury; O ☐ Other Major Injury; T ☐ Loss of Teeth; U ☐ Unconsciousness; S ☐ Stabbing; C ☐ Strangulation/Choking

RELATIONSHIP OF VICTIM TO THE SUSPECT: (For Multiple Suspect Relationships, enter suspect number(s) in circle)

SE ☐ Spouse; CS ☐ Common-Law Spouse; PA ☐ Parent; SB ☐ Sibling; CH ☐ Child, Juvenile; GP ☐ Grandparent; GC ☐ Grandchild; IL ☐ In-Law; SP ☐ Stepparent; SC ☐ Stepchild; SS ☐ Step-sibling; OF ☐ Other Family; AQ ☐ Acquaintance; FR ☐ Friend; NE ☐ Neighbor; BE ☐ Babysitee (Baby); BG ☐ Boy/Girlfriend; CF ☐ Child of BG above; HR ☐ Same Sex Relationship; XS ☐ Ex Spouse; EE ☐ Employee; ER ☐ Employer; OK ☐ Otherwise Known; ST ☒ Stranger; RU ☐ Relationship Unk

SUSPECT

Susp #1 — Name (Last, First MI) — Alias — DPD #

# of Susp — Home Address — City — State — Zip — Home Phone

Employed by — Business Address — Business Phone — Social Security #

☐ Arrested ☐ At Large	Charge ☐ Offense 1 ☐ Offense 3 ☐ Offense 2 ☐ Other	DOB/Age	Sex	Race	Hgt	Wgt	Hair Color/Style	Eye Color
		30	M	Blk	6' 1"	180	blk/afro	brn

☐ Ordered-in Date	Scars Marks and/or Tattoos	Clothing
/ /	Scar on left cheek	Jeans

Misc.

WITNESS

Total # of Witnesses

	Witness #1	Witness #2
Name (Last, First MI)	Bennet, Scott	Payton, Rodney
Address	2900 Race Ave, Denver	4647 E. Bellaire Aurora, CO
Home Phone	757-5432	345-6789
Cell Phone	757-6586	344-7643
Business Phone	321-1234	321-4758
DOB	2/18/62	6/27/58
Statement Made	☒ Yes ☐ No	☒ Yes ☐ No
Ordered to Appear on	/ /	/ /

ADMIN

Reported By ☐ Victim ☐ Officer ☐ Other — DOB/Badge # — Home Phone

Residence Address — City — County — State — Zip — Business Phone

Officer Taking Report/Serial #: M. Bates/1122-3340 — Approved By/Serial # — Reason for Paper Report: ☐ Off-Duty ☒ System Down ☐ No Laptop - Unit # — I affirm this information is true and correct. X

Counter Reports/Telephone Reports/Mail-in Reports – **Fill in shaded areas on front and back.** DPD 250 REV (7/07)

Chart 6

<table>
<tr><td rowspan="2">SUSPECT</td><td>☐ Arrested
☐ At Large</td><td>Charge ☐ Offense 1 ☐ Offense 3
☐ Offense 2 ☐ Other.</td><td>DOB/Age
30</td><td>Sex
M</td><td>Race
Blk</td><td>Hgt
6' 1"</td><td>Wgt
180</td><td>Hair Color/Style
blk/afro</td><td>Eye Color
brn</td></tr>
<tr><td>☐ Ordered-in Date
/ /</td><td colspan="4">Scars Marks and/or Tattoos:
Scar on left cheek</td><td colspan="4">Clothing
Jeans</td></tr>
</table>

Chart 7 below displays identifying information provided by the witness to the reporting officer, concerning the description of the robber.

Chart 7

Descriptive items available within page 1 of the police report		
Age Race Sex Height	Weight Eye color Hair color	Hair style Scars Clothing

For purposes of illustration, concentration will be on the building of the "height" page. While this is just one of many topics to be covered, the building of topic pages is replicated for each topic and each witness.

From page one of the police report (Chart 5), it is clear that the officer has obtained a description of the height of the robber. The lawyer is ready to begin the topic page, which will carry each description given by witness Bennett of the height of the robber.

Chart 8

Bennett: *Height*
6-1

The height, 6′1″, is taken off the source document (Chart 6) and put on the Bennett-Height page (Chart 8).

Because of the rules of impeachment, the lawyer also needs to show on the index page where in the discovery she found the points of information being transferred onto the topic pages. The lawyer must therefore write the source of the information "offense report, page 1/5." (See Chart 10, upper left hand corner.)

Chart 9

Bennett: *Height*	
6-1	Off Rpt. p.1/5

A trial lawyer must always assume that the witness may forget, deny, or change this description no matter how often he was consistent before trial. Thus, the topic page must contain all other types of information needed for the laying of a foundation to introduce a prior inconsistent statement: the date the statement was given, and the person to whom given (see Chart 5). Now these are added to the topic page so that now the page is complete as to this one version of the witness's description of height.

Chart 10, below, graphically sets out how the lawyer has taken the necessary information off a source document and transplanted it to a topic page.

Chart 10

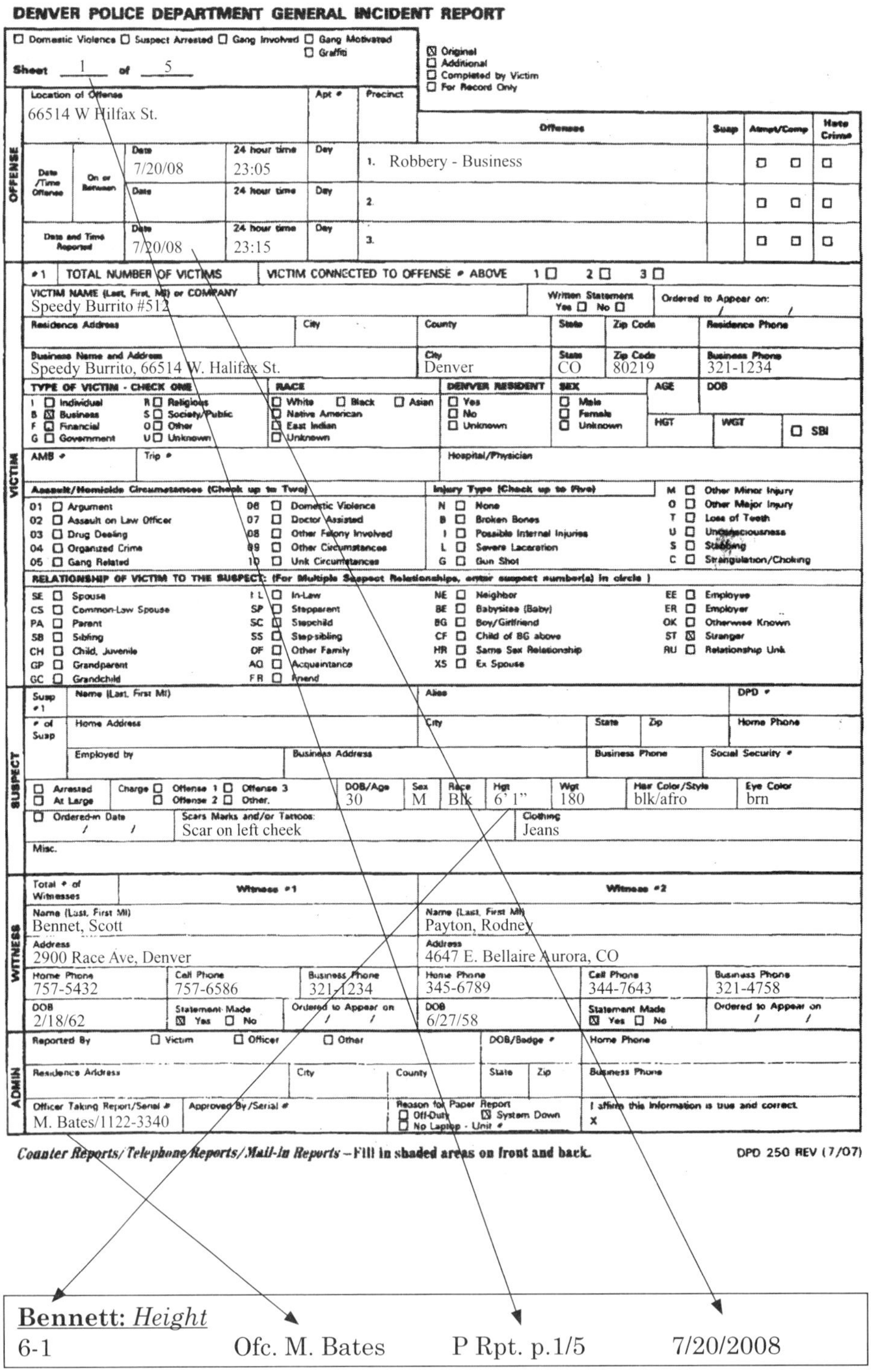
DENVER POLICE DEPARTMENT GENERAL INCIDENT REPORT
Sheet 1 of 5
Original
Location of Offense
66514 W Hilfax St.
Date 7/20/08
24 hour time 23:05
1. Robbery - Business
Date and Time Reported
7/20/08
23:15
TOTAL NUMBER OF VICTIMS
VICTIM NAME (Last, First, MI) or COMPANY
Speedy Burrito #512
Business Name and Address
Speedy Burrito, 66514 W. Halifax St.
Denver
CO
80219
321-1234
Business
Stranger
Susp #1
DOB/Age 30
Sex M
Race Blk
Hgt 6' 1"
Wgt 180
Hair Color/Style blk/afro
Eye Color brn
Scars Marks and/or Tattoos:
Scar on left cheek
Clothing
Jeans
Witness #1
Bennet, Scott
2900 Race Ave, Denver
757-5432
757-6586
321-1234
2/18/62
Witness #2
Payton, Rodney
4647 E. Bellaire Aurora, CO
345-6789
344-7643
321-4758
6/27/58
Officer Taking Report/Serial #
M. Bates/1122-3340
System Down
Counter Reports/Telephone Reports/Mail-In Reports – Fill in shaded areas on front and back.
DPD 250 REV (7/07)
Bennett: Height
6-1
Ofc. M. Bates
P Rpt. p.1/5
7/20/2008

This, then, is an overview of the process by which the lawyer transfers a *single description* point of a *single fact* from the source document onto the index page guard.

Step Two: Build Topic pages by Exhausting All Useful Information on Each Single Page of Discovery Material Before Moving to the Next Page of Source Material.

At this point, the lawyer has *not* completed this topic page. The lawyer has only completed the first entry onto the topic page. In order to complete the topic page, the lawyer must find every description of height given by this witness in all of the discovery material. Finally, the lawyer will also eventually add on a reference to client's actual height.

In order to accomplish this, the lawyer does not need to, and should not go through the stack of discovery looking for every height description. Such a method would force the lawyer to reread every page of discovery innumerable times as she builds each topic page. That is a gross misuse of precious time. Instead, the lawyer should go through the remainder of the first page of discovery, copying onto the appropriate topic page each "fact" dealing with any other topic of the identification issue or any other topic in which she is interested.

As the lawyer builds a set of identification topic pages from this first page of discovery, the other identifying descriptions given on page 1 of the police report (Chart 5) require the generation of additional topic pages at this point.

Chart 11

SUSPECT	☐ Arrested ☐ At Large	Charge ☐ Offense 1 ☐ Offense 3 ☐ Offense 2 ☐ Other.	DOB/Age 30	Sex M	Race Blk	Hgt 6' 1"	Wgt 180	Hair Color/Style blk/afro	Eye Color brn
	☐ Ordered-in Date / /	Scars Marks and/or Tattoos: Scar on left cheek					Clothing Jeans		

That is, the items in Chart 11 alone would require the lawyer to create entries on separate entitled topic pages for "age," "hairstyle," and "weight."

There are always many facts that are not in dispute. Such facts do *not* require a topic page. For instance, the witness says the robbery happened at Speedy Burrito. Unless something comes up to cast doubt on this, the issue is not worth reducing to a topic page. Similarly, the race and sex of the robber are not in dispute, and therefore, no topic page need be made — unless it should later occur that this or another witness disputes that the robber was a black male.

When all of the facts gathered from the first page of discovery have been transferred onto appropriate topic pages, we can begin on the next page. Counsel must now work through all offense reports, police supplements, preliminary hearing transcripts, grand jury testimony, suppression hearing transcripts, defense interviews, statements by any third persons who have also discussed that topic with that witness, and all of the discovery, whether formal or informal.

§ 3.18 Digesting Second and Subsequent Source Documents

The same process just completed for the first source document is repeated for the second and subsequent source documents. In this example, Chart 12 shows a partial page out of the second source document, a preliminary hearing transcript.

Chart 12

Second Source

Partial Preliminary Hearing Transcript

p19

Q: Mr. Bennett, can you describe the man who entered Speedy Burrito?

A: Yes, sir. He was about <u>five feet seven</u> inches tall and weighed about 175 pounds. He had a small afro. I can't recall the clothes he was wearing.

Bennett: ***<u>Height</u>***
6-1 Ofc. M. Bates P Rpt. p.1/5 7/20/2008

about 5'7" PH. p. 19:3

Second Source Partial Preliminary Hearing Transcript

The height (about 5′7″) is transplanted to the height page. Note the exact quote is moved. Nothing is added. Nothing is deleted. The foundational information is transferred, including, in this case, the exact page and line number, and that it was at the preliminary hearing (PH.). While the prosecutor's name, title, and date of statement are included in Chart 13, by coding the lawyer can shorten the transfer.

Chart 13, below, shows the height page with the addition of a description of height found in the preliminary hearing transcript, including all identifying information.

Chart 13

Bennett: *Height*			
6-1	Ofc. M. Bates	P Rpt. p.5	7/20/2008
about 5'7"	DA: Simpleton	PH. p.19:3	11/15/2008

§ 3.19 Tracking Imprecise Descriptions

Often a witness will not give a precise answer concerning a fact or issue but will describe the fact or characteristic in some indirect way. Such information is as much a form of identification or assertion as a more precise answer and may prove equally useful. However, such descriptions are subtler and more difficult to catch. For instance, suppose the witness stated: "I was standing right across from him and I had to look up." That phrase is pertinent to the height topic, though not as precise an answer as 5′7″. It needs to go on the height topic page, as an identical quote (see Chart 14).

Chart 14

Bennett: *Height*			
6-1	Ofc. M. Bates	P Rpt. p.5	7/20/2008
about 5'7"	DA: Simpleton	PH. p.19:3	11/15/2008
We were standing in front of each other and I had to look up.		HRG. 78:21	2/20/2009

In any case, civil or criminal, in which the perceptions of a witness are in issue, any topic in which the witness has been given an opportunity to show inconsistency, confusion, or an inability to observe or recall a detail is fertile for cross-examination. Besides the raw descriptive data of the assailant, other topics can be of equal importance in casting doubts on the credibility of the witness. Perhaps the victim is confused about where an event happened, when it happened, how long it took, how many participants were involved or what was taken. All of these issues require separate topic index pages. Descriptions of the weapon, words spoken by the assailant, the color or model of the getaway car, and all other things that can be shown to be inconsistent, or unlikely to have occurred in the sequence or manner suggested by the victim/witness, are useful to the lawyer, and therefore she needs to keep track of them.

Regardless of the nature of the case, for every subject that may be of interest, a separate topic page should be prepared so that the facts found in discovery may be distilled onto the pages. Remember, a topic page entry is incomplete unless the source page and line number or number of the page of discovery is noted so that the fact can be instantaneously relocated. Never assume the factual entry will be easy to relocate. In the stress of the courtroom, it is not.

§ 3.20 Coding the Topic Pages for Source

A single document or transcript may be the source for a great many entries on many different topic pages. The lawyer may repetitively write the date of the hearing or report, the name of the reporting person, or, in the case of court hearings, the names of the judge and the district attorney who were also present, as these items are needed each time in order to lay a proper foundation for impeachment. As a short cut, it is useful to make a summary source page detailing the foundation information as to each of these discovery documents. In that way the topic page need only say "PH" for preliminary hearing, or "Mtn Hrg" for motion hearing, and the page and line, while the source code page will show that the preliminary hearing was conducted November 15, 1992, in courtroom 111 before Judge Frey, and deputy district attorney Larry Simpleton.

Chart 15

Bennett: SOURCE CODES FOR SOURCE DOCUMENTS		
Off Rpt	Ofcr. Mike Bates	7/20/2008
PH Ct 111	Judge Frey/DA Simpleton	11/15/2008
Def. Interv.	(D.I.) Bob Lucas	1/12/2009
MTN HRG. Ct 17	Judge Hutt/DA Hines	2/20/2010

Having created a source page, the lawyer can now greatly reduce the amount of source information needed to properly show on the topic entries:

Chart 16

Bennett: *Height*			
6-1	Off. Rpt.	1/5	7/20/2008
about 5'7"	PH	19:3	11/15/2008
We were standing in front of each other and I had to look up.	MTN HRG.	78:21	2/20/2009

However, even when using this source code page, it is absolutely critical that every notation on the topic pages have the name and page number of the source document. Page and line should be used wherever page and line numbers exist (see Chart 16, entries 2 & 3). If no line number is available, at least the portion of the page should be noted. Some lawyers prefer to use T for top one third of the page, M four middle one third of the page and B for the bottom one third of a page. Others use arrows "[arrow up]" showing on the upper half of page or "[arrow down]" showing on the lower half of page, or any other helpful codes. This may seem overly precise; however, it is always harder to find the information in trial than the lawyer would think, and the time spent looking for the appropriate entry on a page seems excruciatingly long. Moreover, when we can easily find exactly what we need, our level of confidence goes up, the jury's confidence in its goes up, and correspondingly, confidence of the witness is somewhat shaken.

Multiple Witnesses Single Topic Comparison

Chart 17

Bennett: *Build*	
160-175	P. Rpt. p.2/5
175-180	PH 80:21
Pretty good shape	PH 80:25
Trim	PH 81:4, 81:1

Chart 18

Dudley: *Build*	
Medium to heavy	Off. Rpt. 2/5
Very heavy set, big belly protruded all the way around	PH 63:14-20

Chart 19

Paxton: *Build*	
Little stockier than LSP	PH 25:23
Could not tell shape the guy was in	Mtn. Hrg. 31:6

§ 3.21 Tracking the "Non-Answer" Answer

If a witness, when asked about a particular topic, says, "I didn't see it," "I've forgotten," or "I'm unsure," or any other words along these lines, that answer needs to appear on the appropriate topic page, as well (see Paxton's page, above). Such statements may prove inconsistent with other testimony of that witness or another witness on that topic. Such "non-answers" are also useful in crafting a cross-examination that requires the witness to repeatedly answer, "I can't remember" or "I didn't see." This may be the safest of crosses, and equally telling or helpful to the cross-examiner.

Occasionally, the lawyer discovers in her source material no answer whatsoever. The answer isn't, "I didn't see it," but a blank where an answer could have been written, or a failure to describe something that elsewhere the witness does describe. Such a failure to describe a fact requires both a notation on the appropriate topic page and further investigation. For instance, if in the initial police offense report, which formed the first source page for the topic pages, there was a blank under "glasses" and a blank under "beard/ mustache," during the initial reading of discovery, done to verify the theory of the defense, the lawyer may have mentally noted whether a "glasses" or "beard and mustache" description was given.

This information should be noted on the appropriate page (see Chart 20). If a description of that item is ever given by that witness, then the failure to give such a description to the police officer in the course of the offense report is something that must be noted on the proper topic page (see Chart 21). A failure to report to the officer a description of these items is inconsistent with later giving a description of that topic. The blanks found in descriptions may translate to either the answer, "None" or "I don't know." Further clarification may be required.

Chart 20

Bennett: *Glasses*	
No info given	Off. Rpt. 1
I think he had wire-framed glasses	PH. 17:6

Chart 21

Bennett: *Items Absent*	
Glasses: No description	Off. Rpt. 1
Tattoos: No description	Off. Rpt. 1/5

Furthermore, if the lawyer recalls and notes that another witness saw glasses or a beard or mustache, the theoretical "none" answer by this witness sets up an external inconsistency. Compare Chart 21, above, with Chart 22, below. Once again witness Bennett has given internally inconsistent answers and has given answers inconsistent with witness Paxton.

Chart 22

Paxton: *Glasses*	
Black framed	P. Rpt. 1/5
Heavy black	OH. 56:19

§ 3.22 Tracking "Did Not See" and "None" Answers

The process and necessity of tracking definitive information provided by a witness and tracking "non-answers" of the witness has been presented. There is another type of answer — the answer in the negative. Answers in the negative are answers in which the witness affirmatively admits a lack of knowledge on a particular topic, i.e., "I didn't see if he was wearing glasses." Just as was true from the other forms of answers, the lawyer must keep track of such negative answers in order to be prepared to impeach with them or to bring them out in cross-examination as a means of showing how little the witness saw or recalls.

§ 3.23 Tracking Facts on Which All Information Is in the Negative

There are invariably a great many topics that the witness did not see or describe in the discovery, the hearings, or the pre-trial investigation. It is helpful to create a general topic page for all of the items that are consistently not seen, or those seen, but not remembered (see Chart 23, below). Later, if a specific fact becomes significant or is contradicted by this or another witness, the "didn't see" answer can be transferred to the appropriate witness/topic page (see Chart 24). In this way, the cross-examiner is shielded from the requirement to reread all of the discovery. This "did not see" page can now also serve as the basis of a cross-examination on what was not seen (see Chart 25).

Chart 23

Bennett: *Did not see / Can't remember*	
Shirt — Can't recall	Off. Rpt. 1/5
Hair style — Couldn't really see it	PH. 20:13
Shoes — I didn't see them	PH. 33:2

Chart 24

Bennett: *Shirt*	
Can't recall	Off. Rpt. 2

§ 3.24 Generic Topic Pages

There are some pieces of important data that do not fit conveniently into any one topic, but are important to a great many topics. For instance, the opportunity to observe the robber is important as to every single item of description given by the witness. However, it is too time consuming and redundant to put that information on topic page after topic page. Therefore, it is easier to create a single topic page such as "Opportunity to Observe" that contains upon it all appropriate information. See Chart 25, below.

Note, however, that when filling out such generic pages, such as "Opportunity to Observe," if the lawyer happens upon an inconsistency, the information is now deserving of its own topic page. Inconsistencies on any topic rate their own page, since each area of inconsistency may well be worth its own chapter of cross-examination (see chapter 5, *The Chapter Method of Cross-Examination*).

For instance, if at one point the witness states that the robbery took no more than 30 seconds, but at another point the lawyer finds a claim by the witness that the whole thing took about five minutes, such material is worthy of its own topic page (see Chart 26). The lawyer might call it "duration of robbery" or some other term that reminds her of what she is talking about, but any meaningful inconsistency is worth its own topic page, since inconsistencies are of utmost importance to the cross-examiner.

Chart 25

Bennett: *Opportunity to Observe*	
The store was real well lit.	Off. Rpt. p. 3
He walked right up to me and was standing across the counter from me.	Supp. p.7
I didn't see him walk in the door and the first time I noticed him was when he walked up and asked for the money.	Supp. p. 9
The whole robbery took no more than two minutes and then he turned and ran out.	PH. 19:60

Chart 26

Bennett: *Duration of Robbery*	
30 seconds	Off. Rpt. p.5
It took about five minutes	PH 19:12

§ 3.25 Coding in Externally Verifiable Facts

A completed topic page will immediately demonstrate any internal inconsistencies (inconsistencies within the statements given by that witness on any topic). By comparing completed topic pages of more than one witness in the same topic, the lawyer has identified one form of external inconsistency. Further work is needed to locate and show other forms of external inconsistencies.

Externally verifiable facts include, but are not limited to, other witness descriptions, exhibits, documents, photographs, drawings, videotapes, audiotapes, experiments, physical evidence, tangible evidence, and the verifiable laws of nature such as time of sunrise and the direction in which a landmark is located.

The significance of much of the information on a particular topic page can only be appreciated when compared to some other externally verifiable fact.

For instance, if the client has a prominent facial scar, there deserves to be a topic page on that characteristic, so the lawyer can enter onto that topic page every single instance where the witness has been given an opportunity to describe the face of the assailant, but made no mention of a scar. This remains true even if the direct question of a scar did not arise. The witness can explain all she wants that she was not directly asked about that fact. But jurors may doubt that a person who stood face-to-face with a robber, described him and picked his picture later, did not notice or mention the facial scar; or having noticed it, failed to tell anyone about it.

In other instances, while all of the entries on a particular topic page may be consistent with each other, and even consistent with other witnesses, they, of course, must be considered in relationship to absolutely unquestionable realities. In a criminal case based on identification testimony, the defendant's physical characteristics will generally fall into the category of physical evidence. If a witness consistently describes the assailant as being in good shape and the client has a noticeable beer belly (which was not recently acquired), then that aspect of the witness's description is very relevant to a theory of the case based on misidentification. Every instance where the witness has said something about the assailant being in good shape may be externally inconsistent with the client's actual build. Hence every one of those descriptions needs to be noted on the topic page, regardless of the fact that they are consistent with each other. Similarly, in civil cases, what the witness perceived, and the consistency of those perceptions, may be at odds with reality: the stop sign the witness insists was not there, the "hill" that does not exist, or the patient's spiking temperature.

§ 3.26 Sourcing External Facts

In order to make the necessary comparison of a witness's version of facts to any externally verifiable fact, it is necessary to code in information on the topic page concerning that externally verifiable fact. Such externally verifiable facts also need to have a source. If the only source of that information is the client, the lawyer is mentally boxing herself into needing to call the client to the stand. There may well be cases where that is not a desirable tactic. In a civil case where the client may be called by deponent, the lawyer is boxing herself into dependence on the client's credibility in order to establish that particular fact. It is far better to look for ways to independently prove the external facts than to rely solely upon the client. For instance, on the height page. Assume the lawyer can develop an inconsistency between the description given by a witness and the height of the client, and further assume that the lawyer wants the jury to know the height of the client. It is important to mark the height of the client on the witness height page along with a source that can introduce that evidence. Example:

Chart 27

Bennett: *Height*			
6-1	Ofcr. M. Bates	Off. Rpt. 1/5	7/20/2008
about 5'7"	DA: Simpleton	PH. p.19:3	11/15/2008
We were standing in front of each other and I had to look up.		MTN HRG.	78:21
Pretty tall — at least 6 feet.		Def. Int.	p.3
5'8"	**client**	**Booking slip**	**9/15/2008**

§ 3.27 Facts from Other External Sources

So far, the witness topic pages have assumed the witnesses to be live people. However, there are many occasions in both civil and criminal cases when facts speak for themselves, though a witness must take the stand to introduce the fact. For instance, the coroner's report shows: (1) the blood alcohol of .20; (2) three stab wounds to the back; or (3) a bullet trajectory entering the chest and angling upward, exiting in the back. All of these topics themselves are facts that need to be coded into appropriate topic pages. In a civil case, the highway diagrams, the accident scene diagrams, and the pathology lab report are all facts from external sources that need to be coded into the appropriate topic pages.

Similarly, in a contract case, a document may use a particular phrase. If this is a fact having some bearing on the case, it needs to be coded into the appropriate page. In a products liability case, another example may be a warning label on a machine, or a user's manual that either contains or omits a particular warning. Language or lack of language is itself a fact and best yet, is a fact beyond change. The document says what the document says, the photo shows what the photo shows, and the number of stab wounds noted in the autopsy is almost surely the number of stab wounds. These facts may contradict the witness, either by their introduction in raw form or by their introduction through the testimony of the witness, such as a coroner interpreting the fact. Similarly, the physical dimensions and mechanical characteristics of a machine are fixed facts. Testimony inconsistent with these physical characteristics is testimony that can be exposed as unbelievable. In all such instances, the lawyer must move the facts, the documents, exhibits, and reports onto the appropriate topic pages. In a civil wrongful death action:

Chart 28

Distance of Collision from Intersection	
The car hit him in the middle of the intersection.	Witness Mackey PH. p.3:9 (Preliminary Hearing of Defendant)
The car "hit the guy that died" right under the red light The body fell "right there"; "no movement."	Mackey Depo. p.22:7
Body found on sidewalk 36 feet from corner.	Coroner's Report p.7
Only blood stains from 32-34 feet from corner.	State Accident Lab Rpt. 4 p.2

As Chart 28 indicates, Mackey's testimony is consistent in his version of events, yet inconsistent with both the anticipated testimony of the coroner and the anticipated testimony of the investigative lab technician. These external inconsistencies can either be coded directly onto the appropriate topic page or they can each have their own page (see Charts 29 and 30 below).

Chart 29

Coroner Whitney: *Distance of Collision from Intersection*	
Body found on sidewalk 36 feet from corner	Det. Police Rpt. 6/14

Chart 30

Investigative Lab: *Distance of Collision from Intersection*	
Blood stains from 32-34 feet from corner	Jim McHughs Rpt. 3/6

In this way, the lawyer looks at external facts as witnesses. In the same way that witnesses testify, documents, photographs, and measurements can communicate. Though all may require an interpreter, they are as much testimony in the case as the words spoken by witnesses. Therefore, they need to be coded into the topic pages so that the lawyer can find both instances where witnesses are inconsistent with external facts, and instances where witnesses are consistent with external facts.

§ 3.28 Summary of the Preparation Technique

At the conclusion of this process, the lawyer has taken all of the information in discovery, added information gained in hearings and transcripts of any kind, added material derived from investigation, and then systematically grouped the material together by topic so that the lawyer now has categorized and systemized the information available.

Thousands of facts have been chiseled down into a far fewer number of topic pages. It is within these topic pages that the lawyer now has the vast majority of the facts needed to prepare tight, accurate, penetrating cross-examinations. In writing the cross-examinations, the lawyer will refer almost exclusively to these pages, rather than to the discovery from which they were distilled (see chapter 6, *Page Preparation of Cross-Examination*). Remember, even if many of the pages generated reveal no inconsistencies, they must be retained. They may have tremendous value at trial. No trial lawyer can ever predict when a witness will vary a story or detail that has previously been thought to be rock solid. This will be further discussed in chapter 8, *Seven Steps of Impeachment by Inconsistent Statement*.

Chapter 4

THE ONLY THREE RULES OF CROSS-EXAMINATION

§ 4.01 Control Through the Only Three Rules of Cross-Examination

This chapter sets out the foundation methods of obtaining and maintaining control of the witness and the subject matter of the cross-examination question by question. There are only three rules. The rules are all positive. These rules are simple and allow the cross-examiner to understand and apply the rules of controlled damage. Finally, the rules apply to every type of case — whether jury trial, judge trial, arbitration panel, or mediation. Because the rules of cross-examination are positive, the cross-examiner knows a rule is about to be violated before the question is verbalized rather than after it is asked when the damage has already been done. Because the rules have universal application, they afford safe and predictable results. The cross-examiner is not required to learn or employ different systems or techniques of cross-examination based on the personality, intelligence or hostility of the witness. The only three rules of cross-examination are:

(1) leading questions only,

(2) one new fact per question, and

(3) questions move in a logical progression to one specific goal.

Many of us have had the privilege of seeing Professor Irving Younger's excellent lecture entitled "The Ten Commandments of Cross-Examination." While the rules he espoused are valid, they are difficult to employ in trial. First, there are few cross-examiners who can remember ten rules while cross-examining. In addition, many of the rules are phrased in the negative (e.g., don't ask one question too many). Unfortunately, when a rule is phrased in the negative, often the practitioner only recalls the rule has been violated. There are no points for error recognition. We need error avoidance. The only three rules of cross-examination allow us to recall what it is we are to do, instead of what we must not do.

§ 4.02 Cross-Examining to Enable Real-Time Learning

The three rules of cross-examination are designed to maximize the amount of useful factual information coming before the jury in a context in which the facts may immediately be understood for their impact on the opposing theories of the case.

The three rules are designed to permit the fact finder to learn the cross-examiner's theory of the case and understand effective attacks upon the opponent's theory of the case in real time. Real time is defined as being the instant when the questions and answers are spoken in trial. The opposite of real time is to suggest that the jury will only understand the significance of a question and answer in the closing argument, or worse, in the jury room. The jury must understand the significance of the questions and answers at the time of trial. It is only through the building of these facts, one at a time, that the fact finder can appreciate the significance of the testimony and the relationship of that testimony to other testimony that has come before this witness and will come after this witness.

The jurors must be able to say to themselves, "I understand why the lawyer is asking this question and I understand the significance of the admission." Juries vote for what they understand.

§ 4.03 Rule 1: Leading Questions Only

The Federal Rules of Evidence and the rules of evidence of all states permit leading questions on cross-examination (Fed. Rules Evid. Rule 611(c); 28 U.S.C.A.). Simultaneously, the right to use leading questions is almost wholly denied the direct examiner. This is the fundamental distinguishing asset of the right to cross-examine. It is the critical advantage given the cross-examiner. This singular procedural advantage must always be pressed.

Despite this incredible opportunity, many lawyers do not take advantage of this right and instead, by habit or design, ask primarily open-ended questions. This is unwise at best and foolhardy at worst. The cross-examiner must never forfeit the enormous advantage offered by the right to question using leading questions.

The "leading questions only" technique means that, in trial, the cross-examiner must endeavor to consistently phrase questions that are leading. No matter what the rationale, a non-leading question introduces far greater dimensions of risk and occasions far less control than a question that is strictly leading.

One of the greatest risks occasioned by the use of open-ended questions is not the answer that may be given to that particular question. The answer may be perfectly acceptable to the cross-examiner. However, by asking the open-ended question the cross-examiner has failed to consistently train the witness to give short answers to leading questions and not to volunteer information. With every open-ended question the cross-examiner teaches inconsistently. By occasionally asking open-ended questions we send the clear signal that long narrative responses are an acceptable method of replying to our questions. We actually invite explanations. Even if we gain a satisfactory response to a particular open-ended question, we sow the seeds for later problems in the cross-examination. As will be discussed, the cross-examiner must teach a consistent lesson to the witness concerning how the cross-examination will proceed: The cross-examiner will pose the leading question and the witness may verify or deny the suggested fact. The consistency of teaching through the repetitive form of the leading question is fundamental to the goal of witness control.

§ 4.04 Leading Questions Allow the Cross-Examiner to Become the Teacher

If the lawyer is to teach the case, the lawyer must demonstrate that she understands the case. The leading question positions the cross-examiner as the teacher, while the open-ended question positions the cross-examiner as a student. The open-ended question converts the witness into the teacher of the facts. The open-ended question focuses courtroom attention on the witness. The leading question focuses attention on the cross-examiner. The cross-examiner seeks the jurors' attention not for ego gratification, but for purposes of efficiently teaching the facts of the case. The cross-examiner/teacher using leading questions places the cross-examiner in control of the flow of information. The leading question also allows the cross-examiner to select the topics to be discussed within the cross-examination. These topics will be referred to throughout the book as the chapters of cross-examination.

§ 4.05 Use Short Declarative Questions

Leading questions are often defined as questions that suggest the answer. This is too broad a definition. True leading questions do not merely suggest the answer; they *declare* the answer.

Review the following three questions:

1) How do you feel about drinking?

2) Do you like to drink?

3) You like to drink?

Most lawyers will recognize that the first question is not a leading question. There is no answer suggested in the question. It is completely open-ended, allowing the witness to respond in any manner that he or she chooses. Worse, it invites a narrative response in which the witness may elect to include unsolicited information that relate in some distant way to drinking. Did the witness's parents drink? When did the witness start drinking? Does the witness suffer back pain and use drinking as self-medication? Has the witness worked hard to teach his children the dangers of drinking? You ask broadly about drinking, you invite a broad range of responses.

There are many experienced trial lawyers who would argue that the second question, "Do you like to drink?" is a leading question, as it indicates that the person should respond only with a monosyllable. It is not, however, a leading question for cross-examination. It does not *require* the desired answer. It does not *declare* the answer.

The third question, "You like to drink?" is leading, and unquestionably more confining and suggestive of the answer desired than question number one or two.

Why is this? The answer is quite simple. The fact that question number three begins with a non-verb means that it will be more closed-ended, more conducive to a restricted, monosyllabic answer. Especially when phrased as a statement, it *tells* the witness to answer with the answer the questioner requires. It *declares* the answer.

If the question mark is taken away from question three, it would be a short declarative sentence. Leading questions on cross-examination must be short declarative sentences. While the court reporter will type them all with a question mark at the end, the cross-examiner's voice need not even inflect a questioning tone.

§ 4.06 Declarative Questions Allow Immediate Understanding by the Jury

We are not in court to create great literature. We are seeking to communicate and short questions aid in that regard. The accomplished cross-examiner asks questions the way Ernest Hemingway wrote. Here is the thought process of the old man seeking to catch the great fish in *The Old Man and the Sea.*

> Maybe today. Every day is a new day. It is better to be lucky. But I would rather be exact.
>
> *The Old Man and the Sea*

We understand what he is saying. We can immediately digest the thoughts without saying to ourselves, "Now what did he say again?"

The cross-examiner does not ask questions the way James Joyce wrote:

> And by that way went the herds innumerable of bellwethers and flushed ewes and shearling rams and lambs and stubble geese and medium steers and roaring mares and polled calves and longwools and storesheep and Cuffe's prime springers and culls and sowpigs and baconhogs and the various different varieties of highly distinguished swine and Angus heifers and polly bullocks of immaculate pedigree together with prime premiated milchcows and beeves: and there is ever heard a trampling, cackling, roaring, lowing, bleating, bellowing, rumbling, grunting, champing, chewing . . .
>
> *Ulysses*

Unquestionably, both Hemingway and James Joyce had great talent. Unquestionably, each wrote beautifully. Which one was understood more quickly?

Juries and judges understand when a leading question is put in a declarative style. The fact proposed is immediately understandable. It is learnable in real time.

Take question three from the preceding section: "You like to drink?" If Hemingway were to ask this question, he would use two questions rather than one. The understanding for the jury would be more precise and more immediate. The resistance from the witness would be minimized:

> 4) You drink?
>
> 5) You like it?

Examine what has been accomplished with breaking the question down to a more understandable form. The witness is given a question about drinking and responds. Once the witness has said "yes," the witness must say that he likes it or subjects himself to ridicule, humiliation, or at the very least illogical thought.

§ 4.07 Dealing with Witnesses Who Don't Want to Answer

Most cross-examiners have encountered a witness who feigned a lack of understanding that the leading question requires a response. The lawyer asks: If the witness doesn't answer, what do I do?

First, that is a rare situation. Yes, there are some witnesses who will pretend they do not understand that they are being asked to verify or deny the truthfulness of the fact within the leading question. But these witnesses are rare and are almost always witnesses who have testified a great many times before and who are recognized by the jury as advocates of the position taken by the lawyer who called them to the stand.

First consider the vast majority of witnesses. They come to court, reluctantly perhaps, once in their lives. These witnesses are not interested in game playing. They want to tell their story, answer the questions, and get off the witness stand. If they are schooled in the method of examination based on leading questions, they will freely and quickly provide answers to those questions. For these witnesses it is imperative that the cross-examiner teach consistently. It is imperative for the cross-examiner to use leading questions exclusively so that the witness will understand that that is the exclusive method by which witnesses are to be cross-examined.

The use of leading questions to establish facts is not confined to the courtroom. In everyday conversations most people do not speak in perfectly grammatical sentences. People use shorthand. They don't necessarily even finish their questions. The flow of the conversation establishes a context. In everyday life people understand each other even when the grammar or punctuation would earn a failing grade on an English final. In everyday life, we do not add ". . . don't you?" to our sentences. At the last social function you attended, people did not ask questions such as, "You want a drink, don't you?"

There may be the rare judge who interrupts and offers that your declarative question is not, in fact, a question. In this case, occasionally add the ". . . don't you?" or other introductory or concluding phrase that turns the declarative question into a true question. This will undoubtedly satisfy the bench. Experience has taught that this method is so conversationally common that interruptions from the bench soon stop.

§ 4.08 Avoid Enemy Words that Give Control to the Witness

The adept cross-examiner *never* uses questions that begin with the following:

1) Who
2) What
3) When
4) Where
5) How
6) Why
7) Explain

These words create the polar opposite of closed-ended questions. These words invite uncontrolled, unpredictable, and perhaps unending answers. These words *invite the witness to seize the action*, to become the focal point of the courtroom. They take the jury's mind off the fact the cross-examiner is trying to develop and allow the witness to insert a mishmash of facts, opinions, and stories that focus the jury on the issues the witness thinks are most important.

Cross-examiners are not journalists looking to present both sides of a story or even all aspects of one side of the story. Cross-examiners are not interested in having the witness explain everything that the witness wishes to explain. Cross-examiners strive to introduce or expand on the facts that most aid the cross-examiner's theory of the case or that most damage the opponent's theory of the case.

Some lawyers maintain that they are so skillful that they can pose open-ended questions, the answers to which will always be of assistance. These lawyers are fond of saying, "I didn't care how she answered," or "There were no possible answers that could hurt me." In response, those lawyers have only eliminated the answers they have thought of. They have falsely projected a closed set of responses to an open-ended question As we have discussed, the open-ended question invites the witness to answer tangentially, providing information that touches upon the subject matter of the question but does not squarely answer the question. None of us is so omniscient that we can confidently state that we have eliminated every possible negative or explanatory answer. There are truly both bad answers and non-responsive answers awaiting the open-ended question. Why take that unnecessary chance? This applies to the most experienced trial lawyer as well as the novice. No one outgrows this advice.

For example, the cross-examination of the government's major witness — an admitted "large-scale drug smuggler" for the drug cartel in a federal criminal prosecution — was proceeding well as a result of thorough and controlled questioning by a very skillful lawyer. One slip into the enemy words, however, devastated the cross-examiner:

Q: How much cocaine did you import into the United States?

A: With or without the assistance of your client?

Or

A. I had been dealing in ounces until I hooked up with your client. He convinced me to up it to pounds.

Or

A: I was about done until your client told me I either bring in the drugs or he kills my wife.

And it goes on and on. The variety of bad non-answers is without limit.

But you say this isn't fair. If the witness would only answer the question asked, the answers would be safer. True enough. So let's more carefully control the information we seek and thereby more carefully prescribe the limits to the answers we are inviting. The leading question accomplishes this.

The flip side of that coin is: Why give up the advantage of the leading question? If, in fact, the cross-examiner has eliminated all other possible answers, why take the chance in asking anything but a leading or declarative question that dictates the answer? Remember to always control the witness. Keep the focus of the questioning on the cross-examiner instead of the witness.

§ 4.09 Open-Ended Questions Encourage Long-Winded Answers Even to Later Leading Questions

Of course, not every witness will respond in a devastating manner to a single open-ended question, but that is no reason to run the risk. In fact, the risk of a bad answer to that particular question is only one of the risks created by the open-ended question. A far greater risk is that the cross-examiner is now teaching inconsistently. By mixing open-ended and closed-ended questions, the cross-examiner is, in effect, instructing the witness that it is completely permissible or expected that the witness will volunteer long explanations to the cross-examiner's questions. The result of this inconsistent teaching is that the witness can no longer be counted on to give short answers even to the simple leading questions. Seen in this regard, every open-ended question damages the cause of witness control so ardently sought by the cross-examiner.

§ 4.10 Leading Allows Control of Mood and Emphasis

Another great advantage of the leading question is that it permits the cross-examiner to choose the emotion of the answer and the facts to be stressed. When leading questions are used, the cross-examiner can ask in a cold, hard, factual tone of voice, in a matter-of-fact tone, with sarcasm, or with incredulity. The choice belongs to the cross-examiner. If the witness is left to choose, it is unlikely that the opposing witness will independently adopt the favored tone of voice. Yet, the cross-examiner can create the tone of the facts by using tone of voice to set the emotional stage, allowing the witness only the right to answer "yes."

§ 4.11 Leading Facilitates Word Selection

One of the most important benefits of the leading question is that it permits the cross-examiner to select the desired adjectives and adverbs. Or, if you hated this stuff in junior high, just think of them as the descriptions. In this way the cross-examiner can give color to the facts of greatest importance. Opposing witnesses can hardly be counted on to provide vivid descriptions of facts or events that do not aid the theory they endorse. If we use open-ended questions, we allow the witness to characterize the fact or event or to leave out any of the description whatsoever. The one predictable statement that could be made is that the word will not be selected to consciously help the cross-examiner's theory of the case.

By use of a leading question, the cross-examiner controls the word selection and may more descriptively and vividly describe that which has occurred. This is critical in that the vivid picture is far more memorable than the bland fact.

> We say: "Please describe the road."
>
> The witness answers with an evasion: "What do you mean?"
>
> We try again: "What effect did the weather have on the road?"
>
> The witness partially answers: "It wasn't dry anymore. "
>
> We try again:" "Did the road look icy?"
>
> The witness partially dodges: "It had a little snow."

And so it goes. We don't suggest an answer. We hope for one. And we get answers, but not the ones we want or deserve. It would be so much easier if we used leading questions to assert what we believe to be the facts and we insert the described descriptions:

> "It had been snowing for several hours?"
>
> The road was coated with snow?
>
> The traffic had packed down the snow?
>
> And now you could see the headlights glisten off the thin sheet of ice that had formed?

You think the witness might not give "yes" answers to these facts? Well, he certainly won't if you don't ask. By painting the picture in the terms you feel are appropriate, you have upped the chances of getting the answers you want. And you have forced the witness to work from a starting description you have provided.

Compare the following three questions:

1) What did you see after the accident?

Vs.

2) You saw a man lying on the side of the road?

Vs.

3) You saw a man hurled from the car?

The first question provides no picture and leaves the witness with a clear opportunity to evade or to provide only the facts and descriptions selected by the witness.

The second question offers some minimal description of a potential plaintiff in a personal injury suit. At least the subject is narrowed. But the question begs for some further description. As is it remains a colorless picture.

It is only in the third version that the cross-examiner uses the leading question to both control the subject of the inquiry while simultaneously providing a useful description. The insertion of the descriptive word "hurled" in the third question adds context to the picture.

The lawyer's conscious word selection can make the fact finder, both judge and jury, react differently to the explanation of events by the witness. Beyond that, careful word selection makes the witness feel differently about himself and his role in the activities.

Do not be discouraged if a witness, particularly a professional expert witness, will choose to disagree with a vivid but fair word selection.

Example:

Q: You saw a man <u>hurled</u> from the car?

A: I would not call it that, counselor.

Initially this response may cause the cross-examiner to rethink her descriptive word. Once she has determined that it is a fair word to describe the actual facts and events, it is then up to her to make the fact finder and the witness realize that the word is fair and will not be abandoned.

Q: You saw the man exit the car?

A: Yes.

Q: He did not voluntarily exit?

A: No.

Q: He exited through the window?

A: That's true.

Q: He exited through the side window?

A: Yes.

Q: That side window was rolled up when he exited?

A: Yes.

Q: He exited through the window head first?

A: Yes.

Q: His head broke through the window as he exited?

A: Yes.

Q: The man was hurled from the car?

A: That's correct, counselor.

Once the trial lawyer determined that the descriptive word that she used was a fair, accurate, and vivid word, the non-answer is dealt with by more detailed questioning, more precision, and more time. Do not abandon the vivid word.

§ 4.12 Leading Allows Word Emphasis

Similarly, by use of the leading question, the cross-examiner can use her voice to place the emphasis on the selected words.

The open-ended question results in the following:

Q: Did you put that in your report?

A: No, I didn't.

The leading question, on the other hand, results in the same information, but with a different emphasis:

Q: You wrote an entire 27-page report, but you never mentioned any such thing?

A: No, I didn't.

In the leading question the cross-examiner controls word selection, tone of voice, and word emphasis. All of these devices of persuasion are forfeited when the cross-examiner offers up the open-ended question.

§ 4.13 Word Selection Describes Theory

When the cross-examiner carefully selects words to describe her theory of the case, the cross-examiner never has to verbalize or have the witness agree to the conclusion that represents the theory of the case. As an example, in nine questions the cross-examiner by word selection conveys to the jury her entire theory of the case:

Q: She confided in you that this was her life savings?

A: Yes.

Q: She cautioned you that her goal was safety?

A: Yes.

Q: She was sixty-six years old?

A: Yes.

Q:. She was on a fixed income?

A: Yes.

Q: She was retired?

A: Yes.

Q: She was on a fixed income?

A: Yes.

Q: She told you it was her nest egg?

A: Yes.

Q: She told you it was her life savings?

A: Yes.

Q: She told you it was all the money that she had?

A: Yes.

Does the cross-examiner need to explain to the jury that the plaintiff was a conservative investor?

§ 4.14 Rule 2: Ask One New Fact per Question

In Rule 1 we used the leading question for many reasons. It controls the field of discussion. It suggests the answer. It provides a fact to be accepted or rejected by the witness.

We now add another measure of control. In Rule 2, we ask only one new fact in each question. In this way we further narrow the field of evasion by specifying the fact to be discussed. By placing only a single new fact before a witness, the witness's ability to evade is dramatically diminished. In addition, when we ask short, narrowly focused questions containing only one new fact, both we and the jury immediately understand the significance of the answer. A "yes" answer means we now own that fact. A "no" answer tells us exactly what fact is in dispute. A question that contains only one new fact enhances the ability of the fact finder to comprehend the significance of the fact just proved.

§ 4.15 Fixing the Multiple-Fact Question

When we violate Rule 2 by asking a question containing more than one new fact we create problems regardless of the answer. Let us begin by supposing a "no" answer. When we ask a leading question that seeks agreement to multiple new facts and the witness answers "no," we are unsure to what fact the denial applies. This is a problem of the cross-examincr's creation. By including in any question more than one new fact, we have created a situation in which a denial can apply to more than one fact. In such instances, the cross-examiner must first back up and start the chain of questions back at the last fact to which she has gotten an affirmative answer:

We begin the process of fixing the problem by locating the fact the witness is really denying. Once we isolate the fact in dispute, we can decide if it is worth fighting over and, if so, we can elect the methods we might use to gain a "yes" answer.

> **Q:** You saw the blue car come around the corner and speed through the red light?
>
> **A:** No.

This compound question contains five facts and one adjective. There are five possible "facts" to which the answer "no" might apply. Now the examiner must decipher to what "no" refers: The color of the car? The speed of the car? The color of the light? Whether the witness saw anything at all? Even if the opponent does not object on the basis of compound questions, the witness has just as effectively done so by answering "no." If the lawyer has established *any* of these facts, she must now back up to the last fact established, re-establish it and then continue one new fact at a time:

> **Q:** You did see a car?
>
> **A:** Yes.
>
> **Q:** It was blue?
>
> **A:** Yes.
>
> **Q:** The blue car came around the corner?
>
> **A:** Truc.
>
> **Q:** It drove through the red light?
>
> **A:** True.
>
> **Q:** As it drove through the red light, it was speeding?
>
> **A:** It depends on what you mean by speeding.

By backing up to the last *safe* point in the above sequence, the cross-examiner can now begin the process of isolating the fact in dispute. The cross-examiner can now concentrate her efforts on clarifying that issue.

In addition, many times the lawyer immediately assumes that a negative answer to a compound question means the witness is fighting the cross-examiner about something that must be proven. As the following exchange shows, often the witness is not fighting the lawyer about what she must prove, only about her word choice in describing certain things:

Q: You saw a car go through the light?

A: Yes.

Q: The light was red for the car?

A: Yes.

Q: The car that was speeding through the red light was blue?

A: No.

Q: No, it wasn't speeding?

A: No, it was gray. (Pause.) Well, it could have been light blue.

Q: Well, a light blue or gray car was speeding through the light?

A: Yes.

In this case, the word choice was "gray" rather than "light blue." It may be that this simply doesn't matter. (However, one may appropriately ask the cross-examiner why was the question asked, if the color of the car truly did not matter?) The witness may not be disagreeing about anything of relevance, and the cross-examiner may be able to accept the answer. However, it would serve the cross-examiner well to be careful of this witness, as he has shown not only the willingness to dispute facts, but the ability to potentially prevail in the dispute.

A "yes" answer to a leading question that asks for agreement to multiple new facts also provides problems. The "yes" answer may not mean "yes" to all the facts and may not be understood as meaning "yes." The more new facts in a question, the harder it is for a juror to comprehend all the new facts. This is especially true if more than one fact is important. Different jurors may focus on different facts within the leading question. We have lost our ability to focus attention where we desire.

In addition, "yes" to a multiple-fact question allows the opposing counsel to attack the multiple-fact question in a redirect examination. The standard method is for the direct examiner to call the witness's attention to the multiple-fact question, point out that the witness said "yes" to the question, and then ask the witness to clarify if they meant "yes" to all the facts in the question? If necessary, the direst examiner may draw the witness's attention to a particular fact in the multiple-fact question. The witness is thereby signaled that the direct examiner hopes the witness will clarify their answer by saying that their yes was only as to one or more other facts in the offending question.

§ 4.16 Avoiding the Compound Question Avoids an Objection

This method of asking only one new fact per question also allows the cross-examiner to avoid the valid objection "compound question." This alone is an important reason to avoid asking multiple-fact questions. But there are additional benefits. Often an opposing lawyer will interpose multiple objections to a question. The cross-examiner may try to reply to one or more of the objections, but may fail to answer all the objections. By avoiding compound questions, counsel sidesteps at least that part of a multi-tiered objection, allowing counsel to better meet any forthcoming objection. Witness this interchange:

Q: You were charged with murder in this case as well?

A: Yes.

Q: So in exchange for your testimony, you have worked out some kind of back room deal that will keep you out of prison or at least the State might not ask that you go to prison?

Opp.: Objection. That is a compound question. It calls for a conclusion on the part of the witness, and also it is argumentative.

Q: Your Honor, I believe I have a right to show motive, interest, or bias.

Judge: Sustained.

The cross-examiner has focused on the right to attack credibility, and likely would win the ruling if that were the only grounds for the objection. However, counsel has failed to solve the valid objection that this was a compound question. An objection sustained on that ground could easily be overcome by rephrasing the question into a series of questions each asking one new fact. Had counsel broken the question into its component parts, the cross-examiner could easily have established the facts of the plea bargain and its likely consequence on the sentence that could be imposed on the witness. The objection could easily have been overcome. In fact, it could have been avoided had counsel placed before the witness a series of leading one-fact questions.

By failing to solve the compound question objection, counsel allows the court to validly sustain the objection.

§ 4.17 Facts, Not Conclusions, Persuade

This second rule of one fact per question tightly controls the witness. The witness has before him but a single new fact. It is hard for the witness to express confusion or be evasive. Moreover the jury is more easily educated by this technique of factual presentation. Because the facts are so detailed and because the facts are presented one at a time, the jury will reach the conclusion to which the facts inevitably point. The jury will embrace the same logical conclusion suggested by the cross-examiner.

Remember it is the lawyer, not the jury, who is intimately familiar with the facts. The jury must slowly and carefully be brought to the conclusion sought by the advocate. It is far safer to let the jury reach its own conclusion based on the facts rather than demanding that conclusion from a hostile witness. The structure of one fact per question meticulously builds the picture so that the jury reaches the cross-examiner's desired conclusion, even though the conclusion itself may never be put to the witness. See chapter 5, *The Chapter Method of Cross-Examination* and chapter 6, *Page Preparation of Cross-Examination*.

§ 4.18 Conclusions Are Not Facts

Cross-examiners always feel the need to move faster in a trial. Judges become impatient. Juries send signals of boredom. Witnesses show a willingness to become uncontrollable. All of these facts make the cross-examiner want to move quicker. Unfortunately, cross-examiners tend to think that moving to conclusions, opinions, generalities and legalisms makes for faster movement. It does not. Worse, conclusions, opinions, generalities and legalisms inadequately teach the cross-examiner's theory of the case.

Individual, precise, detailed facts will always trump or overcome conclusions, opinions, generalities and legalisms. The reason? Facts —multiple and precise — paint a mental image. Conclusions, opinions, generalities and legalisms paint no image at all.

Q: Only a wealthy man could live at that address?

A: I wouldn't call myself wealthy.

The lawyer has created a problem for herself by falling into word usage that is conclusionary. It results in a distraction to the cross-examination and does not teach the details necessary for the jury to come to the conclusion that the witness is wealthy. The cross-examiner moves to facts and away from the conclusion to fix the problem:

Q: You are not poor?

A: No.

Q: You wear custom-made suits?

A: Yes.

Q: You ski in the Alps?

A: Yes.

Q: You own a 2008 Porsche Carrera.

A: Yes.

Q That costs $128,000.

A: Yes.

Q: You own your own Lear Jet.

A: Yes.

Q: That costs $3,600,000.

A: Yes.

Q: You own three homes?

A: Yes.

Q: One of those homes is in Aspen, Colorado?

A: Yes.

The lesson is that witnesses can always disagree with our conclusions and the cross-examination on conclusions usually degenerates into an argumentative battle with the cross-examiner lacking any way to force acceptance of the desired position. If we stick to facts, we can place the witness in a position where they admit the truth of our factual assertion, and the jury can and ordinarily will draw our desired conclusion.

Let us look back at the last series of questions and add a final denial by the witness of the conclusion the cross-examiner earlier wanted;

Witness: But I wouldn't call myself wealthy.

Or

Witness: I know a great many people who would not consider me wealthy.

Or

Witness: In comparison to many others, I am not all that wealthy.

Imagine what a juror will think of such answers. When we fill our chapter with facts that graphically illustrate the expensive possessions and life style of the witness, we do not need to ask the witness to agree with our desired conclusion. Moreover, attempts by the witness to deny or even qualify the obvious will not be successful. The facts tell the story. The facts persuade.

§ 4.19 Legalisms Are Not Facts

Not only do legalisms fail to teach the trial lawyer's theory of the case, they are often met with appropriate objections. In a personal injury case coming out of a collision between an eighteen wheel commercial truck and a car, the defendant was asked on cross-examination:

Q: You were negligent?

A: No.

Opp.: Objection. The question calls for a legal conclusion.

Judge: Sustained.

The lawyer moves into one true fact at a time to better prove and teach her theory of the case:

Q: It was dark, but you didn't slow down?

A: No.

Q: It was raining, but you didn't slow down?

A: No.

Q: The road was slick, but you didn't slow down?

A: No.

Q: The traffic was heavy, but you didn't slow down?

A: No.

Q: The traffic was bumper to bumper, but you didn't slow down?

A: No.

Q: You were passing every car that you came up to, but you didn't slow down?

A: Yes.

The jury may not understand negligence. The jury does understand someone who would not slow down.

§ 4.20 Creating Impact One Fact at a Time

By establishing one fact at a time, the cross-examiner achieves another laudable goal: The cross-examiner adds impact to the answers. By letting each fact have its own moment of revelation, the jury is allowed to concentrate on the development of the picture long before the whole picture is revealed. Example:

Q: You saw the six-foot, five-inch, 225-pound guy with the bloody fists beat down the five-foot, seven-inch, 155-pound boy with the bloody face?

This question was put to the state's only eyewitness to an assault. The answer received was "yes." The cross-examiner was elated. In one fell swoop, she had gotten an admission to numerous favorable facts. In the process, however, she deprived herself of the opportunity to create a truly memorable picture of self-defense.

The reason this question and answer never impressed the jury was because the jury was not given the time to absorb the eleven facts.

Q: You (1) saw the (2) six foot, five inch (3) 225-pound (4) guy with the (5) bloody (6) fists (7) beat down the (8) five foot, seven inch (9) 155-pound (10) boy with the (11) bloody face?

Had the individual facts been put to the eyewitness a single fact at a time, the cross-examiner would have had 11 times as many opportunities to use voice and emphasis to create drama. The cross-examiner could choose the pace of each individual question, building emotion, and creating interest as the individual facts piled up. Slowly, inexorably, the picture emerges of the bigger man beating mercilessly on the much smaller boy. For example:

Question 1:

Q: You saw the fight?

A: Yes.

Question 2:

Q: John, the big guy, was fighting?

A: Yes.

Question 3:

Q: John was six feet, five inches tall?

A: Yes.

Question 4:

Q: John is a big man?

A: Yes.

Question 5:

Q: Dave is only five feet, seven inches?

A: Yes.

Question 6:

Q: Dave is a much smaller boy?

A: Yes.

Question 7:

Q: John weighed 225 pounds?

A: Yes.

Question 8:

Q: Dave is 155 pounds?

A: About that.

Question 9:

Q: John was a much bigger person.

A: Yes.

Question 10:

Q: John was a much heavier person.

A: Yes.

Question 11:

Q: And then John was hitting Dave?

A: Yes.

Question 12:

Q: He was hitting Dave with his fists?

A: Yes.

Question 13:

Q: He was hitting Dave in the face?

A: Yes.

Question 14:

Q: John was hitting Dave, and his fists were bloody?

A: Yes.

Question 15:

Q: And as you watched, you saw the blood on Dave's face?

A: Yes.

Question 16:

Q: You saw John beating down on Dave, in the face, with his fists?

A: Yes.

The eleven individual facts now are spread over sixteen questions. Note that the cross-examiner used more questions than the number of facts within the initial compound question to establish all of the desired facts. Sometimes it takes many more questions to paint a picture than the number of hard facts in the picture. As discussed earlier in dealing with subjective questions, it may take multiple questions to establish just one important descriptive word or fact. Sometimes the added questions are simply ways of adding interest or better filling out the picture. In this example, the cross-examiner has been able to expand the material by use of summary questions and looping facts already introduced (see Chapter 10, *Loops, Double Loops, and Spontaneous Loops*).

§ 4.21 Infusing Emotion Question by Question

The "one fact per question" technique allows the cross-examiner to infuse various emotions on a question-by-question and fact-by-fact basis. Because each question contains only one new fact, the cross-examiner has created the flexibility necessary to drive the jurors emotionally into the story. It is for the cross-examiner to determine which facts deserve a change of voice or an emotional inflection that signals to the fact finder the importance of that particular fact.

In contrast, when multiple new facts are stuffed into a single question, it becomes exceedingly difficult to place different emotional tones on different facts. The multiple-fact question was already too cumbersome, and the addition of changes of voice, tone, and emphasis would sound preposterous. In the example above, the last, sixteen-part breakdown of the facts presents the facts more in a more digestible manner. Not every fact deserves an emotional overlay. In fact, relatively few facts should receive extra emphasis. When every fact is treated as extremely important, it becomes extremely difficult for the fact finder to accurately pick out which fact is truly the most important.

When only one new fact is asked per question, the picture of violence is made more graphic than could be provided by any conclusory statement. There is a true sense of drama to the unfolding scene. The jury is given time to absorb the picture. This evidence is brought to the front of the jury's mind.

Generally speaking, the more subjective the fact to be established or, at the other end of the spectrum, the more complex the fact to be established, the more careful and detailed the questioner must be. Therefore, the questioner must ask multiple questions to establish facts at either end of the spectrum.

When trying to compress too many facts into one question, the cross-examiner becomes sloppy with her word usage. There are too many facts to deal with, so the cross-examiner cannot select adequately descriptive words. As the questions improperly encompass multiple new facts there is a tendency to minimize the descriptive words. To the cross-examiner, the question already seems overly long, and the addition of descriptive detail serves only to further complicate the question. Hence, by enlarging the field of inquiry within the question, the cross-examiner has simultaneously diminished the ability of the sentence to create a vivid word picture. The technique of one new fact per question provides the solution. Each question has to be short enough to allow the cross-examiner the flexibility to infuse the descriptive words helpful in explaining that fact.

When the cross-examiner presents one fact per question to the jury, not only is the jury led step by step to the ultimate completion of that factual picture, but the cross-examiner has the freedom to concentrate on individual emotionally evocative facts within each question. The more concentrated the focus of the individual question, the more opportunity for descriptive, emotion-inducing word choices. Just as the jury can better envision the picture because of a more regulated flow of facts, the jury can better sense the desired emotion created by better word selection. Introducing one new fact per question permits the examiner to better control the flow of facts.

§ 4.22 Word Selection Made Easier by Envisioning the Event

While presenting one fact per question, the cross-examiner must make certain that the words used are adequate to create the desired scenario. There is a technique to aid the cross-examiner in selecting the descriptive words that can make the picture clearer and the facts more vivid. If the cross-examiner forms a mental image of what she is seeking to describe and then presents that mental image through leading questions, the result is a series of leading questions of more granular texture. The cross-examiner wishes the fact finder to see a particular picture, so it would only stand to reason that the cross-examiner must first see that picture:

Q: You saw the big boy hit the little boy?

A: Yes.

Compare that question with the following question that adds no new facts to the question, but is intended to heighten the image of the fight's unfairness by painting a more vivid picture:

Q: You saw the big boy beat on the little boy?

"Beat" is a more powerful and descriptive word than "hit." "Beat on" not only shows stronger impact than "hit," it emphasizes the height and size advantage that ultimately will be played out fact by fact to the jury. By seeing the fight in greater detail, the cross-examiner can describe, through leading questions, that same fight in greater detail.

Q: He pounded Dave with his fist?

Q: He punched him in the ribs?

Q: He smacked him in the face?

The cross-examiner must strive to use descriptive words to describe accurately the facts questioned upon. The descriptive words will come naturally when the cross-examiner will look into her own mind to see the event.

§ 4.23 Rule 3: Break Cross-Examination into a Series of Logical Progressions to Each Specific Goal

We are now a long way toward establishing control of the flow of our cross-examinations. Through Rule 1, use of leading questions, we have positioned ourselves as the teacher of the facts. Through Rule 2, one new fact per question, we have both controlled the flow of information and channeled the witness's range of likely responses. We are now in position to take the third step in control by linking the individual questions to drive the cross-examination toward preselected, comprehensible goals.

Cross-examination of a witness is not a monolithic exercise in which one question follows another endlessly until the entire experience is ended. Instead, the cross-examination of any witness is a finite series of goal-oriented exercises. The third technique of the only three rules of cross-examination is to link together a group of leading questions to establish a particular goal. It is equally helpful to think of this method as putting together a group of related facts in order to paint a particular picture. This is the heart of the chapter method of cross-examination and is explored at greater length in chapter 5, *The Chapter Method of Cross-Examination.*

In Rule 3, we assemble the facts into logical groupings. In order to engage in this process of chapter creation it is first necessary to break the cross-examination into separate and definable goals. Each section of cross-examination must have a specific goal. It must be so specific and clear that the cross-examiner, if asked at any time without notice (as judges are inclined to do), can identify the factual point she is seeking to make. Another way of envisioning this is to see cross-examination as a series of pictures that must be painted.

In almost every instance, the cross-examination of any witness will have multiple specific goals. However, the cross-examiner should produce a chapter at a time in order to establish a single identifiable goal at a time. Cross-examination is thereby envisioned, written, and finally performed as a series of specific goals. Each goal, in turn, must individually be factually developed. In trial, each individual chapter should be completed before moving to the next chapter.

Too often advocates envision the cross-examination of a witness as having a single, overriding goal such as:

- "destroying the credibility of the witness"
- "showing the defendant drove negligently"
- "proving the defendant robbed the store."

When we conceive of cross-examination in such a manner we make it exceedingly difficult to prepare and present the cross-examination. A cross-examination described in such global terms is too big to be workable. Where would we begin? How would we accomplish such global goals? How would we know when we had accomplished such a vast, overarching goal? Furthermore, we should notice that these are all conclusory goals, not factual goals.

Cross-examination is ideally suited for the establishment of factual goals. Cross-examination is ill-suited for the establishment of conclusory goals. There is a method to get a jury to accept a conclusion. In order to bring the jury to a point where they have accepted a desired conclusion, we need prove a set of facts which, in the context of this case, logically lead a jury to arrive at our desired conclusion. Remember, a cross-examination whose goal it is to get a hostile witness to agree with the cross-examiner's desired and important conclusion is a cross-examination likely to fail. Setting aside for the moment the fact that jurors are unpersuaded by hearing an advocate's conclusions, witnesses called by the adversary are extremely unlikely to agree with the cross-examiner's conclusions. It is therefore improper and unnecessary to conceive and plan a cross-examination in global legal terms such as breach of fiduciary duty, or failure to mitigate damages, or in such global factual terms such as driving too fast for conditions or failure to heed facts which should have been red flags. Instead, it is a far easier and more productive technique to break down every cross-examination into its individual factual goals. As the lawyer accomplishes those factual goals, the fact finder is led to the appropriate and desired conclusion.

There are sound reasons for developing each cross-examination around specific factual goals. First, it is easier for the jury to follow any line of questioning if it clearly and logically progresses to a specific goal. An organized presentation that is broken down into several individual points invites attention. Even a reluctant listener can focus attention when there is clear sense of organization and defined points made by the speaker. When a jury does not know where the facts lead, they pay less attention and can fail to get the take-away — the point counsel is trying to make.

Breaking cross-examination into individual factual goals also allows the judge to know where the cross-examiner is proceeding so that she will permit the cross-examiner to continue. When judges do not understand why we are cross-examining in a particular area, they are more likely to sustain relevancy objections.

Long gone is the age when a trial was a civic event. Trials are now statistics. Judges want cross-examiners to "move it along." There is undoubtedly a general right to cross-examine witnesses. But that is insufficient. There must be a reason to cross-examine the witness. Before rising to cross-examine, the advocate must have firmly in mind the individual goals of that cross-examination. When the cross-examiner clearly has built the chapters of cross-examination around specific factual goals, the cross-examiner could always answer a question by the court "Where is this going?" or the more formal "What is the relevancy of this line of cross-examination?"

Eventually the trial judge and the opponent learn that, for this cross-examiner, there is always a specific goal. When in doubt, opponents will not object, nor will judges sustain the objection if made. This gives the cross-examiner even greater latitude in her examination.

Each specific goal within a cross-examination should either assist the cross-examiner in building her theory of the case or assist the cross-examiner in undermining the opponent's theory of the case. It is unnecessary and unwise to pursue factual goals that do not impact the contrasting theories of the case.

§ 4.24 From the Very General to Very Specific Goals

Each individual goal is developed through a logical progression of leading questions, each putting into evidence one new fact. These two techniques work best when the questions dictated proceed from the very general to the specific goal. We start with general facts and become more specific as we develop the desired picture. It helps to envision this questioning technique as a funnel. The general questions are the wide end of the funnel. As we introduce more detail, it is detail that further clarifies the general facts. We are moving the witness, and the minds of the jurors, down the narrowing funnel. Remember, the end of a chapter is seldom a conclusion, as the witness is free to deny the conclusion. Instead, the end of the chapter funnel is often nothing more than a last fact that adequately finishes a desired picture. We build our safest and most productive cross-examinations out of factual admissions. We funnel the witness toward admissions to helpful facts. We funnel the jurors to understanding of those helpful facts and the conclusion that logically comes from those facts.

Our questioning in a chapter begins with general facts. We begin by setting the stage for more important facts. If we want to talk about a meeting, we might begin by establishing that the meeting occurred. Witnesses will find it easier to agree to general issue questioning before they are brought to specifics. This is true particularly when specific facts will be harmful to the witness. A tightly controlled witness will often give a very short answer, preferably "Yes." As we develop more facts around a point, the witness is more tied to their earlier factual admissions. The logic of the chapter hems in the reluctant witness. The witness is more likely to respond in a monosyllabic manner when each factual question is logically linked to an earlier admitted fact. As we draw a picture from the general to the specific, logic is our silent ally. Witnesses do not like to appear illogical, and jurors can see for themselves the factual development of the picture.

As has been discussed, it is ordinarily unproductive to ask a witness to agree with a conclusion harmful to their side of the case. For instance, a witness is unlikely to admit at the onset of cross-examination that he is a chronic liar. However, a series of facts may well establish that the witness can understand why people would lie, has been in situations where a lie benefited the witness, and has lied in those situations. The cross-examiner should start out generally and proceed slowly and methodically, one fact at a time, to the specific goal of establishing that the witness is a "liar." The cross-examiner is advised to recall that "liar" is a conclusion, and one that the witness is unlikely to adopt. That is not the goal of the cross-examination chapter. The goal is to provide the fact finder with sufficient facts by which they may infer that the witness is a liar. The technique, as always, is to provide facts to the witness through leading questions, making it more likely that the witness will give truthful "yes" answers. The cross-examiner should strive to score the points factually, leaving it up to the fact finder to draw the appropriate inference.

§ 4.25 General Questions Lock in and Make Easy the Specific

The following cross-examination contains questions indicating that the witness is willing to lie:

Q: In December the police questioned you about this case?

A: Yes.

Q: You told Detective Wylie you knew nothing about the case?

A: Yes.

Q: That was not the truth?

A: No, it wasn't.

Q: Instead of telling the police the truth, you chose to lie?

A: Yes.

Q: You did not want to tell him the truth?

A: No.

Q: The truth was likely to get you in trouble?

A: Yes.

Q: So you lied?

A: Yes, I did.

Q: The reason you lied was because you believed a lie would help you?

A: Yes.

Q: You are willing to lie if a lie will help you?

A: Yes.

Q: You are a liar?

A: On occasion.

Q: On occasion when you need to be?

A: True.

The questions set out above are not necessarily the only ten questions in this line of questioning. It may take twenty questions to move the witness to the point of giving in to the cross-examiner's goal. As the witness admits a particular fact, other facts not yet admitted may be logically inferred. Through this process the cross-examiner funnels the witness toward the desired factual picture or goal by establishing sufficient facts so that the witness must either answer further questions with a logical response that aids the cross-examiner, or with an illogical response that is likely to be rejected by the fact finder. When the fact finder, judge or jury, sees the logic in a picture, the fact finder provides their own logical response and a witness who answers illogically is unlikely to be believed. Such an examination may end as follows:

Q: You are a talented liar?

A: Yes.

Q: You can make up and tell lies very quickly?

A: Yes.

Q: You can think of elaborate lies and work on them a long time?

A: Yes.

Q: You are the best liar that you know?

A: Yes.

A witness's body language may tell as much as his answers. At the end of the above examination, a carefully questioned witness, when asked if he is the best liar he knows, will not shrink, hesitate, or act defensively towards the jury. The witness will act as if he were proud of his status as a liar. The jury will not be proud of him.

§ 4.26 Proceeding One Fact at a Time Makes the Specific Answer Inescapable

The following line of questions illustrates several points. The facts are put in through leading questions. The questions insert one new fact at a time. The chapter develops from the general to the specific. The logic of the situation becomes apparent to both the hostile witness and the jury. The picture develops one fact at a time logically and inevitably, both for the witness and the jury:

Q: When you got back to the apartment you noticed you were missing your lighter?

A: Yes.

Q: You discussed it was missing that night?

A: Yes, a little.

Q: It was the lighter you had used to light a cigarette when you got into the van?

A: Yes.

Q: It was a metal lighter?

A: Sure.

Q: You realized that it had spilled from your purse?

A: Yeah.

Q: You figured out you had left your lighter in the van?

A: Yes.

Q: You knew your fingerprints were on file.

A: Yes.

Q: And that your fingerprints on that lighter were going to lead the investigation to you?

A: Yes.

§ 4.27 The General to the Specific Creates Interest

This method of questioning can make the mundane issue of the size of the carry-on bag in a drug courier profile case interesting:

Q: Airlines have regulations that are backed up by federal law on what size of bag you can carry on the plane, don't they?

A: Yes.

Q: It has to fit under the seat?

A: Yes.

Q: Or in the overhead compartment?

A: Yes.

Q: And you have been on these airlines that travel in our country?

A: Yes.

Q: There is not a lot of room under the seats.

A: Correct.

Q: The overhead compartments are small?

A: True.

Q: So the bags that were carried onto the plane would have to fit legally under the seat or in the overhead compartment?

A: That's true.

After that line of questioning, each juror can visualize the size of the bag that travelers have become accustomed to fitting under the seat or in the overhead compartment. The idea is to make the jury see, hear, or otherwise "sense" the evidence. They must "experience" that evidence.

§ 4.28 The "Yes" Answer Is the Most Understood Response

The techniques discussed in the only three rules of cross-examination are designed to produce a great many "yes" answers. When the cross-examiner has placed a fact before the witness and the jury through a leading question, the "yes" answer efficiently allows the fact finder to understand what has been proven. The short leading question followed by the short verification is the best teaching method. All answers other than "yes" require more concentration and risk more misunderstanding. That is not to say that in order to be successful the cross-examiner must always get a "yes" response. As will be discussed there are other ways of making important points even when a witness denies the leading question.

Phrasing a question so that the desired and expected answer is "yes" is a far more efficient method of teaching. Dr. Herbert H. Clark, a psychologist at Johns Hopkins University, has performed studies that show that the average person takes forty-eight percent longer to understand a sentence that uses a negative than to understand a positive or affirmative sentence.

It is very difficult to comprehend a question phrased in the negative answered in the negative. Example:

Q: That document wasn't provided to the investors?

A: No.

What has the witness said? It is true that with a little concentration the listener may realize that the witness has confirmed that the document was not provided to the investors. But the chance for misunderstanding is greater, as is the concentration needed to assimilate the information. That is not to say that a question phrased in this manner is impermissible, or represents poor technique. Where possible, the question should be put to the witness in such a way that the desired and expected answer is "yes."

If the cross-examiner wants the jury to remember Mr. Kay, a witness who is a liar, she will phrase every question so that the answer must be "yes," so that the jury remembers, "Yes, he is a liar."

Picking up our prior example:

Q: You lied to the police?

A: Yes.

Q: You lied to your probation officer?

A: Yes.

Q: You lied to your wife?

A: Yes.

Q: You lied to the bank?

A: Yes.

Conclusion? He is a liar. If, in a divorce case, the cross-examiner wants the jury to remember that the husband viewed the wife (his client) as a wonderful mother, all questions will be put to that witness in such a way as to receive a "yes" answer.

Q: Your wife was a volunteer when the children were in Boy Scouts?

A: Yes.

Q: Your wife was president of the Parent/Teachers Organization?

A: Yes.

Q: Your wife always placed the children first?

A: Yes.

Conclusion? What a wonderful mother!

§ 4.29 The Techniques of the Only Three Rules Can Lead to Unexpectedly Honest Answers

The cumulative effect of the use of the modern techniques of cross-examination is to encourage the witness to tell the truth more often and more quickly. An additional and very important reward for the use of such techniques is that the witness may begin to concede honest answers to leading questions that the cross-examiner could not independently prove. In other words, cross-examination has proven so successful that the witness is willing to admit even harmful facts in circumstances where the cross-examiner believes the question to be accurate, but cannot directly impeach a "no" answer.

Once the witness is conditioned to rapidly verify the leading questions, the cross-examiner is in a better position to take risks. The cross-examiner can ask leading questions for which no independent proof is available, but for which she has a good faith basis of belief.

Assume that an important document has been changed. The cross-examiner believes that the superior instructed the subordinate to make the change. However, there are no independent witnesses to the conversation, and the only way to prove the fact is through an admission by one or the other of the two people involved. The cross-examiner may choose to address the issue in this way:

Q: When you came out of the meeting, the memo had changed?

A: Yes.

Q: The meeting involved only you and your boss?

A: Yes.

Q: It was changed because your boss ordered you to change it?

At this point the witness might deny the truthfulness of the assertion. If the chapter has been set out with a logical progression of facts toward this fact, it may be possible or even likely that a jury will conclude that this is precisely what occurred despite the denial of the witness. In a best-case scenario, the witness may see the logic of the progression of facts and concede the truthfulness of the leading question. With the application of sound cross-examination techniques, including the employment of the only three rules of cross-examination and the chapter method of cross-examination (see chapter 5, *The Chapter Method of Cross-Examination*), the cross-examiner will enjoy many of these moments.

§ 4.30 The Three Rules: Building Blocks for Advanced Techniques

It must be stressed that these three rules are the basic building blocks for all additional techniques. Every technique works more reliably when the witness is under control, when the questioning method narrows the field of evasion, when the jury can understand how the fact impacts the two competing theories of the case. When we can perform thc three building block techniques in every question, we can advance to the more artistic techniques. Each new technique builds upon the solid foundational techniques of: (1) leading questions only, (2) one new fact per question, and (3) building toward a specific goal.

Chapter 5

THE CHAPTER METHOD OF CROSS-EXAMINATION

§ 5.01 The Chapter Method Explained

We need a structure to the questions asked within any cross-examination. That structure is the chapter method of cross-examination. The term "chapter method" is meant to reinforce our understanding that the cross-examination of any witness is not a free-flowing discussion of the entire case, nor is it ordinarily a focused discussion with a single unifying purpose. Instead, the cross-examination of any witness is a series of targeted introductions of facts (chapters) on individual topics of importance to the cross-examiner. Cross-examination is a series of focused discussions, each with its own factual purpose. One cross-examination is almost always designed to accomplish several factual goals.

Cross-examination in the chapter method seldom flows smoothly from one topic to the next. Instead it moves from preselected topic to preselected topic, and not necessarily in chronological order. Cross-examination virtually never covers everything a witness might know about the case. Chapters sometimes relate to each other. Sometimes the transition from one chapter to another chapter is an abrupt jump to a separate area of the case. What can be said is that there is a beginning and an end to each chapter. The beginning and the end are largely mapped out before the cross-examination begins. The chapters are designed to maximize the good evidence available. As a result, chapters do not trail off. They end crisply. A chapter that has not accomplished its purpose using the best facts available is not likely to get better through additional questions. If the best evidence didn't work, the second best evidence or the unknown evidence is likely to produce worse results.

A trial is a book of information. The individual witness examinations are themselves large accumulations of information: parts of the book. The individual topics within the cross-examinations are the chapters of the book. Each chapter has a designed goal. The jurors can understand the purpose of each chapter as the cross-examiner assembles related facts into one logical sequence, designed to paint one picture. The chapter method is the polar opposite of the freewheeling style of cross-examination. The chapter method of cross-examination is designed as the optimum teaching model in an adversary system. An advocate working without benefit of the chapter method of cross-examination can establish many important facts but does so in no particular order. As a result, the jurors must reassemble the facts in order to understand the points being made by the cross-examiner.

§ 5.02 Chapters Defined

We now understand that cross-examination is a series of goal-oriented exercises. Each of these individual exercises is a cluster of related facts grouped to establish one particular point useful to the questioning party. The chapters of cross-examination are each composed of a series of goal-focused, leading questions. The questions are ordinarily very short. The facts are often not going to be disputed by the witness. Many times the purpose of several questions within a chapter is to give context to other facts or chapters. Any one goal of cross-examination will be presented through one or more chapters of cross-examination.

Of course within any cross-examination there are many types of goals, each accomplished by a chapter or a grouping of chapters (chapter bundle). For instance, the goal of a chapter may be to prove existence of a fact or a scenario, to build a sufficient body of facts from which may be deduced a helpful inference, to introduce facts that will weaken the fact finder's belief in a fact or scenario suggested by the opponent, or to establish a particular fact or facts that affect the credibility of a witness.

Once the advocate becomes comfortable with the concept that the cross-examination of every witness is a series of goal-oriented questions, the advocate should recognize that thc logical form of a series of goal-oriented questions is a chapter. Each chapter is itself a goal-oriented device designed to marshal together a group of facts that leads the jury to make a favorable conclusion on a particular issue or fact. Many chapters are not confrontational in nature. Instead, in a modern method of cross-examination, we seek to convert our opponent's witnesses into a source of facts helpful to our theory of the case. We use leading questions to place the witness into a position in which that the witness will admit facts we have selected, though those facts may hurt the party the witness favors. As will be demonstrated, the chapter form marshals related facts so that a juror may arrive at the desired conclusion even if that conclusion or its supporting facts are not admitted by the witness. Each chapter has an individual theme that supports the theory of the case. Each chapter has its own beginning and ending.

§ 5.03 Chapter Bundle Defined

A chapter bundle is a grouping of related chapters that need to be used together in order to create a full picture of a topic. A single topic within a cross-examination may well require several chapters. For instance, let us consider a civil suit alleging that a customized computer software program was defective and therefore required no payment. The large topic of proving that the software was defective might require a great many chapters, each focusing on one of the various alleged defects within the computer program. In addition, there would almost certainly be one or more chapters detailing the consequences of each of those defects. The overarching topic can be thought of as "The Software Was Defective." Proving this large issue to a jury will require many individual chapters. That is a chapter bundle. Each chapter takes on one aspect of the overall issue of our theory that the software was defective. The entire bundle of chapters represents our complete effort to introduce facts exposing the computer program's defects and the consequences.

One might erroneously think that the entire cross-examination of a witness is a chapter bundle. However, a chapter bundle is a more limited exercise. It is a part of the entire cross-examination. It explains a discrete topic. We need to recognize the construction of a chapter bundle, as the chapters that make up a chapter bundle need to be performed one after the other in a grouping in order to be best understood by the jury. While we are free to separate many different goals within a cross-examination and to attack those goals in many different sequences, we should perform the chapters within a chapter bundle one right after the other, never splitting up the chapters or interrupting the bundle to attack a different goal unrelated to the chapter bundle.

Let us return to the example of the chapter bundle designed to expose the multiple defects of the computer software. While performing chapters devoted to that topic, we should not break the flow of that story by venturing into chapters on a lack of damages, or on the credibility of the witness. These may well be chapters of importance, chapters we will perform, but we should perform the chapters that make up a bundle one after the other until the overall picture is painted. Then we can move on to a different goal accomplished by a different chapter or bundle.

§ 5.04 The Chapter Method Gives the Cross-Examiner Control of the Topics

The chapter method is a closely controlled series of factual revelations of topics selected by the cross-examiner. The chapter method both allows and requires that the cross-examination be broken into a series of questions designed to accomplish well-defined goals. Those goals support the advocate's theory of the case or undermine the foundation of the opponent's theory of the case. To the greatest extent possible, chapters are drafted in advance of trial.

Using the chapter method of cross-examination, the lawyer selects for use only those areas she believes to be necessary and fruitful. The lawyer divides those areas into individual chapters. She can then draft cross-examinations that develop within each chapter all of the facts that drive the jury to the acceptance of the goal in that chapter (see chapter 6, *Page Preparation of Cross-Examination*). We may well draft chapters that we later elect not to use as we judge them to be unnecessary or unworkable.

The chapter method of cross-examination is predicated upon the realization that cross-examination is very much a positive endeavor designed to prove one's case, not simply a defensive reaction to the opponent's direct examination. Cross-examination in the chapter method is decidedly not an opportunity to repeat or explain the direct examination. Direct examinations ordinarily require the witness to recite in chronological order all of the events of a topic or topics that favor the opponent's theory of the case, so that the witness has told what appears to be an entire story — although ordinarily not the entire story. In contrast, cross-examinations are selective revelations in individual areas of the story. Many of these chapters of cross-examination address parts of the story that have been omitted or require greater focus. In this process, many parts of the story told on direct examination will be ignored because they are unproductive or unnecessary.

§ 5.05 Spotting Opponents Who Have Not Adopted the Chapter Method

Lawyers working without chapter organization often wander from topic to topic and thereby adopt ill-defined goals, never marshalling all of the supportive facts at any one place. This lack of chapter organization becomes apparent during the cross-examination when the lawyer is forced to skip back and forth among areas of cross-examination as the lawyer remembers some of the facts left out of earlier questioning on the same topic. Lawyers using a disorganized approach flit from topic to topic, never knowing what has been established and never confident that they have made their point. These lawyers often are interrupted by objections of, "Cumulative" or "Asked and answered," and rulings by the judge to "Move it along."

§ 5.06 The Chapter Method Gives the Cross-Examiner Witness Control

The chapter method is fundamental to the process of witness control. If the witness was called by the opponent, the opponent has worked with the witness to ensure that the witness discusses the facts most relevant to the opponent's theory of the case. If we allow the witness great latitude in our cross-examination questioning, the witness is likely to take the jury into areas calculated to help the opponent. On the other hand, we can achieve far greater witness control by using the technique of asking leading questions only, and by channeling the discussion into only the areas (read: chapters) selected by the cross-examiner. The process of grouping questions into narrow fields of inquiry selected by the cross-examiner results in far greater control over the matters discussed by the witness.

Cross-examination ordinarily occurs only after a direct. However, in civil cases, and in a very few criminal cases where a witness is declared adverse or hostile, the cross-examination may precede the direct examination. When a party calls for purposes of cross-examination an opposing party, or the agent of an opposing party, the same three rules apply. We should use leading questions, asking one new fact per question and putting our facts together from the general to the specific to prove a particular goal. In such circumstances we are calling the witness to make our points. The process is actually more positive in design, as the direct examination has not occurred. It is therefore easier to concentrate on supporting one's own theory of the case.

The chapter method recognizes that the cross-examiner is not going to attack or retell the entire story of the direct examination, nor the entire story of the case. Not every part of the opponent's story is capable or deserving of attack. There are parts of the direct examination that potentially help the cross-examiner, and there are parts that cannot successfully be disputed. There are other parts of the direct examination that simply do not matter. It is critical that the cross-examiner work from a method that ensures only the topics of importance to the cross-examiner will be discussed.

The cross-examiner is going to attack, introduce additional evidence concerning, or highlight only portions of the direct examination. In addition — and it may be a very large addition — the cross-examiner is likely going to seek facts from the witness that have not come up in direct examination. We will undoubtedly agree with many facts testified to on direct examination. As to these facts, we may choose to offer no cross-examination. In some instances, some cross-examination will address agreed facts — not to weaken a factual assertion but to highlight these facts. We do this in order to put those admitted facts into their proper context in relation to our theory of the case, and show the fact finder that those facts have greater significance than revealed by the opponent's direct examination. In such instances, the purpose of cross-examination is not to cast doubt upon such facts, but to make sure that these facts indeed receive the full attention of the jurors. They can appreciate the significance of those facts in an alternative context — the context created through cross-examination.

By way of example let us assume the prosecutor calls an eyewitness/victim to testify to his identification of the defendant as the perpetrator of the crime. Assume the defense is one of mistaken identification. There may be parts of the direct examination we will ignore as they lack good cross-examination material. There may be aspects of the description we will bring out in greater detail as they are parts of the description that do not match our client. There may be aspects of the identification that were never discussed but deserve substantial cross-examination. For instance, we would want to expose any motive or bias the witness may have to testify against our client. In addition, the lighting conditions may have been poor, or the entire event could have happened in a matter of seconds. These are subjects the direct examination may have omitted. Our cross-examination chapters are based on our needs and are not dictated by the opponent's selection of topics.

Often a whole series of questions have been asked in direct examination that will go unchallenged for a different reason: They simply have no significance to the cross-examiner's theory of the case. The tendency in all direct examinations, both civil and criminal, is to "tell a story in chronological order." As a result, direct examinations tend to cover much more material than is truly useful or at issue. The skillful cross-examiner will let most of these facts go without comment, as most of these facts assist neither side. But the cross-examiner should still listen for "spontaneous loops" and theme phrases (see chapter 2, *Developing a Theory of the Case* and chapter 10, *Loops, Double Loops, and Spontaneous Loops*).

§ 5.07 Modern Cross-Examination Still Employs Destructive Cross-Examination Chapters

Modern cross-examination uses the chapter method to both attack the opponent's theory of the case and support the advocate's theory of the case. Too much of the literature of the field has focused on cross-examination as a destructive device whose purpose is primarily to attack the direct examination testimony. This is an old-fashioned and overly defensive view of cross-examination. The defensive aspect of cross-examination remains very much a part of modern cross-examination. We will still develop attacks on selected chapters related in direct examination. We will continue to draft chapters of cross-examinations that are solely destructive in nature, attacking the opponent's theory of the case. We will continue to assemble chapters that are intended to harm the credibility of the opponent's case. It is entirely appropriate to build chapters that expose inconsistencies. In all such instances, we will not invite open-ended testimony of the witness but require the witness to admit or discuss particular facts that are selected by the cross-examiner.

§ 5.08 The Chapter Method Builds Support for the Advocate's Theory of the Case

An opposing witness may well know many additional facts not brought out on direct examination that help the cross-examiner's theory of the case. These facts need to be introduced, placed into their context, and made more memorable to the jury. This is the modern or advanced use of cross-examination as a method of building the cross-examiner's theory of the case.

This is the "positive" or "constructive" aspect to cross-examination. The opponent probably will have guided their witness to avoid discussion of various facts. As a result there are gaps in the story told by the witness. Our cross-examination chapters are designed to insert facts into the case that fill that gap — but only to the extent that filling in those gaps helps us "prove" some further aspect of our case or that does damage to the opponent's theory of the case.

The presentation of facts in our chapters may require the witness to agree with the theory of the cross-examiner's case, or the presentation of facts through this witness may greatly undermine a witness to be presented by the opponent later in the trial. These positive cross-examinations or "constructive" cross-examinations are also selective. They do not tell an entire story, but only portions of it.

§ 5.09 Purpose of a Chapter

A chapter is a group of leading questions designed to introduce facts that accomplish a goal. The facts within a chapter are presented through the leading questions in a logical sequence. The goal of a chapter may be to highlight a fact, dispute or weaken a fact, introduce a new fact, or affect either positively or negatively the credibility of a witness (not necessarily the witness being questioned). The goal is always to allow the jurors to gain an understanding of the significance of the facts in relation to the opposing theories of the case. A chapter might simultaneously accomplish more than one of these goals. A chapter is only worth pursuing if it advances the advocate's theory of the case or undermines the opponent's theory of the case. Embodied within this rule is the concept that a chapter that diminishes the credibility of an opposing witness simultaneously diminishes the credibility of the opponent's theory of the case.

The purpose of drafting a chapter is to use the best available admissible evidence to push a jury toward the recognition of a well-defined, fact-specific goal. A chapter is performed to establish one goal or complete one picture. In the process of establishing the goal, the lawyer often establishes many subsidiary points. The cross-examiner is trying to communicate an image. A series of leading questions puts before the jury many facts, each contributing to the intended image or goal. While seeking to establish a goal or paint a picture of an event, the advocate may simultaneously demonstrate the credibility of a witness. For example, the process of impeachment by inconsistent statement establishes the goal of demonstrating that the prior statement of the witness was more believable. At the same time, by establishing that the witness has previously testified in a manner inconsistent with their current testimony, the advocate has scored a subsidiary goal of diminishing the credibility of the witness.

A chapter composed of leading questions performed in a logical order reduces the lawyer's risk while increasing the comprehension and impact of the evidence. A logical sequence of leading questions within a chapter requires that the lawyer move the jury and the witness through a progression of related facts. It is the job of the cross-examiner to compile the facts that relate to each other so that the jury is not burdened with the responsibility of assembling the facts established by the cross-examination chapter. The goal fact, or last question of a chapter, is not necessarily the culmination of all the supporting facts (often mistakenly posed as a conclusion) but simply the last fact in the logical sequence of facts on a point. The last fact is not necessarily the most important fact or even a disputed fact. It is often simply another fact that helps complete a picture. The important concept is that each chapter is an organized sequence of leading questions designed to show the significance of the goal of that chapter. The facts of a chapter are its context. They are the details that flesh out the desired picture.

The goal of a chapter may assist in the establishment of a goal in conjunction with the cross-examination (or possibly the direct examination) of another witness. By way of example, a fact to be highlighted through witness A may achieve its importance only when considered in conjunction with a fact disputed during the cross-examination of witness B. Simultaneously, that fact highlighted during the cross-examination of witness A may indeed affect the credibility of witness B. Therefore, two goals are accomplished. In this way, a single chapter may accomplish more than one goal, even though the information within the chapter only establishes a single goal-fact.

§ 5.10 Breaking Cases into Understandable Parts

> "Divide each problem into as many parts as possible; that each part being more easily conceived, the whole may be more intelligible."
>
> Descartes, *Discourse on Method* (1637).

An entire case contains an enormous amount of information. No judge or jury can learn the entire case at once. Even a simple case is made out of an enormous number of separate parts, which come together to create the issues and events in dispute. The chapter method allows the trial lawyer to divide even the most complex case into individual parts such that the jury can understand those smaller parts and thereby gain an understanding of the entirety.

A crime, a contract case, an auto accident, the division of assets or the deciding of custody in a divorce — or virtually anything leading to a lawsuit — is not a single fact or event, but a group of facts and events that together form the case. In order to recognize the facts the lawyer will dispute, highlight, or create (put into context), the lawyer needs first to break cases into their component parts so that they may be studied individually.

Below is a representation of a simple homicide, first presented with a broad-brush overview:

Barbie and Ken have been living together. Barbie says she is broke. Ken suggests she prostitute herself with Ken acting as her pimp. They leave the apartment with that plan. Ken arranges with a man to have sex with Barbie. Before the man can have the sex, Ken kills him. Barbie subsequently reports Ken to the police.

Although this is an accurate overview of the case, it is the barest outline of the case. It is worthless to the cross-examiner, since the lawyer is left with many questions, such as:

"What is the nature of their relationship?"

"Did they know the man?"

"Did Barbie see the murder?"

"How did the murder occur?"

The facts of the case are too few, compressed, and conclusory to be useful in preparing cross-examination.

In order to find the vulnerabilities of a case, the lawyer will first break the case into smaller parts so the facts of each event can be scrutinized. Within these facts there may be many opportunities for successful cross-examination, but the lawyer cannot find them without first breaking down this case into component parts.

Here, then, is a second, more detailed, telling of the facts:

Barbie and Ken have been living together for a few weeks. Also living with them was Barbie's girlfriend, Midge. Barbie is the single mother of an infant child. Barbie is on welfare and receives Aid to Dependent Children and food stamps. According to Barbie, on the night in question, she was broke, had no food for her baby, and her baby was starving. Ken suggested that she commit one or more acts of prostitution to raise some money. She agreed to do this solely out of desperation.

Ken and Barbie left the house and walked around in a part of Cleveland where prostitutes are frequently contacted. First, they stopped by a hotel where a friend of Barbie's worked. She and the friend had a social conversation, after which Barbie and Ken left.

Barbie committed her first act of prostitution in a deal negotiated by Ken. Barbie and Ken then went to the Beef Bowl where they ate some dinner. They then went back on the street, at which time Ken negotiated a second act of prostitution with a man in a white van. Barbie and Ken got in the van, and they drove to a secluded area. As Barbie was climbing into the back of the van to get undressed, Ken pulled out a knife and killed the man. He then took the man's money, and he and Barbie fled. A few blocks away they got into a taxi and went back to the house.

Barbie was quite upset and cried herself to sleep. The next day she saw a news broadcast and read a newspaper report on the homicide, and decided to call the police. She called a police officer that she has known for some time. The cop came to the house and arrested Ken for the homicide.

This second version is a more useful case narrative. A case narrative is a story told as a series of parts. Each part is, in turn, made up of numerous facts. This expanded case narrative allows the lawyer to better view the story as a series of individual facts, but the events still need a further division into fact chapters. In order to find opportunities for cross-examination, the lawyer must further dissect the story as grouping of facts.

§ 5.11 Events or Areas Versus Chapters

Bear in mind that identifying the events of a case is not the equivalent of identifying the chapters of cross-examination. Creating a list of the events of a case does not create the chapters for cross-examination, as this broad breakdown is still far too large to be studied carefully. A list of the events may well suggest possible areas for cross-examination, but the lawyer must find within these events the chapters that require detailed exploration before the jury.

In surveying the events, the lawyer is looking for facts that can be used to build her theory of the case. Simultaneously the lawyer is looking for weaknesses in the opponent's theory of the case, i.e., any suggestion that further inquiry is merited. Such weaknesses represent overall concepts for cross-examination and are not in themselves a cross-examination. For instance, on first reading the narrative of Barbie and Ken, the lawyer may well recognize the implausibility of the central feature of Barbie's story: Because her child was starving, she decided to turn to prostitution. Yet the mother has family in the city and knows people who live in the multi-unit apartment building. The explanation causes the lawyer to realize she needs to cross-examine in this general area, although the exact form of chapters of the cross-examination is undetermined.

§ 5.12 Time Is the Measure of Importance

Time is the measure of importance in the courtroom, not the inflection or volume of the cross-examiner's voice. Important information deserves and requires more time. We spend time developing our most important facts and scenarios. Case-critical events deserve far more context than peripheral events.

As a component of this relationship of cross-examination to time, the trial lawyer must understand that the more important a fact or series of facts are to the theory of the case, the more time the jury expects to be spent on those facts. If facts are not important to the theory of the case, no time should be spent on developing those facts.

When in cross-examination we wander into areas that are unnecessary or unproductive, we send the message that these areas are important. When we get into battles over less important facts, we make those unimportant issues important by virtue of the time we spend fighting the battle. We cannot blame a juror for attaching importance to things that seem to greatly interest or trouble us. We must therefore strongly resist the urge to prove ourselves correct when the battle is over an inconsequential fact. It is okay to pass on some fights. In fact, by passing we send a clear message that the fact is not worth our time as the fact has no real bearing on the case.

Because in trial time is the measure of importance, it follows that we need to create the greatest factual development to the issues of greatest importance to our theory of the case. This translates into more chapters on matters of greatest importance.

§ 5.13 The Development of Chapters: The Process

After the lawyer has broken down the major components of a case into smaller parts, she should be in a position to recognize facts, groups of facts, and parts that may be suitable for examination. These will need to be studied at their chapter level. A quick method of recognizing potential chapters is to use a part process.

1. Divide the case into its important scenarios. A single scenario may be composed of many events.
2. Divide the important scenarios into their component events. A single good event may contain many good issues.
3. Analyze the component events for issues of assistance. A single good issue may require more than one chapter.

Let us apply these steps to a commercial case brought by shareholders alleging that a corporation hid from its investors its declining financial health. The overall theory of the case may be that, in order to keep its share price up, the corporation deceived the market. The proof of that theory is dependent upon many factual scenarios. One of those scenarios involved a meeting in which an outside auditor reported troubling financial news concerning the corporation to the chief financial officer (CFO) of the defendant corporation. Within that meeting the outside auditor reported discovering many facts concerning bookkeeping irregularities. Those irregularities were themselves composed of several erroneous or impermissible bookkeeping entries.

Follow the three-step analysis in reviewing a single scenario.

Step 1. Identify a single important scenario:

> The meeting between the outside auditor and the chief financial officer is a large event that contains many potentially useful facts.

Step 2. Identify a single component event in that important scenario:

> The outside auditor reported on the bookkeeping entries relating to sales of computers to XYZ Corp.

Step 3. Identify a single good issue inside of that one aspect of the meeting that deserves development through one or more than one chapter:

> Chapter: The sale of computers was booked the last day of the corporate year, but the contract was not signed until 20 days into the following corporate year.
>
> Chapter: The sale was booked in an amount that far exceeded the actual dollar value of the contract.
>
> Chapter: The sale was booked in a most improper way. The computers were shown as being in inventory as of year end, and thus were counted as an asset. However, because the sale was also booked as occurring before year end, the resulting account receivable was also counted as an asset. This resulted in a double counting of the asset.

Let us summarize the process we have engaged in. Our theory of the case is that executives either participated in or covered up improper financial reporting devices in order to conceal the deteriorating financial condition of the company. We have identified the meeting between an auditor and a corporate executive as an important event to our theory of the case. We believe that we can use the events of that meeting to show that high ranking corporate executives were aware that there were substantial irregularities in the corporate books and that, as a result, there was known fraud in the business. There may be many parts of the meeting in which we are interested.

We have begun the process of drafting chapters by focusing on a specific component of the meeting. Within the bookkeeping entries of that single large sale of computers to XYZ Corp. certain bookkeeping irregularities were noted and disclosed to the corporate executive. This one example of improper accounting requires more than one chapter. Hence it is developed as a chapter bundle. As we find other financial irregularities that were disclosed in the meeting, we will develop other chapters to describe those irregularities.

This segmenting of events is at the heart of the chapter method of cross-examination. Instead of talking in global terms about bookkeeping irregularities, the cross-examiner produces factual evidence of the irregularities, explaining the significance of each irregularity and allowing the jurors to come to their own conclusion that this was fraudulent conduct, and that the corporate executive was advised of these irregularities.

§ 5.14 The Most Important Topics Ordinarily Deserve the Most Detailed Presentations

The most important topics or areas within a case ordinarily require more than one chapter in order to create the several pictures or establish the several goals within that topic or area. Within each chapter are the leading questions, which minutely form the picture or establish the goal. The most important topics will ordinarily require the most detailed factual presentations. In the above example, the topic of the meeting and the revelation to the CFO that there were bookkeeping irregularities is critical to the theory of the case. It follows that this subject deserves a richly detailed presentation requiring many chapters.

The proper form of the question to the CFO is not: "Did the outside auditor tell you about any financial irregularities?" Such a question is far too broad and deeds control of the facts to the witness who can now elect what facts to stress, what to minimize, what to skip.

The proper form of the question is not: "Isn't it true that the outside auditor told you about some problems with the XYZ contract?" This question is only slightly more specific, and provides no reference to the specific facts that compel a jury to the conclusion that the witness was on notice of particular problems in the audit. Even if the witness answers "Yes," the jurors have no picture of the ugly facts. This question might serve as an introduction to a string of far more specific leading questions.

We need to fashion a chapter that sets up the importance of the outside audit. That chapter can be constructed using facts that paint a clear picture of the definition and importance of an outside audit. We can then create a chapter that proves the importance of the meeting between the CFO and the auditor. This chapter is constructed with leading questions, which provide facts that paint a clear picture that the meeting was important. What is next needed is a chapter that exposes the conversation concerning the computer sale to XYZ. And then there is a single chapter that discusses the entire sub-issue of booking the sale before it actually occurred. This will be followed by a chapter that lays out factually the separate issue of booking the sale in an inflated amount. There is a single chapter that lays out factually the double counting of the computers as both an asset and as a sale.

This may seem like it will take a long time to accomplish, but a chapter could be less than a dozen facts. The facts are put into leading questions so the process of establishing a single chapter may amount only to a minute or two of courtroom time. The pictures created by such a detailed presentation in areas important to the theory of the case are truly quite stunning. Too often the backhanded compliment to a good cross-examiner is: "Sure it went well. You had great facts." In reality the compliment should be: "Sure it went well. You made excellent use of the facts you had."

If there were 50 such transactions, the cross-examiner might at some point begin to shorten the chapter presentations as to each of the frauds. But at first the cross-examiner would establish why these bookkeeping entries distort the financial picture of the company. In order to establish the prosecutor's theory of the case, it is critical that the jury be educated as to why such bookkeeping entries are impermissible. Once these types of chapters are used, it is not necessary to repeat those same chapters in relation to other alleged frauds that use the same pattern. It is necessary that each fraud be given attention. They cannot be grouped into a single chapter called: "Isn't it true you booked a lot of things erroneously?" The heart of the theory of the case is the individual events alleged to be fraudulent and the chapters that reveal the facts at that level.

§ 5.15 Recognizing Events Suitable for Cross-Examination

The cross-examiner may have many chapters suitable for cross-examination, but she still needs to cull the best. The cross-examiner may be capable of cross-examining upon a matter — but that matter may still be unworthy of cross-examination. "Suitable for cross-examination" does not mean that the lawyer must inevitably cross-examine on these issues, groups of facts, or specific facts. It means only that an area appears to be a likely area for cross-examination. In order to be a likely area for cross-examination, the event must have within it a fact or facts that: (1) cast doubt on an opponent's assertion; (2) are likely to be conceded by the opponent yet need to be highlighted or more firmly placed in the proper context; (3) are likely to be omitted in direct examination but need to be added to the picture, since they assist the lawyer's theory of the case; or (4) reflect upon the credibility of a witness. In all instances, to qualify as a potential area for cross-examination, a topic must contain a fact or facts that assist the lawyer in developing her theory of the case. This, then, is only a preliminary screening of the facts. A more thorough analysis is required to actually deliver the cross-examination chapter.

§ 5.16 Possible Chapters Deserve Preparation, Even Though They May Later Be Dropped

After the lawyer begins developing her potential chapters of cross-examination, she will often reserve judgment on some chapters initially thought to be useful. Perhaps the potential chapters do not bear directly enough on the theory of the case or perhaps they are too tangential to be of assistance.

Perhaps further investigation is warranted to discover facts that, if added to the area under study, would make the chapters in this area useful in cross-examination.

As the lawyer begins a deeper study of the facts, she will inevitably find topics that she originally passed over that she now recognizes as useful. Fear not, as nothing that has been done so far in cross-examination preparation is permanent. The addition or deletion of areas of cross-examination is still easily accomplished.

§ 5.17 Examples of Preliminary Analysis of Chapter Development in a Particular Case

The development of chapters is altogether a natural act for a trial lawyer. It is virtually impossible for a trial lawyer to hear a client's story without beginning to think of the chapters she will need in both direct and cross-examination. Perhaps the lawyer is unaccustomed to recognizing the topics as chapters. But cases always break into chapters and the most relevant chapters ordinarily suggest themselves after the advocate formulates a first draft. The analysis considers the theory of the case likely to be advanced by the opponent. The lawyer need only play out in her head what the trial will look like in its broadest terms. Within each case there are some topics or events that by their very nature indicate their importance to cross-examination and signal the need to formulate a specific chapter or chapters of cross-examination.

In a domestic relations case where the wife is asking for alimony and child support, the cross-examiner immediately knows that there will be a chapter or chapters concerning the husband's assets and liabilities.

In a personal injury lawsuit resulting from a car collision, the cross-examiner (whichever side of the case she may be on) will know that there will be multiple chapters on liability and, in all likelihood, multiple chapters on each statute allegedly broken that resulted in the collision. Each injury deserves its own development. A single injury may require several chapters in order to be fully explained.

In an eyewitness examination, inconsistency as to items of description will automatically cause a lawyer to think in terms of chapters on inconsistencies. Each area of inconsistency, such as height, weight, or facial hair, deserves its own chapter or chapters.

In a self-defense case, the angry words spoken by the deceased will be recognized as forming the basis for a chapter or chapters on cross-examination. When defending a case built around the testimony of an immunized "flip" witness, the snitch's prior bad acts will, of course, be recognized as fertile areas (multiple chapters) for cross-examination.

In a copyright infringement case, the extent of the copyright will need to be examined for purposes of liability. The damages aspect of the case will necessitate studying the history of sales of the copyrighted materials.

In the defense of a wrongful discharge claim, the work history of the fired employee may require many chapters. If there was a single precipitating event, a single straw that broke the camel's back, that event will probably require the development of several chapters.

§ 5.18 Putting Facts into Context

Not every chapter is suggested by a consideration of the broad outlines of the case. Some chapters appear only after the advocate has engaged in a detailed analysis of the facts. There are some facts or groups of facts that take on significance only when viewed in juxtaposition to other facts, testimony or exhibits. For example, take the following fact pattern:

A witness who has turned State's evidence asserts that he got involved with the defendant in this crime before the defendant begged him to go along and help on some aspect of the crime, and based on their friendship he did so.

Found elsewhere in the discovery is a debriefing of that cooperating witness where he claims that he hated the defendant, ever since the defendant beat him up in a bar fight a couple of years prior to the crime.

The first paragraph of the story, viewed in isolation, may be insignificant to the theory of the case, or the lawyer may consider that the negatives of cross-examining on this issue outweigh the positives. However, when the two paragraphs are compared, the lawyer realizes that both events may deserve cross-examination, as they relate to each other and make implausible the witness's story as to why he cooperated with the defendant in this crime. In effect, the greater the witness's description of the bar fight and his resulting hatred of the defendant, the more unlikely the witness's story of why he went along with the defendant on this crime.

In any event, after reflecting on the significance of various facts or areas of the case and determining which may be useful for exploration in cross-examination, the lawyer moves to the next step, breaking chapters out of the analysis.

§ 5.19 Using Chapters to Avoid Global Cross-Examinations

The tendency of less experienced trial lawyers is to examine in global terms (headlines, generalities, conclusions, or summaries). Frequently, the less experienced the lawyer, the more global is the cross-examination. The less experienced lawyer often tries to stretch for a quick and helpful admission to either a critical fact or conclusion. This cross-examiner is attempting a global rather than a specific cross-examination. A global cross-examination is one that seeks to sum up a point of view about the facts rather than establishing the facts with such specificity that the jury can come to that conclusion on its own. An example of a global cross-examination is this question: "You were driving negligently?" The more global the cross-examinations, the fewer facts are used within the leading questions. Instead, the cross-examiner asks the witness to agree with the cross-examiner's conclusion.

The fewer facts relied upon to build a chapter, the more risks the cross-examiner runs in terms of receiving unfavorable answers and failing to advance favorable facts. Global methods of cross-examination deprive the cross-examiner of control (see chapter 4, *The Only Three Rules of Cross-Examination*). By proceeding one detailed fact at a time, the cross-examiner uses her self-discipline in moving slowly, thoroughly, and methodically through the best material available.

In order to move from the global to the chapter form of cross-examination, it is necessary to break a case into identifiable goals. Each goal of cross-examination will require at least one chapter of cross-examination, though some goals may be accomplished only through a group of chapters known as bundles. The mental movement from the overview of the case to the narrow focus on finite goals of cross-examination is accomplished by examining cases first as component parts and then examining these component parts of the case as potential chapters.

An event, topic, or component part of the case is a major section of the case. Some sections of the case will be neutral to the theory of the case. Some sections will be positive or favorable to the theory of the case. Some sections will be negative or unfavorable to the theory of the case. Analyzing the case information in another light, some facts will appear to be unassailable. Other facts will appear to be subject to great dispute.

A single large event can in turn be seen as a series of smaller events. Each small event may be worthy of cross-examination deserving of at least one chapter. By using the chapter method, the cross-examiner will analyze more thoroughly the individual facts that may be developed within each chapter. By doing this, the cross-examiner may find smaller, more detailed chapters within a negative chapter that are in fact positive to the theory of the case.

A chapter is built one question at a time, but it is not just one question or one fact. A chapter is a series of questions and facts that lead logically to the one factual goal. One "event" may contain many chapters, many helpful factual goals.

§ 5.20 Even Bad Events May Contain Good Facts Deserving of a Chapter

A criminal defense lawyer is defending a case based on a theory of missed identification. If a witness picks the defendant out of a photo lineup, that can be viewed as harmful to the defense. However, if the witness has been told, before coming down to view the lineup, that the police have a suspect ("we have arrested the man"), and they want to see if the witness can pick him out of the lineup, then that is evidence worth its own chapter. Those facts may be worthy of cross-examination because they show that when the witness went down to the police station, she had been advised that the culprit had been arrested. Now, armed with this advice, the witness felt a need to pick somebody out of the lineup because the police had "the man."

Furthermore, if there are six photographs in the photographic lineup (sometimes referred to as a "show up"), and two of the photographs simply do not fit the description given by the witness, the defense lawyer may have two additional chapters on how those people could easily be excluded.

Assume the witness views the lineup for five to ten minutes before circling any number. That unusual length of time may itself be worthy of a chapter of cross-examination. If, after the witness circles a number, the officer says something in confirmation such as, "You've done well," or "Yeah, that's what we thought," it is yet another chapter. The police have clearly indicated to the witness that she has picked correctly. Of course this means the witness should keep picking that individual throughout the remainder of the case. How many chapters could an able lawyer generate out of a single part of the case (the photographic lineup)? The lawyer could have as many chapters as she can find positive or helpful. The lawyer has as many chapters as she has distinguishable goals.

In this example it first appeared that the photo lineup evidence would be negative or unfavorable to the defense counsel's theory of the case. Undoubtedly the prosecutor will take the witness through the lineup selection during the direct examination. Indeed, the fact that the witness picked the defendant out of the lineup is a bad fact. But a more detailed analysis by the cross-examiner has developed multiple chapters that in fact are favorable to the theory of the case. It can put the opponent in a position of having to explain to the jury why his presentation of the larger issue in direct examination did not deal more particularly with the multiple details of the cross-examination.

In another example, the defendant has been arrested for driving under the influence of alcohol. One large part of the prosecution case involves roadside sobriety tests, a series of physical tests and observations supposedly designed to allow the officer to determine whether the driver is likely driving under the influence of alcohol.

One of the standard roadside tests is called the "heel-to-toe" test. In this test the officer requires the driver to walk a prescribed number of steps down an imaginary or real line, beginning with the foot designated by the officer. The officer instructs the driver that after taking the prescribed number of steps, the driver is to turn around, begin with a designated foot, and walk another prescribed number of steps. All of this is to be accomplished with the driver's arms at his sides. Officers explain to the jury that this test is a test of memory and a test of coordination and balance. Very frequently the officer testifies in direct examination in conclusory form: "The witness failed the heel to toe test." Or the officer testifies that the witness failed the heel to toe test because of particular enumerated errors: "On steps six and seven the defendant lost his balance and had to raise his arms to stay on the line."

Assume that the defendant cannot contradict that assertion but does challenge the notion that he "failed" the heel-to-toe test or that the test was even a valid indication of whether he was driving while intoxicated. The cross-examiner might well begin with a study of the terrain where the test was conducted. Potentially favorable facts:

- The officer conducted this test on the roadside of a busy highway with 18-wheeled trucks whizzing by at 70 miles an hour.
- The defendant was ordered to perform this test on an uneven and unpaved shoulder of the road.
- The shoulder of the road was covered with gravel.
- There was only an imaginary line in the gravel.
- Did the officer's cruiser continue to flash all of its lights during the tests?
- As a result of the way the officer conducted the test, the defendant was required to walk toward several sets of high beams blinding him while doing the test.
- It was snowing during the test.

These and many more facts may be assembled into several convincing chapters that factually display the difficulty for any driver of performing this test at this location. Such facts would lead to one or more chapters on the site of the test and the testing circumstances.

Those chapters concerning the site of the test and the conditions of the test alone could give jurors great pause in deciding whether the test is valid evidence that the defendant's ability to drive was impaired by the use of alcohol.

Take note that the above chapters do not even touch upon the test itself. If the defendant was told to take nine steps before turning around, and did take nine steps before turning around, then the defendant perfectly passed the memory part of the test. If the defendant was told to begin with his left foot and did begin with his left foot, he perfectly passed that part of the test. If the defendant was told that after reaching the end of the line he should turn to his right before coming back, and he did turn to the right, he perfectly passed that part of the test. If the defendant was told that after turning he was to take six steps toward the officer, and the defendant did take six steps toward the officer, he perfectly passed that part of the test.

As can be seen, it may be that the advocate must concede some or even many facts to the opponent. But even in a scenario used by the opponent to his supposed advantage, there may well be a great many facts that assist the cross-examiner. The appropriate method is to examine any scenario in detail in order to find those facts that may be marshaled to form a coherent picture of assistance to the cross-examiner.

In the above scenario there may well be one or more chapters concerning the things done right by the defendant that paint a picture at odds with the incomplete picture painted by the direct examination. The cross-examiner is reminded that no fact in isolation can draw the vivid pictures created by chapters. The cross-examiner must gather the facts that relate to each other to build a chapter designed to accomplish a single goal. There may well be several goals accomplished by breaking down the heel-to-toe testing performed by the officer.

§ 5.21 Chapter Size

How big is a chapter? A chapter is only as big as the number of good facts available to accomplish a single goal. It is conceivable that you may have more facts than you need to accomplish a particular goal. This then requires a further analysis. It may be that the goal is both minor and undisputed. An event took place on August 26. But is this important to either theory of the case? We may have many facts to prove it, but do we really need to prove it at all? If not, this chapter should be omitted, or the fact that the event took place on August 26 can be done in a single question.

However, if the goal is important to our theory of the case, or important to undermining the opponent's theory, it is deserving of factual development. Even then, we must consider whether this important goal is disputed or undisputed. If undisputed, we certainly need to use our best facts but not all our facts. However, if a goal is both important and disputed we should be reluctant to discard any facts that help must prove that goal.

When there is more than one goal that can be obtained through discussion of an event or topic, it is likely that there is more than one chapter that needs to be considered for cross-examination. It is impossible to decide how far to break down a part or topic of the case until we understand how many favorable facts it contains. In addition, it is impossible to decide how far to break down a topic until we understand the importance of that topic to the competing theories of the case.

Trial lawyers must train themselves to think in greater detail. Cross-examiners diligently study in a search for those facts that are useful to a theory of the case. In court the lawyer can always back up to a more general presentation, but it is very difficult to start with only a very skeletal notion of a chapter and develop the appropriate leading detailed questions at the podium. Within an event there is often more than one point of importance.

§ 5.22 Draft Chapters Backwards

A helpful way to approach the development of chapters is to engage in a four-step process designed to efficiently move the advocate from chapter concept to chapter completion. It is easy to think of the process in this way: Draft chapters backwards. Below is a diagram of the process followed by a description of the four steps:

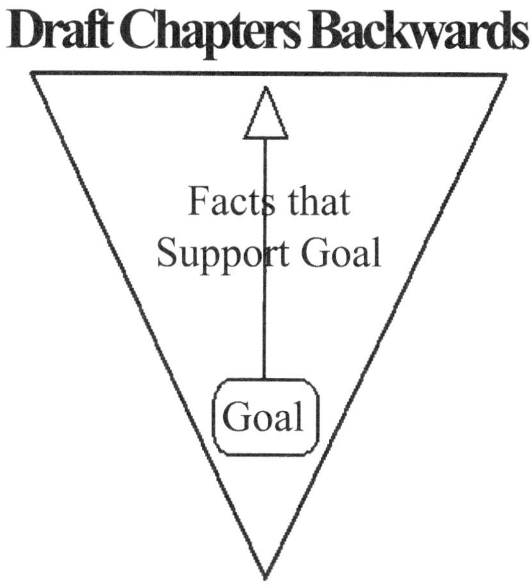

Step 1: Identify any one single factual goal to be achieved in the course of the cross-examination that is congruent with the theory of the case.

Step 2: Review cross-examination preparation materials for all facts that lead toward acceptance of that single factual goal.

Step 3: Draft a single chapter that covers those facts, leading to the factual goal as set out.

Step 4: If, while in the course of drafting a chapter an additional worthwhile goal is identified, separate that goal and its supporting material into its own chapter.

This simple technique of chapter building permits lawyers to gather facts quickly and assemble them around their goals. Many experienced trial lawyers have informally adopted the chapter method of cross-examination, often without recognizing it as a system.

§ 5.23 Detailed Notes for Detailed Chapters

In addition, working from notes prepared in the chapter form increases the lawyer's opportunity to convince the jury of the theory of the case. With inadequate notes, the trial lawyer's questioning becomes unfocused and uncertain. When chapters (and their goals) are not handled crisply, witnesses are encouraged to fight back. Often, facts that support the lawyer's theory are omitted under the pressures of the moment. As a result, goal answers are not firmly anchored by all available supporting facts, and jurors are thereby permitted to remain uncertain concerning the trial lawyer's goal-facts. The methods of preparing our notes for courtroom use in the chapter method are further described in chapter 6, *Page Preparation of Cross-Examination*.

§ 5.24 Give Each Chapter a Title

Each chapter concerns itself with one factual goal. The materials collected for chapters are not miscellaneous; they are facts related to each other. The chapter stands for a logical proposition. That proposition is the title of that chapter. Chapter titles create a very organized method of preparing not only cross-examinations, but opening statements and closing arguments as well. Because the cross-examiner has identified all of the chapters that are favorable to her theory of the case, she can use the same topics in closing argument.

§ 5.25 Examples of Chapters in a Domestic Relations Case

In a domestic relations setting, which can be a jury or a non-jury trial, the cross-examiner must convince the jury that the defendant husband is wealthy in order to support the plaintiff/wife's claim for child support, equitable division of property, and periodic alimony. Without the chapter method, the cross-examiner could establish what would appear at first blush to be a rather strong admission from the defendant in one question:

Q: You are wealthy?

A: Yes.

In a theoretical world, that admission would be sufficient to sustain a large verdict against the defendant husband in all three areas of financial prayers in the lawsuit (child support, equitable division of property, and alimony).

Trials are not conducted in a theoretical world. They are conducted in front of people who want to feel that they have done right and want to feel that they had sufficient factual grounds to justify their award.

The cross-examiner could break down the overall component of the case (wealth) into many other categories:

WEALTH

(1) Land

(2) Cars

(3) Vacation Home

(4) Marital Home

(5) Bank Accounts

   (a) Nations Bank

   (b) First Union Bank

   (c) Wells Fargo Bank

(d) Citibank

(6) Retirement Funds

(7) Profit Sharing

(8) Gun Collection

LIABILITIES

(1) Less than 10% of Assets

(2) No Contingent Liabilities

In this rather elementary breakdown, the cross-examiner has greatly enhanced her ability to cross-examine successfully and convince the jury of the magnificent wealth of the defendant.

As these chapters are more thoroughly developed, they may in time be split into more detailed multiple chapters. For instance, the chapter on cars may divide into three chapters of its own:

CARS

(1) 2004 Mercedes

(2) 1990 Jaguar

(3) 2003 Land Rover

As these examples bear out, the establishment of a goal is enhanced by a systematic approach whereby the overall part, topic, or event is divided into chapters. This remains true whether the finder of fact is a judge or a jury. Each chapter drives toward its own conclusion.

In the domestic relations example above, the cross-examiner first viewed a potential subpart of the case as "wealth." The initial chapter breakdown was in accordance with specific assets. Finally, a part of it was broken down into three vehicles. By simply reviewing the chapter heading from the cross-examination, the cross-examiner will be prepared to give a factual opening statement about a 2004 Mercedes, 1990 Jaguar, and a 2003 Land Rover. No longer will the cross-examiner, who is pressed for time, have to speak in abstract or global terms (for example: "a bunch of cars") about subjects that are important to the theory of the case. Both in opening statement and in closing argument, the cross-examiner can be extremely fact-specific by reviewing her chapter headings.

§ 5.26 Example of a Series of Potential Chapters in a Commercial Case

In this next example an investment executive (Sharp) must be cross-examined concerning his failure to monitor an investment. This failure to monitor the investment is the foundation of the lawsuit. As a result, the cross-examination of the single witness will likely have a great impact on the verdict. The cross-examination preparation might yield more than 200 potential chapters of cross-examination. The actual cross-examination might require a full day and more than 100 chapters of cross-examination. The partial listing of some of the chapters that might be prepared for this witness includes the following:

Selected potential cross-examination chapters for James Sharp:

- Job is to do due diligence on investments.
- Sharp decided which companies were strong enough to be sold to clients.
- Sharp's job is to monitor safety of ABC insurance company.
- Sharp surveyed the insurance market on a constant basis.
- Sharp was the only person employed by the defendant to monitor the safety of ABC insurance company.
- Brokers were told to call Sharp with insurance questions.
- Sharp determined what information the brokers received.
- Clients deserved correct information.
- Clients look to their brokers for correct information.
- Brokers look to Sharp for correct information.
- Sharp monitored ABC on behalf of the brokers' clients.
- Sharp relationship with Kane.
- Kane tells Sharp to get clients out of ABC.
- Sharp never warned brokers Kane felt ABC unsafe.
- Sharp relationship with Rogers.
- Rogers told Sharp he was getting his clients out of ABC.
- Sharp told his boss about Kane's and Rogers' concerns.
- Sharp learns ABC lost $3 million.
- Sharp learns ABC took high management fees.
- Sharp learns ABC paid extraordinary dividends to its owners (management).
- Sharp learns ABC sold to new owners.
- Sharp learns ABC no longer trying to sell insurance.

These are just a sampling of the many chapters that might be prepared for a single witness. The purpose in laying out these chapter titles is to make clear that the cross-examination of a witness is best accomplished in chapters, each chapter making a single point, establishing a single factual goal or picture. The chapters are not complex, though the accumulation of chapters is the best method for proving a complex story.

§ 5.27 Examples of a Series of Potential Chapters in a Simple Scenario

Every witness who may be cross-examined deserves to have their cross-examination constructed in the chapter method. However, not every witness will necessitate many chapters of cross-examination.

Let us assume a lawsuit in which the plaintiff company sues the defendant company for unfair competition. As part of that unfair competition suit, plaintiff seeks to show that the defendant company tried to lure away all of plaintiff's key employees, while knowing that these employees were bound by contracts containing covenants not to compete. One of the witnesses called by plaintiff is a current manager who testifies in direct examination that he talked with the defendant's executive, who made it clear that the defendant was interested in hiring this witness. The necessary cross-examination chapters might be quite short:

- You called Mr. Jones.
- You brought up the subject of employment opportunities.
- Mr. Jones reminded you of the covenant not to compete.
- Mr. Jones said he could not talk to you until the covenant was up.

One cannot call these chapters unimportant. In fact, these chapters help with the bigger picture that the defendant is competing fairly. However, as to this witness, this is all we need and may well be all we can get that is both safe and productive. So be it. Using the chapter method, we stand up and do the chapters we have prepared. Then we sit down.

§ 5.28 Example of a Series of Chapters Necessary to Portray a Complex Character Impeachment

A more complex example of the need to divide the matter into its component chapters and how to make that chapter division is found in the following scenario:

Fact Pattern: The prosecution calls a snitch witness. As part of their plea negotiations, they have promised not to file a particular case against the snitch. That case involves a complex fraud: The snitch applied for a bank loan to buy an eighteen-wheel, over-the-road truck, purportedly to haul coal. He filled out a fraudulent bank application claiming that he had a contract to haul coal. His loan application also listed several small trucks as assets. He got a $55,000 bank loan for the truck and operating expenses. The bank closed the loan, the defendant took the check for the truck to his friend, who signed it as if

> the friend had sold him a truck. In fact there was no truck. The defendant used a portion of the bank loan to buy insurance coverage on the non-existent truck. He made none of his loan payments. He then reported the truck as stolen and collected on the insurance, which went to repay the bank loan. Through this complex scheme, the snitch made about $50,000 in the swindle.

All of this evidence could be covered as part of a single chapter of cross-examination on this witness's deal. As part of the chapter on "the deal," the lawyer could simply require the witness to admit that he committed a fraud and is getting immunity for the crime. However, the elaborate nature of the fraud is extremely critical to the lawyer's closing argument: This is a person lacking in credibility; that the witness is a person experienced in lying, cheating and stealing; and that this witness is a person capable and willing to mislead jurors as much as he was willing to mislead bankers, insurance companies, and the police who took the report on the stolen truck. Hence, to milk those facts for more value, it can be broken down into, at least, the following chapters:

Example of a single crime (immunized) planned and executed by the snitch

a) The Loan Application (full of lies)

b) The Loan Payment Schedule (promises made were really lies, as snitch had no intention of repaying loan)

c) Loan Payments Made (none — no intention of keeping word)

d) $48,000 to Tumbleweed (got friend to sign check as if defendant had bought a truck — a big lie)

e) Insuring the Truck (insurance application is all lies — there is no truck)

f) Reporting the Theft (big lie — even names a real person as a scapegoat, showing snitch's ability to concoct false story blaming real people and places)

g) Collecting the Insurance (snitch solves a lie with a lie — gets insurance company to use its money to repay bank, and thereby bail out snitch who has paid nothing on the loan)

h) Just Keep on Trucking (snitch runs a con to get out of a con and, having cheated everyone, keeps the $50,000 from the original bank loan as profit from his ability to lie, cheat, and steal)

By breaking this one fraudulent scheme into its component chapters, the lawyer shows the jury that in actuality there are a number of crimes (and more lies), including defrauding the bank, defrauding the insurance company, conspiracy, and filing a false police report.

This chapter breakdown permits the lawyer to explore and reveal the snitch's ability to lie convincingly to sophisticated business people and police, all according to a plan that nets the snitch a great profit. In chapter (f), "Reporting the Theft," the lawyer recognized an opportunity to prove through cross-examination that the snitch can use real people and places to concoct a wholly fictitious set of events, which he can then sell to the police. The worth to the lawyer's closing argument of such detailed chapters is incalculably high.

§ 5.29 The Chapter Method Gives Clarity to an Event

How can the lawyer recognize facts that lead toward acceptance of a factual goal? An easy and effective technique is for the lawyer to view a chapter as a very brief documentary film on one small scene in the case. Now the lawyer can better focus on those additional facts that give that scene more depth and texture. Our pretrial task is to search for the facts that we will need to construct our desired chapters. Our task in trial is to develop the facts we have available to make the picture more vivid for the fact finder. In cross-examination, ambiguity is the cross-examiner's enemy. Ambiguity allows each juror to paint his own picture. Because we have been less than specific with our facts, we have allowed each juror to paint his own picture and believe that the picture he has painted is not only the accurate picture, but the picture we have suggested. It is the job of the cross-examiner to place facts into a context that will assist the fact finder in understanding and accepting the fact goal of that chapter, to see our picture.

If the cross-examiner desired that a particular factual event remain muddy or testimony remain ambiguous, she would not have cross-examined on it in the first place. Chapters, by their very nature, give clarity to an event. By choosing to cross-examine on a particular subject, the cross-examiner has elected to establish that fact goal more clearly than if it was discussed in direct examination.

It may well be that the picture presented through cross-examination will conflict with a previous picture drawn on direct examination, and thus create an ambiguity for the fact finder. The cross-examiner prevails on that issue when the jury finds the picture she has painted to be more vivid and more believable. Facts are the tools for these tasks. The purpose of the chapter is to assemble for the fact finder related facts around a central point.

§ 5.30 Conclusions May Be Disputed, But Supporting Facts Are Not as Easily Disputed

Ordinarily we do not cross-examine by asking a witness to agree with our conclusion concerning a group of facts. We avoid this style because it is very easy for a witness to deny a conclusion sought by the cross-examiner. Furthermore, while denying that conclusion, the witness is automatically led into a position where they wish to explain either why they are denying our conclusion or why they are suggesting an alternate conclusion. By cross-examining in the chapter method, the cross-examiner can present an accurate picture of facts that compel the fact finder to agree with the cross-examiner's desired conclusion without ever asking the witness to agree with that desired conclusion. This is accomplished through chapters establishing factual goals that are themselves incapable of dispute.

For example, in a commercial case the cross-examiner wishes to show the jury that the opposing party/witness was at a specific time under great financial pressure. The witness will never concede that conclusion. In fact, he can be counted on to vigorously dispute it. Cross-examining in the chapter method shows that there is no need to offer up that conclusory question and engage in the fight that will inevitably occur. Instead, the technique most helpful is to factually demonstrate aspects of the financial situation of the opposing party/witness at the time in question. Listed below are some of the chapters of the cross-examiner might develop in order to win the disputed issue:

> Chapter: In 2006 you borrowed $12 million from Giant National Bank.
>
> Chapter: The payments on the $12 million loan were as follows. (List payment terms.)
>
> Chapter: The money was borrowed to finance your acquisition of the Ajax Company.
>
> Chapter: You were going to make the loan payments using the profits from your housing development.
>
> Chapter: Details of the housing development profit picture as projected.
>
> Chapter: But in 2007 the housing market tanked.
>
> Chapter: In particular, your housing development went under.
>
> Chapter: In May 2007, when the $12 million loan payments began coming due, you failed to make the payments.

The cross-examination would continue with a series of chapters factually demonstrating the financial crisis facing the opposing party/witness in 2007. We could continue with any other chapters that factually demonstrate the deteriorating financial condition of the witness. Perhaps the witness sold his car collection, a corporate jet, let his membership in their country club lapse, sold a family vacation home in Vail. All of these chapters are built on facts. The witness may deny forever that they were suffering any financial problems, but the accumulation of facts plays on the common sense and life experiences of the jurors. The jurors arrive at our conclusion whether or not the witness agrees. The lesson is that we do not need to and should not ask the witness to agree unless in a pretrial setting the witness has signalled to us that he will agree with our desired conclusion.

§ 5.31 Facts Trump Conclusions

Keep in mind that we do not need a witness to agree with our conclusions; we do not even need to state our conclusions. We build our case using facts in such a way that a rational fact finder arrives at our desired conclusion. When we marshal facts in support of an idea, we are working as lawyers. When we get into fights about our desired conclusions, we are only arguing with the witness. The facts are far more persuasive than the fights.

As the above list of chapters shows, the cross-examiner can best make a disputed point by displaying the chapters of facts that paint the picture. Each chapter is factually accurate. The hostile witness is left with the very difficult task of answering yes but wanting to explain why yes does not matter. The cross-examiner is best advised to ignore the explanations and stick to proof of the facts. It is unnecessary to ask the witness to agree with the fact finder's desired conclusion that the witness was under great financial pressure in the spring of 2007. Instead, the cross-examiner must be satisfied that the systematic grouping of facts within each chapter will allow the jury to arrive at the desired conclusion regardless of the witness's protests. We should remember that when the witness denies a conclusion, whether in direct or in cross-examination, his denial itself is merely a conclusion and conclusions can't paint a picture. The cross-examiner's facts are more vivid and more dependable than the mere rhetoric of the witness. What a chapter factually proves is far more powerful than what a witness orally denies in a conclusion.

§ 5.32 One Question Is Never a Chapter

Facts must be established in sufficient context so that a jury will accept the goal-fact as having been proved. A single leading question can never fully create a dependable context. A group of facts can create context. A group of facts can paint a believable picture.

It is never enough just to receive a favorable answer to a goal-fact question. The goal must be supported with the strongest available factual details. The factual details that support the proposition give the jurors the strongest basis to accept the inference suggested by a chapter (see chapter 6, *Page Preparation of Cross-Examination*).

Anyone who has tried a case knows the frustration of a juror coming up to the lawyer after the case and saying: "You are a good lawyer, and if I ever get in trouble I will call you, but you had nothing to work with." An equally experienced lawyer will know the satisfaction of having properly developed fact goal chapters when a juror will approach the lawyer after a trial and say: "You are an okay lawyer, but that case was easy."

It is the purpose of the cross-examiner to make the critical decisions easy for the jury by providing such detailed and multiple supporting facts that the decisions seem inevitable or at least fully supported by the facts. The chapter method of cross-examination prepares the lawyer to establish many important facts through witnesses called by the opponent. A fact admitted by an opponent is more easily accredited by the jurors than if the same fact was testified to by a witness aligned with the cross-examiner's side of the case.

§ 5.33 In Matters of Importance, a More Exacting Breakdown Is Preferred

Sometimes we hear the criticism that a lawyer was "overly prepared." Frankly, we do not know what that means. If it means that a lawyer prepared one area of the case exquisitely but in so doing ignored the other areas of the case, we might be willing to accept that criticism. However, being too well prepared is a rap most of us can live with.

It is our belief that most lawyers under-prepare rather than over-prepare their cross-examinations. We are better off spending more time adequately breaking down scenarios and analyzing the value of the available facts. Having developed our theory of the case and an understanding of the opponent's theory of the case, we are well equipped to recognize the topics of greatest importance. These topics should be prepared in great detail. The best evidence deserves the greatest time and attention in the trial. And it is easier to combine two potential chapters into one larger chapter on very short notice than to attempt to break one chapter down into two smaller chapters on short notice.

When in doubt, analyze the material more closely for a more refined focus. Events are understood only in a context. And jurors make decisions between two competing inferences by comparing the facts that support each alternate inference.

§ 5.34 How to Avoid Spending Time on Unproductive Chapters

Can the lawyer break the evidence down too far and into too much detailed information? Yes. The breakdown can become too small. What is deserving of the greatest attention is the evidence that has the greatest impact on the theory of the case. A chapter having no bearing on the opposing theories of the case has no business being done at all. If an event happened on Wednesday, or it happened on December 9, but the day or date have nothing to do with the contrasting theories of the case, there is no reason to discuss those facts and certainly no reason to develop a chapter concerning the day or date.

If the educational background of the witness has no bearing on the case or on the credibility of that witness, then there is no reason to discuss that background. There are many areas of discovery that can be recognized before trial as having no impact on the case. One of the advantages of the chapter method of cross-examination is that it allows the lawyer to skip over large amounts of facts that can be recognized as undeserving of attention at trial.

Time not spent preparing for irrelevant issues is time saved. That time can then be used to more fully develop chapters that matter to the theory of the case. When faced with a potential topic of cross-examination, the cross-examiner need only compare that topic to the competing theories of the case and ask what difference it would make if that topic were well established. In order to be of value, the topic or proposed chapter must have impact on the two competing theories of the case or on the credibility of a witness. Topics or chapters that accomplish none of these things are not worthy of the cross-examiner's time or preparation effort.

Chapter 6

PAGE PREPARATION OF CROSS-EXAMINATION

§ 6.01 Philosophy of Page Preparation

The trial courtroom is a venue devoted to the orderly adjudication of disputes. We apply a set of rules and procedures in a controlled setting with the thought that such procedures will assist us in arriving at a just result. Then how is it that we, the people most trained to work in this setting, experience feelings of disorganization, of confusion, even of chaos? One of the most difficult challenges facing the teacher of trial advocacy is the necessity of communicating how arduous is the day in trial. The trial lawyer is bombarded with thoughts, judgments, decisions, obstacles, doubts . . . and more. We are required to pose questions, listen to information, respond to objections, and gauge the judge or jury's response to the flow of facts.

In this highly interactive venue we cannot afford to load ourselves down with unnecessary tasks. The overwhelming goal of cross-examination is to introduce and discuss facts. The overwhelming purpose of page preparation is to make that task easier.

The science and techniques of page preparation are designed to work on many levels to free the cross-examiner in trial from tasks that could be performed before trial, thereby leaving the cross-examiner better able to listen and respond to the witness.

§ 6.02 Technique One: One Chapter = One Page

A chapter is a sequence of questions designed to establish a goal. It therefore makes sense that each chapter of cross-examination is composed as a separate entity entitled to its own page. A chapter is often factually linked to another chapter. This is referred to as a chapter bundle. In fact, it may take several chapters to adequately cross-examine on an entire event. Even when several chapters are factually linked, each linked chapter also needs its own page. The chapter method of cross-examination is weakened by drafting multiple chapters on a single page. The best form of preparation for chapter method cross-examination is to devote one page to each chapter.

By drafting no more than one chapter per page, we encourage ourselves to fill out the chapter with as many facts as necessary to establish a goal or create a context by which a fact may better be understood. When we start with an empty sheet of paper and a chapter goal, the blank page encourages us to fully develop the important facts in a chapter. Conversely, once we begin to list multiple chapters on a single page, we physically encourage ourselves to abbreviate our preparation of each chapter. A page crowded with multiple topics drives us to write fewer notes for each topic.

A corollary to the technique that each chapter deserves its own page is that no chapter should require two pages. When a chapter runs more than one page, we are encouraged to recognize that we really have multiple chapters that are being unwisely and unnecessarily combined. Undoubtedly there will be occasions when a topic requires multiple chapters (a chapter bundle). But when the strong facts centering on a particular point consume more than one page it is very likely that the material would be better presented as two separate chapters with two smaller goals.

§ 6.03 Technique Two: Never Write on the Back of a Page

There is a practical problem with drafting a chapter that requires more than one page. Our quest is to create a system that repeats. Variations on a system really mean more than one system. One chapter = one page is a system. One chapter = one page or sometimes one page and the back of another page = two systems. When a chapter spills over onto the back of a page, in the controlled chaos of trial, it is easy to forget the additional questions on the back of the page. When we ignore Rule 1, we force ourselves to remember to turn each page over to see if this is one of the chapters that has additional questions on the back side of a page. It is one more thing to remember. It is one more thing to go wrong. It seems the easiest thing in the world until an opponent is objecting, a hostile witness is evading, and the judge is becoming impatient.

§ 6.04 One Chapter = One Page Creates the Ability to Sequence Our Chapters

Each chapter needs to be separately drafted for another important reason: Individually drafted chapters can be easily reorganized to shift sequences of presentation. When chapters are separately drafted and placed one per page, the lawyer can add, delete, and change the order of chapters at any time prior to and even during trial. When two or more chapters are placed on a single page, the chapters are now locked into an inflexible sequence. It will be hard to separate the chapters and, as our eyes go to the page, we are more likely to venture into all the chapters on the page even if one or more of the chapters should be omitted. We may try to change our sequence by scribbling a note on a page indicating that a certain chapter is to be deleted or performed later. However, in the heat of trial, it is hard enough to follow that plan. It is almost impossible to recall what we intended to skip and which subject we intended to revisit at a later point in the cross-examination. Multiple chapters on a single page encourage lawyers to use each chapter even if we later determine that one of those chapters should be abandoned.

§ 6.05 Multiple Chapters on One Page: A Recipe for Confusion

When two chapters are placed on one page and the lawyer attempts to integrate the direct examination, exhibits, and other "happenings" at trial, the page becomes a series of arrows, scratched-out directions, and a potentially indecipherable list of priorities and stage notes. This becomes confusing and frustrating at trial:

Chart 1

Source	Questions	Notes
	Chapter I. Good Father	
Deposition 43/13	"pretty good"	"OK"
Deposition 44/1	"certain activities"	
Deposition 2/9	"thought of self'"	
Deposition 116/8	"worked long hours"	
	Chapter II. Good Husband	
Deposition 16/14	"most of the time"	"Not good"
Deposition 16/22	"better with children"	
		Photo of Family

Chart 2

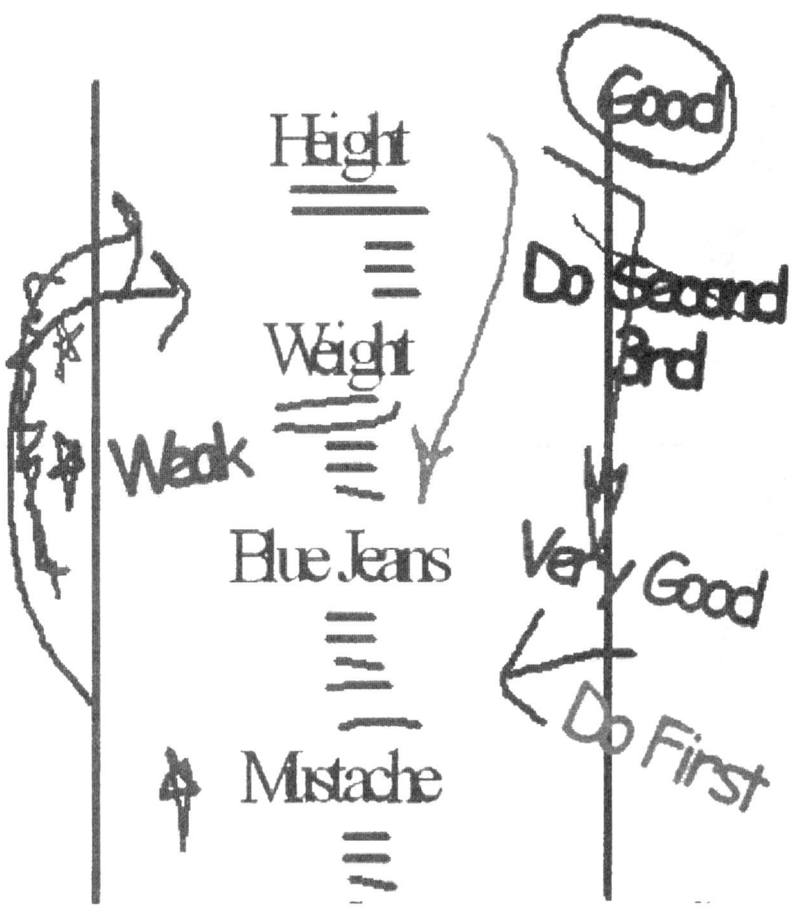

These two examples of pages of cross-examination (chart 1 and chart 2) are samples of the confusion that comes from the failure to adopt a cross-examination preparation system. There is so much going on the courtroom that the last thing the advocate needs is the stress of trying to remember what she was thinking when she wrote those cryptic notes. The advocate is warned: More colored pens will not make a system. Colored tabs on the side of pages will not improve the situation but instead create another confusing system within a system.

§ 6.06 Prepared Pages of Cross-Examination: Required, Not Optional

The techniques of page preparation of cross-examination ensure that the lawyer will move toward a single goal at a time and that she will present to the fact finder the best facts on that topic. If working from instinct or scribbled notes rather than from a prepared page of cross-examination, the lawyer is more likely to skip many supporting facts that establish context and instead skip to the goal questions. In addition, individual page preparation is the best technique of ensuring that the lawyer will complete a selected goal before moving to another goal.

The lawyer works from a script in cross-examination, so she can avoid the "Oh no!" syndrome. All attorneys who have worked without full preparation of their cross-examination chapters have suffered this result. The first variation of the syndrome: The lawyer has done what she perceives to be a brilliant cross-examination. The witness has been wrung dry of useful information. The lawyer confidently tells the judge, "No further questions." The witness is excused. After he has left the courtroom, the lawyer returns to counsel table where she looks down at her list of things to cover and sees one or more that she forgot completely to address. The lawyer says to herself, "Oh no!" (Authors' note: We are likely to say something far worse).

The "Oh no!" syndrome also manifests itself at or near the time of closing argument. The trial has concluded and the lawyer is drafting final notes and mentally rehearsing her summation. The lawyer realizes that she has forgotten to put into evidence a fact or a chapter upon which she intended to rely on closing argument. Now it is too late. A chapter that the lawyer failed to get into evidence is a group of facts that do not exist for closing argument. As a result, the case has been weakened by the advocate's own actions, not the actions of opposing counsel or a hostile witness. Who knows what would have been the effect of the additional facts had the lawyer just taken the time to outline the chapters properly.

Prepared pages of cross-examination protect us from the failure to introduce our best facts in an organized method. Questions not asked are the equivalent of facts thrown away and arguments squandered. Inevitably, even the best-prepared lawyers will forget to write some things and ask some things in trial. This is the penalty all lawyers pay for being human. We do not need to add to that list of errors and omissions those things that we could have cured with thorough preparation of a script for each chapter of cross-examination.

§ 6.07 Three Critical Questions That the Cross-Examiner Must Be Instantly Able to Answer

Cross-examination is a mentally and physically exhausting affair. And that's on a good day. There are a lot of decisions made during the cross-examination. In the midst of all of stress, the advocate is trying to guide a hostile witness through a mass of facts with the intent of proving several important goals. What is most needed is a system and set of techniques that allow the cross-examiner to remain focused and in control of the cross-examination regardless of the situation. At any moment in the cross-examination the cross-examiner must be able to answer the three fundamental questions of cross-examination:

1. What chapter am I in at this moment in my planned cross-examination? (Where am I?)
2. What is the goal of this chapter? (Where am I going?)
3. What facts do I have to achieve my planned goal? (How am I going to get there?)

The techniques of page preparation of cross-examination provide the cross-examiner with immediate answers to these issues. In the heat of trial, the ability to answer these questions instantly provides great stability to the cross-examiner and a predictable level of success.

Witness: Wes Martin **Robber was more than 6' tall**	← **(Q1: Where Am I? A1: I am in a Chapter on Height)**
You were face to face with the robber. Standing directly across the counter from him. Robbery took several minutes. Looked the man up and down. Noticed you had to look up at him. You are 6' tall. You found yourself looking up at a man taller than you. ↑	**(Q3: How do I get there?** ← **A3: My list of leading questions)**
(Q2: Where am I going? A2: Chapter Goal: Original description was of a robber taller than the witness.)	

[1] Using Page Preparation to Answer "Where Am I? "

Cross-examination is a series of goal-oriented exercises. As the cross-examination proceeds from topic to topic, without a script it is easy to lose focus. Where are we going now? Where are we going next? The advocate needs to be able to immediately determine what goal she will now be developing. "Where am I?" represents that moment when the cross-examiner either shifts focus to a new chapter or loses focus due to some distraction. Because the cross-examination does not necessarily proceed in chronological order, and because the cross-examiner ordinarily wishes to avoid certain topics, cross-examinations are not a stream of consciousness event. With this simple technique, the cross-examiner has planned the chapters that she wishes to cover and placed them into persuasive sequences. The cross-examiner does not have the time, energy, or need to memorize either the chapters or the sequences in which they should be used.

Every chapter is a single page. Every chapter needs to carry its title at the top of the page. The title of the chapter often announces our goal for that chapter. For instance, a series of chapter titles may be:

- March 1, 2007: Sallie Mimms tells CEO of duplicate invoices
- CEO tells Frank Slade (CPA) of the Mimms revelations
- CEO and Slade agree not to tell auditors
- Slade understood auditors would want this information

Here are examples of only some selected chapters that might be used in the cross-examination of an expert witness:

- You are a structural engineer, not an accident reconstructionist
- Your report is based on photos, no on-scene analysis
- You have no new information since April 6, 2007
- Crash tests are valid and useful

Some witnesses do not require a great deal of cross-examination. Their role in the cases quite limited. The entire cross-examination may occur through a handful of chapters. Below are a group of chapters designed to show that an employee of the plaintiff was the one who initiated contact with the defendant corporation, not vice versa.

- It was you who called John Flanagan
- You wanted to check out your employment options
- Flanagan asked if you had a noncompetition clause
- Flanagan said he could not talk to you until after non-competition period expired

In order to answer the question, "Where am I in this cross-examination?" the cross-examiner need only glance at the top of the page and she will be instantly oriented to the subject of the cross-examination she is about to perform.

[2] Using Page Preparation to Answer the Question "Where Am I Going?"

"Where am I going?" is shorthand for the goal the cross-examiner is seeking in the chapter. Often the goal is signified by the title at the top of the page, such as "Pullman had no background in insurance" or "the formula in the software is taken directly from the IRS code." But the question "where am I going?" also signifies that there is an end point. It is important to recognize where we are going, as we often get into trouble by questioning beyond our goal. We use the structure of our prepared questions to reinforce the notion that this is but a single chapter. Alone it may work, fail, or be abandoned. But the chapter will not be used as a springboard for other subjects. If those subjects arise in other chapters, we will get to them when we get to those chapters. But once we reach the end of our prepared chapter, it is time to turn the page and move on.

[3] Using Page Preparation to Answer the Question "How Am I Going to Get There?"

Finally: How am I going to get there? What facts do I discuss in order to create the desired context or establish my factual goal? This is an extremely difficult question for the unprepared cross-examiner to answer. It is the inability to answer this question that causes cross-examination to meander into open areas that are harmful to the cross-examiner. The techniques of page preparation allow the cross-examiner to know — at any moment — exactly how she intends to question the witness to accomplish her chapter. The facts to be adduced are listed on the page itself. No matter how stressful the court environment, the cross-examiner need only look down to remind herself of the leading questions to be asked and follow that script to its completion. Of course there is room to change questions, add facts, drop questions that seem unnecessary, and customize the chapter based on circumstances. But these changes in judgments become much easier because the cross-examiner has a firm starting point or outline of how to accomplish this chapter of cross-examination.

Armed with individual chapters of cross-examination laid out using these page preparation techniques, the cross-examiner can instantly answer the three questions:

Where am I?

Where am I going?

How am I going to get there?

The result is both the feeling and the reality of control. Knowing where we are in our cross-examination, where we are going, and how we intend to get to our factual goals allow the cross-examiner to think about other issues — ones that can be decided only as the cross-examination occurs. We can better listen to the answers and judge how our material is playing to the jury.

§ 6.08 Forms of Written Chapters: Room for Flexibility

It is appropriate to note that there are different ways to prepare the pages of cross-examination. The technique of one chapter per one page remains the fixed starting point. Where possible, questions should be sourced. The degree to which the details of the cross-examination questions should be written is a matter of personal choice. Some advocates are more comfortable writing every key factual question they intend to ask in each chapter. In contrast, some lawyers believe that outlining thoroughly and sourcing some individual questions is the preferable method.

Neither school is right or wrong. The goal is to provide the cross-examiner with pages of prepared cross-examination that reduce anxiety and increase control of the flow of information. The decision as to how detailed to make chapter notes is the preference of each lawyer. We will find our own comfort zone. We should not assume that one style is a starter kit and that another is what we grow into. Instead, we all experiment with our chapters and come to our own individual conclusions of the detail needed for our cross-examination pages. The critical factor is that substantial planning of the content of each chapter is called for in order to maximize the favorable facts we introduce in any chapter. This maximizes the opportunities available in cross-examination.

§ 6.09 The Architecture of Control — Laying Out the Page

There are three fixed components of a prepared page or chapter of cross-examination. These components can be arranged in various ways — again depending on the comfort of the individual. However, each form of the page must include each of the three critical components of a prepared chapter: the facts to be introduced (which can also be in the form of the questions to be asked); the source of the fact, if known; and a space for notes.

We start by dividing a page into three unequal columns: one wide column for the questions or outline of the questions; a second narrow column for the source of the answer, if known; and a third column for many possible uses, which might but does not necessarily include such notes as tactical comments or the use of exhibits, quotes from direct examination, and quotes from the prior cross-examination.

In setting up the page, the cross-examiner should choose the order of columns that feels best. After experimentation, one method will seem more natural. One method uses the column on the left side of the page for the source, the larger middle column for the questions or outline of questions for cross-examination, and the column on the right side of the page for tactical comments and quotes. The techniques of "sourcing" a fact are discussed at length in sections 6.12, 6.13, and 6.14.

In method 1, below, the columns are set out with the source of the fact, where available, on the far left, leading questions or facts in the center, and notes on direct examination or tactical considerations on the far right.

An alternative page format uses the column on the left side of the page for tactics, a narrow middle column for sourcing, and the right-side column for the cross-examination questions or outline of questions. See method 2, below.

Lawyers are encouraged to use either format or any other format with which they are comfortable.

Four samples of alternative page layouts

Method 1

Bennett (Witness) Sourcing	HEIGHT (Chapter Title)	Tactics
	(Leading Questions)	

Method 2

Bennett (Witness) Tactics	Sources	HEIGHT (Chapter Title)
		(Outline of Questions)

Method 3: Some lawyers drop the source column altogether and simply put the source in parentheses following the leading question or outline of questions. See method 3 below.

Method 3

Bennett (Witness) HEIGHT (Chapter Title)	Tactics
You were face-to-face with the robber? (Leading Questions) (77:9) (Source)	

Method 4: Some lawyers with the benefit of great quantities of discovery find that their courtroom presentations are so heavily dependent on their pre-trial preparation that any notes they might take in direct examination are of minor consequence only. They therefore develop their cross-examination pages using only a column for the facts they wish to assert and the column for the sources, where available.

Method 4

BENNETT CROSS-EXAMINATION	
SOURCE	HEIGHT (Chapter Title)
	(Leading Questions)

§ 6.10 Leading Questions Format

Each cross-examination chapter is a series of leading questions. The importance of preparing cross-examination as a series of leading questions cannot be overemphasized (see chapter 4, *The Only Three Rules of Cross-Examination*). A page of cross-examination questions is designed to be a page of answers. Hence, what the lawyer is really drafting is not a series of questions, but factual statements the lawyer wishes to establish. It is the lawyer's desire that the witness agree with these factual statements. In addition, we have many techniques designed to deal with those occasions when a witness answers other than with a "yes" (see chapter 9, *Controlling the Runaway Witness*, chapter 10, *Loops, Double Loops, and Spontaneous Loops*, and chapter 8, *Seven Steps of Impeachment by Inconsistent Statement*).

Below is an example of the questions column in a single chapter in a multi-chapter cross-examination where the general theory of the case is misidentification. This chapter concerns itself only with the witness's (victim's) version of the height of the robber:

Height of the Robber (Chapter title)

Q: You were face to face with the robber?

Q: You were standing directly across the counter from him?

Q: The robbery took several minutes?

Q: You looked the man up and down?

Q: And you noticed you had to look up at him?

Q: You are 6 feet tall?

Q: You found yourself looking up at a man taller than you?

In a driving under the influence case, where the theory of the case is that improper subjective observations are being coupled with unreliable objective evidence, the next example shows the question column of a single chapter on *one* of the inaccuracies of the Breathalyzer:

The 2,100: 1 Ratio Is Only an Average (Chapter title)

Q: You are certified as an Intoxilyzer operator?

Q: You must take a course to get that certification?

Q: Requirements of that course are set out by the Health Department?

Q: Its rules determine what's in the course?

Q: Principles of breath testing and physiology of breathing are taught in that course?

Q: You know that it is the alcohol in blood that affects you?

Q: Breath testing is a way of trying to find out how much alcohol is in the blood?

Q: The reason it assumes that is because there is an average relationship of breath to blood in people's bodies?

Q: But of course people's bodies are all different?

Q: If you took the average height of everybody in this room you might come up with 5'6"?

Q: That doesn't mean everyone is 5'6"?

Q: In fact, most people aren't 5'6"?

Q: They're either more or less?

Q: Same with breath-to-blood ratio?

Q: The Intoxilyzer assumes everybody's breath-to-blood ratio is 2,100 to 1?

Q: But 2100: 1 is just an average?

Q: Most people are either higher or lower?

Q: But Intoxilyzer assumes everybody is 2,100 to 1?

Q: If a particular person's breath-to-blood ratio is less than 2,100 to 1, the Intoxilyzer will give an inflated reading of the BAC?

Q: You have no idea if the defendant's breath-to-blood ratio is 2,100 to 1?

The next example is drawn from a sexual assault case. The complaining witness is a 16-year-old female who alleges that her schoolteacher had sex with her on numerous occasions. The defense theory is that the complaining witness is psychologically disturbed and seeking attention. She is seeking revenge on a teacher who was friendly to her but now is no longer friendly.

This chapter immediately follows a chapter in which the expert witness has described the victim as complaining about a previous (claimed) rape while the victim was in the hospital. This previous claimed rape is now conceded by the victim never to have occurred.

The general goal of this chapter is to show that the complaining witness suffers inadequately treated victimization fantasy.

Victimization Fantasy (Chapter title)

Q: Fair to call this (falsely alleged hospital rape) a victimization fantasy?

Q: A very intense and very real one?

Q: A psychological name for it is a dissociative episode?

Q: Certainly possible that this is not the only time in E's life when she has had one of these?

Q: In fact, you know about other times that it has happened to her?

Q: One of the reasons you had for keeping her in the hospital when you evaluated her progress on August 16 was that she might have more of them?

Q: If she's going to have problems perceiving reality, you would rather have her in the hospital?

Q: But you had to let E out of the hospital on September 6, 2005?

Q: The reason for that was her insurance coverage had run out?

Q: You really would have liked for her to stay in the hospital longer?

Q: You can't cure someone of borderline features and problems with reality in three weeks, can you?

Q: It is possible for someone to have these episodes of blurring fantasy and reality when there isn't a psychologist around to convince them it was unreal?

Q: You agree that if a person had a fantasy that she believed was true and, rather than anyone telling her it was unreal, people told her it was true, her belief that it was true could solidify?

The fourth example comes from a commercial case. In this example a high-ranking employee had written a letter citing facts and stating a product was defective and denouncing the conduct of his company. That letter has now come to light through discovery, and at trial the employee will attempt to back away from the letter. This particular chapter attempts to portray the very contentious meeting that occurred between the employee and his superior as a result of the letter.

The Ron Lane Meeting (Chapter title)

Q: Ron Lane was angry?

Q: He told you that your letter did not make people in Chicago headquarters happy with you?

Q: You discovered that the management of Blaine was angry at you for putting these facts in writing?

Q: Ron Lane made it clear to you that you were being called in because of your letter?

Q: The meeting lasted an hour and a half to two hours?

Q: It was not a pleasant meeting?

Q: Ron Lane used obscenities?

Q: Ron Lane yelled?

Q: Lane said that this letter about how Blaine handled the engineering problems in the Blaine 2000 all terrain vehicle (ATV) was a more serious matter then you understood it to be?

The following example comes from a commercial case. It involves the cross-examination of an employee of the corporate defendant. The allegation is that the corporate defendant and his employee aided in the cover-up of a fraud.

Q: ABC Corporation clock operated in your desire to audit a different month?

Q: You did not agree that the results of the audit of August sales was an accurate representation?

Q: You wanted to pick another month to audit?

Q: ABC agreed to let you pick any month you wanted?

Q: Once again, he knew in advance exactly what month would be audited (no surprises)?

Q: And again, ABC's auditor (Bob Ellis) agreed to give you a list of exactly which claims he would audit?

Q: Your job: to assemble the appropriate paperwork to justify ABC's rebate dollars?

Q: This was all paperwork you were to have ready for the auditors?

Q: Auditor (Bob Ellis) arrived November 17, 2005?

Q: He began work on the list of invoices he had given you?

Q: You could have audited this list yourself?

Q: You could have compared actual customer invoices to the prices you sent in to ABC but you didn't?

§ 6.11 Safely Asking Questions to Which the Answer Is Not Known

The often (too often) cited maxim of cross-examination is: "Never ask a question to which you do not know the answer." But this rule is both misunderstood and misapplied. The misunderstanding comes from too narrow an application of the term "know the answer." This shorthand phrase implies that the cross-examiner must have proof that the witness has previously admitted this fact or be armed with a witness or exhibit capable of impeaching the witness should she deny the fact asserted in the leading question. This self-imposed limitation on cross-examination is too restrictive and foreboding. It might mean that, in some critical issues, the cross-examiner blindly obeying the letter of this supposed rule is left with little or nothing to ask. In reality "never ask a question to which you do not know the answer" is not advice to be obeyed if the advice is interpreted so narrowly.

First: Not all answers can be known prior to trial. This is particularly true in criminal law since the defense ordinarily faces significant discovery limitations and the prosecution must contend with its own limited ability to obtain discovery from the defense. In addition, the Fifth Amendment shields defendants from having to make any statement until the moment they choose to take the witness stand. Discovery limitations are becoming more frequent in civil cases as well. Arbitrations ordinarily allow very limited discovery rights. In every forum, regardless of the amount of discovery available, it is impossible for pre-trial preparation to document every fact needed for the cross-examinations.

This often-cited advice to never ask a question to which you do not know the answer is better understood as a caution that the cross-examiner should plan the cross-examination. Planning minimizes risks and avoids unnecessary risks. In this sense the advice is of some assistance. If the definition of "know the answer" is broadened to include situations where a particular answer may not be independently provable, but may be logically indicated, then the advice has greater utility. By constructing chapters using known facts in combination with facts that logically flow from those known facts, leading questions can be asked to which the answer is less than certain but predictable. The applications of the techniques of the only three rules are instrumental in substantially reducing the risk inherent in any question to which the answer cannot be independently proved.

The cross-examiner needs to proceed carefully within a chapter from the general to the specific. Then, the cross-examiner can ask a series of leading questions to which the only logical response is evident by the time she asks the question whose answer is not known. The third rule of the only three rules is that questions should follow the logical sequence to a specific goal. If the cross-examiner constructs a series of questions so that the answer to any one question is logically deducible from the previously admitted facts, then the witness either must answer the question with a logical "yes" or risk denying the leading question and providing an illogical answer. Illogical answers harm the witness's credibility. Furthermore, logical fact finders are incapable of confidently picturing the illogical response. In other words, while every witness is free to answer illogically, the minds of the fact finders will continue to process information logically. Any fact or series of facts that logically leads to another fact or inference will cause the fact finder to picture the logical answer and reject the illogical answer or denial.

We encourage a witness to answer honestly through a variety of techniques, including the grouping of leading questions in a logical sequence. Another important technique that reduces the risk of asking leading questions that produce unknown answers is to document as many other facts as possible so that if a witness denies a leading question that has a known answer, the cross-examiner can immediately impeach the answer. Through this method the witness is taught that he takes a risk by denying the leading question. The witness cannot be sure of what answer he may have previously given in a deposition, what facts may have been previously provided by other witnesses, or what facts may be ascertained from documents.

Every time the witness denies a leading question and is immediately impeached, the witness is schooled in the danger of denying a fact when that fact is true. The techniques of impeachment are discussed at some length in this book (see chapter 8, *Seven Steps to Impeachment by Inconsistent Statement).* Within the science and techniques of page preparation is a technique critical to witness control in the ability to instantly impeach. That technique is referred to as "sourcing the answer."

§ 6.12 "Sourcing" the Answer

"Sourcing" is the process of finding and entering the designation of where, within the materials, a particular answer can be found. Knowing the answer, and knowing where the answer can be documented, is the highest plateau of witness control. When we know and can document the answer to a leading question, we erase any fear that the witness will successfully deny the leading question, plead a lack of memory, or substitute a different answer. While witnesses can still attempt all of these evasions, they are unlikely to do so because of the high degree of control the lawyer has gained through use of the technique of sourcing the answer, leading to very efficient impeachments. As a result, witnesses learn that they cannot succeed in these evasions because the lawyer is now prepared to impeach on anything other than the answer "yes."

This physical preparation for the possibility of impeachment represents a quantum leap in control of the witness. The lawyer's ability to prepare at this high level is derived from the cross-examination preparation system discussed in chapter 3, *Cross-Examination Preparation: Topic Charts,* and chapter 5, *The Chapter Method of Cross-Examination.*

In the preparation system discussed in this book, the lawyer gathers not only the multiple versions of a fact or event given by the witness, but also the specific location in discovery of each version. At that point, the lawyer has created a preparation system in which she has sourced the answer. When preparing the pages of cross-examination, the lawyer needs only add to the leading question a notation as to the source of the answer that is suggested by the leading question.

For instance, in the lawyer's preparation for a civil trial of a wrongful death case she may have prepared a topic card on how fast the defendant driver was going when he first saw the truck (see chapter 3, *Cross-Examination Preparation: Topic Charts*). The index card or chart, whichever is being used, might appear as follows:

SUE SHANE	SPEED WHEN FIRST SAW TRUCK
Unsure of speed limit	Interrogatory No. 26
Looked at speedometer just a minute before	P. Rpt. p.3
Saw going 45 mph	P. Rpt. p.3
Thought going 45 mph	Dep. 126:21

In the cross-examination of the driver, the lawyer established a chapter on when the driver first saw the truck. In that chapter, the lawyer is going to ask a series of questions to prove that single issue. One of those chapters will be how fast she was driving when she first saw the truck. That chapter includes the leading questions: "You looked down at your speedometer?" and "You saw that you were going 45 miles per hour?" The lawyer knows that the answers should be "yes" because the preparation system establishes that fact. In order to properly source the question on the lawyer's page preparation of cross-examination, the lawyer will systematically fill the page of a chapter with all of the sources for as many of the answers as the lawyer can within the body of the chapter.

As it would appear in Method 2, for example, on a single page of paper, the lawyer has the leading questions that make up this single chapter. Of course, they are not questions as much as they are facts. Now, to the left of that group of questions, the lawyer may draw a line creating a column running down the middle of the page. In this column, the lawyer should write the source for as many of these facts as can be found in discovery. The safest cross-examinations are those in which the lawyer has a source for the most important facts within the chapter, though there will often be leading questions to which the facts have never been established previously. The more facts that the lawyer can source, the safer the cross-examination chapter.

Take the first example above when, through a series of leading questions, the lawyer established the height of the robber. Now, working from one of the cross-examination preparation systems, the lawyer feeds into this middle column the source for each of the facts to be established.

Chart 3 below illustrates the page preparation of a single topic, "Height of the Robber," documenting the source of each of the answers.

Chart 3

Source and Question Portion of Chapter

Bennett NOTES	SOURCE	Height of robber
	Suppression Hearing 77:9	You were face to face with the robber.
	Police Rpt. P3 T	You were standing directly across the counter from him.

Bennett NOTES	SOURCE	Height of robber
	PH 20:12	The robbery took several minutes.
	S HRG 23:11	You looked the man up and down.
	PH 20:14	You noticed you had to look up to him.
	PH 36:21	You are 6' tall yourself.
	S HRG 79:4	The robber was taller than you.
	PH 36:12 SHRG 22-5	You found yourself looking up at a man taller than you.

The result of this process of sourcing the answer is that we are now instantly prepared for an impeachment by inconsistent statement. We have literally prepared for the worst-case scenario. If the witness were to say to a leading question, "No, I wouldn't agree with that," or "Gee, I don't think that's correct," or "I cannot recall," we are immediately prepared to impeach. The source notes in the source column tell the lawyer where, within even the largest file, the lawyer can find that precise answer.

The topic chart tells the date of the hearing, report location, and the persons present (see chapter 3, *Cross-Examination Preparation: Topic Charts*). Because of our preparation, we may now immediately impeach after laying an appropriate foundation. This instant and seemingly effortless impeachment reassures fact finders that the cross-examiner is the best guide to the facts.

Simultaneously the immediate impeachment schools the witness in the risks of denying a leading question. This preparation technique establishes and reinforces credibility with judges as they instantly recognize that the cross-examiner is well prepared.

In addition, judges grant more leeway for additional impeachments once they recognize that a witness has been successfully impeached. Finally, immediate impeachments by inconsistent statement strike fear in the hearts of opponents. They are weaponless in this battle. A correctly handled impeachment offers no valid objection. The opponent completely understands that the cross-examiner is not troubled by evasive answers, but in fact uses the opportunity to both establish the fact desired and impeach the witness. The opponent becomes less confident that his witness can answer the redirect examination questions without tripping and thereby opening up other opportunities for impeachment by inconsistent statement. This realization impacts the willingness of the opponent to engage his witness in any redirect examination.

The preparation technique of sourcing the fact allows the lawyer to avoid the anxiety of the unexpected answer. The lawyer no longer fears the loss of the goal itself or a loss of momentum.

§ 6.13 Know Where to Find the Fact

Opponents who cross-examine without sourcing the facts are easy to spot. After getting the unexpected denial, the lawyer utters the hollow phrase, "Your honor, may I have a moment?" The jury focuses on the confrontation between the witness and the cross-examining lawyer. With tension clenching their bodies and everyone staring at them, with the cross-examiner's client wondering how badly this is going to hurt her case, the lawyer desperately combs through exhibits, transcripts, or answers to interrogatories. In the fruitless search for the expected answer, every second is painful. It will take longer for the cross-examiner to find the impeaching material than most lawyers can endure.

In desperation some lawyers try to bluff the impeachment, saying something that suggests they could find the prior statement if required to do so; "Isn't it true you've said something different before?" And of course, the lawyer gets back a flat "no" or "I don't think so, not to that question." The witness can often sense lack of preparation or lack of confidence in the cross-examiner. Sometimes, the lawyer tries to bravely cover up the utter agony and embarrassment by saying, "Well, I'll come back to that." Not very likely. The lawyer is not going to come back. She is not prepared to come back. There may never be an opportunity to come back. The strength of the chapter has been wasted.

Because of inadequate preparation (attributable to just one small shortcut in page preparation), the cross-examiner has, at least as to this point, turned victory into defeat. The lawyer has embarrassed herself at having lost the point. She has yielded the momentum of the cross-examination to the witness and she has proven her own fallibility to the jury. The client and the case are hurt, while the witness is strengthened. The witness has unfairly denied a point and gotten away with it. This encourages further obfuscations.

The lawyer has lost both control and credibility at the same time. Worst of all, the lawyer has suffered all of those negative consequences on a point where the lawyer was right. Please take note of that lesson: The lawyer has suffered grave damage to her case by questioning in an area in which the truthful answer should have been "yes." If the lawyer can do that kind of damage to her credibility when she is right, imagine what damage the lawyer could do when she is wrong. The point is that because of a failure to source the fact, the lawyer might as well be wrong. For all the jury knows, the lawyer was wrong. The lawyer's credibility is now in tatters.

§ 6.14 Sourcing the Answer: Eliminating Risky Business

All of this damage could have been avoided, and the dodge by the witness could have been turned substantially to the lawyer's advantage by sourcing the leading question. When the lawyer has written out the source of the fact next to the leading question, the minute a witness denies, dodges, or feigns a lack of recollection, the lawyer can begin her systematic attack through impeachment:

> **Q:** You noticed you had to look at the robber?
>
> **A:** Well, I wasn't exactly taking a survey. He had a gun in my face.
>
> Or
>
> **A:** No, I don't think I had to look up at him, I looked more across at him.

Or

> **A:** I can't recall.
>
> Impeachment begins:
>
> **Q:** You came to this court for another hearing in this case?
>
> **Q:** It was on July 1, 2002?
>
> **Q:** The prosecutor, Ms. Brewsterman, was there asking questions?
>
> **Q:** We were in Courtroom T on the first floor of this building (etc., establishing the foundation). (Cross-examining attorney visibly reading from transcript.)
>
> **Q:** You were asked, by Prosecutor Brewsterman at page 20, line 12: "Did you get a look at the man?" Your answer at page 20, line 14: "Yeah, I did, and I gave him a good look up and down, and I noticed that I had to look up to him." (Cross-examiner goes on to complete impeachment.)

The contrast between the two scenarios is dramatic. In one, the cross-examiner is working without having sourced the fact. In the other, the cross-examiner is working from a sourced chapter of examination. For the prepared cross-examiner, something electrifying has happened. Although the point was not major, the very act of impeachment has bestowed a string of benefits upon the cross-examiner. First, the witness is brought up short. He has been defeated easily. The attempt to deny, evade, or alter the answer has immediately been defeated by impeaching the witness with his own previous answer. The witness now must confirm having given the previous answer. Instead of losing a point, the cross-examiner has scored the original point (the goal of the question or chapter) and has simultaneously scored the bonus of reducing the credibility of the witness, which is the consequence of a successfully performed impeachment.

§ 6.15 Always Source the Facts

The cross-examiner cannot safely predict when the opportunity to impeach will come up. As a result, sourcing the fact is a technique not reserved for the most important chapters or facts. Sourcing a fact should become a matter of routine. While the task might have seemed difficult at a point in the lawyer's development when she did not use the chapter method of preparation, once the lawyer has adopted this method and is transitioning that material into chapters, the source for a fact is immediately at hand and easily noted as the chapter is written. Below is an example of a typical chapter adequately sourced:

Firing Francine

Notes	Source	
	Depo 91:15	You fired Francine on July 2, 2004?
	91:17	You were her immediate supervisor?
	167:11	You fired her abruptly?
		There was no warning?
		There was no probationary period?
	168:15	You had a few notes scrawled on a piece of paper?
		You read the note?
		And that was the end of it?
		Francine asked if she could discuss it?
		You said no and walked out of the room?
		<u>Francine tries to get her personal items</u>
		Before you walked out Francine asked if she could go back and collect her personal things from her desk?
	167.21	You told her she was not allowed to go back to her office?
		You did not even allow her to pick up her personal items?
		You had one of your guards bring Francine her purse?
	168:12	2 or 3 days later you let her back into the building with a guard?
		The guard stood beside her while she cleaned out her desk?
		Then the guard escorted her out of the building?

As can be seen, not every fact has a source. Many times the cross-examiner knows or believes a fact because her client or another witness has related that fact. Sometimes the cross-examiner knows a fact because it is logically demanded. It is not critical that every fact in a chapter be sourced. Many questions are based on logic, on things told us by our client, or on interviews or background investigation that may not be admissible. It is critical that the facts that can be sourced are sourced.

§ 6.16 Other Benefits of Sourcing the Fact

By sourcing the fact, the cross-examiner is preparing to broaden the field of cross-examination. This occurs through the psychodynamics of trial. Judges appreciate and reward prepared lawyers. Judges acknowledge lawyers who are on a roll. Judges recognize when a cross-examination is going well. The cross-examiner who appears prepared to immediately impeach is the cross-examiner who will likely later be rewarded when she moves into areas of impeachment that may draw an objection. A judge who has previously observed successful impeachment of this witness is more likely to allow further inquiries into credibility.

A successful impeachment captures the attention of the jury. As one impeachment follows another, the jury gives its silent approval for the lawyer to continue to impeach.

In contrast, the lawyer who has the material but is unprepared and botches the easy opportunities to impeach often finds herself stopped by a judge. The reason for the ruling is not so much because the impeachment was collateral, but because there is no longer a belief that the lawyer can efficiently accomplish the impeachment.

A judge has many discretionary calls to make in the course of trial. The surest way to encourage calls that go the cross-examiner's way is to take advantage of every opportunity to demonstrate thorough preparation, pinpoint cross-examination, and steady advancement toward meaningful goals.

§ 6.17 The Drama of Instant Impeachment

When the cross-examiner has sourced a fact and suddenly encounters a full or partial denial of the sourced fact, the end result will always be the opportunity for a successful impeachment of the witness. The cross-examiner has the opportunity to impeach but not the necessity. There may be those changes of story that assist the cross-examiner and therefore do not call for an impeachment. There may be situations in which the fact is judged to be so minor or the impeachment so complex that the cross-examiner, for some tactical reason, chooses not to impeach.

When the cross-examiner elects to impeach using a prior inconsistent statement contained in a deposition or a document, this technique has an interesting byproduct. When a witness denies the truth of the leading question, and the cross-examiner immediately begins impeachment from a document, there is an undeniable urge on the part of the opponent to grab the cited transcript, chart, or report. Should the opposing counsel have some difficulty locating the document, so much the better. It graphically illustrates the opponent's diminished degree of preparation. This in turn demonstrates the opponent's lack of factual control, which can prove fatal when the jury deliberates on which version of the case to trust.

Assume that opposing counsel can quickly find his transcript or report. He will hurriedly shuffle through the document to find the page and line to which the cross-examiner has referred. The jurors' eyes turn toward opposing counsel, expecting to hear a loud objection. They, along with the witness, are wondering if the opponent will stand up and say something along the order of, "Your Honor, nothing like that appears in this transcript." Or, "Your Honor, counsel is misquoting the former testimony of the witness." They are waiting and wondering, but that is not what they are going to hear because exactly at the page and line of the document the cross-examiner has specified will be the information that she has demanded of the witness in the leading question. Now, that portion of the drama having been played out, the cross-examiner may elect to confront the witness with the document, requiring him to acknowledge his prior inconsistent answer.

After the cross-examiner has acted out this mini-drama several times in a case, there are some opponents who will forgo searching their documents and resources to verify the fact that the lawyer is suggesting through her leading question. When this happens, and the jury notices that the opponent no longer tries to retrieve a transcript or document, the jury understands the opponent to be saying, in essence, "If that lawyer says it, it's true." At that point, the cross-examiner has sealed her credibility with the fact finder, witness, and even with opposing counsel.

Sometimes, the opponent chooses to verify every reference cited by the cross-examiner. The jury will watch as the opponent searches for the cited material and then chooses not to object. Each of these mini-dramas further signals the jury that the cross-examiner is superbly in control of the facts.

This drama is not lost on the witness, who notices that the lawyer who put him on the stand is unable to protect him from the cross-examiner. This encourages the witness to save himself by granting the lawyer the "yes" answer that the leading question first demanded. This, in turn, decreases risk for the remainder of the cross-examinations. All of these benefits stem from one simple technique — sourcing the question.

§ 6.18 Tracking the Witness's Direct Examination

There is another benefit derived from drafting no more than one chapter per page. This technique gives us the ability to integrate new answers or facts produced during the opponent's direct examination of the witness. The cross-examiner may also use the page of prepared material to track facts developed within the cross-examination. When chapters are separately prepared, we can easily add notes, quotations, or new questions directly into the subject matter where they belong. As a result, we avoid taking several pages of notes mixed up by topics during the opponent's direct examination, covering a variety of subjects in no particular order — or worse, in the order selected by the opponent. Trying to cross-examine from such notes leads the lawyer to partially cross-examine the witness on a variety of issues, none fully developed. In the resulting confusion, facts get taken up out of context and chapters are awkwardly developed. Under these circumstances, the cross-examiner will often ask questions suggested by the notes taken during direct examination and then return to the same area of inquiry later when she comes to her prepared chapter of cross-examination. By then, however, all semblance of control, precision, or sequence is lost. For all of these reasons, the best method is: a page of cross-examination = a chapter of cross-examination. The simplicity of this system makes note taking and note integration easier.

When a witness is on direct examination there ought to be little reason to take notes. His direct examination should be the same old story. It ought to be what the lawyer has anticipated hearing. Both the bad parts and good parts ought to accord very much with what the cross-examiner anticipated when she wrote her cross-examinations. It is therefore not necessary to take extensive notes over the entire course of a witness's direct examination.

There are, on the other hand, some portions of the direct examination that the lawyer may want to document. For this reason, the lawyer makes a third column along the side of the prepared page of cross-examination (see diagrams below). In this third column the lawyer will keep track of what may be called "tactical issues." The first tactical issue may deal with the witness's direct examination.

Chart 4

Method 1

Source	Chapter Title	Tactics
	Cross-Examination Questions	

Method 2

Tactics	Source	Chapter Title
		Cross-Examination Questions

§ 6.19 Responding to the Witness's Direct Examination

A witness may change a story during his direct examination. It may be a new statement inconsistent with a previous statement, a fact that has never been asserted previously, or any other thing upon which the lawyer wishes to cross-examine. When such change occurs in direct examination, we need only turn to our chapters to locate the prepared chapter of cross-examination that is relevant. Having located the appropriate chapter, we can make a note in the **tactics** column on the new information. Then, when we cross-examine in this chapter, the new material shows in a visible reminder to consider in the course of cross-examination.

Of great importance is that the new story will be found precisely where it belongs — on the page of prepared questions that deal with that issue, referenced with the relevant sources. In this way, instead of accumulating on one page a string of unrelated notes on several issues arising in the direct examination, each note finds its way to the proper chapter page.

While it is critical to pay attention to the witness's direct examination, it is not particularly difficult to find the appropriate chapters in the prepared pages to insert a new issue. As direct examinations almost always proceed in chronological order, it is easy to follow the direct examination. Since the cross-examiner is listening for issues, it is easy to page through the chapters of cross-examination, although those chapters are almost certainly not in chronological order. If the cross-examiner is uncomfortable taking even a moment to turn to the prepared chapters to make a notation in the appropriate page, the lawyer may resort to the system of keeping notes on new items or reminder slips of any kind on a separate piece of paper. However, these notes should be transferred to the appropriate chapters of cross-examination at the next available recess (see chapter 5, *The Chapter Method of Cross-Examination*).

There is another method of integrating the direct examination into our cross-examination chapters. We can take notes on the direct examination by thinking of the direct as if it is being performed in chapters. We take notes on separate sheets of paper, just as if we were preparing a new chapter of cross-examination. As the opponent moves to a new area, we move to a new sheet of paper and take necessary notes in a chapter format. Then we marry up our chapter notes from direct examination with our prepared chapters in those areas.

Whatever else recesses are for, they are not for relaxation of counsel. Transferring direct examination notes onto appropriate cross-examination chapters or looking through cross-examination preparation materials for inconsistent answers or source locations of impeachment material, or otherwise ingraining new materials into the cross-examinations are but some of the things to be performed during recesses.

Chart 5 below shows the use of the "tactics" column to record a witness's helpful testimony given on direct examination. This exact quote, properly recorded in the tactics column, can be retrieved by the cross-examiner when performing this chapter and looped back to the witness. Because the quote is recorded where it needs to be, its usefulness to the cross-examiner is increased.

Chart 5

Method 1

Witness **Bennett** Source	Height of the robber	Tactics
S HRG 77:9	You were face to face with the robber?	
Police Rpt. P. 3	You were standing directly across the counter from him?	"I was no more than 3' from him."
PH 20:12	The robbery took several minutes? And you looked the man up and down?	
PH 20:14	And you noticed you had to look up at him?	
PH 36:21	You are 6' tall yourself?	
SHRG 79:4	The robber was taller than you?	
SHRG 22:5	The robber was 6'3"?	

Method 2

Witness **Bennett** Tactics	Source	Height of the robber
	Suppression Hearing 77:9	You were face to face with the robber?
"I was no more than 3' from him."	Police Rpt. P. 3	You were standing directly across the counter from him?
	PH 20:12	The robbery took several minutes? And you looked the man up and down?
	PH 20:14	And you noticed you had to look up at him?
	PH 36:21	You are 6' tall yourself?
	SHRG 79:4	The robber was taller than you?
	SHRG 22:5	The robber was 6'3"?

In chart 6 below, the notes column contains a new answer, given on direct examination, which is contradictory to the prepared script:

Chart 6

Method 1

Bennett Source	Height	Notes
SHRG 79:4	The robber was taller than you?	"The robber was shorter than me."

Having noted the new inconsistency in the notes column of the correct chapter, when reaching that chapter during cross-examination, the properly prepared lawyer may confidently confront the witness on this new and dramatic change of testimony after reaching that chapter during cross-examination. The lawyer can then use the witness's exact words as a jumping off point for impeachment. This is only one of several ways to handle this impeachment. See chapter 8, *Seven Steps of Impeachment by Inconsistent Statement* for other methods.

§ 6.20 Responding to the Witness's Earlier Cross-Examination Answers

Often when a cross-examination is going well, a witness will offer bait, which is an answer designed to entice the lawyer into changing her predetermined sequence of cross-examination. When we say that a witness baits us we mean that the witness gives some answer that tries to deflect us from the chapter we are in by moving us to a topic or area in which the witness is more comfortable. Cross-examiners working without scripted cross-examinations too often take the bait for fear that if they do not do so, they may forget to return to the baited issue. The lawyer armed with prepared chapters of cross-examination will easily resist the bait. We can respond to offered bait not by immediately questioning the witness in their desired area, but by taking a second or two to leaf through the cross-examination chapters, locate the appropriate place within the appropriate chapter to mark the offered quote, and then return to the sequence of cross-examination we chose before trial ever started. If necessary, the cross-examiner can code a quote with a D or an X in the tactics column to indicate whether that quote was from the witness on direct or cross-examination.

By using the tactical issues column to note a witness's exact words, whether given in direct or cross-examination, the lawyer is equipped to capitalize on the quote, either on cross-examination or in closing argument. See chart 7 below.

Chart 7

Bennett Source	Height	Notes
P. Rpt. P3	You were standing directly across the counter from him?	D "I was not more than 3' from him." "I was so close I could smell his breath."

Perhaps this new statement contains a better or more favorable recitation of facts than the cross-examiner previously possessed. In that case, the lawyer might want to loop off the exact words of the witness (see chapter 10, *Loops, Double Loops, and Spontaneous Loops*) or even spontaneously loop (in a delayed manner) off the statement by in essence forcing the witness to reassert the desired phrase during cross-examination.

As an example of the spontaneous loop the lawyer asked:

Q: You were standing directly across the counter from him?

A: Yes.

Q: When you were standing so close to him that you could smell his breath, you were no more than three feet away?

A: Yes. (This is a delayed spontaneous loop from the direct examination.)

§ 6.21 Keying in the Exhibits for Use as Impeachment

Exhibits have multiple uses in a cross-examination. Their placement on a page is dependent on how they will be used. If an exhibit is being used as the source of an impeachment, the trial exhibit number, page, and line should be noted in the source column. In this use, the exhibit is the functional equivalent of a deposition. It contains the previous statement of the witness. Chart 8 below is a representation of a chapter demonstrating how exhibits can be keyed in as sources of a fact:

Chart 8

SOURCE	ANOTHER PART TO TYUR DEAL
	September 2000 as part of the sale of JY Ltd. to TYUR you formed a new private company, JY Ltd. (bought back name).
Ex. A-5 (6) ¶ 15	You owned 90% of company.
Ex. A-5 (6) ¶ 15	Charles Moore, the Executive V.P., owned 3.2%.
	You knew private company JY Ltd. brought back many properties from TYUR.
Ex. A-5 (7)	1) Kola (U.S.) 2) A resort property in Mexico 3) A Gulfstream III jet 4) Furniture, vehicles (your car collection), 12 other cars in Montreal, office space
Ex. B article	5) Spare parts for the Gulfstream jet 6) A contract to buy an even more deluxe Gulfstream jet 7) Lease on top 3 floors of skyscraper Provencal building in downtown Montreal 8) 2 furnished suites in NYC 9) A Cadillac in Japan
	And your company gets a coal commission contract.

§ 6.22 Building Chapters Designed to Admit an Exhibit

Some exhibits may come into evidence by stipulation. In fact it is becoming increasingly common in both civil and criminal cases for the court to require the parties to meet in advance of trial and narrow their objections to exhibits. Some exhibits go in with relatively little effort. The foundation for the exhibit is simple and straightforward. The witness can lay that foundation and the opponent really does not believe he can block the admission of the exhibit, or intend to object to its admission. In such instances the exhibits can be shown in the body of the prepared page with the simple note "mark and introduce Exhibit 17, the nursing notes."

However, there are those situations in which the introduction of the exhibit is itself the purpose for the chapter. In such circumstances it is important that a chapter be written to lay the foundation or do anything else necessary to accomplish the admission of the exhibit. Chart 9 below is an example of a chapter written for the express purpose of admitting an exhibit:

Chart 9

SOURCE	Intro of E-5: Game Plan for default (overcoming attorney/client privilege)
Ex. E-5	You were afraid Mr. Harlan would default on his payment to you. So afraid that you wanted a game plan for default. That game plan is contained in Exhibit E-5. E-5 was written at your request.
E-5: pg. 1 Bates: 02759	You made it on June 1st. You shared E-5 with your management team. Your management team were business people, not lawyers. E-5 was not modeled by an attorney/client communication. And it is fact E-5 was distributed to your employees so they would know which percentages needed to have liens placed on them.
Ex. E-5	Move to admit E-5.

§ 6.23 Keying in Exhibits as a Tactical Reminder

Another use of the notes or tactics column is to key in exhibits. It may be that the cross-examination can benefit from showing a witness a particular exhibit. It may be that a particular exhibit must be introduced through this witness. It may be that an exhibit can be impeached or explained through this witness. In all of these events, this tactics column can be used to remind the cross-examiner of the exhibit to be introduced or discussed.

The chapter in chart 10 below is designed to impeach a portion of the story of a high school student who claims to have had multiple consensual sexual experiences with her principal. The school janitor has been called by the prosecution to establish seeing the two together at school long after classes were over. This cross-examination chapter is designed to impeach the girl's story that the sex acts took place in certain locked rooms. Note the use of the tactics column to key in a useful exhibit.

Chart 10

Goal: Show inconsistencies between testimony and physical evidence

HEAD CUSTODIAN SHAW SOURCE	DOORS	NOTES
	You are the head custodian at Fitzmunkers Middle. You were in the late 2000 and early 2001. Familiar with work that was done on doors and locks over the last few years. Back in late 2000 the lock on the office nurses' bathroom door didn't work. That was because back in 1999 the lock on the door to the main office didn't work but the nurse's bathroom lock did so they were switched. You personally saw to it that the lock was switched. To do this, you created a work order.	
	More important to be able to keep the office locked than the bathroom.	Introduce work order — EX.11
	Aware that it was common for the principal and the office staff to use the bathroom in the health office. So they were all aware that the lock didn't work.	
4-2	You had a conversation with Mr. Hardin when he first became principal in fall of 2000 about the locks.	
4-2	Remember telling him that lock on bathroom in health office didn't work.	
	You are also familiar with the lock on the door to the principal's office. It requires a key. Can only be locked from the outside. No button or keyhole on the inside.	

While the introduction of an exhibit often forms its own chapter, once an exhibit is in evidence, discussions concerning it require a stage note within a chapter prompting the lawyer on when and how to make use of the exhibit. See chart 11 below.

Chart 11

Example: Page Preparation of Chapter Involving an Exhibit

Ms. Farr	*The Lighter*	*Tactics*
Preliminary Hearing 12-7:25	When you got back to your apartment you noticed your lighter was missing.	
PH 167:4	That night or the next morning you discussed it being missing with Midge.	
PH 167:15	It was the lighter you had used to light a cigarette when you got into the van.	
	It was a metal lighter. In fact this is your lighter.	Show her ex ________
PH 167:9	You realized it was in the van — that it had spilled from your purse.	
PH 167:19	You believed that your prints were on it.	
PH 167:22	And that your prints on that lighter were going to lead the police to you.	

Similarly, there are times when the lawyer marks an exhibit for identification, but it may not be introduced. For instance, items may be shown to a witness for purposes of refreshing recollection, impeachment, or as a demonstrative aid. The court might very well ask that the item be marked for identification so that the record is complete. That same item, whether it is a transcript containing an inconsistent statement, a record used to refresh the witness's recollection, or any other type of document that is not going to be introduced, is still a prop that needs to be set in place. This tactics column is an appropriate place to keep notes concerning such exhibits and props. Alternatively, we are free to note the intended use of such items within the fact or question portion of the page.

The chapter in chart 12 below is prepared as part of the impeachment on a "snitch" witness. It deals with several exhibits that may be shown to the witness in telling the story of a prior fraud committed by this witness. Hopefully, the snitch will admit the truth of the leading question, but should he hesitate, the appropriate exhibit is keyed in, ready for use.

Chart 12

Example: A Chapter of Cross-Examination Keyed with Exhibits for Identification Purposes

Mark Nautiluss (Snitch) SUBJECT – THE INSURANCE FRAUD GETTING THE LOAN		
Source		*Tactics*
Cooling GJ	9/18/82 you went to People's Bank and asked	see Cooling GJ
5:22	for a $50,000 loan	5:22 GJ Ex 17 loan app. ID ______
Cooling GJ	You said you need $ to purchase over road	
5:23 PH	tractor/trailer for your coal loading business	
154:17		
	They made you a $55,000 loan	GJ Ex. 18: loan 11/9/82 pkg p1 ID # ______ GJ Ex 18: loan pkg p7 ID # ______
	The money was to purchase a new Kenworth	GJ Ex 18:
	Tractor and some cash for operating expenses.	loan pkg p3 ID # ______
Cooling GJ	The bank wanted to inspect the 1982 Kenworth,	
10:1	but you said your dealer had not received it yet.	
Cooling GJ	So, bank gave you one ck for $48,000 to	GJ Ex. 19:
10:10	Tumbleweed Ent. for 1982 Kenworth.	Bank ck ID # ______
Cooling GJ	And bank gave you a ck for $7,000 for	GJ Ex. 20:
10:16	operating expenses.	Bank ck ID # ______

Sometimes the note in the **tactics** column is not about an exhibit to be used during the cross-examination or an item to be marked for identification when shown to the witness, but it is a reminder to counsel of the existence of a piece of evidence that will contradict what the witness is saying. The lawyer may want to key in the note about the exhibit just as a reminder that the lawyer is setting the witness up for impeachment through either the previous or upcoming use of that exhibit.

By way of example, examine this case involving a witness who allegedly murdered the defendant's business partner so that the defendant might recover some insurance. One of the chapters of the cross-examination (see chart 13 below) involves the witness's description of where he stood as he stabbed the victim, who was lying in his bed. While preparing the witness statement charts, it was noted that the alleged hit man's description of the homicide did not match the coroner's report and photographs, either in the number of stab wounds, or in the place where the assailant must have been standing in order to inflict the stab wounds.

The witness is not going to be confronted with these differences. To do so would only point up the inconsistency to the witness and perhaps allow the witness to give a credible explanation. Part of the theory of the case is that the alleged hit man is not the hit man at all, but is covering up for a far bigger conspiracy not involving the defendant. Therefore, a chapter that demonstrates the alleged hit man's unfamiliarity with the homicidal act is a benefit to the lawyer.

Chart 13

The Stabbing		
Source		*Tactics*
GJ 12/11/81 p 36	You were standing by his left side.	
DA	You held the knife in your fist so that the sharp edge was facing toward you.	(demonstrate with rubber knife)
GJ 12/11/91 p 36	The first time you stabbed	
DA 12/9/81 p 33	him was on the right side.	
GJ 12/11/81 p 36	You believe it entered his right lung.	
GJ 12/11/81 p 34	You raised up the knife	
DA 12/9/81 p 36	and plunged it in full length.	
DA St 12/9/81 p 31	You stabbed him 3 times.	Pres EX _____, _________, _________, photos of deceased 5 stab wounds all made by person at his head

The Stabbing		
Source		*Tactics*
GJ 12/11/81	From side to side — across his body.	Pros Wit Dr. Toll (Coroner) Make sure details of wounds in Ev. during cross of Dr. Toll Chapters: # of wounds Direction of wounds Where assailant prob standing

§ 6.24 Tracking Inconsistencies with Other Witnesses

When a chapter is designed to show that a witness has been inconsistent on a prior occasion, we are engaged in a one-witness impeachment scenario. One witness has given two or more versions of a fact. However, in some instances one or more chapters of the cross-examination of one witness are performed to set up an impeachment of or by another witness. In this instance it is important to note the fact that the current testimony or chapter is part of a two-witness impeachment. In such instances, the chapter the lawyer is covering may not make sense to the jury, even though they have heard the testimony of both witnesses. In the tension of trial, it is possible for even the cross-examiner to lose track of how a particular chapter will be used to frame up an inconsistency with another witness. In such instances, it is helpful to make notes in the tactics column, adding in the text from another witness or in some way noting that another witness has or will testify inconsistently with the material found within this witness's chapter.

In Chart 14 we see a workup of testimony dealing with the topic of the negotiations between the witness and Gary Goundery. In the source column we show the testimony of the witness on that point. Note however that we have added the testimony of Gary Goundery as well. If we had conducted a private interview of Mr. Goundery, we could note his thoughts on this subject, even though we would not try to intruduce those notes. We are simply preparing ourselves to draft the leading questions for the witness. We might well ask a leading question based on something revealed by the witness in an interview or recollections of a witness contained in some other item that may or may not have been part of the formal discovery process.

Chart 15 is an example of the next step in the process of chapter preparation. This chart moves information from the draft topic pages into chapters to be used in the courtroom. Within the tactics column we see notes to ourselves reminding us of what another person has said on this point. We may or may not call that witness, but by including the other person's specific recollection on a point, we encourage a hostile witness to admit the truth and thereby often alleviate the necessity of calling a witness in our case to establish the point.

Chart 14

SOURCE	**1992 NEGOTIATIONS BEGIN WITH GARY GOUNDERY**
EK 304:4-10	You admit that you sent Hank Putter to negotiate with Gary Goundery in 2000 about Gary Goundery's purchase of Rust Financial?
EK 304:3-307:8	And it's your testimony that you allowed Putter to do this, even though you had no interest in selling Rust Financial to Mr. Goundery?
GG 10:16	And you were aware Hank Putter and Gary Goundery flew to S.C. to work out the details of the contract with Hank Putter concerning the negotiations to sell 100% of your interest in Rust Financial.
	You are still trying to hold off bankruptcy of your business EKJU (US)
GG 30:23	Hank Putter would suggest direct calls to you from Gary Goundery.
GG 31:1	Hank Putter would relate your specific requests on negotiable items.
GG 31:7	Hank Putter made it clear that he was in regular conversations with you.
	Many phone calls, much exchange of information and you kept assuring Gary Goundery team that your revenue and expense projections were reasonable.
EK 304:4	"I was not particularly interested in this, and so I did not take an active participation in the exercise myself."
GG 22:13	But at the same time you tried to communicate with real time pressure to get deal closed.
GG 30:17	It was a 4-month period of negotiations leading up to the final session July 4, 2000, weekend in Madison.
	But there was one last step: the buyer gets to look at the detailed financial records of the business

By way of further example, see the notes concerning Coroner Toll set out in the "tactics" column of the preceding murder trial example.

Chart 15

Traffic Reconstructionist Lindy		
Source	*NO SKID MARKS*	*Tactics*
Dep 1/12	You investigated the scene?	
Dep 4/4	You looked for skid marks?	

Traffic Reconstructionist Lindy		
Source	*NO SKID MARKS*	*Tactics*
Dep 4/6	You found none? None on the road?	Ex.___________ Photo from Tech I. Corbit showing skid marks
	None on the curb? None on the sidewalk?	Ex. __________ (Skid marks on road, curb, sidewalk)
Dep 63/19		Plaintiff expert Corbit: "They were faint because it was black rubber on blacktop pavement, but I have no doubt they are skid marks."

§ 6.25 Customary Order of Questions within a Chapter

The most frequent purpose of a chapter of cross-examination is to introduce or highlight a particular fact or set of facts or to create a vivid picture of a particular moment or event. Although establishment of this goal-fact or picture may often serve to impeach the witness, a chapter that introduces or highlights a fact that impeaches a witness takes a form different from that of a chapter devoted to impeachment by inconsistent statement. The form of a chapter designed to impeach by inconsistent statement will be discussed separately (see chapter 8, *Seven Steps of Impeachment by Inconsistent Statement*).

The introduction or highlighting of a fact through cross-examination can best be accomplished through an ordering of questions that begins with the chapter's general area of questioning and moves to the specific. It is ordinarily envisioned as an inverted triangle:

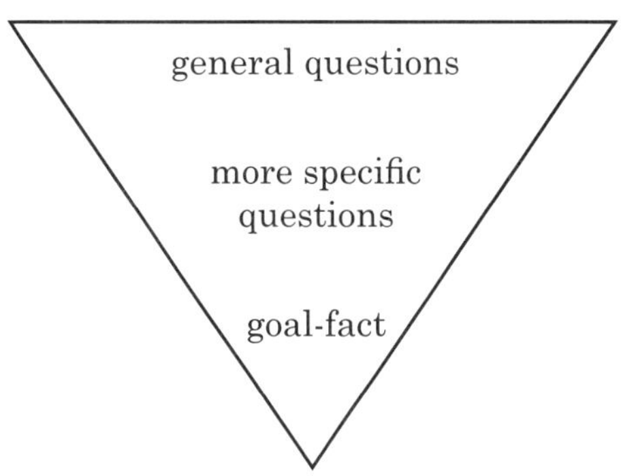

When it is said that a chapter moves from the general to the specific, it is meant that the chapter begins with a series of questions that establishes the broad nature of the topic. Then the cross-examiner, through a series of leading questions, pulls the witness along an ever-narrowing path until, at the conclusion of the chapter, the witness answers the specific question that completes the goal. Charts 16 and 17 below exemplify this frequently employed format:

Chart 16

Example of General to the Specific

Type of Case: Employee Sues Employer Claiming Sexual Harassment Overall

Goal: To discredit the complaining witness's allegation that on several occasions the employer took her into his office during work hours and locked the door so that he could engage in sexual activities with her.

The Employer's Secretary DOORS NOT LOCKED		
	Your desk is immediately to the left of Mr. Lewis' door. Your desk is less than 3 feet from his doorway. Your desk is perpendicular to his door. So when you are seated at your desk you can see into his door. His door has a lock. It is a push button lock. It makes a distinctive "click" when it is pushed or locked.	Show diagram Defendants Ex. 9

Chart 17

Type of Case: DUI
Area of Inquiry: Roadside examination
Specific Area: Improper administration of the Horizontal Gaze Nystagmus Test
Goal: Undermine police officer's expertise

DUI Officer Bloomingdale	Horizontal Gaze Nystagmus Test
	Method of Conducting Horizontal Gaze Nystagmus Test When you give HGN you look for three different things in each eye. Look for whether the eye follows pen smoothly. Then look to see if the eye jerks when it is all the way to the side. Then look to see at what angle the eye begins to jerk. Means you have to move the pen in front of each eye a number of times.
DMV Hrg. 28:23	And when you gave the test to Mr. S. you moved the pen at the same speed each time.

DUI Officer Bloomingdale	Horizontal Gaze Nystagmus Test
	But that's not the right way to give the test, is it?
DUI ENF Man p12	The Colorado manual on correct procedures for roadside test says you're supposed to move the pen at a high speed when checking for smooth pursuit.
DMV Hrg 29:16	But you are to move pen at half that speed when checking for the angle the jerking begins.
DUI ENF Man p16	And the State of CO DUI ENF Man says if you move the pen at the wrong speed you will mistake the normal movement of the eye for nystagmus. In other words if you give the test incorrectly you will think you see nystagmus when it really isn't there. You did not give the test in accordance with the manual. Since you moved the pen at the same speed each time, then you did at least half that test incorrectly.

The other examples in this chapter demonstrate the common sequence of questions within a page or chapter of cross-examination. Our questioning moves from the general to the specific. All have in common the same structure: First, the cross-examiner establishes the opportunity for the witness to observe an event or understand an event. Then there is a narrowing of the scope of the questions to show an ability to observe and understand events in this particular situation. Finally, there is the observation or goal-fact itself.

Alternatively, the chapter begins with the general statement of principles or a general orientation to the event or topic of the chapter. The chapter proceeds with more finely detailed facts and concludes with a completion of the picture. The goal of such a chapter is not to set up and win a battle with the witness but to use the witness as a method of educating the jurors on an important fact or issue. The chapter may well contain no facts in dispute. The power of the chapter is not in confrontation, but in the use of a hostile witness to establish facts that assist the cross-examiner's theory of the case. Remember, a fact admitted by the opponent's witness is a fact that the opponent can no longer easily dispute.

Moreover, a fact admitted by the opponent's witness is one less fact that must be proved by one of our own witnesses. If there are fewer facts that must be proved by our client or witnesses, there are fewer opportunities for our witness to fumble an answer or create an opportunity for productive cross-examination by the opponent. We significantly improve our tactical position when we craft a series of chapters that allows us to establish many facts of importance and paint many necessary pictures. By building our chapters to constructively introduce facts that support our theory of the case, we can fashion a series of chapters that cause even the hostile witness to provide a series of "yes" answers.

§ 6.26 Use of Theme Phrases as a Secondary Goal of a Chapter

Ordinarily the chapter has ended once the single picture is completed or a goal fact is established in its context,. Often, the goal is accomplished by the grouping of questions and not simply the final question of a chapter. However, there is a technique in which the desired picture or goal-fact of a chapter is followed by another question. This additional leading question is often a question designed to insert the theme phrase. In such instance, the chapter truly has two goals: establishment of the fact, and establishment of verification of the theme phrase upon which the lawyer intends to capitalize in closing argument. Chart 18 below is an example of such a chapter, moving from the general to the specific, and then ending with the theme phrase:

Chart 18

Witness: Snitch
Goal: Destroy credibility through character attack
Chapter: Willingness to involve innocent wife in lies for snitch's own benefit

Mary A. Dennis worked at the United States Trays of Snarp Association in Chicago.	General introductory material
You knew that because Mary A. Dennis is your wife.	
She didn't know about the scheme. She wasn't part of the fraud.	Specific questions designed to demonstrate witness's ability to cheat and lie
She was just a handy name. An easy way to handle things. She had no idea you were doing this. She didn't get the money. She didn't cash the checks. You cashed the checks. You signed her name. That's forgery.	
You just kind of pulled your wife down into the middle of your own crimes.	Chapter goal: witness's total lack of morals
You put your wife in a position where she would be arrested.	Theme phrase of "you put your wife in a position . . ." also used
You put your wife in a position where she would be charged.	
You put your wife in a position where she would be convicted.	
You put your wife in a position where she could go to prison.	
Fifty-six times.	

It was dishonest.	Establishment of theme
But it was good for your business. It was good for you.	Theme phrases: ". . . good for your business"; "good for you"

In the example below drawn from a trademark infringement action, the cross-examiner wishes to establish a goal fact that a high ranking corporate employee had reason to believe that his company would be infringing on the trademarked name of a competing cat food, but that he cared so little for the rights of the plaintiff that he proceeded anyway. That goal alone makes the chapter quite valuable. Equally important is the use of this chapter to establish the theme phrase, "It wasn't your problem." The resulting chapter accomplishes both its factual goal and the added goal of theme integration.

Using the Name Purrcat — Not Your Problem (Chapter title)

Arden Heller told you that there was a cat food on the market named Purrcat?

And Purrcat was a direct competitor to your cat food?

You didn't call the legal department and say, guys, we're putting Purrcat on our bags?

You didn't call Moffat, the head of marketing, and tell him we're putting Purrcat on the bags?

You didn't call anybody?

You just rolled it out?

Tens of thousands of bags with Purrcat on them?

Because using Purrcat on your bags wasn't your problem?

§ 6.27 Creating a Strong Inference as the Goal of a Chapter

Besides the factual goal, in many instances there is an unstated additional goal of a chapter: creating an inference — the conclusion that the jury is to arrive at concerning the testimony given by a witness in this or related chapters. Such a goal inference is in reality a conclusion. A conclusion should directly be asked of the witness only rarely, since the witness will likely be unwilling to admit our desired inference or conclusion. However, a chapter can more safely lead to a conclusion concerning facts or an inference when the witness has given up the desired conclusion in a deposition or pre-trial hearing, or within an exhibit. In such instance the denial of the inference is less likely and the denial can easily lead to an impeachment by inconsistent statement.

A common chapter that employs this technique is a "things-not-done" or a "things-not-done-correctly" cross-examination. Ordinarily it is dangerous to ask a witness to concede either of these forms of conclusion. The far safer approach is to show through education or through some other independent source that there is a correct way of doing something and the witness has not performed up to that standard or has failed to do the task at all. In such instance the very **fact** that there is an inappropriate task or way to do a task set against the **fact** that the witness has either failed to do a task or has done it incorrectly will lead to the desired inference without asking the witness to agree with the inference. When we ask the witness at the conclusion of the chapter to verify that he has improperly done a task, or has conducted the investigation poorly or incompletely, we place the witness in a situation where the witness will want give an explanation. The better approach is to set out facts and allow the jury to come to its own conclusion or inference as to the significance of the task not done or done improperly.

Again we see that the conclusion that the lawyer wishes the judge or jury to draw from the testimony is based on a factual presentation and does not require agreement by the witness. Methods of confronting the witness with the facts and asking the witness to agree with our conclusion are outdated and unnecessarily risky. We cause the fact finders to embrace our desired inference by our introduction and use of facts. If we wish for a finder to draw a particular conclusion or inference the least risky technique is to provide the hard-edged facts in a context that causes the reasonable person to say that our inference or conclusion is logical. Of course, the chapter method is the ideal form in which to introduce those facts, and to establish the logic that flows from those facts. The desired inference is thereby built upon facts, not oratory. There is no use trying to persuade a hostile witness that they are being illogical. To the extent that a witness feels it necessary to work out his own inference or conclusion that is illogical when compared to the facts they have admitted, a fact finder will administer the appropriate punishment. While we will often discuss our desired inferences or conclusions during closing argument, by that point in the case, the battle over the inference has largely been decided, and it has been decided based upon facts rather than rhetoric.

To obtain the jurors' agreement with the desired conclusion or inference, the lawyer should follow the customary format of building a chapter from the general to the specific. Below (chart 19) is an example from a civil case about a securities investment gone bad. The stockbroker for the investor complained to management that the research department of the brokerage firm had provided incomplete and misleading information to the stockbrokers in an attempt to bolster the price of the stock. After receiving the complaint the brokerage firm took two actions. It paid back the investors the money they had lost, and it levied a substantial fine against the stockbroker. The fine was allegedly for some unspecified violation of securities rules.

The purpose of the cross-examination chapter is to drive the inference that the stock broker was fined as a way of warning this and other stockbrokers not to complain or take a position adverse to the interests of the company. At the time of the cross-examination the stockbroker still worked for the brokerage firm and was unwilling to testify against his brokerage firm. However, a fact-based chapter that compels an inference does not require a hostile witness to change his attitude, only that he honestly answer factual questions. This chapter is part of a chapter bundle that explains the entire sequence of complaint letters and actions by the brokerage firm. While only one of the chapters within the bundle is presented, it is possible to see how the facts point to the inference that the actions by the brokerage firm were retaliatory and not based on a violation of rules or industry standards.

Chart 19

Alleged compliance violation

Exhibit 50 (letter)	In June 2002 you wrote your first letter of complaint?
	You received no reply from your company?
Exhibit 53 (letter)	In January 2003 you wrote another letter about this investment?
	Again, you heard not a word of reply from your company?
depo 112:21	Mary Allen, the head of compliance, never called?
	She never told you in any way that you had violated any rule?
186:07	Your client did not even know you had written these letters?
186:19	You wrote these letters solely because you had your customer's best interests in mind?
190:22	You never believed telling your brokerage firm how you analyzed a situation was any violation of a securities law?
190:25	Telling your brokerage firm how you saw the facts was the exercise of your judgment is an investment executive?
199:9	The National Association of Securities Dealers never wrote you saying that you had violated any rules?
199:15	The Securities and Exchange Commission never wrote you that you had violated any rules?
201:18	In fact the head of your compliance department, Mary Allen, never even talked to you about your letters?
202:19	Instead what happened was that you wrote a third letter setting out the facts as you saw them?
Exhibit 57 212:11	That is when your boss Norm Spiegel called you in and said you were fined $75,000?

Such a factual chapter, used in conjunction with other chapters (a chapter bundle) that educate the jurors on the letters of complaint and the settlement with the client, is the most effective way of equipping the jurors to find the inference that the broker was fined for speaking out. Through this entire chapter that hostile witness is never asked to agree with the inference but is asked only to agree with the factual leading questions.

Let us discuss another example of a factual chapter designed to compel an inference: "Investigating defendant's whereabouts at time of arson." It concerns a detective sent to interview a homeowner who is suspected of burning down his house. The theory of the defense is that the police department always assumed the defendant to be guilty and never investigated anyone other than the defendant. Regardless of the evidence, the police intended to charge the defendant with the crime.

Cross of the Investigator:

Investigating defendant's whereabouts at time of arson

Q: You do not know what time the fire on April 11, 2006, was called in, was reported?

A: No, I don't.

Q: You do not know the person who called in the first report of the April 11, 2006, fire?

A: No, I don't.

Q: It was part of your assignment to see if you could find out where Robert Lucans was at the time of the fire on April 11, 2006?

A: No.

Q: You interviewed him about where he was at the time of the fire?

A: Yes.

Q: And you interviewed his family?

A: Yes.

Q: About the events of April 11, 2006?

A: Yes.

Q: You were assigned to interview Robert Lucans and his family about the events of April 11, 2006?

A: Yes.

Q: And it could have been that you would have developed evidence that would prove he couldn't have been at the house at the time of the fire?

A: My purpose was to gain information.

Q: You were sent out on this case as part of the investigation of an arson of April 11, 2006?

A: Yes.

Q: Robert Lucans was a suspect in that?

A: Yes, he was.

Q: You wanted to know his whereabouts at the time of the fire?

A: Yes.

Q: The fact of the matter is you interviewed him because he could have been the perpetrator of the arson?

A: He could have been.

Q: You needed to know his whereabouts at the time of the arson?

A: Yes.

Q: The purpose of the interview was to pin down his whereabouts at the time of the arson?

A: Yes.

Q: That was your assignment?

A: My assignment was to interview him.

Q: About that subject?

A: About his whereabouts right after the fire.

Q: And at the time of the fire?

A: Yes.

Q: And you didn't know the time of the fire?

A: I didn't know.

The investigating detective, sent to check out the defendant's alibi, did not know when the fire started or even when it was called in. He may well have an explanation for how he could interview the defendant concerning his whereabouts at the time of the fire, but that fact he will never be asked. Instead, the cross-examiner will save the issue until closing argument — when the witness is no longer able to drum up an excuse or scenario to explain the curious method of investigation.

§ 6.28 Planning Chapter Bundles

It may take several chapters to explain one event in a case. When several chapters are required to tell a full story, each chapter within the bundle should be built using the inverted triangle form, in which the chapter is headlined with the general proposition or statement of fact and progresses toward increasingly specific questions until the goal is established or the picture painted. In addition, this grouping of chapters will itself create its own inverted triangle form, as the beginning chapters of a chapter bundle will ordinarily establish general propositions. Subsequent chapters will provide the specific and most important facts in the concluding chapter. This process occurs automatically. When we think about a story that requires several chapters, we intuitively put first those chapters that introduce jurors to the story so that they can understand the significance of later chapters. The important thing to realize is that a story or important event may require several chapters and we are free to arrange those chapters in a way that we feel best walks the juror through the sequence of events.

For example, in cases involving the testimony of an expert witness, it is often important in the early chapters to show exactly how a thing should be done, and then in the later chapters to show how the thing was done. The outline of how this multi-chapter presentation moves from the general to the specific is outlined below:

Witness:	Expert in child abuse case
Goal:	Undermine expert opinion that abuse has occurred.
Chapters:	1. Not all injuries are the product of abuse
	2. Factors that experts look for to determine if child abuse has occurred
	3. Type of medical examinations needed to determine if abuse occurred
	4. Lack of such examination in this case

The questions contained within chapters 3 and 4 of this chapter bundle are set out in charts 20 and 21 to demonstrate the sequence of chapters moving toward the goal. (For trial, each chapter will be prepared on a separate page.)

Chart 20

Chapter 3 — Information needed to determine if abuse occurred:

You want full medical histories

You want all medical reports

You want a complete physical

Sometimes type of injury may tell you how it occurred:

Fingerprint from a slap

Scalding water creating a burn

Cord marks from a whipping

Marks made by a coat hanger

X-rays

Lab data

Incidents that happen in the past, or the lack of past incidents

You have to do a very thorough and careful evaluation using these tests and interviews to determine if abuse occurred

Chart 21

Chapter 4 — Diagnosis without an examination:

Never saw Melissa in person

Never spoke to her by phone

Never had your staff examine Melissa

Never reviewed CAT scans

Never reviewed X-rays

Never reviewed head measurements

Never saw the results of any medical tests performed on Melissa

Never got any lab results

Never saw a single medical report that chronicled any other examinations of Melissa

Within chapter 3 the questioning moves from the general to the specific, but the whole sequence of the four chapters also moves from the general to the specific:

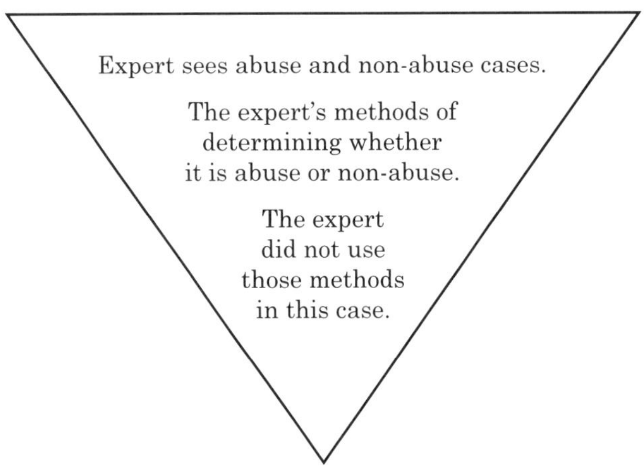

§ 6.29 Preparing Credibility Chapters

While the obvious goal of a chapter may be to introduce, highlight, or explain the significance of a fact, often the less obvious goal is to affect the credibility of the witness. Even in such instances, we may find ourselves establishing a factual point as we are working toward a more generalized goal of affecting credibility. It is important to keep in mind that the credibility of a witness overall or in any particular testimony is still a fact-based decision. If we show jurors a series of facts that indicate it would be difficult or impossible for a witness to see what they claim to have seen, the facts attack the credibility of the witness. When we factually show the financial motivation of a witness, the facts allow the jurors to infer a reason the witness may be less than candid. When we factually establish the prior felony conviction of a witness or cause the witness to admit that they have lied in the course of this case, we are engaged in a fact-based chapter affecting the credibility of the witness. In all of these instances, the lawyer uses a series of facts to paint the picture, but the true apex of the triangle or the goal of the chapter is two-part; showing the facts that paint the desired picture and thereby allowing inferences concerning credibility that flow from that factual scenario. Again, the techniques discussed above in section 6.27, Creating a Strong Inference as the Goal of a Chapter, are the techniques we use in attacking credibility. We show the operative facts to the jury and they arrive at their own conclusions concerning the credibility of the witness, either in total or as to a particular piece of the witness's testimony. We need not the witness to concede that he is a bad witness. At the farthest extreme, and while we may be able to fashion chapters that show the witness has lied previously or chapters that show the witness has reasons to lie in this matter, it is rather fruitless to ask the witness to admit that they indeed are lying. Far better to factually demonstrate prior lies or the witness's motivation to lie and allow the jurors to make their own judgment or inference.

Two examples of such chapters are set forth below: In this first example the city auditor has testified that he believed that the defendant Raceway was charging more for tickets than their city lease contract allowed, but that he remained silent because the city gained increased tax revenue. It is the position of the defendant that the auditor studied the contract and actually came to the conclusion that Raceway was within its rights. Of course, the hostile witness will never agree with that conclusion. While the cross-examiner would undoubtedly perform several chapters dealing with the contract itself, this particular chapter is designed to reflect on the credibility of the witness:

"I do not audit things that do not make the city money."

The city charter establishes the position of auditor?

The auditor is the general accountant for the city?

It is your job to make sure the city fairly and accurately accounts for the money it owes and the money that is owed to it?

You pride yourself on your integrity?

Your job is to be fair and accurate no matter who it helps?

And no matter who it hurts?

But in direct examination you said your job is to look out for the city's financial interest?

You say you did not audit what Raceway was charging for admission because you thought they were charging too much?

It is your position that if a company has a contract with the city but they violate that contract by charging people too much, so long as the city makes more money it's not your job to blow the whistle?

In fact, you would say it is your job to keep quiet?

In the next example we are confronting a snitch witness. Part of our larger strategy is to perform chapters which cause the jurors to appreciate the witness's lack of morals. We are seeking to demonstrate that the witness lives by his own code and that part of that code is that he can prey upon weaker people with no sense that to do so might be wrong.The facts demonstrate how he charges interest at an astonishing rate. The impression or take-away is that he is person not to be trusted as he will do whatever makes him a buck.

Chart 22

Witness: Snitch — Drug Conspiracy
Goal: Damage credibility by impeachment on character issues
Chapter: Cross-examination on being a loan shark

Money Lender = Loan Shark
You are a money lender, aren't you, Mr. Arden?
You loan your money out.
And you ask a reasonable return on your investments.
You ask 30% a week.
120% a month.
1,500% a year.
So a $1,000 loan from you costs $15,000 in interest a year.
Plus, of course, the original $1,000.
That's called loan sharking, isn't it?
That's just good business.
If somebody wants to pay it, why not let him, right?
You never promised it was a good rate.
You never promised it was a fair rate.
But if somebody is desperate enough, your attitude is: Why not?

§ 6.30 Format for Expert Witness Chapters

In a series of chapters performed in sequence to prove that an officer has not investigated properly, that an expert has not tested or analyzed properly, or in any other sequence of chapters performed with a goal of showing things not done, or things done improperly, the general format of the chapter is:

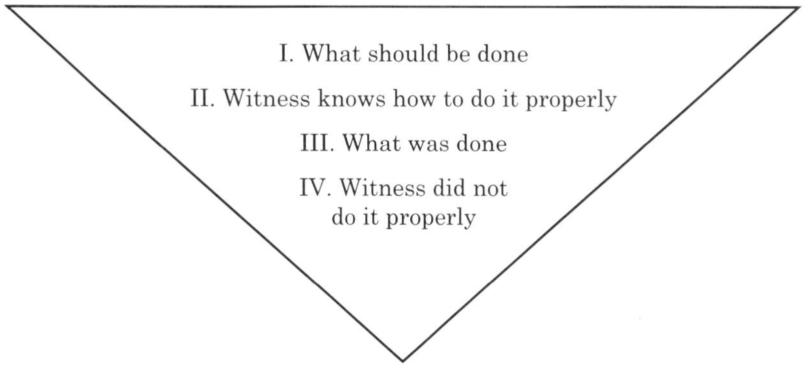

If the expert witness denies part II, so much the better for the cross-examiner. After gaining that very damaging admission, the lawyer could still press ahead to establish parts III and IV.

If chapters I, II, and, III are done well, it may not be necessary or prudent to perform chapter IV. It is in the case by inference that the cross-examiner may elect to discuss chapter IV in closing argument, when the witness is no longer in a position to explain away the errors and omissions.

If a lawyer were cross-examining an expert witness in an attempt to show that, while they did certain things, they did not do them in accordance with the proper procedures, the inverted triangle formed by the sequence of chapter is as follows:

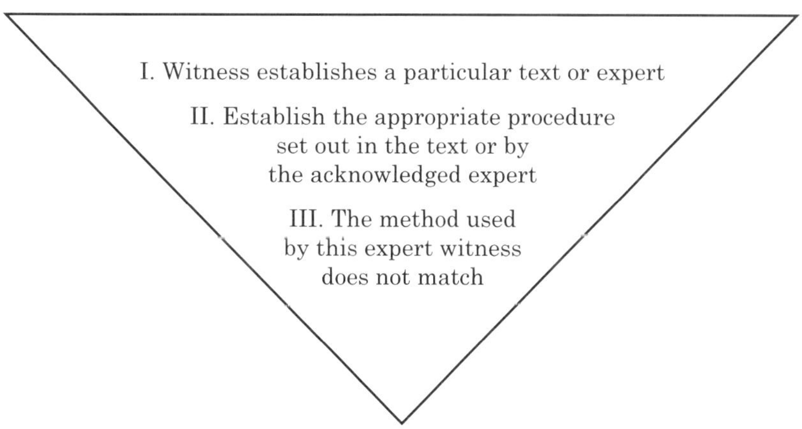

§ 6.31 It Is Not Necessary That Witness Recognize Goal-Facts

Often the witness does not appreciate the significance of the goal-fact or picture the lawyer is creating in a particular cross-examination chapter or chapters. This may occur because the witness does not realize that another witness, or some item of physical evidence, contradicts the witness's assertion. It may occur because in constructive cross-examination the witness does not appreciate that his answers are helping establish our theory of the case.

Sometimes the witness does not appreciate the significance of the questioning area simply because he has not considered the inferences that will flow from the facts he is admitting. In all such instances it is unnecessary and often harmful to our overall strategic goals to require the witness to acknowledge that we are making a good point or that our case is growing stronger and the opponent's case is growing weaker. It is not necessary for the witness to understand that the lawyer is driving toward or has achieved a goal. It is only necessary that the jury understand the significance of the fact admitted or testified to by the witness.

In all such instances, the inverted triangle form of questioning remains the same, though the witness does not sense the value of the goal achieved. The chapter can be diagramed in the customary way. It is an inverted triangle. By the bottom of the chapter, hopefully the jury gets the point. Although the witness does not necessarily feel the pinch of the narrowing triangle, the jury appreciates the significance of the goal. In fact, it is to the lawyer's advantage that the witness does not recognize the goal. The lawyer is likely to encounter a less directed fight by the witness. That is, the witness may still resist leading questions where possible, but the fight is not properly aimed, since the witness is unsure where the cross-examination is heading. It appears to the jury that the witness is just being hard to get along with.

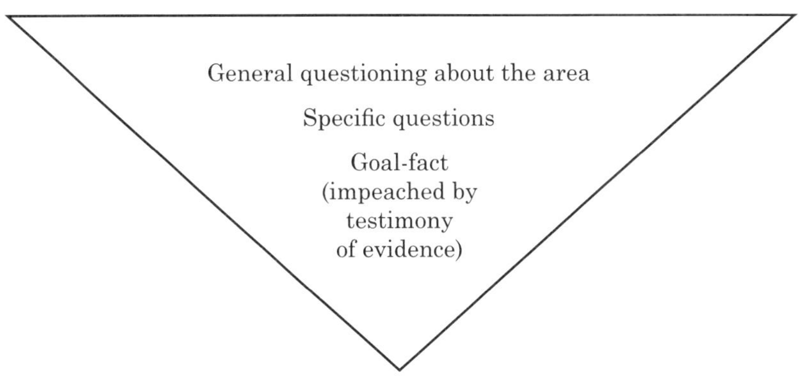

Many chapters look innocuous on their face. A witness can be led into a series of answers that is directly contradictory to the statements of another witness on the same topic. Opposing counsel, who has called both witnesses, realizes the damage being done but is helpless. The leading questions are not objectionable. The witness is not being frontally impeached and therefore feels comfortable with his answers. But the jurors understand the significance. A portion of the story of the opponent is now disputed by two witnesses called by the opponent. Such chapters often go rather smoothly, though they are effective impeachments.

§ 6.32 Sequence of Questions Impeaching with an Inconsistent Statement

Impeachment by inconsistent statement is a subject of such importance that it is discussed at length in chapter 8, *Seven Steps of Impeachment by Inconsistent Statements*. This discussion is limited to the sequence of questions in a chapter designed to impeach with an inconsistent statement.

The ordinary rule of moving from the general to the specific applies in such chapters. However, the introductory material at the top of the triangle may be the introduction, in some form, of the current version of a fact about to be impeached. The lawyer may begin by putting in some form of the witness "today's version" of a fact and then proceed through the introductory questions (foundation impact questions) before arriving at the goal of the chapter — introduction of the prior inconsistent statement. This can be diagrammed as follows:

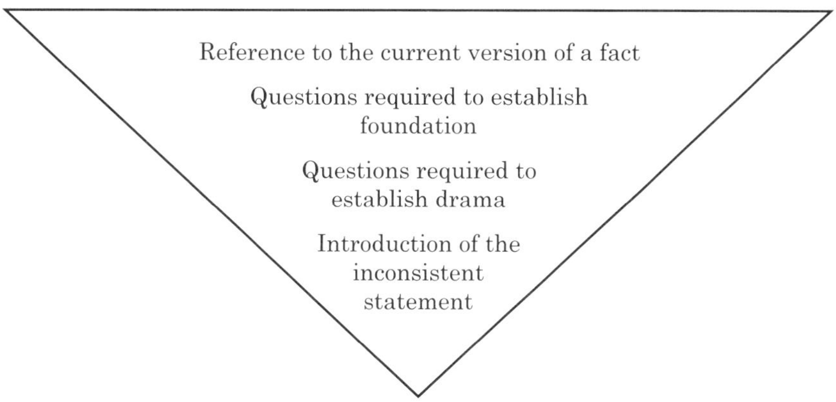

Keep in mind, however, that there is a seven-step process to impeach by inconsistent statement (see chapter 8, *Seven Steps of Impeachment by Inconsistent Statement*).

In written form, an abbreviated form of such an impeaching chapter might read as follows in Chart 23:

Chart 23

Differing Stories on Why Embezzle from TBC	
	On 3/25/86 when D.A. Inv. Abe Hendrickson interviewed you (to get you ready to testify for this case), you had a new story:
	This fraud arose out of your bookmaking activities.
Bertolli st to Hendrickson 3/25/86 p.19	Some execs at TBC had lost on some football bets and they would not pay, but they did authorize you to steal the money for the corporation.
	[Use of Foundation Questions]

Differing Stories on Why Embezzle from TBC	
(Bob Cantor, Pres, TBC)	And when you were caught you told your employers a story.
	A story on why you needed to cheat them
	to defraud them
	to lie to them.
Police rpt. 8/10/85 p.21T (st of Bob Cantor)	Your story:
	You needed to steal the money because you were getting a divorce and you need the money to pay bills.
(D.A. Inv. A. Hendrickson)	A different story for a different audience.

This description implies each page is a series of leading questions all ordered around a single chapter and leading to a specific goal. By posing these leading questions to the witness, the lawyer seeks to compel a series of "yes" answers, thus establishing the goal of that chapter. Establishing the goal in turn enhances the theory of the case.

Some lawyers believe that it is possible to perform good cross-examinations without a script. This is rarely true. It is also possible for a visitor to find her way in a city without a map, but it would be quicker and safer if she had one. It would be even easier if she had studied the map and outlined a route in advance.

§ 6.33 Thinking of Cross-Examination in Terms of Chapters

Each chapter is a finite goal. For instance, take a personal injury case about a car collision. If the lawyer has done her topic chart or index cards, whichever is being used, and finds that she has an important inconsistency concerning what the driver saw immediately before the accident, and that previous version is more helpful than a later version given by the same witness, there will be a cross-examination chapter on what the driver saw immediately before the accident. This will be drafted as a single chapter on a single page.

Further assume that the witness heard something of importance immediately before the accident. There will not be a chapter titled: "What the driver saw and what the driver heard immediately before the accident." Those will be two separate chapters. The lawyer must completely finish one chapter in her cross-examination before going to another chapter. In order to make sure that the lawyer has done this, she drafts a single chapter and dedicates a sheet of paper to each chapter. The chapter has a chapter heading at the top of the sheet. It has every question on that chapter in an appropriate order on that single page.

Chapter 7

THE RELATIONSHIP OF OPENING STATEMENT TO CROSS-EXAMINATION

§ 7.01 The Relationship Between Opening Statement and Cross-Examination

The goal of the opening statement is not to cause the fact finder to keep an open mind. Bluntly stated, the purpose of the opening statement is to aid in winning the case rather than simply explaining the case. Too often, trial lawyers are conditioned to expect interruptions and objections, such as, "She is arguing the case," or "Opening statements are not evidence and counsel is giving the jury her opinion of the evidence." As a result, lawyers tiptoe through their opening statements, hoping at best to outline the case without setting off an objection. However, the powerful, factual opening statement does not necessitate arguments. In fact, the opposite is true. A factual opening statement avoids arguing the evidence. Valid objections are eliminated by the techniques in this chapter. Instead, by grouping facts through the chapter method, the facts argue that the lawyer's side is the more believable.

At their best, opening statements are both much more and much less than an encyclopedic explanation of all of the evidence and witnesses in the case. On the more side: Opening statements are a vehicle to teach the advocate's theory of the case, point out the facts that most support her theory of the case, place her best facts into an understandable context, enhance the credibility of her witnesses, undermine the opponent's theory of the case, and attack the credibility of the opponent's witnesses. In the course of accomplishing these goals, by dwelling on well-organized facts arranged around a central theory of the case, the trial lawyer's credibility is established and enhanced.

On the less side: The advocate need not discuss every witness or every issue in the opening statement. Just as the lawyer cross-examines only on selected material, the opening statement points only to the critical issues in the case. The lawyer needs to determine "where the case breaks" — that is, the area of the factual dispute that must be won if the lawyer is to prevail. The advocate will inevitably spot these battles long before trial. Within the opening statement, the trial lawyer must deliver the deepest, most detailed factual presentation in precisely these areas.

§ 7.02 Recognizing the Power and Strategic Place of the Opening Statement

Cross-examination consists of a series of goal-oriented chapters, each designed to reinforce the advocate's theory of the case or undermine the opponent's theory. A proper opening statement not only introduces the advocate's theory of the case to the fact finder but also initiates the process of teaching, which leads to persuasion by familiarizing the fact finder with the most important chapters of the cross-examinations to come. Similarly, the critical chapters of the advocate's direct examinations will also be highlighted in the opening statement. However, the true power of an opening statement in the modern method is to highlight the favorable aspects of the cross-examinations to come and launch the factual attacks that weaken the opponent's theory of the case so that the jury is positioned to understand our theory of the case, comprehend the most telling facts we have in support of that theory, and recognize the factual barriers to acceptance of the opponent's theory.

§ 7.03 Cross-Examinations Lead to Opening Statements, Not Vice Versa

Opening statements are largely defined by the cross-examinations to come. Opening statements promote the favorable testimony we anticipate obtaining from the direct and cross-examinations we have drafted. Our opening statement details for the jury the admissions we are confident of obtaining in our cross-examinations. Remember, an admission is not necessarily a fact painful to the hostile witness. As we are now using our cross-examinations to build our theory of the case, we will be putting many leading questions to the witness that should result in a "yes" answer.

In a modern method of trial advocacy the opening statement is of enormous importance. This is a lawyer's opportunity to speak directly to the jury. It is an opportunity to share detailed facts that are meant to cause jurors to question testimony long before that witness takes the stand. In order to do that, we must have developed at least the most important chapters of our cross-examinations. By working backward from our prepared pages, we are supremely equipped to discuss in detail the most important facts we will develop in our cross-examinations. As will be discussed, this aggressive use of an opening statement can have gigantic impact on the acceptance of our theory of the case and a correspondingly devastating impact on the credibility of the opponent's theory and the credibility of witnesses the opponent will call in support of his theory.

§ 7.04 Opening Statement May Not Be Evidence, But It Is Teaching

What is the difference between evidence and teaching? Yes, jurors are routinely instructed that what the attorneys say in opening statement is not evidence. Our revealing a fact in opening statement does not put that fact into evidence. But jurors understand that lawyers are not allowed to just make up evidence. If we state a fact, jurors rightly expect that we have support for it. Therefore, they accept our assertions of fact with the unspoken understanding that we had better be able to back them up with testimony and exhibits. They may later choose to believe or not believe a witness, but they already know an outline of what they hear. Through our opening statement the jurors are learning about our theory of the case and how we will prove it.

Just as judges tell jurors that opening statements are not evidence, they also tell jurors that they are not to form any opinions about the case until the taking of evidence has concluded and deliberations have begun. But the instruction itself recognizes that people begin forming beliefs about the case based on what they hear in the opening statement. We can order people not to vote based on the opening statements but we cannot order judges or jurors not to learn from the opening statement. When we hear a story, we all begin to form impressions, working hypotheses — if not full-blown theories — as to what has happened and who is. Strong opening statements are theory driven, fact intensive, and organized around the chapter method of presentation. Opening statements are designed to teach, not to give an impartial overview of the evidence. The overall purpose of the opening statement is the opportunity to teach our case and thereby allow understanding of our theory of the case and what evidence we have to support it. Thus armed, the jurors may indeed begin to form not only an understanding of some of the most important scenarios in the case; they may also begin to judge the validity of the two opposing theories.

Example: In a civil trial alleging breach of contract, the plaintiff complained that the defendant had failed to pay sums due for construction of a home. The defense centered on the many alleged construction defects in the home. The plaintiff's opening statement centered on amounts owed for various portions of the construction. Plaintiff discussed in detail the letters written to the defendant, the numerous requests for payment, and the general unfairness of the situation. The defendant's opening statement did not deny any of the facts concerning the letters, requests or nonpayment. Instead, defense counsel gave a fact-intensive presentation, detailing the most important defects in the construction methods used by the plaintiff. Instead of talking about fairness, or arguing that there were two sides to the story, defense counsel confined her argument to her best chapters of cross-examination. Defense counsel showed the jury pictures of the water damage attributed to improperly laid and broken roof tiles. Defense counsel detailed how a window should be flashed to avoid leakage, and then showed how the flashing was misapplied in this home. Defense counsel discussed how the copper water pipes were laid in corrosive soil and were now leaking, and then discussed how a simple and inexpensive sheathing would have prevented this. The case settled after jury selection and opening statements. Reacting to the opening statements alone, a juror approached the defendant after the court instructed the jury that the case had settled and the jury was dismissed, and said, "I hope you didn't pay that crook [the plaintiff] any money." Is this surprising in light of the fact that no witnesses had yet testified? Not at all. People are accustomed to making decisions on available information. Opening statements can provide a tremendous amount of information. That the information is not yet reduced to admissible evidence may diminish the current value of the information, but it is valuable information nonetheless. Jurors, even judges, come to the courtroom eager to find out what happened, who was right, and who was wrong. The process of deciding a dispute begins subtly but instantly during attorney-conducted voir dire. It is in full gallop by the conclusion of opening statements.

§ 7.05 The Construction of Opening Statement: The Three Elements of an Advanced Opening Statement

The lawyer goes to trial with the goal of teaching her case so that those facts, when combined with the law, cause the fact finder to vote her way. The opening statement must reveal to the fact finders the essential facts that compel them to accept her theory of the case. She came to court to win this lawsuit, not merely to explain it. In order to get the most value from the opening statement, she must deliver theory-driven, chapter-organized, and fact-intensive openings.

Three elements are necessary to the structure of the successful opening statement:

(1) Construct the opening statement around the lawyer's theory of the case;

(2) Present fact-intensive detailed descriptions of the events that create pictures, not generalizations; and

(3) Base the opening statement on chapters of witness examination.

Structuring a powerful opening statement is simple if counsel has prepared the case using the chapter method. Successful opening statements (defined as openings that use facts to move the fact finder toward conditional commitment to the theory) have a great deal more to do with structure than with oratory. As with cross-examination, oratorical devices such as loops (see chapter 10, *Loops, Double Loops, and Spontaneous Loops*) can add great impact. But what is true of cross-examination is also true of opening statements — use of the chapter format to support a theory and organized communication of the detailed facts are of dominant consideration.

§ 7.06 Opening Statement Must Be Theory Driven

A theory of the case provides a fixed point by which the fact finder can judge the evidentiary progress being made by the advocate.

Particular jurors are selected because the advocate believes that they are the persons most likely to accept her theory of the case; that these fact finders are most likely to respond to the facts that the lawyer intends to produce in cross-examinations (and in any direct examinations that are necessary). The opening statement offers the advocate an uninterrupted opportunity to talk to these jurors.

What is the advocate going to tell them? They must be told the advocate's theory of the case. By educating the jurors about the theory, the advocate provides a framework or point of reference for the otherwise unrelated facts that are going to be adduced through witness examinations.

It is essential that the fact finders understand the theory of the case before witness examinations begin. This is especially true in cases where any significant portions of the theory are dependent on facts adduced through either the cross-examination of an opponent's witnesses or through the questioning of certain "adverse" witnesses for purposes of cross-examination. While direct examinations often tell a coherent chronological story, cross-examinations are designed to highlight or introduce only selected chapters of the story. Cross-examinations are most often disjointed with the evidence flowing out of chronological order. Generally, in cross-examination the advocate must cover small increments of the story, and even then the strategy of sequencing most often dictates a non-chronological approach. It is crucial to structure opening statement around a cognizable theory of the case so that, as the facts are developed in cross and direct, the fact finder can immediately, in real time, recognize the significance of the facts established and place them in context.

It is the theory of the case that gives direction to the cross and direct examinations. It is that same theory that must give direction to the opening statement. The goal is to educate jurors so as to allow them to both understand and believe in the lawyer's case — even if only conditionally. To keep these conditional votes, the lawyer must verify the opening statement by introducing the facts through the testimony of witnesses and the introduction of exhibits. Knowing the theory, the fact finders are able to say to themselves, upon hearing the cross-examination, "I see where you're going." When the jurors hear the recitation of the facts, they are in the position to say, "Now I see how you're going to get there." Jurors need to understand where the lawyer is going (the theory of the case) and how the lawyer is going to get there (facts).

In order to communicate our theory, it is not necessary to boldly announce, "Our theory is that . . ." or "We submit that . . ." Instead, the lawyer needs only to collect and present individual facts in such a way that the theory becomes obvious. For example, if a theory of the case and an opening statement based on that theory are truly effective, the lawyer need not say: "This is a divorce case. The wife, who is the plaintiff, is asking for alimony and child support. If she does not get at least $2,000 a month, her situation and that of her children will become desperate." The reason for the request for relief, the need, and even the consequences of a lesser award, become obvious from the proper recitation of facts.

Example:

> This case is about a man who ten years ago married a woman when she was eighteen years of age. They had a child, Alicia, a beautiful and bright child. The mother dropped out of school to nurture the child. Since the parties needed an income while the father continued his graduate school studies — first a Master's degree and then a Ph.D. — the mother worked as a teacher's aide in the public school system. Her schedule permitted her to take care of the child, and there was a day-care center at the school. Not much income, but enough. Once the husband received his Ph.D., the mother continued to work as a teacher's aide, and through the husband's early days of teaching, the mother continued to nurture Alicia because her schedule was the same as the child's. Now the husband is a full-time professor teaching early childhood education, earning a fine salary of $82,000 per year, with benefits, and lifelong job security, commonly referred to as "tenure." This man has now decided to abandon his family — a family that consists of a wife and child who still adore him, to live with a recent student of his who is nine years his junior. Younger, fresher, and better educated than his present wife.
>
> Despite his education and his understanding of education, he says that his wife and the mother of his child should receive no alimony, no educational allowance, and no security. He feels that she should get

> out and work a "real job" to better support their child regardless of the child's schedule. (More details to follow in the balance of the opening statement.)

Intensive use of facts without generalizations, conclusions, opinions, or legalisms "explain" the case to the fact finder. It is the gathering of facts around central themes that persuades the fact finder. The urgings of the lawyer are unnecessary and unavailing. Intensive fact presentations are not argumentative in the legal sense. Objections to them fail. The facts argue themselves.

§ 7.07 Give a Fact-Intensive Opening Statement

Of the three elements of an advanced method opening statement, the one most often lacking is the intensive use of favorable facts. Rhetorical devices alone cannot close this deficit. Oratory provides power only when used to highlight particularly helpful facts. By themselves, these techniques have no significance. Elegant words, phrases, and tones may mark the advocate as articulate, and they undeniably assist the lawyer in emphasizing her best facts, but it is the factual content that is persuasive. Between the facts or the flourishes, the best teaching lawyer always relies on the facts to win the case. The fact-intensive opening statement needs few embellishments to ensure its success.

Building the persuasive, fact-intensive opening is a far easier task once the lawyer has developed the cross-examination chapters. Abandon generalities, conclusions, legalisms, and opinions. The lawyer must concentrate on the specific facts that support the chapters that have already been prepared. There is no persuasive value in saying in a firm voice, "We will prove the defendant drove in a negligent (a legalism) manner, in fact, in willful and wanton disregard for the rights of others, and in a callous and . . . (legalism #2) manner." These are conclusory statements only. They give the jury nothing to envision, no facts to rely on, and no story to believe in. A fact finder cannot be persuaded by such conclusory phrases, as these phrases provide no facts upon which to base a judgment. The lawyer must provide the judge or jury with facts that support the conclusion she wishes them to embrace. The jury or judge can thus form their own conclusions and opinions, which will not be easily challenged or changed — by anyone. A direct, chapter-organized presentation of the facts that graphically shows negligence, for example, is far more valuable than all the posturing of the most articulate lawyer who speaks in legalistic generalities about concepts of due care and the reasonable man standard.

Example of an opening statement example based on facts rather than conclusions:

> The night was dark. The clouds were low. There was a misty rain. The traffic that night was unusually heavy for so late an hour. The defendant, barely nineteen, had not driven this road before — not in good weather and certainly not in conditions of a dark, cloudy, and rainy

> night with heavy traffic. Burt Baker, the defendant, knew that he was tired, knew that he was fatigued, and knew that he was distracted by other worries. Defendant Burt Baker will admit that those worries that distracted him from paying complete attention also drove him to drive faster and faster as the night got later and later. Defendant Burt Baker will admit, and the physical evidence will show, that he didn't just break the speed limit. In fact, he was speeding at least twenty-two miles per hour over the speed limit.
>
> Defendant Burt Baker will admit that Mary Jo's car was not the first car that he tried to pass. He will also admit that when he went to pass this car, he saw that the double yellow line was just up ahead. This is the manner in which defendant Burt Baker drove his vehicle head on into Sally Luke's vehicle.

In an example where the driver was drunk, it is not enough to tell the jurors, "We will prove the defendant drove in an intoxicated condition." The phrasing is stilted, the story is conclusory, and the impact is negligible. At best, the words create an unspecified picture; at worst, no picture at all. Of course, the lawyer undoubtedly had available all the ingredients of a truly compelling opening on this aspect of the case.

Example:

> It was just a few minutes before midnight when Dan Caplan finished his last drink. He had started drinking at about 9:45 that Friday night, and he had one drink after another for that entire two hours. His bar tab shows 7 vodka and tonics. At 11:55 p.m. Dan Caplan decided to get in his car and drive home. In fact, after the crash he told the police that, having swallowed the equivalent of at least seven ounces of liquor, he felt just fine. His blood-alcohol level an hour after the collision was .196, putting him at more than twice the legal limit.

If jurors are given the facts, they will inevitably begin forming their own mental pictures, inferences, and conclusions. Given facts on the primary issues of a theory, the jury may adopt the lawyer's theory, or one that is sufficiently similar. If the jury adopts the theory, the ensuing cross-examinations will verify what the jurors already believe. The mental pictures may not be identical to the ones in the lawyer's mind, but they will be similar enough to carry the day.

A lawyer is not permitted to "argue" her case in opening statement. However, the facts that the lawyer reveals, the order in which the lawyer discusses them, and the emphasis the lawyer gives them, are all permissible devices that teach the theory of the case and "argue" for a certain result. For example, if the advocate is championing a medical malpractice case based on a failure to diagnose, the opening statement should contain several chapters that reveal the opportunities the physician had to diagnose the illness and the list of telling facts that were available to the defendant/doctor. These should include how, when, and where the non-diagnosis or missed diagnosis occurred and should describe the damages that flowed from the failure to diagnose. As a capstone to each of these missed opportunities to diagnose, plaintiff's counsel might well choose to add a theme phrase such as: "But Dr. McDermott did not put the slide under the microscope. He did not see the dangerous cancerous cells," or "Since Dr. McDermott saw no cancer, Cheryl McGill got no treatment."

A very short theme trilogy might include:

(1) Dr. McDermott saw no cancer.

(2) Cheryl McGill got no warning.

(3) The tumor grew uninterrupted for another month.

While the detailed facts of the chapters for cross-examination provides the text of the opening statement, it is neither necessary nor possible to provide the fact finder with every fact that the lawyer intends to adduce through the witnesses. Equipped with the chapters as an outline for the opening statement, the advocate will recall enough of the specifics to flesh out a sufficiently detailed opening statement covering all of the important issues relating to the advocate's theory of the case.

No persuasive technique is more helpful than a fact-intensive opening statement. All of the argument is provided by the facts. The well-organized facts argue themselves. It becomes completely unnecessary (and remains completely objectionable) to tell the jurors how to vote. The jurors have already formed their first impression of the facts. They are already drawing their own conclusions. This technique of fact-intensive opening statement advances the credibility of the advocate's case long before the jurors have heard the first witness. In a larger sense, the fact finder has already heard from the witnesses before they have been called.

§ 7.08 The Fact-Intensive Opening Statement Brings Credibility to the Theory of the Case

Trial is a duel of information systems. This is a most unusual teaching environment. Instead of one professor, there are two, and they don't agree on much. The jurors will hear that the facts are disputed. They will be told of differing — even opposite — inferences that may be drawn from those facts. The two sides will attack the credibility of each other's witnesses. Both sides will speak through lawyers who sound sincere. So how are we to gain even conditional acceptance of our theory of the case? The credibility of our case is all important. In order to establish its credibility we best establish our own.

It is human nature for fact finders to judge the credibility of the advocates as well as the witnesses. Trial lawyers gain credibility by giving concise, fact-intensive and organized opening statements that clearly explain their theory of the case. Even with attorney-conducted voir dire, a newly sworn jury does not understand the nuances of the case. The detailed recitation of key facts in an opening statement tells the jury that this lawyer is prepared, that this lawyer understands the facts in detail, and that this lawyer can explain the facts in a way that assists the jurors in understanding how the facts support the advocate's theory of the case. The lawyer giving such an opening statement becomes a trusted guide to the evidence.

Our common experience is that when we stop for directions, we are willing to follow directions that are clear and detailed. Nebulous directions may be accurate, but the listener will not feel a sense of certainty and will follow these directions reluctantly, if at all. In fact, under this common scenario, the listener may well stop again soon to ask directions from a different person. The listener has graphically demonstrated a lack of trust in the first guide.

Good directions: Make a right hand turn at the third intersection. There is a traffic light at that corner. Travel 2.4 miles to a red light. There is a grocery store on the right-hand corner. Make a left at that light. It is the third house on the left. It is yellow. Poor directions: Hang a left at the first traffic light you come to. Go down a ways, not very far, and there is some sort of store at the corner. Make a left. It is somewhere on that block or the next block.

Whose directions would the listener confidently follow? Transport this scenario to the courtroom.

Included is a portion of an unpersuasive opening statement on the credibility of the plaintiff's theory of the case in a commercial case:

> "You're going to hear from Mr. Thomas. He will say his company was badly damaged by the defendant Acme's conduct. He will say that, but for Acme, in 2008 he would have sold tens of thousands of copies of his software. But the evidence will show a different story. The evidence will show that his company never did very well. You are going to hear evidence to challenge his version of damages. In fact, the evidence will show that he really wasn't injured by Acme."

The same material can be covered in a far more educational method by teaching the facts:

> "Wayne Thomas will ask you to give him $500,000 in damages. He will tell you that that is the amount of profits he lost in 2008 due to what he claims was a violation of his copyright software program. So let us look at the evidence of just how well his company, Money Mine, had performed in the two years he had tried to sell this software before the Acme software went on the market.
>
> In 2006, Money Mine revenues were $52,300. But Money Mine expenses were $78,800. Money Mine lost $26,500. How many copies of the Money Mine software were sold in 2006? Not tens of thousands of copies. Not even thousands of copies. The plaintiff sold 632 copies.
>
> In 2007, Money Mine revenues were $61,500. But Money Mine expenses were $89,400. Money Mine lost $27,900. How many copies of the Money Mine software were sold in 2007? Not tens of thousands of copies. Not even thousands of copies. The plaintiff sold 721 copies."

Of course, a great deal more would be said in this opening statement. But just this snippet shows how devastating a picture can be painted with facts rather than conclusion-filled rhetoric. We do not tell the fact finders that the evidence will convince them of the rightness of our position. Instead we tell the fact finders our position and the facts that support the position. The fact finders will embrace their own conclusion far more than any conclusion we urge upon them.

§ 7.09 The Fact-Intensive Opening Statement Earns More Room to Cross-Examine

The trial lawyer enhances her credibility with the judge and jury by demonstrating an intimacy with the operative facts of her theory of the case. As we articulate detailed facts that support our view of the case, we also use our best facts in such a way that they drive the inferences we cannot discuss in opening statement without fear of objection. Through the facts we preview for the jury, we educate the judge as to what we consider to be important aspects of the case. Quite often, even a well-prepared judge cannot envision how the facts will come together to establish a claim or defense. A judge left to speculate on the importance of a particular line of questioning may disallow the line of questioning at the time of the cross-examination. The judge may erroneously entertain the objection "irrelevant" because the judge cannot envision how the chapter fits into the cross-examiner's theory of the case. Alternatively, the judge may urge the lawyer to hurry the cross-examination, causing the lawyer to shorten the presentation of important material. Once the judge understands the factual goals of the cross-examiner stated in a positive light, and how those goals will be accomplished through various witnesses, the judge is more likely to permit the cross-examiner latitude.

Observe this example from a commercial case: The plaintiff sold his sports franchise to the defendant in 2007. Within the sales contract the seller required a warranty that the defendant was the sole purchaser of the franchise and was not acquiring the franchise on behalf of any other buyers. The plaintiff now alleges that the defendant was buying the business as a representative of a group of investors. Plaintiff sues on theories of breach of warranty and fraud, and seeks rescission of the contract. The defendant denies plaintiff's claim of fraud, stating that he bought the franchise solely for himself, though later others guaranteed the loans needed to finance the purchase. The defendant also challenges the materiality of the alleged false representation, stating that the plaintiff would have sold the franchise in any event, as the plaintiff was desperately in need of money. The defendant intends to cross-examine the plaintiff on his several failed business deals from 2003 through 2007. Once the court understands that these chapters on earlier business failures directly attack the materiality element of fraud, their relevancy becomes obvious. When a judge understands the relevance of particular areas of cross-examination, the judge need not interrupt the lawyer to ask, "Where is this going?" The powerful, fact-intensive opening statement that ties facts to our theory of the case inoculates us against the relevancy objection.

The opening statement needs to make the link between the plaintiff's earlier failed business deals and the need to sell the subject business in 2007. A factually weak or abbreviated opening statement on this issue could leave the judge with the impression that these chapters on failed business deals amount to little more than an attack on the business acumen of the plaintiff (a peripheral issue at best). On the other hand, when the cross-examiner gives a detailed opening statement linking these failed business deals in earlier years to the plaintiff's urgent need to sell this business, both the court and the jury can appreciate the relevance and the importance of these chapters. The factually detailed, theory-driven opening statement allows the judge and jury to better understand the cross-examiner's theory of the case. It also encourages the judge to grant the cross-examiner more latitude to prove these failed business deals during the course of the cross-examination.

The inherent power of the opening statement to bolster a subsequent cross-examination is often unrecognized or undervalued. In fact some lawyers so misunderstand the value of an opening statement that they waive their right to give one. They have voluntarily renounced their opportunity to teach. The jurors correctly see the lawyer as not having assisted them in their need to learn the case. Some trial lawyers recognize opening statement as having only minor value. They view the opening statement as a time to remind the jurors that there are two sides to the story and they request that the jurors keep an open mind until their side of the case is aired. Burdened by this minimalist view of the benefits of an opening statement, such lawyers may add a few unlinked facts just to let the jurors "know" that the lawyer has some facts worthy of discussion. They make a half-hearted attempt to discuss the facts by saying "Just for instance . . ." and then adding a few facts. They spew out their disagreements with many of the assertions made by opposing counsel, and then tell the jurors, "But you will hear more about that as the trial progresses." The promise of information is not a substitute for information. Once we prepare our witness examinations, we are so factually attuned to our case that we can easily avoid the tendency to rush our presentation. Our fact-intensive, non-argumentative opening statement dominates an opponent so foolish or unprepared that they give only a cursory opening statement so they can get down to the business of taking "real" evidence.

The truth is that the opening statement is far more valuable a persuasive tool than the closing argument. Twenty-five minutes of strong opening statement will prove more valuable than fifty minutes of equally strong closing argument. This makes perfect sense in the real world. Each person worries about making a good first impression, not necessarily making a good last impression. The first impression in front of the jury is the most important opportunity to tell the theory of the case.

A fact-intensive opening statement leaves many jury members perceiving the rightness of the advocate's position. Even those jurors not fully committed to their vote at the outset will have a mental map of the path that the advocate wants them to travel to the desired verdict. When a theory-driven and fact-based opening statement is matched against an opponent's weak opening statement, the opponent is left with the necessity of dissuading fact finders of what they have already begun to believe. The lawyer's strong opening statement must be overcome before the opponent can even begin to persuade the fact finder of the worthiness of his own case. In this way, the skillful, powerful opening statement gains an immediate advantage in the task of teaching the case.

§ 7.10 Using the Fact-Intensive Opening Statement to Affect the Credibility of Witnesses

Jurors are instructed to judge the credibility of each witness. An opening statement organized by chapter can and should provide jurors with facts that will aid the jury in determining who and what to believe or disbelieve, before those witnesses ever take the stand and before the testimony is formally offered.

Credibility is primarily a fact-based judgment. While jurors are instructed that they may use the demeanor of a witness as an aid in judging credibility, such indirect clues are less important (and less understood) than the direct method of judging the story that the witness relates. Jurors will first ask, "Does the story make sense?"

It is not enough to tell the jury that "a witness will testify that . . ." or "the evidence will show that . . ." Fact finders learn from the detailed recitation of facts, compiled in such a way as to tell a story and to paint a mental picture. (See chapter 4, *The Only Three Rules of Cross-Examination.*) If the lawyer wants the fact finder to believe a particular person as to a particular fact, the lawyer must provide enough supporting detail so either the person or the story or, ideally, both are invested with particular credibility.

Compare two approaches:

Example 1:

> The evidence will show that Henry Hawkins admitted that his company, A.B. Cobb, withheld vital information from its clients. Henry Hawkins admitted this to his friend. His friend will testify. He will tell you what Henry Hawkins said to him about this critical issue. Henry Hawkins will deny he ever said it but you will have an opportunity to decide for yourself who is telling the truth. There is a lot more to this story, and you will hear more of it during trial.

Example 2:

> James Snow worked with Henry Hawkins for six years. They rose together through the ranks of management. Both are now senior vice presidents. They shared responsibility for several projects. They

came to trust each other, professionally and personally. Their families exchanged Christmas presents.

They and their spouses occasionally shared dinners together. So it was not out of the ordinary when Henry called James one day in the fall of 2004 and asked if he could spare a little time to talk with him. What struck James as unusual was Henry's specific request that they meet outside of the office building. Henry picked the place — the Portland Athletic Club. James marked his daily calendar, "Lunch with Henry, PAC 11:30 a.m." James remembers the meeting. Henry was unusually nervous. He picked at his food. He seemed distracted. He even lit up a cigarette — something James had not seen Henry do in almost two years. James waited until Henry was ready to talk, and finally that moment arrived. Henry began shaking. "Remember the SUJITSO bond offering? Well, there were problems. Big problems. It looks like the bonds may not be so good. It seems the research department failed to perform some basic financial checks before selling those bonds."

"Well," asked James, "Why not just get the clients out?" And James remembers Henry's reply. "That's what I asked management and I was told, 'No way, no way. ABCO clients own a majority of those stocks, and if we tell them to get out, the stock prices will drop through the floor. Somebody will start asking questions about why we sold these shares in the first place. When that happens, ABCO is going to end up in court and our research department personnel will look like morons."'

Yes, James Snow well remembers that meeting and the words "our research department personnel will look like morons." Henry Hawkins will testify, because we will call him to testify. Henry Hawkins will tell you that he just can't remember using those words. He can't recall even discussing SUJITSO shares with James Snow. In fact, he can't even recall the lunch — not the Portland Athletic Club nor the phone call. He can't recall any of these events.

What does the second version of this brief portion of the opening statement accomplish that the first version does not? It has painted a factual picture of the lunch meeting. The fact finder has specific times, places, and even words. The advocate has organized this portion of the opening statement around the prepared chapters of cross-examination of Henry Hawkins, using a fact-intensive chapter presentation to sell the credibility of her witness while diminishing the credibility of a witness, Henry Hawkins, all without arguing whom to believe. By offering details that reveal the factual strengths or weaknesses inherent in a witness's testimony on a particular issue, the lawyer provides the fact finder with a logical and just method for reaching conclusions that the lawyer wants the fact finder to reach.

In the previous example concerning the conversation between James Snow and Henry Hawkins, both are senior vice presidents at ABCO. Would you be more inclined to believe James Snow or Henry Hawkins? In that short portion of the opening statement, the credibility of James Snow is elevated and the credibility of Henry Hawkins is deflated. It is done by facts, not conclusions.

The alternative, saying, "Snow and Hawkins will disagree, but you will find Snow is more believable," is both factually unsupported and objectionable. It is merely a statement of personal opinion, not a fact. A solid chapter of facts culminating in a particular point builds the foundation for credibility. In the above example, the cross-examiner could launch a far more effective attack on the credibility of Hawkins by citing facts that are likely to cause a fact finder to doubt the credibility of Hawkins. If Hawkins has given contradictory versions of events, reveal those contradictions to the jury. If Hawkins has authored documents that tell a different story than Hawkins will relate in court, tell the jury about the documents.

If a witness has a motive, an interest, or a bias, tell the jury the facts that allow them to judge these factors. It is insufficient merely to say, "The evidence will show that witness X has a motive to testify as he does." It is argumentative to say "I believe you will find that witness X has a motive to testify as he does." In all instances, give the jurors the facts. Make it possible for the jurors to arrive at their own conclusion, supported by the facts we have assembled for the jurors.

Most importantly, if the lawyer hopes for the fact finder to accept her theory, she must explain her case in enough detail so that the fact finder can follow the theory through recognizable chapters. Counsel cannot afford to leave the jury guessing at what she will try to prove or disprove, or what facts are important. Opening statement puts the lawyer at the head of the classroom. We must use our position to begin teaching our case. Tell the full factual story in the opening statement. Teach. Do not promise that you will teach soon. Teach now.

§ 7.11 Focus the Opening Statement on Our Best Material

If the goals of focusing on the theory and selectively enhancing or attacking credibility sound the same as the goals set forth for cross-examination, that is because they are the same. Opening statements are given for the same reasons that cross-examinations are conducted. Both are a means of communicating the facts to the jury. Both are an opportunity to teach. Both are times when the cross-examiner is talking the vast majority of the time. Their differences, however, hold the key to the successful opening statement.

Teaching through use of the opening statement offers several distinct advantages over teaching through the other trial phases. Trial lawyers understand that the testimony of witnesses on both direct and cross-examination is fraught with hazards. Witnesses do not always explain the facts succinctly. Witnesses may offer facts that do not make sense until linked with other facts introduced by later witnesses. Witnesses fight. Opponents interrupt with objections. The opening statement has none of these disadvantages. The advocate controls the sequence and rhythm of the opening statement. It is not dictated by the order of witnesses. The opening statement brings together pieces of evidence from many sources and groups them into understandable chapters. The bulk of the case can be set forth in pertinent detail in a fraction of the time necessary to adduce the live testimony. Opening statements have the added benefit of being uninterrupted by the unresponsive or tangential statements of witnesses. In fact, the supreme benefit of a proper opening statement is that it is a concise and persuasive recitation of the key evidence, choreographed by the advocate in a manner designed to teach the case.

To achieve this potential, the facts that need to be communicated in the opening statement must be distilled from the far larger number of available facts. Given enough time, a trial lawyer could literally tell the jury all the testimony that the jury was about to hear. While it might explain the case, it would not efficiently teach the case and it definitely would not explain the case persuasively. The best techniques of opening statements, like those of cross-examinations, have little to do with quantity and a great deal to do with focus. Just as in cross-examinations and, to a lesser extent, direct examinations, the advocate in opening statements should utilize time in accordance with the importance of the facts addressed. Remember: In the courtroom, importance is measured by the time spent on the subject matter, not the volume or oratorical flair of the lawyer. When the lawyer speaks calmly, factually, and forcefully in the advancement of a recognizable theory of the case, the jury is alerted as to the key issues.

The effective opening statement must compress the case. In a case that will take a day, the judge might allow an opening statement of 15 minutes. A matter that may be on trial for two or three weeks might need to be covered in an opening statement of 45 minutes. Whatever the amount of time available, it is never enough to cover the entire case, nor should we use our time to summarize the entire case. We have limited time and we have limited needs. We must concentrate our efforts on only the scenarios of greatest importance to our theory of the case.

It is easy to find the facts of greatest importance to our opening statement. To the extent that certain chapters of cross-examination are critical to the theory of the case, they are critical chapters in the opening statement. The chapters of an opening statement must help the fact finder focus on how the lawyer is going to win. From the fact finder's point of view, the opening statement assists in deciding the case. At a minimum, the opening statement provides the fact finder with a system or context in which to view the facts. The fact finder does not absorb all the facts, but absorbs the key pictures that come together in a cohesive theory of what really happened and how that equals a verdict. Therefore, the first measure of the quality of an opening statement is the degree to which it results in an individual fact finder's understanding of the advocate's theory of the case.

The value of an opening statement is measured by the degree to which it causes an individual fact finder to prejudge or, in the case of a more cautious juror, to favorably consider the merits of the lawsuit from the advocate's point of view. When successful, the opening statement will cause even the fair-minded fact finder to silently say, "If you can prove the facts you have told me about, I am prepared to decide the case your way." This state of mind is referred to as "conditional commitment." The fact finder is not making an unconditional guarantee, as the salient facts must be produced as promised in the opening statement. It is seldom possible to bring all the jurors to a state of conditional commitment, but that is certainly the goal. The goal often heard in opening statement, "Keep an open mind," is not the goal desired by the lawyer. The opponent who uses that phrase is simply fearful that the other side's opening statement will overpower his case. He betrays his fear by asking the jury to remain neutral. But people do not remain neutral in the face of the facts promised in opening statement. They cannot help but begin to pre-judge the case, based on the assumption that these promised facts will be produced.

§ 7.12 Using the Chapter Method to Craft an Opening Statement

The lawyer who has organized her cross-examinations (and any necessary direct examinations) using the chapter method (see chapter 5, *The Chapter Method of Cross-Examination*) is instantly prepared to give a powerful, theory-driven opening statement. By preparing to examine witnesses by chapters, the lawyer has automatically outlined the opening statement. All that remains to create our opening statement is to put the chapters into the order that makes the most sense for a fact finder at the opening statement phase of the case.

In a civil case in which the insurance defense lawyer concedes liability but the defense's theory is that damages are minimal, five cross-examination chapters dealing with lack of objective evidence to support damages might be headed as follows:

(1) X-rays — Negative

(2) MRI — Negative

(3) Straight Leg Raise Test — Negative

(4) Patient Climbing on Table — Without Substantial Difficulty

(5) Patient Walking Down Hallway Away from Doctor — Gait Appears Normal

The lawyer uses these chapters as an outline to talk to the jury in a fact-intensive manner. It is unnecessary for the lawyer to draft an outline in great detail or write out her opening statement in its entirety. She can remember the details of the facts and verbally embellish the simple outline presented above, because she has already written the individual chapters for cross-examination to be used on the plaintiff's doctor and on the plaintiff. An example of this portion of the opening statement could look like this:

> The plaintiff, Becky Tam, complained of back pain and so her doctor, being a careful and compassionate man, ordered X-rays of her back.

Those X-rays were negative. They revealed no broken bones. They revealed no injuries. The doctor found absolutely nothing objectively wrong. Plaintiff, Becky Tam, continued to complain about pain in her back and so her doctor, being a careful and compassionate man, ordered an expensive MRI test. It too was negative. It did not reveal any broken bones. It did not reveal any injuries. The doctor found absolutely nothing objectively wrong.

Of course, the doctor had already performed what doctors refer to as a "straight leg raise test," which is a test designed to determine whether or not there are abnormalities or problems or injuries to someone's back. Becky Tam's straight leg raise test was negative, indicating no injuries. Again, the doctor found absolutely nothing objectively wrong.

Doctors observe their patients in more ways than just performing tests on them. That is, they watch their patients get on and off the table in the examination room. Ms. Tam's compassionate and careful doctor noted that she could get on and off the table without substantial difficulty. In other words, she could climb up and climb down without showing any back pain. He found absolutely nothing objectively wrong. The doctor also observed her walking away from the examination room, walking down the hallway, and the doctor noted and thought enough of it to note it in his records, that Becky Tam's gait (that is, the way that she walked) appeared to be normal, as if she had no back problems. He found no injuries. He found absolutely nothing objectively wrong.

§ 7.13 The Relationship of Opening Statement to Direct Examination

Opening statements incorporate those portions of our anticipated direct examinations that are critical to the theory of the case. Remember, however, that a fact finder is much more likely to believe an admission of an opposing witness than the identical testimony obtained from the trial lawyer's own witnesses. When our witness helps our case the testimony may be viewed as self-serving and predictable. Although opening statements must often present facts that the advocate's own witnesses will substantiate, the opening should place emphasis on the cross-examination and the admissions by the other side's witnesses. In other words, focus on admissions of opponents, in preference to testimony that the lawyer's own witnesses will reiterate.

If a key point is proven by the lawyer's own witnesses and is admitted by the opposing witness, the lawyer should use both forms of evidence in opening statement — stressing the solid admission and backing it up with direct examination testimony.

Example 1:

Ladies and gentlemen, Homer, the defendant, will testify that he was not at any of the locations at which the United States Government will tell you that the conspiracy occurred. More importantly, and even

> more significantly to you, each of the Government's witnesses, all of whom were at those locations where the Government tells you that the conspiracy occurred, will say that they never saw the defendant present, never heard of the defendant being present, and that they have no evidence to give you that the defendant was present at any one of those locations.

Note: Accent was put on the defendant's testimony, but below the admissions by the Government witnesses are stressed. The burden is lifted from the defendant, Homer. This fact now appears as an admission.

Example 2:

> Ladies and gentlemen, two of the Government's witnesses will admit on cross-examination that the defendant was never at any of the locations where the Government alleges that the conspiracy took place. Of course, Homer, the defendant, is also going to say this. He was not at any of the locations where the conspiracy took place.

§ 7.14 Emotion in Opening Statement

The use of emotion in opening statements — in fact in trial in general — is overrated. There are as many downsides to an emotional pitch as there are upsides. And both upsides and downsides are hard to predict. A discussion of the facts is a far more dependable form of opening statement. We seek a conditional pre-judgment by jurors — not a vote of sympathy but a vote of confidence. We will settle for understanding. Emotions are transitory. Perhaps we can generate them now, perhaps never again in the trial. But understanding of the facts is more likely to remain constant or grow as we put on the case. While it would be nice if the lawyer could cause the fact finder to feel a particular way about the case, a fact finder's emotional reaction to the evidence is difficult to predict. It is difficult to maintain a particular emotion up to the time that the jury actually votes — be it hours, days, or weeks later. A successful case cannot be premised purely, or even largely, on an emotional pitch. Certainly, the opening statement should spark a reaction, but that reaction should be driven by logic. Stated differently, the facts recited in a particular area may compel a juror to feel angry, but it is the grouping of the facts that drives the emotion, not the urging of counsel or the emotion of counsel. A tightly crafted, fact-intensive opening statement may generate a predictable and desirable range of emotions within the fact finders. But even if it doesn't, the fact-intensive opening statement should generate a belief about the key issues in the case. The goal is to create a predisposition as a result of the facts recited. Any emotional reaction to the facts recited is simply a byproduct.

By way of example, envision a prosecutor's opening statement in a simple drunk driving case in which there was no accident. Let us now add that the driver was coming home from his college graduation party. The prosecutor should compile the facts so as to leave no doubt that the defendant was driving and had been drinking, and that consumption of alcohol had affected his ability to drive. Once this picture has been painted, the jurors should all come away convinced of these critical facts. Depending on strategy and presentation, which includes phrasing, timing, and word choice, the fact finders may experience emotional reactions that could range from understanding, even sympathy, to anger. If each fact finder could be conditionally committed to voting guilty, regardless of their individual positions on the emotional spectrum, the opening statement has succeeded.

However, if the prosecutor sets out with the goal of persuading each juror to feel anger at the defendant for his conduct, she has assumed an unnecessary burden and risk — that some jurors will not respond with the desired emotion and will therefore come away from the opening statement lacking the conditional commitment to a guilty verdict. By making a particular emotion a goal of the opening statement, the advocate has made that "emotion" a fact in dispute. Jurors who do not feel that target emotion are not likely to be persuaded by the theory that stands behind it. Further, the advocate has confused the issues by elevating an emotion to a degree of proof. Those jurors who come up short on that emotion will feel themselves out of synch with that fact.

In all cross-examinations, the advocate compiles facts in an attempt to compel desired conclusions. The lawyer uses facts combined with the judicious use of voice and timing to generate the appropriate emotion. The same works well in opening statements. In fact, the lawyer can be more effective in opening statements because she is able to spell out facts from different witnesses' testimony and weave those facts into an overall picture. In cross-examination, trust is placed in the grouping of facts, not the oratory or emotional delivery. Opening statements must share this trust. Emphasize facts not emotion.

§ 7.15 Opening Statement in Non-Jury Trials — Same Rules Apply But More So

The informality of bench trials, motions hearings, preliminary hearings, temporary injunctions or orders, or alternative dispute resolutions often deludes the lawyer into believing that no opening statement is necessary. Sometimes the judge or mediator or arbitrator will signal to the lawyers that opening statements will not be helpful, suggesting that they can pick the case up "on the fly." It is unlikely, however, that judges will fully understand the gist of the case solely from the pleadings. It often seems that the legal issue is straightforward, e.g., whether there was a contract, a fraud, or negligent conduct. However, the facts always come together in strange and unique ways. The judge may have heard a hundred preliminary injunction hearings based on breach of employment contract, but she hasn't heard the facts in counsel's case. A brief recitation of the key facts coupled with a clear communication of your theory of the case will aid, not bore, the court. The persuasive facts needed in order to prevail, are not fully understood without a proper context. The opening statement provides that context.

No case is immediately understandable without an appropriate opening statement. Every case needs "explaining." No presentation of evidence ever flows in purely chronological order. Certain witnesses tell their entire story in one sitting, but much of what they say has importance only if understood in context. Without an appropriate theory-driven, fact-intensive opening statement, the fact finder is left to either guess at the context or remember all the facts for subsequent mental insertion into a context later to be learned. When? In closing, or worse, after the court has taken it under advisement for days or weeks?

Judges and arbitrators want to assure that they can follow the case without the benefit of our opening statements. Even if the advocate gives the fact finder the benefit of the doubt, she needs to remember that teaching the fact finder how to follow the facts in context is only one of the goals of opening statements. Persuading the fact finder is the ultimate goal. By skipping the opening statement, the advocate makes absolutely no progress toward teaching and eventually winning the case. By voluntarily giving up the right to opening statement, the advocate gives up an opportunity to focus the fact finder's attention in the appropriate areas and affect the credibility of witnesses before they testify. Ask permission to give your opening statement. Our obligation is to teach the case. The fact finder should honor our need and their need for a factual opening statement that makes clear our theory of the case.

If the other side wishes to defer to the intelligence and professionalism of the judge by waiving the opening statement, so be it. Equal respect for intelligence and position can be shown by giving a concise, fact-intensive opening presentation that educates the fact finder and begins the task of persuasion. Does the giving of an opening statement to a judge show disrespect? No. The lawyer shows disrespect to the fact finder by being unprepared to try her case. The well-crafted opening statement acknowledges the all-important role of fact finders — whether they are jury, judge, mediator or arbitrator. It is designed to assist them in their task. The rule is simple: It's show time. Get up and start winning your case. Give a strong, fact-intensive opening statement every time.

§ 7.16 Reveal Important Inconsistencies in Opponent's Stories

When an important part of the lawyer's strategy is the exploitation of inconsistencies in the opponent's case, there are sound tactical reasons to reveal those inconsistencies in the opening statement. A preemptive strike at opening statement is important, as a trial lawyer should expect even a moderately skillful opponent to have anticipated the inconsistencies. There is not much the opponent can do, however, about inconsistencies already contained within a witness's pre-trial statements.

The lawyer prepared with cross-examination chapters built around important inconsistencies, should reveal the inconsistencies in opening statement in order to fully exploit their persuasive potential. Lawyers ordinarily explore inconsistencies as a method of attacking the credibility of the witness. Telling the fact finder about the important inconsistencies will serve to weaken the credibility of that witness before the witness even takes the stand. If the lawyer hides the inconsistencies out of fear that revelation in opening statement will allow the opponent to remedy the problems, she will have bypassed the opportunity to weaken the opponent's case.

A lawyer might hesitate to air these inconsistencies in her opening statement because she fears the opposing lawyer will alert the witness to an inconsistency and thereby encourage the witness to change his story. If the opponent rises to the bait, the inconsistency is not lost but multiplied. A documented contradiction does not disappear when a witness changes his story a second, third, or fourth time. All the witness has done is add an additional inconsistency, and so a changed story favors the impeaching party, not the party being impeached. Furthermore, by changing his story during trial, the witness opens a new line of impeachment on the fact that he is changing his story (again) during trial. This will seldom prove reassuring to the jurors.

The trial lawyer should expose the inconsistency during the opening statement. In such a situation, the opponent is forced to deal with our theory, and this distracts the opponent from advancing his own theory. Every time an opponent spends part of his opening statement explaining why the inconsistencies exist, he is using precious time and energy talking about the trial lawyer's theory of the case. He is arguing with the jury that they should not be persuaded by her case but, in so doing, he is not advancing his own case. Armed with demonstrably inconsistent statements that will be used in cross-examination, the lawyer must exploit them in detail in the opening statement.

Example:

Within minutes of the robbery, Mrs. Edlestein told the police that the defendant had light brown hair "that was kind of long." Within two hours of that statement, the police brought Tommy James back to Mrs. Edlestein's store. Mrs. Edlestein will tell you that he was "bald as a cue ball," but that he was the robber. She will tell you that she has seen cue balls. She will tell you that she knows that they are smooth, glossy, with absolutely no hair on them and certainly not light brown hair "that was kind of long."

Further, as a result of having heard in opening statement that the witness has changed her story on one or more facts, the fact finder will likely be more cautious in accepting other uncontradicted parts of the witness's testimony. The witness then takes the stand as "damaged goods," having been tainted by these contradictions and inconsistent statements that damage credibility. Additionally, by revealing in opening statement prepared cross-examination chapters on motive, prejudice, and bias, the lawyer has pre-conditioned the jury to be skeptical of the opponent's direct examination, long before the cross-examiner has had her turn to cross-examine on these issues.

§ 7.17 Never Waive Opening Statement

Never waive your opportunity to give an opening statement. The opening statement is an unparalleled opportunity to influence the fact finders, so why would an attorney give it up? The argument in favor of waiving opening statement is usually predicated upon the assertion that the lawyer's case is too weak to be discussed. If that is true, then it is all the more reason to give as strong an opening as possible in order to try to win the case. If the lawyer has already decided that she is likely to lose, it is time to take more risks. Most jurors equate waiver with silence, and silence with weakness or — even worse — concession. When an advocate is offered the opportunity to tell her side of the story and she passes, the clear implication is that the lawyer has no story to tell and no strong disagreement with the opponent. A situation may hypothetically exist where waiving opening statement makes sense, but we have not yet found that situation.

§ 7.18 Open Immediately; Do Not Reserve Your Opening Statement

In accordance with the doctrine of primacy, whether plaintiff or defense, whether the trial is criminal or civil, whether it is being tried to a judge or a jury, the lawyer must give her opening statement at the first possible opportunity. "Flexibility" is not gained by reserving the opening statement. A delayed opening statement abandons the field of persuasion to the opponent. She can then present her entire case without any of the persuasive impediments caused by the opponent's opening statement. This one-sided persuasive void leaves the jury with a clear understanding of the opponent's case, and no understanding of the advocate's.

Forget any advice about keeping options open by reserving opening statement. This is not a strategy; it is a dodge. A trial advocate's options are always limited. That is why trial lawyers study the facts that cannot change in order to develop the best potential theory of the case (see chapter 2, *Developing a Theory of the Case*). If the phrase "keeping my options open" means leaving the lawyer in a position to later advance one of several "possible" theories or for "playing for the fumble," she is setting herself up to perform a series of unfocused or contradictory cross-examinations. Under this scenario, counsel won't have any credibility left by the time she gives her reserved opening statement.

§ 7.19 Factual Openings Gain More Than They Give Away

Alternatively, lawyers sometimes rationalize that it would be better to waive or reserve their openings in order to keep their strong case or theory secret. Of all the purported reasons to reserve or waive opening, this is the most seductive. The justification sounds good because it is based on a claim of superior strength, but it is wrong.

The overriding problem with the tactic of hiding from the opponent the advocate's best facts woven around her theory of the case is that she will be hiding her case from the fact finder as well. The net result is that the fact finder hears only one side of the facts, and understands only one theory of the case — and it isn't ours. The price of concealment comes too high, even if the advocate manages to create some confusion or uncertainty on the part of the opponent.

In any event, there is great reason to doubt the primary premise of this tactic — that an advocate can successfully hide her theory from an opponent. There are, after all, only limited theories of the case available to an advocate, and in most cases the major strong and weak points of the case are already known to both sides. If an opposing lawyer is so poorly prepared that he has not focused on the advocate's theory, he is ill-equipped to combat that theory.

By allowing the opponent unchallenged access to the jurors' minds in opening statement, the lawyer has unnecessarily promoted the opponent's credibility. The first and only objective of trial must be to educate the jurors, not to embarrass or confuse the opponent. The advocate can best accomplish that task by giving her opening statement and detailing for the jury the factual reasons to vote her way. If her theory of the case is strong, a fact-intensive, chapter-organized opening statement makes it stronger.

§ 7.20 Plaintiffs and Prosecutors Must Always Give an Opening Statement

It is impossible to conceive of a situation in which the party bringing the case would pass up the opportunity to brag about the case. Either a plaintiff or a prosecutor got this trial started and bears the burden of persuasion. The plaintiff/prosecutor surely must have a theory of the case and is about to call witnesses in support of that theory. Plaintiff's/prosecutor's counsel has no excuses and no options. She must open. If she doesn't, defense counsel will present his opening argument unchallenged, and then dominate the battlefield.

§ 7.21 The Defense Must Open Now, Not Later

It is the defense lawyer, civil or criminal, who theoretically has the option of reserving his opening statement until the beginning of his own case. The problem with this option is that the beginning of the defense case is thought to come only after the end of the opponent's case. To forfeit to the opponent the quest for persuasion is never a wise tactic. The plaintiff/prosecutor has given her opening statement, told the jury members where to focus their concentration, and educated the jurors on the decisive issues of the lawsuit, at least from the opponent's point of view. The plaintiff's/prosecutor's opening will boost both the jurors' understanding of her case and the credibility of her witnesses while undermining the credibility of the defense case. After the persuasive advantages of her opening, she can move forward to put up the evidence that will verify all the things the jury was already conditionally committed to from hearing her opening statement. There is only one sensible technique that responds to the opponent's opening. The defense must reciprocate by giving a fact-intensive, theory-driven, chapter-organized opening statement. The defense case begins with the opening statement — not with the first witness.

Perhaps counsel is thinking of reserving her opening with the hope of later developing a theory of the case. Set aside the question of how the lawyer picked a jury without having a theory of the case. Set aside the fact that the lawyer must cross-examine with no theory in mind. A lawyer in trial (and particularly cross-examining) without a theory of the case is not in a position to win the trial. That lawyer has nothing to teach the fact finder. Such a lawyer is not an effective advocate. She is reduced to the role of hacking at the opponent's evidence, hoping that one of her blind thrusts will hit a vital organ and gravely damage the opposition.

Both judge and jury recognize the lawyer's lack of direction. Instead of emerging from opening statement with a clear picture of where the lawyer wants to take the case, they emerge with confusion caused by the lawyer's random and inconsistent attacks on the facts. The jury is likely to miss any rare shots that do hit the mark. With the theory of the case hidden, the jurors cannot understand the factual target of the cross-examinations. A lawyer who lacks a theory of the case lacks sufficiently grouped evidentiary goals, and is left to conduct poorly focused direct examinations as well.

Some lawyers will tell of the time they reserved their opening statement and something wonderful and wholly unexpected developed during the opponent's case. They then took advantage of this development in their reserved opening statement. These lawyers, having once lucked out, are doomed to bet against the odds for the rest of their careers. We hope such lawyers become our opponents.

§ 7.22 Use of Demonstrative Exhibits in Opening Statement

If the cross-examiner intends to use demonstrative exhibits within the cross-examinations, strong consideration should be given to the use of those exhibits in the opening statement. If there is doubt that the judge will permit it, ask in advance. Judges will ordinarily permit demonstrative aids that help the jury understand, as long as the aid is not argumentative and fairly represents testimony that will be admissible. Demonstrative exhibits differ from trial exhibits in that they are not intended to be admitted into evidence, but their display and use is sanctioned as a method of compiling, distilling, or arraying other admissible facts.

Strong demonstrative exhibits do what the name implies: They demonstrate an important concept by pulling together facts that may come from many witnesses or documents. Often, demonstrative exhibits intended for the cross-examination may be used with great effect in the opening statement. For instance, if the cross-examiner wishes to demonstrate the division of ownership interests in a closely held company at various times, a pie chart might prove quite useful with a witness. If the cross-examiner wishes to demonstrate how badly a stock was performing, or the continual decline in income of a particular witness, a bar or line graph would be appropriate. In these instances, the demonstrative aid would also be used with the witness. Instead of the lawyer merely talking the jury through a particular point, the issue is graphically presented by a demonstrative exhibit accompanied by a discussion of the evidence that will be introduced to validate that exhibit.

There are other occasions when the demonstrative aid will not be used in cross-examination but can effectively and ethically be used in an opening statement. In opening statement, the cross-examiner will often highlight the important parts of the testimony of many witnesses. In order to assist the jury in keeping track of these important points, the cross-examiner might fashion a demonstrative aid showing the name of a witness to be cross-examined, their position in the business entity suing or being sued, followed by bullet points of the key admissions expected to be gained on cross-examination. This outline of the testimony of the witnesses will not be used during the cross-examinations but can prove very effective in alerting the jurors to the highlights of the coming cross-examinations.

Care must be taken to fashion such a demonstrative aid in a manner that is not argumentative. The title of an employee/witness should be accurately shown. The witness should not be referred to as "the outcry witness" or "the whistleblower" or any other such subjective description. To do so is to invite objection to the use of the demonstrative aid in opening statement as unduly argumentative. The aid serves only to better equip the lawyer to present and teach the facts.

The cross-examiner may often want to demonstrate that people close to a particular party will offer testimony that disagrees with that party (see Chart 1, below). In such an instance, the cross-examiner may fashion a demonstrative aid that places within a circle the name of the key witness or opposing party. The cross-examiner could then surround that name with the names of witnesses who would seem to be aligned with that party, but who will give up important testimony on cross-examination that contradicts or undermines the key witness/opposing party. Such a demonstrative aid might be entitled "the people closest to (name of key witness)." Alternatively, the board could be titled "(name of witness) closest business advisers." There are many ways to build such a demonstrative aid. It is critical that the title is fair; will one or more witnesses agree that these were the people closest to the party or that they were her closest business advisers? If not, the demonstrative aid must be retitled.

In each case the cross-examiner would place around the name of the key witness the names of close associates who are expected to offer damaging testimony against their friend or business associate within the cross-examination. In opening statement, the cross-examiner graphically demonstrates how the closest associates of a particular person will fail to fully support their friend's/associate's assertions. This demonstrative aid alerts the fact finder that the opponent's case is undermined even by people aligned with the opponent.

At the same time this demonstrative aid serves as a springboard for the cross-examiner's discussion of the particular damaging evidence that the advocate intends to bring forward during the cross-examination of these witnesses. This is another instance in which a demonstrative aid may be used in opening statement, but likely will not be used in cross-examination. Instead, the aid helps summarize an aspect of the cross-examinations.

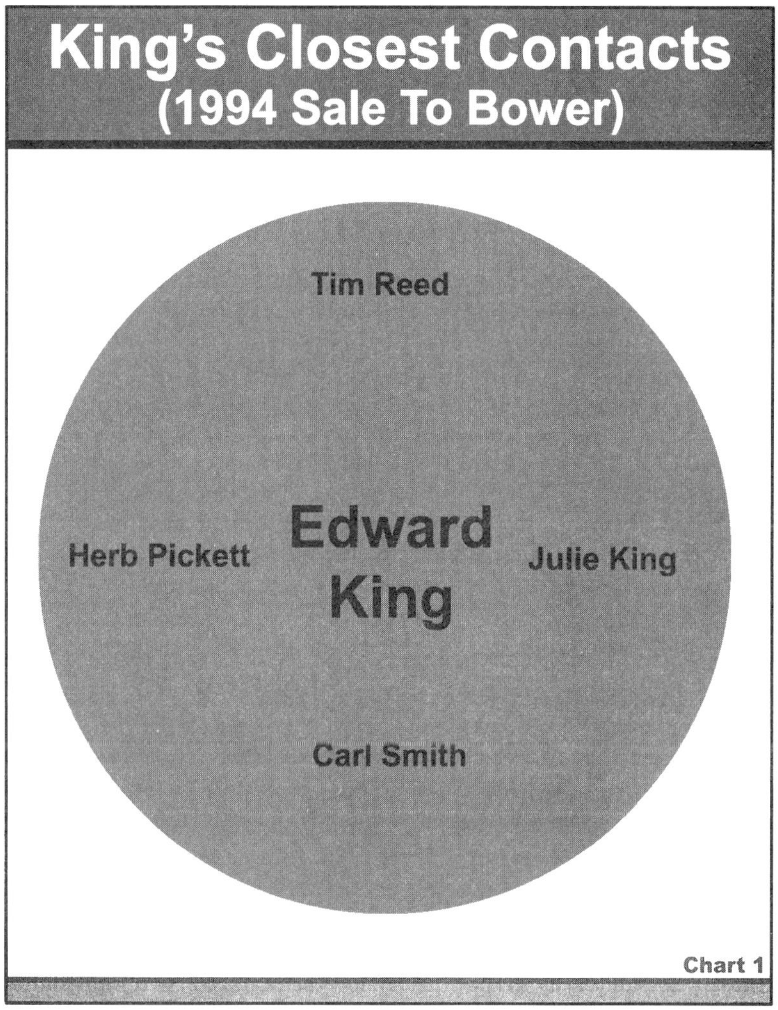

§ 7.23 Use of Timelines in Opening Statement

Timelines are one of the best and most frequently employed examples of a demonstrative exhibit. A timeline is often employed to orient the witness and the fact finder to where a fact fits into the sequence of important facts. The timeline may often be up during much of the trial, but it is not itself an admissible document. The entire timeline can be profitably previewed for the fact finder within the opening statement. In fact, it is at this point in the case that the timeline may be most useful, as it efficiently conveys to the fact finder how the facts will come together to support the cross-examiner's theory of the case. The facts that fill the timeline may come into evidence through multiple witnesses spread over several days or weeks of testimony. Any one witness may provide only a few of the facts and dates, including facts that do not flow chronologically. In other words, the witness may add important facts at greatly separated times on the timeline. If a fact finder can only see the development of the timeline as its facts are introduced in the cross (and direct) examinations, the timeline loses much of its utility. The timeline, used in this manner, rather resembles the television quiz show "Wheel of Fortune." The fact finder is asked to continually guess what the finished timeline will say. The cross-examiner is far better off displaying the finished timeline in opening statement and explaining its meaning to the case at that point. Of course, it remains the duty of the cross-examiner to fill in the timeline through testimony and other admissible documents.

The opening statement explains the evidence and the witness examinations are designed to verify counsel's opening statement. Similarly, the timeline is counsel's submission of the most important facts accompanied by the date or sequence of those facts. Before developing the timeline, the cross-examiner has created the chapters that will introduce those facts and dates. The cross-examiner who has prepared evidentiary sourced chapters of cross-examination (see chapter 6, *Page Preparation of Cross-Examination*) is well prepared to build a demonstrative timeline. The sourced chapters of cross-examination then become instrumental in securing the permission of the court to use a timeline as a demonstrative aid in the opening statement.

The opponent can be expected to try to block the cross-examiner's use of the timeline. The most frequent objection to the use of a timeline in opening statement is that it is an inaccurate statement of the facts, or based on speculation as to what the testimony will show. Judges are attentive to these objections. There is limited utility to the timeline proponent's bald statement that these facts and dates are accurate. A better way to ensure the ability to use the timeline in opening statement is to show the evidentiary source for each item displayed. If the cross-examiner intends to prove that the opposing party took an action on a particular date, then the timeline should show the event, the date, and the exhibit number of the document that will establish those facts. When the cross-examiner intends to prove an event through testimony, the timeline should show the fact or event, the date, and the name of the witness who will testify to that fact. Below (see Chart 2) is a representation of a sourced evidentiary timeline drawn from a medical malpractice case:

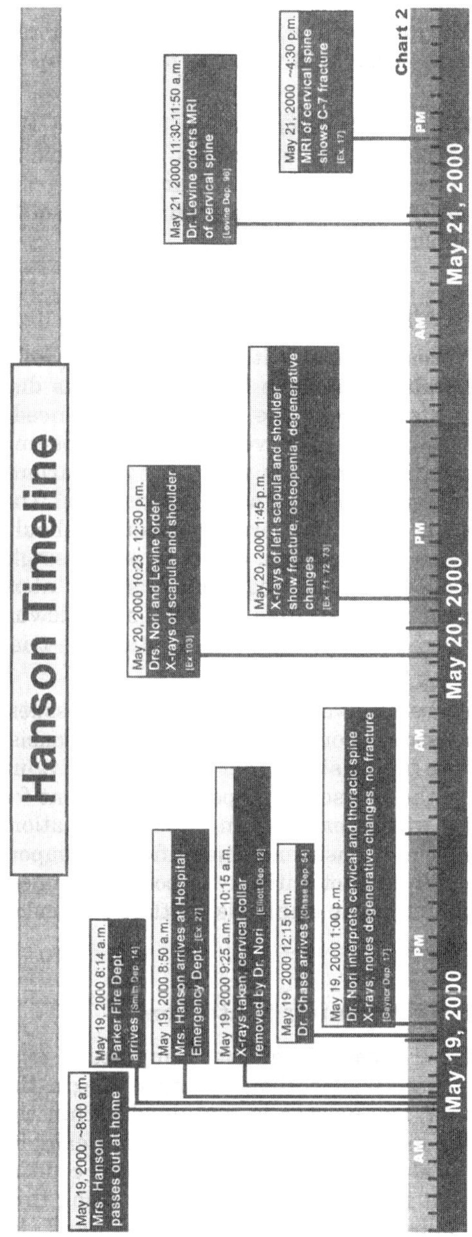

The fact-sourced timeline dramatically alters the likely ruling of the court and the credibility of the demonstrative aid. When a judge is called upon to rule on the opponent's objections that the facts described are incorrect or unsupported by the evidence, the sourced timeline immediately shows the judge that each of the items will be supported by an exhibit or a witness. An additional benefit — one that should not be underrated — is the effect on the credibility of the proponent. The timeline tells the jury and the judge that counsel is well prepared to establish her theory of the case and that the facts line up to support that theory.

Some lawyers find that the exhibit numbers or witness names on the timeline may complicate the picture. In such cases it is advisable to prepare for the judge an 8½-by-11-inch version of the timeline showing exhibit numbers and witness names. A full set of the original or a small version (8½ by 11") should be available for the judge.

§ 7.24 Use of Trial Exhibits in Opening Statement

Counsel should strongly consider the use of her most important trial exhibits in the opening statement. Where should counsel begin the process of selecting the best exhibits? The answer is contained within the chapters of cross-examination. If one or more trial exhibits will be the focus of attention in a critical cross-examination, counsel should consider displaying that exhibit in the opening statement. By doing this, counsel permits the fact finder an opportunity to learn to understand the exhibit and understand the cross-examination that will frame that exhibit. But why not wait until cross-examination to use the witness to explain the exhibit? Answer: Because the trial lawyer is better at explaining the exhibit.

By previewing the exhibit with the fact finder, the trial lawyer highlights its importance. By introducing the exhibit, counsel may shorten the number of cross-examination questions required to explain the exhibit to the fact finder. Furthermore, the use of the exhibit in the trial lawyer's opening statement may well affect the opponent's direct examination of their witness. The jury has seen the exhibit before the direct examination. The jury understands that lawyer's theory concerning the exhibit. If the opponent chooses not to discuss the exhibit, the jury will frequently view that omission as a sign of weakness or fear. If, on the other hand, the opponent decides he must try to soften the force of the exhibit by discussing it with his witness, he gives more weight to the exhibit. More time spent in court on any matter means more significance is attached to it. Time is the measure of importance.

In addition, there is always the chance that the witness will fumble in his response, thereby making the situation worse. Timid trial lawyers would say that the use of an exhibit in opening statement will unnecessarily alert the opponent to the advocate's "take" on that exhibit and signal to the opponent her intention to use the exhibit in cross-examination. Our response would be the same reaction to any notion that the best evidence should ever be hidden. The good opponent has figured out by trial what are the important exhibits and how they will be used. If the document is good, its value should not be diminished because an opposing witness sees it coming. If it is hidden from the opponent, it is hidden from the fact finder. An exhibit hidden from the fact finder cannot possibly help teach and persuade the fact finder.

There is an evidentiary bridge to be crossed before the trial lawyer uses an exhibit in her opening statement. The exhibit must undoubtedly be admissible. The best way to ensure its admissibility is through pre-trial stipulations or rulings on the admissibility of certain exhibits. One of the unwritten rules of trial work is that what is sauce for the goose is sauce for the gander. If the lawyer wishes to use selected exhibits in her opening statement and seeks the cooperation of her opponent, she must be willing to extend the same degree of cooperation concerning clearly admissible exhibits the opponent might wish to use. This does not mean that she should refrain from objecting to objectionable exhibits. It does mean that the two sides should work together to create a list of exhibits that are going to come in during the trial. An important side benefit of this approach is that it may make unnecessary many foundation questions for exhibits to which there is a stipulation.

We must not attempt to use an exhibit in opening statement that may not be admissible. We cannot afford to run the risk, even if it is a good-faith risk. Do not allow opponents to use within opening statements any exhibits whose admissibility remains in question. Always review all exhibits an opponent intends to use in their opening statement. Raise your objections before the jury is brought into the courtroom.

Judges have two forms of rulings or exhibits in opening statements. Some judges rule that no attorney may use any exhibit that is not stipulated to. Other judges take a more sporting approach by ruling that counsel may use any exhibits they believe admissible, but that counsel runs the risk that — if the exhibit is not admitted — the court will later instruct the jury that the exhibit was improperly used and should not be considered. No one wants to be on the receiving end of such an instruction. In other words, play it by the book.

§ 7.25 Time Savings Resulting from Chapter-Based Opening Statements

No lawyer has enough time. Whether the lawyer is a public defender who just has moments and perhaps days to prepare for a trial or an advocate with months and years to focus on a few cases, time disappears and deadlines creep up.

Happily, the three key elements to preparing an opening statement are the same key elements to preparing our chapters of cross-examination. Our cross-examinations are also theory directed, fact intensive, and prepared in the chapter method. This is not to say that direct examination should be ignored; obviously, it should not. However, at least theoretically, direct examinations are cooperative efforts between the witness and lawyer. If the advocate relies on her ability to successfully cross-examine the opponent's witness to win her case and teach the fact finder, then that degree of preparation advances the advocate's ability to give an effective, organized, and persuasive opening statement and closing argument.

The advocate who intensely prepares for cross-examination chapters has prepared much, if not all, of her opening statement, since:

- The chapter headings of important cross-examinations serve as the outline for the opening statement.

- The detailed individual facts that have been developed to cross-examine the opponent's witnesses serve as the text of the chapters of the opening statement.
- The oratorical devices including loops (see chapter 10, *Loops, Double Loops, and Spontaneous Loops*) that will be used in the cross-examinations also will be used and introduced in the opening statement.
- The theory of the case will run throughout the trial consistently.

Chapter 8

SEVEN STEPS OF IMPEACHMENT BY INCONSISTENT STATEMENT

§ 8.01 Impeachment

Cross-examination both teaches the case and shapes the juror's perceptions of the credibility of the witness. The techniques of impeachment allow us to accomplish both of these objectives. There are many forms of impeachment, including demonstrating bias, interest, or prejudice, exposing inconsistencies including, most importantly, impeachment by inconsistent statement. There are many other forms of impeachment including inconsistency with another witness, inconsistency with the physical evidence, inconsistency with common sense, and the revelation of omissions.

Whether the lawyer seeks to show that the witness is honestly mistaken or willfully deceitful, impeachment by inconsistent statement is a superb vehicle. Of all of the forms of impeachment, impeachment by inconsistent statement is the most frequently utilized technique. The techniques of impeachment by inconsistent statement are straightforward and based on common sense. As a result, they are easily understood and used.

§ 8.02 We Ordinarily Impeach to Show the Prior Version Is More Credible

An impeachment by inconsistent statement is only performed when the new version is less helpful than the earlier version. If the story has changed in such a fashion that the new version favors us, we are better off leaving it alone. After all, if an opposing witness wants to change his story in a manner that assists our theory of the case, why would we contradict him? We impeach when we do not like the new version.

The primary use of cross-examination is to tell our story. Similarly, the primary purpose of an impeachment by inconsistent statement is to show a part of the story that the witness has left out. He is now telling a new version. If the jury is ever to hear about the earlier version, it will likely only happen through our impeachment. We impeach not simply to show that the witness has changed his version of a fact but, more importantly, to show that the earlier version is more likely the accurate version.

When we impeach, it is not enough — not nearly — to stop at the point we have shown a change of the story. We must also show that the earlier version is more likely the correct version. We need to bring out the facts that allow the jury to credit the earlier version. In essence, we need to help make the witness a better, more credible witness in his first version. These techniques will be discussed within this chapter, as a part of the process of impeachment by inconsistent statement.

§ 8.03 Identifying the Seven Steps to Impeachment by Inconsistent Statement

There are seven distinct steps in the process of impeachment by inconsistent statement. Each step has its purpose. Some are legally required as part of a foundation and some are done as a matter of technique. By presenting all legally required steps thoroughly and adding other techniques, the cross-examiner maximizes the effect of the impeachment.

1. Uncover the inconsistency;
2. Physically prepare the cross-examination on inconsistency;
3. Establish the current version of the testimony to be impeached;
4. Tie the witness to the current version of the fact to be impeached;
5. Equate or translate the versions;
6. Expose the inconsistent statement;
7. Listen for useful volunteered information at trial.

If completed each time, in order, these seven steps result in predictably successful impeachments. There are occasions when some of the seven steps may be performed in an abbreviated fashion. Nonetheless, these seven steps are the required structure for effective impeachment. The cross-examiner can add impact to her impeachment by carefully selecting words and developing precise chapters designed to maximize the effect of any impeachment. But without the seven steps, no matter how powerfully worded, the impeachment generally will not rise to its full potential and may even appear as a minor diversion, thereby undermining the credibility of the cross-examiner.

§ 8.04 Step 1 — Uncover or Find the Inconsistency

Techniques for discovering and documenting inconsistent statements are discussed in chapter 3. Through the application of these systematic techniques, all witness statements made prior to trial have been broken down, collated by topic, and digested. As a result of the application of the systems, the cross-examiner has uncovered each inconsistency in the witness's previous discussions of the facts. Identifying each inconsistency is different than identifying the big or important inconsistency. "Each" means every inconsistency, whether important or not. The cross-examiner may not recognize that an inconsistency is "important" or "big" at the time of digesting the discovery. That is why the inconsistency should be tracked and catalogued. The cross-examiner must leave herself in a position to make that determination as the case develops during the trial. The cross-examiner can continue preparation for trial confident that, if needed, the source material for the impeachment is readily available.

§ 8.05 Uncovering and Sourcing the Opportunity and Necessity for Accuracy by the Witness

When dealing with impeachment by inconsistent statements as opposed to all other types of impeachments, there is an additional step in preparation. For each statement, document, report, deposition, non-jury hearing, or interview conducted before trial, the cross-examiner should also prepare a separate note page of the trial notebook documenting where the witness has either been given the oath or has, in any way, been cautioned about the necessity to give completely accurate information to the best of his abilities.

§ 8.06 At the Deposition

Oath and Verification Chart

T-2, L4–10	OATH
T-5, L20–T-6, L24	ADMONITION
T-392, L16	"UNDERSTOOD ALL QUESTIONS"
T-392, L18	"GAVE HONEST ANSWERS"

For instance, in a deposition, the cross-examiner should note the page and line numbers where the witness was given the oath. In the chart above those are: T-2, L4-10 oath (read this code as transcript page 2, lines 4 through line 10 — the oath administered).

The cross-examiner should also note the admonition given by the deposing lawyer to the deponent of how important it is that the deponent understands all questions (on the above chart see T-5, L20 and T-6, L24 admonition). It is worth noting exactly where the deposing counsel cautioned that if the deponent did not understand the questions, then it is his obligation to tell the deposing lawyer that he does not understand a question.

As a tactical note, it is wise to caution every deponent that if he does not alert the questioning lawyer of any confusion about the questions, it would be "fair" for the deposing lawyer to assume (and for a jury that may hear all or a portion of the deposition to assume) that the deponent's answers were complete, responsive, and honest answers to the questions (for example: T-5, L20; T-6, L24 admonition of the importance of the deposition):

Q: As I am sure your lawyer has told you, a deposition is a very important process in this lawsuit?

A: Yes.

Q: You understand that the questions are given to you under oath and your answers are given under oath?

A: Yes.

Q: Each of your answers is recorded word for word by the court reporter?

A: Yes.

Q: You realize, of course, that it is extremely important that you understand all of my questions?

A: Of course.

Q: And the reason that is so critical is that we need to understand all of your answers?

A: Yes.

Q: If at any time I do not understand your answers, I will stop and have you clarify. Would that be fair?

A: Yes.

Q: If at any time you do not understand my questions, I want you to stop and tell me that you do not understand them. Would that be fair?

A: Yes, that is fair.

Q: And whether or not you understand the questions means whether or not you have heard it, whether or not you understood the words in it, whether I mumbled so that you could not understand what I said, whether you were unfamiliar with certain words, do you understand that?

A: Yes.

Q: Is that a fair way to handle it?

A: Yes.

Q: It would be fair for all of us to assume that your answers are true, correct, and accurate to my specific question, unless you tell me that you did not understand the question. That would be fair?

A: Yes, I understand.

In order to complete this technique, the cross-examiner should ask, as the last two questions of the deposition or hearing:

Q: Have you understood each of my questions?

A: Yes.

Q: And have your answers been honest, complete, and truthful?

A: Yes.

Deposing counsel should not overlook the importance of the deposition review, correction process, and the correction sheet sent to the deponent. It is important to note the place and manner where these last opportunities for correction were explained to the deponent.

§ 8.07 Look for Signatures on Government Reports

On a collision report, a police report, or other government report, there is a line for the officer to sign attesting to the report. Often such report forms have item numbers for each critical piece of information, including a line number for the space in which the officer attests to the report. In such instances, the cross-examiner's preparation should not only refer to the report (Police Rept. of 6/15/93, p.51), but reference should also be made to the line number (i.e., Line 32, [bottom of the page]) where the signature is located.

In government reports, there inevitably is a separate line item for "approval" by a supervisory official. Likewise, the cross-examiner will have not only the document number, but the line item number for the approval (Police Rept. of 6/15/92, p.1 — Line 33).

Federal and state tax returns contain not only a signature line, but also an attestation that the information is provided under penalty of perjury. A myriad of other government forms have the same language. The cross-examiner should be careful to review all government forms for this language as the fact of its existence can add impact to the impeachment of a witness concerning a statement inconsistent with the statement previously provided under oath.

§ 8.08 Statements, Interviews, and Private Reports

A statement or interview form often requires the signature of the person making that statement or giving that interview. Again the cross-examiner should have the document number, including the page number and the location (upper 1/3-"T", middle 1/3-"M", bottom 1/3-"B"). For a more detailed discussion, see chapter 6, *Page Preparation of Cross-Examination.*

§ 8.09 Purpose of Sourcing the Authenticity of the Statement

This extra level of preparation is important for two reasons. First, in the tension of the courtroom it is quite easy to misplace or overlook necessary materials. It is incredibly hard to search through reports, interview notes, government documents, or depositions before a watchful court and jury. If the necessary information is well documented, it is easier for the cross-examiner to find a specific item.

There is a second reason to fully document the witness's verification of an earlier statement. This reason is built upon the appearance of the cross-examiner's credibility to the jury, the judge, the opponent and — perhaps most importantly — the witness being impeached. When the cross-examiner can routinely, with no significant effort, locate the signature or other stamp of authenticity and recite its source, such specificity intimidates the witness. The unspoken suggestion is that the cross-examiner knows all and that, in times of doubt, the witness is best served by affirming the leading question of the cross-examiner.

§ 8.10 Step 2 — Physical Preparation of the Cross-Examination

Once inconsistencies have been uncovered and the verifying information developed, the physical preparation of the cross-examination becomes relatively straightforward. As is true of all areas of potential cross-examination, an impeachment by inconsistent statement is developed by chapters. Each impeachment by inconsistent statement requires at least one separate chapter (see chapter 5, *The Chapter Method of Cross-Examination*). Each answer to be obtained on the series of questions is written in the form of a leading question. Where the answer is known, the source of the answer is documented.

This systematic procedure is designed to wring the greatest impact out of the impeachment. The cross-examiner is never blessed with enough true inconsistencies. Therefore, none can be wasted. Each impeachment must be maximized.

Once each chapter demonstrating an inconsistency has been developed, the cross-examiner will conceptualize the organization of the chapters in proper sequence. Because each chapter is committed to only one page, the chapters can be reorganized prior to trial. Where necessary, they can also be reorganized as additional information is gathered during direct examination and earlier portions of cross-examination.

§ 8.11 Incorporating the Inconsistency into the Trial Notebook

In any style of chapter preparation, it is imperative that the exact inconsistency and location of that inconsistent statement be noted.

The chart below gives a series of examples:

Chapter: Car Color

		Direct Testimony
Dep T-3: 16 (Blue Notebook)	"The car was blue."	"GREEN" (TIME: 9:45 a.m.)
D-3 ↓ (Black Notebook)	The car was "unknown color."	
D-5 ↑	"I'm not sure."	
Videotape, 0962	Shrugged shoulders and smiled, no response.	

Examine the examples from the chart above in the order they appear. Each shorthand entry is explained. The answer, "The car was blue," is an exact quote. It will be found in the witness's deposition transcript page number 3, line 16. Our pretrial preparation should include segregating each deposition, transcript, or statement of the witness in a separate notebook, folder, or binder. One reason for use of separate notebooks is that it gives a visual signal to the jury and the witness that the cross-examiner has studied the previous statements of the witness. In addition, after the first use of the deposition notebook to accomplish an impeachment the witness understands the meaning of the advocate's movement to retrieve the transcript. Thereafter, whenever the separate notebook is retrieved, the witness and the jury are placed on notice that the witness has testified inconsistently and that the inconsistency will be exposed. There will be a brief period of silence when the cross-examiner goes to the notebook, whether at the podium or at counsel table. This silence will further accentuate the seriousness of the matter.

The answer that the car was an "unknown" color will be found in document 3 (D-3) contained in the black notebook. In the case of many documents, the exhibit number should be marked. In the event that the pages have been Bates numbered, that number should appear in the source column as well. The arrow pointing down (↓) signifies that there are no line numbers on the document, but that it is in the lower half of the document. While the arrow is not as exact as a line number, it has at least eliminated half of the page that ordinarily would have to be scanned. Any other code developed by the cross-examiner may be substituted. However, some code for location is quite helpful, since even one full page of a transcript or a document is too much to survey when searching for an inconsistency during trial.

The answer, "I'm not sure," will be contained in document number five (D-5) in the upper half of the page, as shown by the arrow (↑). Since there is no notebook designation, it is found in the same notebook as previously referenced immediately above that notation in the cross-examiner's notes. Again, if in exhibit number is available before trial, that number should be used in the source column. If an impeachment is from a multi-page exhibit, it is even more important that the Bates number be used in addition to the exhibit number. Hence, an impeachment from a voluminous document marked as an exhibit might be noted this way: def Ex 241, Bates156. This would mean that within defendant's exhibit number 241 at Bates number 156, the impeaching statement will be found.

The answer, "shrugged shoulders and smiled, no response," is a nonverbal response. In this age of video and digital cameras, videotape depositions are common. Our knowledge of the presence of a videotaped response can lead us to become sloppy in deposition techniques. Since we can see the physical response of the witness to the question (i.e., a shrug), we feel we have received a solid answer. However, because the answer is in nonverbal form, its later use for impeachment becomes more problematic. It is extremely difficult to impeach using such a response. It is necessary that, at the time the response is made, the lawyer ask the witness to articulate the response in words so that the transcript may more easily be used later as the basis for impeachment by inconsistent statement.

In any pre-trial matter, hearing, deposition, or interview, nonverbal responses to questions should be immediately clarified, requiring the witness to speak his answer, thereby making the record useful:

Q: Did you see the car?

A: Yes.

Q: What color was the car?

(Witness shrugs shoulders.)

Q: It looked to me like you just shrugged your shoulders.

A: I did.

Q: I take that to mean that your answer is that you don't know the color of the car.

A: Yes, that's what I meant.

Or

Q: When you just shrugged your shoulders, did that mean that you don't know the color of the car?

A: Yes.

§ 8.12 Step 3 — Establish the Current Version of the Testimony to Be Impeached

Of all the steps, this is the least difficult. In almost all cases, the current version of a fact was established in direct examination or was volunteered unresponsively during the cross-examination. Because the new version is favorable to the opponent and detrimental to the cross-examiner, you may expect the opponent to bring it out during direct examination if the opponent is aware of the new version. Frequently, the cross-examiner can anticipate the introduction of the statement in the direct testimony because it has surfaced in some pre-trial hearing or statement. Attention to index cards and charts should pick up the fact that the story has changed.

To maximize the impact for the upcoming impeachment of the witness, the cross-examiner needs to remind the jury one more time of the current version normally stated in the direct testimony. This is the exception to the ordinary rule that the cross-examiner should avoid repeating the harmful portions of direct testimony. There are two separate techniques for accomplishing this step.

§ 8.13 State or Summarize the Text to Be Impeached

Restating the direct examination is potentially dangerous to the cross-examiner. Any repetition of harmful information has the effect of reminding the fact finder of that testimony. Restating is, however, necessary to thoroughly set up the impeachment. In fact, this step requires that the fact finder be reminded of the testimony. The cross-examiner need not present the entire chapter that contains the direct testimony to be impeached; she only must repeat the particular fact to be impeached. Remember, as part of our impeachment we will demonstrate circumstances that allow the jury to view the earlier version as the accurate one.

For example, the witness testified at a pre-trial hearing that he saw truck-tire skid marks — in fact, saw them "quite clearly." However, in his previous statement to the investigating officer, he stated that he had not seen any skid marks. The lawyer might choose to repeat verbatim his testimony in this way: "On direct examination, you claimed you saw skid marks — in fact, you claim you saw them "quite clearly." When the cross-examiner restates the direct examination, the cross-examiner must take care to use the exact quotation from the direct testimony so that the jury will remember that moment in the direct examination. Only extract the minimum verbiage from direct examination to set up the impeachment. Do not repeat the entire direct examination chapter.

§ 8.14 Summarize Rather than Restate Direct Testimony That Is Explosive

Summarizing the direct testimony is preferred, however, when the direct testimony is quite powerful — when it provides strong negative images against the cross-examiner's theory of the case, it is better to summarize. Example: The direct testimony was a vivid account of how the defendant ran a red light and slammed into a parked car, killing the occupant. The original version of the testimony is that the witness only heard the screech of brakes and then saw the accident. He did not remark on who had run the red light. Here the lawyer might isolate and summarize the facts necessary to set up the inconsistent statement by asking only: "Your testimony today that you saw a car run the red light?" Note, even when using this technique, the cross-examiner must not abandon the fundamental rules of cross-examination (see chapter 4, *The Only Three Rules of Cross-Examination*). The cross-examiner should still put the question to the witness in the form of a leading question. To do otherwise is to invite a recounting of the entire harmful story!

The cross-examiner must *fairly* summarize the witness's direct testimony as to the fact to be impeached. Any effort by the cross-examiner to be unfair in the characterization of that testimony risks the loss of her credibility. It may also evoke empathy or sympathy for the witness. This is exactly the opposite effect that impeachment should create. It is therefore ill advised to reword the statement of the witness or in any way tamper with the words of the witness.

Once again, this does not mean that the cross-examiner must quote the entire direct testimony or the entire scenario into which the impeachment fits — or even the entire answer that contained the inconsistency. It means only that the cross-examiner should use the exact quote as to the inconsistent fact at issue. The exact words can be placed in context through a fair summary of the direct testimony so that the jury can recall the context.

In the following example, the plaintiff has testified that she witnessed her former boyfriend brutally stab and kill a man. According to her, the victim was stabbed as he tried to get out of his van. The cross-examiner intends to establish that this alleged attempt to get out of the van is inconsistent with an earlier statement of the witness. For obvious reasons, the cross-examining lawyer does not want to offer the witness an opportunity to repeat her testimony about the stabbing details. Consequently, the cross-examining lawyer will not include in the foundation questions any of the "stabbing" testimony:

Q: As I understand your testimony, Mr. Polidori tried to get out of the van, but couldn't?

A: Brett said, "Give me all your money." He said, "I will if you will let me out."

Q: He could not get out?

A: No.

Q: Your testimony now is that he never left the van?

A: That's what happened.

Q: You can recall that vividly? Is that right?

A: Yes, as far as I can remember.

Q: Your memory is not vague on that, is it?

A: No.

Q: You recall it specifically?

A: I do.

Q: There's not any question about it, is there?

A: As far as I recall.

Q: You have testified under oath before concerning this, haven't you?

A: Yes.

Q: And you were asked before, in May of 2004, what you saw, isn't that correct?

A: Yes.

Q: Ms. Wright, I am at page 163 starting at line 10 of the transcript of May of 2004. You were asked this question: "Question: Did he get out of the van once the van was parked in the alley? Answer: Yes. Question: Did he get all the way out of the van? Answer: Yes, he was on the ground. Question: And how long did he stand outside the van? Answer: About five seconds." That was, in fact, your answer in May of 2004?

A: Yes, sir.

Q: Now you remember testifying that Mr. Polidori was completely out of the van?

A: Yes, that's what I said.

Q: For a full five seconds?

A: Yes.

§ 8.15 Phrases that "Set Up" Impeachments

While establishing the current version to be impeached, the cross-examiner can simultaneously infuse in the question a subtle cue to the jury (and to the judge) that the testimony the jury is about to hear repeated is inaccurate.

An example of establishing the current version of a mistaken witness:

> **Q:** Mr. Jones, as I understand it you now believe the man you remember robbing you was six foot, three inches?

Or

> **Q:** As I understood your testimony on direct examination, your latest thought is that the man who robbed you was six foot, three inches?

Or

An example of establishing the current version of a dishonest witness:

> **Q:** Let me see if I understand this: Today you are telling this jury that you saw Tom hit Alan over the head? (aggressive)

Or

> **Q:** Let me see if I understand today's version of events ... (more aggressive)

Or

> **Q:** What you are now saying is today's truth, that you saw Tom hit Alan? (extremely aggressive)

Courtroom aggressiveness is a matter of contrast. All the aggression we need and that we can safely employ is within the phrasing of the question. We do not need to add an aggressive voice or gesture.

Each of the passages is a "set-up" phrase. It is a code for: "This is a different story." Using these flag-planting phrases, the cross-examiner has put before the jury the fact to be impeached. The cross-examiner signals to the jury that she is not bringing up the subject merely to verify the direct testimony, but instead is rephrasing the testimony as a disputed issue. The cross-examiner has established with the jury and the witness the pattern for impeachment by inconsistent statement.

Because the lawyer has used the opening statement to impress upon the jury the critical inconsistencies in the witness's testimony, the jury has no difficulty in recognizing both the existence and the importance of the inconsistencies. All of these inconsistencies were picked up by a cross-examination preparation system. As a result of the integrated trial plan that allows the lawyer to recognize and focus on the chapters of greatest importance to the competing theories of the case, the cross-examiner has revealed in the opening statement at least the major inconsistencies that she intends to prove. Whether the cross-examiner intends to brand the witness as mistaken or deceitful, the jury has learned through voir dire and opening statement that the credibility of the witness will be challenged. The jurors have been told the basis for that challenge; whether the basis is motive, interest, bias, or inconsistent statements.

An advantage of highlighting to the jury in opening statement the major inconsistencies that the cross-examiner expects to develop is that jurors are alerted to these inconsistencies before ever hearing the direct testimony of the witness. Therefore, when the witness testifies on direct examination, the jury has been forewarned not to accept the story at face value. Instead, the jury is more inclined to suspend judgment on the credibility of that direct-testimony version until such time as the jury hears the cross-examination on that subject.

When the advocate reveals documented inconsistencies in the opening statement, the jurors' first impression about the credibility of the witness is a negative one. This impression remains unless the witness overcomes it. In short, the witness is beginning his direct testimony with a credibility deficit.

§ 8.16 Step 4 — Tie the Witness to the Current Version to Be Impeached

The witness has given today's version of the truth as "advertised" by the opponent's opening statement. If the opponent has failed to discuss an inconsistency, so much the better. In this event it is the cross-examiner who has the opportunity to disclose the fact of the inconsistency to the jury. Then, in cross-examination the advocate can figuratively tie the new version of the story around the witness's (and hopefully the opponent's) neck so that the opponent's case appears to be established only if that new version is accepted. Once the witness is forced to readopt his latest version as being completely truthful, the cross-examiner has, in effect, tied an important part of the credibility of the witness and the opponent's case to the believability of that piece of testimony. By this technique it appears to the jury that much of the opponent's case is staked on the credibility of the particular statement about to be impeached.

The goal is to teach the jury that the accuracy of the entire story is in question because critical parts have changed. In virtually every jurisdiction, the judge will give a standard instruction that reminds jurors that, in judging the credibility of a witness, they may fairly reflect upon whether that witness has been impeached. Impeachments by inconsistent statement will likely be viewed as important reflections on the truthfulness and credibility of both the impeached witness and the side that called that witness.

The cross-examiner can force the witness to tell the jury that his direct testimony is accurate. The witness will be committed to the accuracy of his soon-to-be-impeached testimony. The cross-examiner can irretrievably bind the witness to his direct testimony in a series of leading questions designed to show that the witness has no question concerning the accuracy of direct examination on this particular point.

This method seems to contradict the cross-examiner's mission to show that the witness is unreliable. The contrary is true. By tying the witness to his direct testimony that will be juxtaposed with his contradictory earlier statement, we dramatize the impeachment.

In the face of a witness who claims to be certain, the jury will not understand why the direct testimony is inconsistent with his other statements. In fact, the more certainty the witness has asserted on direct examination, the more unlikely the jury is to accept the fact that the story has changed. Then, when the facts surrounding the initial observation and the initial telling of the story are revealed(see chapter 5, *The Chapter Method of Cross-Examination*), the version of events given prior to trial will be more believable to the jury than the latest version given upon direct examination.

Such a technique of impeachment, done once, raises some doubts in the minds of jurors. When this technique of impeachment is repeated over the course of a cross-examination it leads to outright juror skepticism. After all, the cross-examiner has demonstrated several times that the witness is sure of a fact, but yet at variance with his earlier position on the identical issue. When the cross-examiner repeatedly shows that the story recited in the direct testimony is full of changes, it undermines the ability of the opponent to argue "certainty" of the witness to the jurors or judge.

§ 8.17 Example of Tying the Witness to the Direct to Build Drama

The following is an example from a contract case in which the issue is whether certain signatures were notarized by people present when the signatures were actually placed on the document. The cross-examiner's position is that they were not. On direct examination, the witness testified in general terms that the witnesses' signatures were all properly placed on the document. On cross-examination, the witness will be confronted with a previous statement that the people who signed as witnesses were *not* in the room when the contract was signed. In the initial part of the impeachment, the cross-examiner ties the witness irretrievably to the scene of the contract signing:

Q: You had signed only one contract in your life?

A: Yes.

Q: It was the first professional football contract you had ever signed?

A: Yes.

Q: It was one of the high points of your life?

A: Yes, it was the high point of my life.

Q: The high point of your life?

A: Yes.

Q: It was an unforgettable experience?

A: Yes.

Q: That moment is frozen in your mind forever?

A: Yes.

Q: You can remember the room you were in?

A: Yes.

Q: It was the office of Abe Kane?

A: Yes.

Q: You can remember the day that it occurred, April 12, 2002?

A: Yes.

Q: You can remember the time of the day, about noon?

A: Yes.

Q: You can remember who was in the room?

A: Yes.

Q: Sharon Steinberg and Steve Steinberg were in the room?

A: Yes.

Q: You will never forget those people?

A: That's true.

At this point, the jury can well envision the signing of the contract. It is a vivid image. The cross-examiner has painted an image that is potentially harmful to the cross-examination. It is at this point that the cross-examiner will reveal the real picture (the inconsistency that the witnesses were not in the room) and show to the jury that the direct testimony is only an illusion:

Q: You claim that your signature was notarized by this Sharon Steinberg and Steve Steinberg?

A: Yes.

Q: That is why you remember them being in the room?

A: Yes.

Q: The fact of the matter is, they were not in the room?

A: What?

Q: The fact of the matter is that you previously said under oath that they did not notarize your signature when you signed the documents?

A: Did I say that?

Q: You had your deposition taken in my office on the 13th day of July 2007?

A: Yes.

Q: Your lawyer was there?

A: Yes.

Q: He had carefully instructed you about what the deposition would be about?

A: Yes.

Q: He had told you that I would be asking you questions?

A: Yes.

Q: That you would give answers?

A: Yes.

Q: And that it was all done under oath?

A: Yes.

Q: That each word that we said would be taken down word for word by the certified court reporter?

A: Yes.

Q: He told you that we would be talking about that contract?

A: Yes.

Q: You were placed under oath?

A: Yes.

Q: You were placed under oath in the transcript on page 2, lines 4 through 10?

A: Yes.

Q: In the transcript, page 5, line 20 through page 6, line 24, I particularly gave you an admonition to make sure that you understood every one of my questions and that if you did not, that you would tell me that you did not, correct?

A: Correct.

Q: At page 56 line 17, you said: "The Steinbergs were not there. They didn't see nothing." Correct?

A: . . . looks like it.

Q: In fact, I told you that if you didn't tell me otherwise, I would assume that you understood my questions and you told me in your words that was fair?

A: Yes.

Q: At the end of the deposition at page 392, line 16, you told me that you understood all of my questions?

A: Yes.

Q: Your able lawyer was there for all of that?

A: Yes.

The picture carefully constructed on direct examination has now been shattered.

§ 8.18 Tying the Witness to Emotional and Dramatic Testimony

The following example of tying a witness to the statement is taken from a criminal context:

Q: It must have been very frightening?

A: Yes.

Q: I am sure that it made quite an impression on you?

A: Yes.

Q: There was really no mistake in what happened?

A: That's true.

Q: You watched as Tom picked up the hammer?

A: Yes.

Q: You watched Tom hit Joe over the head three times?

A: Yes.

Q: You stared at the whole thing?

A: Yes.

Q: It is burned into your mind?

A: Yes.

Q: That picture will not go away?

A: Never.

At this point, the cross-examiner must immediately and dramatically shift to the prior version, in which the witness claims never to have seen any of these things.

This technique of marrying the witness to the current version initially appears to be terribly damaging to the cross-examiner. But if the impeachment by inconsistent statement is effective, the damage will not fall upon the cross-examiner but diminish the credibility of the witness and the opponent's case. By making the witness appear certain before revealing the inconsistency, the revelation of the inconsistency in great detail has a powerful impact on the jury.

§ 8.19 Develop a Chapter Showing the Earlier Impeaching Version Is More Believable

When using this technique, the cross-examiner must always make certain that the earlier version is the more believable of the two versions. If we leave the jury with the impression that all we care about is that the story has changed, or worse, that the new version is to be believed, the effort to tie the witness to the current version will backfire. The jurors may hear a repetition of the new version and will read into it our belief in the new version. The technique that solves this problem is to not merely reveal the inconsistent version itself, but also reveal two other critical aspects enhancing its believability:

(1) The original observation was made under circumstances whereby the witness could be expected to be accurate; and

(2) The previous recitation by the witness was made under circumstances in which the witness would want to be accurate and honest.

It is not just the naked fact of a differing version that must be proven; it is that there logically should *not* be a change on this issue. By requiring the witness to testify to facts that prove (1) and (2) above and then demonstrating the change, the lawyer shows that the earlier version is more trustworthy.

This is an important step, deserving of a very complete chapter. The goal of the cross-examiner is to establish that the earlier version is the one to be believed. Therefore any fact that shows that the witness wanted and needed to be accurate, had the opportunity and asserted the facts as accurate, aids the cross-examiner in establishing the reliability of the earlier version.

§ 8.20 Step 5 — Equate or Translate the Conflicting Versions

Sometimes the inconsistency between two versions of a fact is so clear that no translation is needed. Stark inconsistencies make for powerful impeachments. The very words of the witness in the first statement contradict his words in his newest version. In such a circumstance no juror can miss the fact that the witness has testified two different ways on two different occasions. Also, there are inconsistencies that require additional work in order for the jury to understand how the statements are inconsistent. For example: Assume the direct testimony is that the armed robber was five feet, six inches tall, but the statement contained in the police report is that the robber was six feet, three inches. These descriptions are both in feet and inches. Hence there is no need for equating the versions.

However, there are times that the direct testimony must be equated or translated in a way that makes the inconsistency clear.

Assume that on direct testimony the witness states the armed robber was five foot, six inches tall. In the police report the same witness said: "He was taller than me. I looked up to him." The cross-examiner must equate or translate these versions:

> **Q:** The floor you were standing on was level?
>
> **A:** Yes.
>
> **Q:** There were no steps?
>
> **A:** No.
>
> **Q:** You are about six feet tall?
>
> **A:** Yes, I am six feet and one-half inches.

As can be seen, equating or translating often requires the cross-examiner to have made further investigation. As soon as the cross-examiner reads the police report and finds that the robber was described as being "taller than me," the cross-examiner must investigate to determine the height of the witness. She must make sure that the witness and robber were standing on the same level surface. The investigation must ensure that there are no reasons why the earlier statement does not mean exactly what it says: "I looked up at him." Translation: "He had to be taller than 6'½".

§ 8.21 Equating or Translating "I Don't Know"

A more subtle context of equating or translating comes up when a witness has said in a pre-trial statement that the witness "does not know" a particular fact. Such an equivocal statement requires a certain amount of translating in order to set up the impeachment:

> **Q:** You told us in your deposition at page 49, line 36 that, "I don't know the height of the armed robber"?
>
> **A:** Yes.
>
> **Q:** You said that because you could not accurately judge the height of the robber?
>
> **A:** Yes.
>
> **Q:** If you had been able to judge the height of the robber, you would have given it to the police?
>
> **A:** Of course.
>
> **Q:** In fact, you wanted to describe the robber as best you could?
>
> **A:** Yes I wanted him to get caught.

Q: And if you had been able to estimate the height of the robber, you wanted to give that estimate to the officers so they could look for that robber?

A: I wanted them to look for the robber anyway.

Q: But you didn't give the officers the height of the robber because you didn't know the height of the robber?

A: Right.

Q: You did not know if the robber was five feet?

A: I wasn't sure.

Q: You didn't know if the robber was six feet?

A: I guess.

Q: You just didn't have the opportunity to observe the robber's height?

A: True.

The cross-examiner has required the witness to acknowledge that he didn't know the height of the robber because he never got a good look at the robber. Whenever and however the witness has equivocated in pre-trial answers, the cross-examiner must equate or translate that equivocation into more exact concepts. Any words that are nebulous, subject to interpretation, or subjective must be translated into precise concepts for the impeachment to work well.

§ 8.22 Step 6 — Expose the Inconsistent Statement

After tying the witness to the current version, the next thing that the cross-examiner must do is create a change of atmosphere in the courtroom. A certain mood has been built in the courtroom by not only permitting the witness to testify to the version of the fact presented in the direct testimony, but also by irretrievably binding the witness to it. The cross-examiner may have created a sense of tension or expectation that there is more to be said on this subject.

Since the judge and jury know that the cross-examiner is prepared with consistent, goal-directed questions, they sense there is meaning to this repetition of a portion of the direct examination. Because of a detailed opening statement, the jury knows the witness has been inconsistent on several key issues. It may well be that the cross-examiner has foreshadowed this impeachment by explaining the inconsistent versions within the opening statement. If so the jurors understand that this is one of the inconsistencies discussed. If not, the jurors may have observed from the body language and set-up questions that the witness is about to be confronted with another inconsistency. Having learned to recognize the code phrases, the jurors are primed to hear the impeachment. The fact finder has seen and now understands the pattern of impeachment.

§ 8.23 Using Silence to Signal That an Impeachment by Inconsistent Statement Is About to Occur

The cross-examiner must now signal to the judge and jury a change in attitude and direction. There are several devices to accomplish this. With the merely mistaken witness, the cross-examiner can change the pace of the examination. The tone of voice might become more matter-of-fact. The cross-examiner may display a puzzled look. Perhaps the cross-examiner will look down at the prepared chapter as a method of preparing to retrieve the impeaching document.

With the dishonest witness, the cross-examiner can markedly change her tone of voice. The voice can change from understanding or nonchalance to a lower, more pointed voice. The cross-examiner can look directly at the witness. As always, a lower voice is more effective than a raised voice. This is not a movie and we are not actors. The facts supply the drama.

In either case, the lawyer can build drama simply by taking a moment to purposefully return to counsel table to retrieve the first impeaching document, exhibit, or transcript. If that material is close, the cross-examiner should carefully locate the precise page of the transcript, document, or notebook that will create silence to heighten the drama.

This retrieval of impeachment material, whether from counsel table or from a notebook near the podium, may only take seconds, but it will draw the jury's attention to the purpose of the cross-examiner.

Keep in mind that "locating" the exact page of the transcript or the file from counsel table does not require any elaborate search. Because the impeachment has been sourced within the page preparation of that chapter of cross-examination, it is unnecessary for the lawyer to go through numerous pages. The location of the inconsistent statement has been documented before trial. The cross-examiner can now efficiently retrieve the necessary transcript or exhibit and turn to the exact page and line number before returning her full attention to the witness. The cross-examiner is ready to expose the inconsistency.

§ 8.24 Do Not Overlook or Minimize the Foundation

The lawyer must lay a proper foundation for the exposure of the inconsistent statement. This is true whether the witness is merely mistaken or is to be branded as deceitful. The rules require that the witness be oriented to the prior statement: told who was involved, when and where it occurred, and what was said. This is true whether there is a requirement or an inclination to actually show the witness the prior statement. Even if the rules did not require this "orientation," the inherent sense of fairness of juries demands a fair degree of orienting.

Once a foundation for a deposition has been properly laid, continued use of that deposition requires only a cursory foundation. Few judges will require the cross-examiner to endlessly repeat when the deposition was taken, who was present, etc., when such facts have been established. In such a circumstance the cross-examiner might simply state, "Let us again turn to your testimony when we talked about this point in January 2008 at your deposition." There is no precise formula for such an abbreviated foundation, and the cross-examiner is invited to emphasize that part of the foundation that seems most important.

§ 8.25 Foundation as a Tactical Weapon

Mechanically doing what the rules require may be sufficient legally, but wholly insufficient factually. The cross-examiner can convert the required foundational questions into tactical weapons. The pace, phrasing, and tone of the foundational questions provide information to the jurors about the importance of the upcoming impeachment and the attitude of the cross-examiner.

Because it is the prior statement that the lawyer wants the jury to believe, it is to her advantage to do more than the foundation rule requires. The foundation should be laid in a manner that brings the witness back to the "real time" of the prior statement. When the witness is returned to the "real time" of the prior statement, the confrontation becomes more effective, chilling, and disorienting to the witness. The witness now senses that he is in trouble and, more importantly, that the cross-examiner is in control. On the other hand, it appears to the jury that the cross-examiner is being fair to the witness by thoroughly establishing the prior statement.

In this foundation phase, the cross-examiner should always finish with what was said. In other words, finish with the inconsistency. Do not put the inconsistency before the orienting portions of the foundation of impeachment. Doing so would be similar to telling the punch line of a joke before the set-up.

§ 8.26 Foundation in a Civil Case

In the example below, a personal injury case, the cross-examiner lays a foundation before exposing an inconsistent statement on the fact in issue — the color of the car that ran the red light:

Q: Mr. Fraley, on February 12, 2001, you received a subpoena for your deposition?

A: Yes.

Q: You received it by certified mail?

A: Yes.

Q: You had never received a subpoena for your deposition before?

A: No.

Q: That subpoena directed that you go to the law office of Barney Frick?

A: Yes.

Q: It directed the exact time, 10:00 a.m.?

A: Yes.

Q: It directed the exact day, February 20?

A: Yes.

Q: It directed that you give testimony before a certified court reporter?

A: Yes.

Q: You knew what this testimony would concern?

A: Generally.

Q: You knew you would be asked questions about the car collision you saw?

A: Yes.

Q: On the 20th, you got up that morning and prepared to go to the deposition?

A: Yes.

Q: You had to take off work?

A: Yes.

Q: You had never been to that law office before?

A: No.

Q: You went to that law office knowing that you would be giving testimony about this case?

A: Yes.

Q: You knew that it was serious because you had received a subpoena?

A: Yes.

Q: You arrived just after 10:00 that morning?

A: Yes, just a little bit after 10:00. I was nervous and missed a turn and I was somewhat late.

Q: When you arrived a little after 10:00, you were nervous that you might be in trouble because you were late?

A: Yes.

Q: When you arrived I was there?

A: Yes.

Q: Mr. Frick was there?

A: Yes.

Q: The plaintiff was there?

A: Yes.

Q: The defendant, George, was there?

A: Yes.

Q: And there was a certified court reporter there?

A: Yes.

Q: She had a stenographic machine, didn't she?

A: Yes, just like on TV.

Q: That's right, Mr. Fraley, it all looked just like on TV: very official — didn't it?

A: Sure did.

Q: In fact, you were sworn just like you were today?

A: Yes.

Q: You raised your hand and swore before God to tell the truth that morning?

A: Yes.

Q: And it was your intention to tell the truth that morning?

A: Yes.

Q: It was not quite as scary as coming into court because it was only in a law office?

A: I was just as nervous.

Q: You knew that it was just as serious as your testimony here today?

A: Yes, I did.

Q: You took it that seriously?

A: Yes.

Q: You knew it was about this case?

A: Yes.

Q: You knew a lawsuit had been filed once you got your subpoena?

A: Yes, I figured that out.

Q: You knew that it was required that you give honest testimony?

A: Yes.

Q: You were told by both lawyers before you started to testify just how important your testimony was?

A: Yes.

Q: You were told at page 2, line 16 through 23, that it was important that you understood each of the questions and responded truthfully if you understood those questions?

A: Yes.

Q: I also told you that if you didn't understand a question, to say that you didn't understand the question, and not just guess at the answer?

A: Yes, you told me that.

Q: I spoke in such language that you could understand?

A: Yes.

Q: I was seated across the table from you, wasn't I?

A: Yes.

Q: My opponent, Mr. Frick, was on your side of the table?

A: Yes.

Q: The court reporter was at the end of the table taking all of the questions and answers down verbatim word for word?

A: Yes.

Q: At the end of the deposition, page 392 line 10 through 12, I asked you if you had understood all my questions, and you told me that you had?

A: Yes.

Q: In fact, you had understood all my questions, hadn't you?

A: Yes.

Q: And when I asked you at page 73, line 16 of the deposition, what the color of the car was, your answer was, "I don't know."?

A: That's what I said.

The lawyer moves on with the cross-examination after these foundational chapters are completed.

§ 8.27 Foundation in a Criminal Case

The following example from a criminal case exposes an inconsistent statement by a dishonest (not mistaken) witness:

Q: On March 13, 2003, you were interviewed by Detective Sable?

A: Yes.

Q: He questioned you at the Chicago Police Department?

A: Yes.

Q: He questioned you about this crime?

A: Yes.

Q: With him was Detective Caplin?

A: Yes.

Q: You knew why you were being questioned?

A: Yes.

Q: You promised them you would tell the truth?

A: Yes.

Q: You were being questioned about the death of a man?

A: Yeah, Crown.

Q: Dickey Crown was dead?

A: As a bug.

Q: These detectives had your full attention?

A: Sure did.

Q: So, when they asked questions, you made sure to listen?

A: Right.

Q: And then you answered their questions?

A: If I could.

Q: And you answered truthfully.

A: As best I could.

Q: They asked you if you were watching the whole time as Crown was killed?

A: Yes.

Q: But what you told the Detectives Sable and Caplin that day is not what you swore to this jury today?

A: No, it wasn't.

Q: What you told the detectives that day is this (Madam prosecutor, I am at page 27, line 10 of the transcript of the interview of March 13, 2003, question by Detective Sable: "Did you see your father hit him with the hammer?" Your answer, at line 14: "No, no, I wasn't looking, I was walking down the stairs when I heard a noise and I turned around and Crown was falling down the stairs."

§ 8.28 Foundation for the Witness Who Is Merely Mistaken

With a mistaken witness the cross-examiner approaches more gently, but still thoroughly. Tone, pace, and gestures can soften the questions, but the questions still effectively establish the foundation:

Q: Mrs. Hernandez, on direct examination you told the jury the man who robbed you was, "Short, about five foot six?"

A: Yes.

Q: Now Mrs. Hernandez, you were robbed at about 10:30 at night?

A: Yes.

Q: By 10:35 you called the police?

A: That's true.

Q: By 10:40 the police arrived?

A: Yes.

Q: They asked you what had happened?

A: Yes.

Q: You wanted to tell them exactly what had happened?

A: Yes.

Q: You wanted to tell them as accurately as you could?

A: Yes.

Q: The whole event had just happened not more than ten minutes before that?

A: That's true.

Q: When Detective Martin asked you to give a description of the man, that detective was asking you about something that had just happened?

A: Yes.

Q: You told him a description the very best you could?

A: Yes.

Q: What you told him ten minutes after it happened was the man who robbed you was about your height?

A: Yes.

Q: You are about six foot, one inch?

A: Yes.

Q: A tall woman?

A: Rather.

Q: You assured the detective the robber was about six foot, three inches?

A: Yes, I did.

Q: You honestly said six foot, three inches?

A: That's what I believed.

§ 8.29 Have the Fact Finder Visualize the First Statement

It is the prior statement that the cross-examiner is alleging to be the more accurate. As result, the cross-examiner should attempt to make the prior statement as visual as possible to the judge or jury. This is best done by giving the fullest development of the foundation material. The exact exposure of the inconsistency seldom requires more than one question. That question is too short to have the effect needed. The foundation material makes the prior statement more visual to the jury, giving the inconsistent statement itself the depth and texture needed by the jury to absorb its significance.

At this point, the cross-examiner has accomplished two of the three goals of the presentation of the impeachment: (1) exposure of the inconsistent statement; and (2) demonstration that the former statement was made under circumstances where the witness had the desire and opportunity to be accurate. The cross-examiner must now complete the impeachment by proving (3) that the original perception was made under circumstances where the witness could be expected to be accurate.

§ 8.30 Maximize the Damage in Stages

At this point, much has already been done to maximize the damage. The witness has been irretrievably bound to the current version on direct examination. The cross-examiner has used a substantial number of questions to leave no room for the witness to vacillate on the current version.

Just as importantly, the cross-examiner has made great progress in exposing the inconsistent statement through what traditionally was considered a routine foundation phase. By meticulously documenting the foundation process, stressing the reliability of the prior statement, and assuring the truth of the prior statement based on circumstances surrounding it, the cross-examiner has done much to maximize the damage.

§ 8.31 Maximizing the Damage of an Inconsistency by Employing the Chapter Method

Having exposed the inconsistency at this point, the lawyer need only revert to the familiar chapter method of cross-examination (see chapter 5, *The Chapter Method of Cross-Examination).* The cross-examiner proves reliability as if the original version were a goal-fact to be established through conventional cross-examination techniques. Although the goal-fact has been revealed (of necessity), the cross-examiner must still put the fact into context. To do this, the cross-examiner must begin at the top of the chapter that establishes that goal-fact. Through leading questions, the detailed facts will lead a jury to believe that the goal-fact was correctly perceived in the first instance.

In the example above, assume the cross-examiner was not confronted with an inconsistency but wanted to establish that the robber was tall. The cross-examiner would ask the questions in the chapter form. When the cross-examiner has already disclosed this goal, she might simply return to the top of the chapter and establish the facts that make the original version believable.

§ 8.32 Step 7 — Listen to the Direct Examination

The cross-examiner should be aware that inconsistencies occur not only before trial, but also during trial, direct examination, and earlier portions of cross-examination. Every time witnesses speak, they have the opportunity to make inconsistent statements. Listening at all times is, therefore, a requirement. The cross-examiner cannot assume the story will remain the same.

It seems simple, but in trial listening is difficult. In order to deliver consistently strong impeachments, the lawyer must be a consistently attentive listener. Listening is a distinct skill. Like other skills, it must be practiced. The ability to engage in focused listening in a courtroom setting is as much a trial skill as the ability to form appropriate questions. However, listening is far easier when we have prepared our cross-examinations in the chapter method. Because we have drafted our chapters at every point in the cross-examination, we know where we are, where we are going, and how we intend to get there. We can now concentrate on what the witness is saying.

§ 8.33 Dealing with New Inconsistencies Occurring in Trial

This same identification process that is used to properly prepare and document inconsistencies before the trial applies to both the direct examination and preceding chapters of cross-examination. A witness may offer up an inconsistent answer during either direct or cross-examination. Unless the cross-examiner is in a trial in which daily transcripts are produced, and those transcripts are available prior to impeachment, the cross-examiner must develop a method to track the inconsistencies that develop during trial.

Assume that on direct testimony the witness has, for the first time, testified inconsistently with his pre-trial statements on an issue. Witnesses generally change their story on matters of importance. If it is a significant fact, and one that the cross-examiner intends to impeach upon, the advocate needs to note the words as accurately as possible. And then she needs to prepare a cross-examination on this new inconsistency. But how can this be done during trial?

There is a way to handle a new inconsistency. Cynics (the authors included) believe many changes of story — re-remembering an event — occur with the encouragement of someone aligned with one of the parties. The scenarios are too varied to list, but the message is received — "Gee, I remember it this way. How about you?" However it happens, the witness suddenly has a different recollection of a key event.

If the change is on a minor matter, it may not matter that the story has changed. But let us assume that the change matters. If the original version was a fact of importance, then we are virtually certain to have already written a chapter about these facts. We had prepared the chapter in order to prove a point in its context. It was important. It was built on leading questions, sourced where possible. All that has happened is that the witness has given a new version of an important story or fact. Our entire chapter of cross-examination is now simply a prepared impeachment.

§ 8.34 Advantages for the Cross-Examiner When the Witness Changes His Story at Trial

In all other respects, an inconsistency arising during trial will be handled like an inconsistency discovered before trial. However, the impeachment during trial comes very late in the game. This is an added advantage. It offers the cross-examiner an opportunity to point out how many times this new story could have been told but was not. It therefore allows the cross-examiner to close the chapter or chapters exposing this new inconsistency with summary questions that give the history and context of the inconsistency:

Q: Four times we have discussed this case?

A: Yes.

Q: Four times — once on April 1st, 2008?

A: Yes.

Q: Second on June 17th, 2008?

A: Yes.

Q: The third on August 14th, 2008?

A: Yes.

Q: And the fourth time two days before this trial began; isn't that correct?

A: Yes.

Q: You never told me, you never stated, you never said at all what you testified to on direct examination (the car was green) on any of those four occasions, did you?

A: No.

Q: You never discussed it?

A: No.

Q: You never brought it up?

A: No, I didn't.

Q: You never said a thing, did you?

A: No.

§ 8.35 Handling of the Documents and Who Reads the Inconsistency

Generally the rules do not require the cross-examiner to hand the documents to the witness and point out the exact inconsistency. However it is often the better practice to permit the witness to have the inconsistency in front of him. This assures the jury that the cross-examiner is being fair with the witness. In addition, by requiring the witness to visually confront his own inconsistency (or, in the example of an audio, DVD, or videotape recording, to actually hear or see the inconsistency), the cross-examiner permits the witness to react visually to the contradiction in real time. Counsel might consider blowing up a key inconsistency or using an overhead to simultaneously show the inconsistency to both the jury and the witness.

There is no fixed rule defining when to give the witness the documents if the cross-examiner is not required to do so immediately. A major factor in making that determination hinges upon the decision of whether the cross-examiner or the witness will read and expose the inconsistency. There are valid tactical reasons for each of the two techniques. Many advocates are of the school of thought that lawyers should maintain control at all times and should read the inconsistency so that they can give it appropriate emphasis and tone of voice. This technique allows the cross-examiner to choose the tone, pace, and emphasis.

Using the alternative technique, the lawyer requires the witness to read aloud the inconsistent statement. This has the virtue of impeaching the witness out of his own mouth. For these lawyers the disadvantage of losing control over voice and emphasis is compensated for by the impact of the jury witnessing the witness impeach himself. The circumstances of the impeachment, the complexity and length of the impeaching statement, and witness demeanor are all factors to be weighed in deciding whether the witness or the lawyer should read the inconsistency.

A major consideration in determining whether the witness should read the inconsistency is whether it is worth the time to have the witness read it. A witness reading takes longer. However, even if the witness is to read the inconsistency, the lawyer should always phrase the question in a strictly leading manner so as not to permit the witness to run on:

Q: A few moments ago, you told us that you recalled my client performed "adequately" on the straight leg-lifting test?

A: Yes.

Q: But that is not what you said when asked that question in your deposition.

A: I believe it is.

Q: To be precise, at page 20, line 12 of the deposition, I asked you, "How did Julie do on the straight leg-lifting test?"

A: Yes, I recall the question.

Q: Please read to the jury your answer at page 20, line 14.

A: "Well, she had some problems, actually some significant difficulty with that test. She scored quite weak."

In this manner, as little control as possible is turned over to the witness. The only role assigned the witness is to read his own words at precisely the point indicated by the cross-examiner.

§ 8.36 Requiring the Witness to Read the Inconsistency and Repeating It

In deciding who should read the impeaching passage, it is possible for the lawyer to have her cake and eat it, too. Observe the following passage, which is an extended form of the previous example:

Q: A few moments ago, you told us that you recalled my client performed "adequately" on the straight leg-lifting test?

A: Yes.

Q: But that is not what you said when asked that question in your deposition.

A: I believe it is.

Q: To be precise, at page 20, line 12 of the deposition, I asked you, "How did Julie do on the straight leg-lifting test?"

A: Yes, I recall the question.

Q: Please read to the jury your answer at page 20, line 14.

A: "Well, she had some problems, actually some significant difficulty with that test. She scored quite weak."

Q: You answered the same question that you answered on direct examination differently at your deposition, didn't you?

A: Yes.

Q: You answered it at page 20, line 14, didn't you?

A: Yes.

Q: The question was put to you on line 12, wasn't it?

A: Yes.

(The lawyer then reads the question with appropriate emphasis along with the answers.)

As this example demonstrates, it is possible to force the witness to impeach himself and then for the cross-examiner to repeat the impeachment.

Chapter 9

CONTROLLING THE RUNAWAY WITNESS

§ 9.01 The Fear

The question calls for a yes or no answer. The witness is entitled to give either answer. Instead, the witness responds with a narrative. The answer may be long or short. The answer may contain words that amount to "yes" or "no," or the answer may entirely evade the question. In all of these events, we are confronted with a "runaway witness."

The chief problem of a "runaway witness" is his effect on our ability to paint the precise picture in each chapter goal. The more wordy the answer, the more that unnecessary information may distort or muddy the picture. The runaway witness is attempting to take over, if even for a moment, as the guide to the facts. We will ordinarily want to put a stop to this behavior as it is the cross-examiner who is best able to communicate the most important facts to the jury.

The runaway witness often attempts to insert facts, descriptions, and interpretations of his choosing. This type of witness is not merely distorting the picture being painted by the advocate; he is trying to paint a contrary picture of his own choosing.

The runaway witness ranks as one of the greatest fears of the cross-examiner. However, an unresponsive witness is also a great opportunity. An unresponsive or runaway witness often appears when least expected. That is part of the fear. The fear expands because the lawyer is battling to retain control of the cross-examination. It's hard to think of the opportunity as the unprepared cross-examiner struggles to regain control.

Expert witnesses and professional witnesses (those witnesses, expert or not, who have testified at least several times in court or in depositions) heighten the fear of the cross-examiner more often than other witnesses. This age of *Daubert*, where experts and other professionals who testify must do so for a living, poses greater challenges. These professional witnesses are purposefully unresponsive and have refined their skills to artfully dodge the cross-examiner's question.

§ 9.02 Definition of the Runaway Witness

A runaway witness is any witness who is unresponsive to the question put on cross-examination. This unresponsiveness may take many forms. The witness can answer the question on cross, but in such a way as to make the answer unintelligible. The witness can refuse to answer the question put on cross and answer a different question. The witness can answer generally the question on cross, and add many other answers to questions not asked. The witness can volunteer prejudicial information to dramatic effect. The witness (particularly the expert or professional witness) can object to the question posed and in some instances rule on his own objection, ignoring the question.

Example:

Q: Professor, you never measured the circumference of the aluminum alloy tube?

A: I didn't consider it to be relevant. In fact, I don't consider it relevant now. I am sure that it is not relevant. What I did was . . .

§ 9.03 Establishing Control

At times the witness becomes non-responsive so quickly that control was not lost — just never established.

Below is an excerpt from a divorce trial, with the defendant called for purposes of cross-examination:

Q: Raise your right hand, please. Do you swear that the testimony you are about to give this court on the matter pending before the court is the whole truth and nothing but the truth, so help you God?

A: I do. I would like to also make clear, Mr. Dodd, that I was not — it is not manic depressant. It is psychothymic, and there is a big difference.

Q: Thank you. Is that in response to the oath or the question I did not ask you?

Caught by surprise, cross-examining counsel offers up an objectionable question. Worse yet, the only three rules (see chapter 4, *The Only Three Rules of Cross-Examination*) are not followed, therefore providing opportunity for another non-responsive answer:

> **A:** The question you did not ask. I would just like to clear it up, that it was not manic depressant, it was psychothymic that I was dismissed for.
>
> **Q:** The fact is you are still on Lithium?
>
> **A:** Yes.

A quick return by the cross-examiner to the only three rules, and control is beginning to be established. Such witnesses give trial lawyers sleepless nights and make other careers appear safer and wiser. Fortunately, there are a number of tried and truthful techniques that can subdue and, ultimately, control non-responsive witnesses.

Many of these techniques focus on the opportunity presented by the unresponsive answer. All are designed to re-establish control and re-focus the fact finder on the lawyer to guide and teach the case.

As shown in the example above, cross-examining counsel, even when experienced and confident in her own abilities, can react poorly to the unresponsive witness. Whether it is an ongoing argument, a childish remark, or unprofessional conduct to the witness (all of which could be said about the example), counsel "looks bad" to the jury, judge, opponent, and — worst of all — the witness. A resort to one-upmanship invariably leads to the unresponsive witness battling the unwary lawyer. In these moments of near panic, more than ever, the advocate must resist these ego-related impulses and rely instead on the techniques of control. The cross-examiner may well "one-up" the witness, but that teaches nothing and distracts the fact finder from learning in real time the important facts that support the lawyer's theory of the case.

Empirical research has disclosed many techniques for stopping the runaway witness. With these techniques the cross-examiner will be able to stop or take advantage of even the most incorrigible witness's run-on answer. Many times, the most egregious run-on answer comes from the lips of the professional or expert witness. Some techniques work best against the professional or expert witness. Some techniques illustrated will be incorporated into the trial lawyer's regular repertoire of courtroom techniques. Others would be used best on isolated occasions. Still others are better performed in a deposition or other non-jury setting.

Some question why there are so many techniques to control the runaway witness. The answer is that there are different types of runaway witness in many settings. Different techniques are needed for different situations. But a more meaningful answer is found in the varied personalities and styles of cross-examiners throughout the world. Some techniques come naturally for certain lawyers and frustrate others. Some lawyers prefer to use certain techniques over others. Choice of technique is a question of style and personality, as well as circumstances. A wide selection of techniques is helpful for the variations of trial witnesses and situations. Not all will be presented here, but a solid variety shall be shared.

§ 9.04 These Techniques Create Drama so the Lawyer Does Not Have to Speak Loudly

None of the techniques for controlling a runaway witness require or encourage the use of loud, argumentative, or offensive language. Grandiose gestures are discouraged. These techniques are designed to eliminate the feeling that such conduct is necessary.

When we eliminate offensive, inappropriate conduct as a method of controlling the runaway witness, the judge seldom cuts off the cross-examination. Opposing counsel is presented with less opportunity to object. Most importantly, the jury does not observe rudeness, ugliness, and unprofessional conduct from us. Inappropriate or emotional responses are often understood or misunderstood by jurors as proof that the witness is damaging our case. The techniques outlined below rely more on the skill, psychology, and self-control of the lawyer to contain the runaway witness. These techniques verify for the jury that such tactics will not dissuade a lawyer from pursuing the truth of the matter.

Though some techniques allow for a voice different than the tone used in previous questions, each of the techniques can be delivered in any conversational voice. The techniques may be accompanied by a change of position in the courtroom or a gesture, but such physical components rely less on confrontational body language and movement, and more on the change of tone or posture itself. All these techniques can be accomplished with a slower rhythm in the questioning, though again, there may be occasions when we will change the rhythm as a method of enhancing a technique. The important thing to remember is this: The techniques so solidly confront the unresponsive witness that we need not raise our voice, use aggressive or confrontational gestures, or speak faster.

As the trial lawyer gains confidence in her ability to use these techniques to bring the witness back under control, the cross-examiner is likely to adopt a more assured and self-disciplined tone of questioning. Because the cross-examiner is functioning as a teacher rather than an advocate, jurors are more inclined to view the runaway witness as an impediment to the orderly process of trial. The witness's behavior is more akin to an interruption than an exploration of the facts. In teaching our theory of the case to the judge or jury, rudeness, loud voice, threatening movements, and rapid-fire questioning are all counterproductive to the cross-examiner. The techniques discussed within this chapter permit us to quietly and methodically rein in unresponsive runaway witnesses without distracting the fact finder from absorbing our theory of the case. As we eliminate the opponents' objections and the interruptions of judges because of the use of loud and ugly language and body language, there are fewer distractions during the cross-examination. Teaching is improved.

§ 9.05 Relationship of Techniques to the Only Three Rules of Cross-Examination

With one dramatic and seldom-used exception (Story Times Three — § 9.35) the foundation of each of the techniques to control the runaway witness is fully grounded in the three rules of cross-examination (see chapter 4, *The Only Three Rules of Cross-Examination*). We cannot deviate from: (1) leading questions; (2) one fact per question; or (3) a logical progression from the general to the specific ending in one goal. Lawyers who have studied and become comfortable with those building blocks of cross-examination understand how they are the major method of controlling the ability of a witness to evade the question. But as all lawyers still experience discomfort when a runaway witness begins to flee from a question, each lawyer must remind herself of the necessity of employing these three rules in those moments of discomfort. If the three rules of cross-examination are fundamental to the orderly presentation of evidence, they are even more important when the witness seeks to interrupt that orderly presentation. They are the basis for the more specialized techniques used to control the runaway witness.

§ 9.06 Behavior Is Molded by Consequences

Remember Psychology 101 from college? Remember the maze that the little white rats were placed in? The rats learned that if they performed well they were rewarded with a food pellet, but if they performed poorly they received no reward or worse: negative feedback. This was the concept of the Skinner box introduced by psychologist B.F. Skinner. The concept remains true for all thinking organisms.

The people who take the stand as witnesses are thinking organisms. They have learned through innumerable experiences that good behavior will be rewarded and bad behavior will be punished. Many do not understand what is expected of them as a witness. They need cues as to what is acceptable behavior in answering a leading question. Some witnesses know what is expected, but for their own purposes seek to ignore the rules of conduct implicit in a leading question format. For both types of witnesses the cross-examiner uses these techniques to reward good conduct by giving positive reinforcement to the witness who answers "yes" or "no." Likewise, if the runaway witness is engaging in conduct the lawyer wishes to discourage, the cross-examiner applies negative consequences to the runaway answer.

What is an acceptable means of rewarding the short, direct answer to a leading question? When the witness is responding with simple direct answers (preferably yes), rewards include a gentle encouraging nod of the head, a pleasant teaching voice and, most important, efficient movement to the next question, the next subject matter, and the next chapter. Do not create an impediment to the "yes" answer. If the witness has agreed with the fact suggested by the cross-examiner, the witness has earned a reward. A change to a harsher tone of voice, a negative gesture, or a follow-up question that suggests that "yes" is a foolish, illogical, or undesirable answer — all serve to sanction the witness for agreeing with the cross-examiner. The cross-examiner would not punish her coworkers, children, or pets for doing what she wanted them to do. For the same reason she cannot afford to punish a witness for answering "yes."

On the other hand, when a runaway witness uses unresponsive answers, volunteering information, or by a myriad of other evasions, sanctions must be applied. The techniques discussed in this chapter apply those sanctions. Some sanctions are severe by courtroom standards. Some are more gentle and encouraging. With this said, let there be no misunderstanding: They are all negative stimuli. The techniques for controlling the runaway witness all employ negative feedback to counter unwanted behavior.

§ 9.07 Trials Provide a Difficult Environment in Which to Work

Every trial lawyer knows that good evidence presentations — particularly on cross-examination — are built methodically. Trial lawyers also know that a well-planned cross-examination chapter can get off track very quickly. This is a demonstration of Murphy's asymmetrical principle:

Things go right gradually, but they go wrong all at once.

Such is the nature of cross-examining hostile witnesses. A witness who runs away can undermine a lawyer's methodical preparation, careful construction of individual questions, and thoughtful implementation of questions carefully constructed into chapters. Understanding this as the environment in which we toil daily, the need for techniques that are judicially acceptable, non-objectionable, simple to apply, and effective cannot be overstated.

§ 9.08 Techniques That Don't Work

[1] "Just Answer 'Yes' or 'No'"

Television, movies, and, unfortunately, some trial-skill programs in law school have encouraged trial lawyers to fall back on the command, "Just answer my question 'yes' or 'no,'" as a method of controlling the runaway witness. This is *not* a valid controlling technique. First, most judges will not permit the lawyer to do that. They will inform the witness that they may explain their answer, even at length, if necessary.

More importantly, when a lawyer resorts to blunt oratory, it signals to the jury that the cross-examiner is not playing fair. The lack of choice given the witness suggests to the jury that the lawyer is trying to "trick" the witness. Non-lawyers resent this heavy-handed attempt to straitjacket the witness. To them it appears that the lawyer is attempting to "put words in the witness's mouth." A lawyer resorting to this method lowers both her personal credibility and the credibility of the leading question as an appropriate teaching device.

Inevitably the opposing attorney objects to the admonition that the witness "just answer 'yes' or 'no.'" The objection creates an unwanted break in the leading question and short answer technique. There is a break in the teaching of the cross-examiner's theory of the case. The objection is a distraction. More often than not, when there is an objection under these circumstances, the cross-examiner reacts emotionally and overstates her position rather than responding calmly to the objection. This often distracts the jury from the importance of the question.

Expert witnesses have often been trained to respond to the lawyer directing them to "just answer yes or no" whether or not the opposing lawyer objects. Their response is along these lines: "I cannot adequately explain (teach) to the judge or the jury the full answer to your question with just a 'yes or no.'" Whether this is true, the response aggravates the situation. Again, the net result is that the cross-examiner appears to be playing games.

Credibility is the calling card of the successful trial lawyer. When the trial lawyer loses her credibility, the case is lost. Credibility is severely damaged when the cross-examiner utters the words, "just answer my question with a 'yes or no.'" Don't do it.

[2] Asking the Judge for Help

[a] Court-Offered Help

In frustration, some cross-examiners will ask the judge to order the witness to "just answer 'yes' or 'no.'" Asking the judge to help in this way is an impractical way to control a runaway witness. Few judges are predisposed to favor trial lawyers over witnesses. The judge figures, correctly, that since the lawyer was the one who lost control, the lawyer should be the one to suffer the consequences. If the cross-examiner asks for help, the judge is likely to say something to make a bad situation worse. At best the cross-examiner will get, "I will permit the witness to give a full and complete explanation if the witness thinks that explanation is necessary for a complete answer." Who needs that help?

The judge, having been *invited* by the cross-examiner to participate, will often add his own commentary: "You want this court to direct the witness to answer that question? I have been on the bench 40 years and I cannot understand your question!" or "I think the witness is answering your question." Now the cross-examiner has a runaway witness and a runaway judge.

Such responses from the bench should not surprise trial lawyers. The purpose of the judge is not to assist the cross-examiner. The judge's refusal to help sends a message to the witness, opposing attorney, and jury. It is not a good message for the cross-examiner. The witness sees and hears the cross-examiner's frustration. In the event the bench does not sanction the witness, the witness is encouraged to do more of the same offending conduct.

The opposing lawyer now knows that the cross-examiner is not in control of the courtroom. This produces the confidence to make more objections, particularly speaking objections. Alternatively, opposing counsel may feign disinterest in the cross-examination. This apparent lack of interest signals the jury and the court that the cross-examination has degenerated into a personal battle of wills having little to do with the search for truth. This in turn encourages judges to issue their favorite ruling: "Move it along."

During the process, the jury observes the change of dynamics from trial lawyer in control and directing the examination to witness controlling the trial lawyer. The jury notices that now the judge and opposing counsel are active participants. The cross-examiner's voice is no longer the voice of control. The scene is moving from clarity to chaos. The purpose of the cross-examination is to impact the opposing theories of the case, either to promote the cross-examiner's theory of the case or to harm the opposing attorney's theory. None of that is being accomplished now because there is confusion. This is caused *not by the unresponsive witness*, but by the cross-examining lawyer who is fumbling in dealing with that witness. It is therefore essential that the cross-examiner undertake to control the witnesses on cross-examination. Do not invite the help of judges.

Of course, if the court offers help, the lawyer should accept it. Should the court spontaneously instruct the witness to answer, the cross-examiner should accept the power of the bench. When the court voluntarily gets involved in the effort to control the runaway witness, the witness has hurt his credibility, which tells the jury that this lawyer is being fair in her questioning. Permit the court to volunteer; do not seek its assistance. The best way to accept the help of the power of the bench is to remain silent. Do not restate the question unless prompted by the judge to do so, or the witness must admit that he does not know the question by asking for the question again. If the witness has to admit that he does not know the question, the witness admits to all (judge, jury, opposing counsel, and to the cross-examiner) that the witness was not listening to the question and was going to answer randomly.

On the other hand, there are those witnesses who simply are unwilling to answer in a straightforward fashion. There are judges who are skilled at spotting the evasive efforts of such witnesses and who will not tolerate this misconduct. Such judges often lose patience and take it upon themselves to instruct the witness to "just answer yes or no." Jurors will regard such an instruction from the court as a sign that the witness's conduct is inappropriate. To the court, such a judicial instruction means that the witness has lost credibility. Such an instruction from a judge is a most powerful sanction. The witness will likely now change his behavior and answer questions more directly.

[b] "The Deal"

The Deal originates when the cross-examiner, early in the examination, suggests to the witness that the cross-examiner will ask fair questions that need only a "yes" or "no" answer. In exchange for this type of questioning the cross-examiner advises the witness that yes or no answers will prove sufficient. "I am going to ask you a series of questions, each of which can be answered with a yes or no answer. If I do that, will you please provide me with a yes or no answer?"

The Deal is not a recommended method of controlling the witness. It is offered up by a lawyer who fears that somewhere down the road she will lose control of the witness. It is an attempt to control the runaway witness before the witness has run. The Deal sends all the wrong messages to the fact finders in the trial and the opponent, who is made aware that the lawyer believes she will have trouble with the examination. Most importantly, the signal is sent to the witness that the lawyer fears this kind of conduct. If the witness is not friendly to the cross-examiner's cause, wouldn't the witness cause as much difficulty as possible by using this request against the lawyer?

When analyzed, this "deal" is nothing more than a sophisticated method of saying: "Just answer my questions 'yes' or 'no.'" Inexplicitly, the "deal" is most often heard when cross-examiner is dealing with more difficult witnesses. It is heard when a cross-examiner is beginning to question a child witness or opposing expert or professional witness.

The Deal signals to the witness that the lawyer hopes to unduly confine the answers. It also puts the judge on notice that the lawyer is attempting to cut off any explanation. Worse, it tells the jury that the lawyer is attempting to "put words in the witness's mouth." *Worst of all*, the offer of the Deal often generates an immediate objection, followed by a rebuke from the court on the witness's right to answer fully and fairly. As a result, the cross-examination begins at the worst possible credibility level. In an attempt to avoid the witness digging a hole for the cross-examiner, she has dug the hole herself. The advocate has denied her own credibility before the witness ever answered a question. The Deal will not work; do not propose it.

§ 9.09 A General Technique That Assists All Other Techniques: Keep Eye Contact

When cross-examining a difficult witness, always maintain eye contact. Avoiding eye contact is interpreted as weakness. Life experiences verify this both in and out of the courtroom. People who will not make eye contact are uncomfortable and less than forthright. People who will not make eye contact are often afraid. If we suspect the witness will become non-responsive or runaway in their answers, we must keep our eyes fixed on the witness when asking questions and when receiving answers. By directing our full attention to the witness's eyes, we serve non-verbal notice that we will not put up with any nonsense or permit deviation from the question-and-answer approach we have been following. Control the runaway witness's eyes until the witness is off the stand.

Maintaining eye contact with the witness is not an angry stare-down by the cross-examiner. Fixed eye contact on the witness does not have to be unpleasant. The eye contact is telling the witness that we are completely focused and will not be deterred from getting answers to tough but fair questions.

When dealing with expert witnesses, eye contact is even more essential than with lay witnesses. Expert or professional witnesses look for any opening to advance the opposing lawyer's theory of the case. Keeping eye contact deters this behavior by giving the expert witness less psychological room to evade or embellish. Furthermore, there is a useful byproduct of this eye contact. If the expert witness is looking back into the eyes of the cross-examiner, the expert or professional witness is not looking into the eyes of the jurors as such witnesses are so often trained to do.

Of course, we must sometimes divert our eyes from the witness to look at notes and observe exhibits, charts, overheads, or other demonstrative aids. There techniques enable us to divert our attention while maintaining psychological control of the witness. We may take our eyes off the witness after the answer and before the next question, or in limited circumstances even while the next question is being asked. In other words, we may put a question to the witness, receive an answer to that question, and then divert attention to a new task such as putting up an exhibit or consulting notes. Because there is no question pending, there is no permission for the witness to speak. Eye contact should be maintained from the conclusion of the cross-examiner's question through the entire answer of the witness. When there is an interruption of eye contact between questions, cross-examiner should re-establish eye contact before posing the next question.

§ 9.10 Body Movement and Active Listening

With the runaway witness, we must not only maintain eye contact; we must control our body movement during the cross-examination. A question has been asked; the witness has hesitated and is mentally debating whether to give the answer that will undoubtedly hurt the witness or to give a longer, less responsive answer. At that point, all body motion by the examiner must stop. Constant eye contact and no movement is necessary to convince the witness that the only acceptable answer is a simple "yes," and that the cross-examiner is coiled to strike at the unresponsive answer.

It is important to listen to the answer. The lawyer is experiencing many distractions: "loading" the next question, judging the reaction of judge and jury to the question, awaiting the answer, and hoping the opponent does not object. Sometimes the cross-examiner has the "aid" of an activist client, co-counsel, or an investigator at counsel table who wishes to offer suggestions. These suggestions may be worthwhile, but the time to consult is between questions, not when an answer is pending. When the witness has a question pending, has hesitated in answering or has answered but appears to be mentally debating whether to add more, all distractions must be avoided so that the cross-examiner may actively listen to the answer and observe the witness. We are not just using our ears, but our eyes and all other senses and feelings. Jurors and judges focus on the demeanor of the witness, the character of the witness, and the balance of power of the courtroom. Those attentive fact finders often get the real truth about the witness by observing any hesitations that precede or follow the initial answer. We have to be free to observe that conduct as well. We do this best by focusing completely and shutting out other distractions and movement until the pending question is answered.

§ 9.11 Where and When to Use These Techniques

Controlling the runaway witness begins before trial. We should not wait until the jury is empanelled to start conditioning the witness to give "yes" or "no" answers. Recall that behavior is molded by consequences. The witness can and should be conditioned during the pre-trial matters to give responsive answers. In order to encourage short answers and discourage runaway answers, we should begin to exercise control over the witness at all pre-trial opportunities, in order to lessen the need to train the witness in real time before the jury.

The more we believe someone will become a runaway witness, the more control we need to employ in any pre-trial confrontation. The more we have properly trained the witness through pre-trial, question-and-answer sessions, the less the witness is likely to fight the trial lawyer in front of the jury. A witness who has learned to answer responsively has also learned that the responsive answer causes the lawyer to move on. The solemnity of trial sometimes serves to discourage narrative answers. In trial, most witnesses are more nervous. The stress of the trial environment, coupled with the previous education of what works to get through the cross-examination experience, encourages the witness to provide short answers. Certainly this is less exciting for the trial lawyer, but that is a wonderful thing in trial. There will always be too much excitement in the middle of a trial for the cross-examiner.

§ 9.12 Depositions and Other Pre-trial Opportunities

In civil trial work, we have the opportunity at temporary order hearings, motions hearings and, most importantly, depositions and less formal interviews to "teach" witnesses by the use of controlling techniques that any answer other than "yes" will result in unpleasantness for the witness. Each witness is different and calls for the use of different techniques. For example, at a deposition, find a number of techniques that successfully control the witness. Reinforce them several times so that when that technique is used at trial, the witness is already conditioned to respond. If we have conditioned and controlled the witness prior to the jury being empanelled, then control in front of the jury is much easier to maintain.

§ 9.13 Pre-trial Motion in Limine

There are witnesses (particularly expert and professional witnesses) who become so schooled in trial work that every answer is unresponsive. Every unresponsive answer is intentional and malicious. The ability to evade and insert harmful material is one reason opposing counsel has hired these witnesses.

After confronting this type of witness at a deposition (and preferably a videotaped deposition), we may file a pre-trial motion in limine requesting the court to rule prior to trial that the witness shall respond to questions on cross-examination and not volunteer non-responsive information. This motion is best made using excerpts from transcripts and videotaped depositions to illustrate the misconduct.

Even when trial counsel spends a great deal of time illustrating examples, most trial courts will rule that the motion will be "taken under consideration" or "reserved" until trial.

What then is the purpose of spending so much time preparing the motion? Because the judge has been forewarned. When the witness becomes repeatedly unresponsive, the court having been forewarned with examples of what has happened at deposition, will turn on opposing counsel and direct him to control the witness. Often this is the situation in which a judge may order a witness to confine their answers to the question asked. The time spent on the motion is well worthwhile.

§ 9.14 Non-Jury Settings

The right to discovery through depositions translates into excellent opportunities to condition witnesses to answer responsively. In criminal work, the right to depositions is limited. With rare exceptions, depositions in criminal cases are not permitted. As a result, in criminal work there is far less opportunity to confront the witnesses prior to trial. There are still opportunities, however, at motion hearings and preliminary hearings. Regardless of the venue, any question-and-answer scenario provides an opportunity to condition the witness through the use of techniques to control the runaway unresponsive answer.

Do not fear that pre-trial exposure of the witness to the techniques of control will allow the witness to "figure out" the techniques and avoid them at trial. None of the techniques involve trickery, sleight of hand, or unfair advantage. They are valid methods of preventing unresponsive answers. That is precisely why the techniques are so useful in front of a jury. The fact finder sees that the cross-examiner is only seeking to get at the truth in posing a series of questions that call for answers the witness is dodging.

§ 9.15 Opportunities Created for the Cross-Examiner from Unresponsive Answers

Trial lawyers fear unresponsive answers so deeply that they can miss substantial opportunities when an unresponsive answer is given. When the advocate is not actively listening to the answer, particularly when the answer is unresponsive, she misses opportunities. The reason for not listening is that the lawyer can be distracted by her fear of the unresponsive answer. Many times the unresponsive answer will provide two different types of opportunities for the cross-examiner.

The first type of opportunity enables the application of each of the techniques discussed below. That opportunity is to show to the fact finder, be it a judge or jury, that the witness is not being responsive. This elusive answering speaks to the character of the witness, as well as the interest, motive, and bias of the witness. By highlighting the elusive answer, the cross-examiner may undermine the witness's credibility.

The second opportunity offered by the unresponsive answer happens when the witness attempts to avoid assisting the cross-examiner's theory of the case. The witness will refuse to use certain words that are fair in describing what has happened. The witness will refuse to acknowledge certain tough, but fair questions. When a witness does this, he often makes a poor choice of words to explain his position. Remember, the witness is now off the script. No one does that well — not trial lawyers, and certainly not witnesses.

Example:

Q: You heard the cars *smash* together?

(The trial lawyer has chosen a vivid but fair word to describe the collision.)

A: I don't know what I heard. I heard the sound of metal striking metal and then a thud.

The cross-examiner chose the word "smash" to describe the severity of the collision. In an effort to avoid that descriptive word, the witness has chosen even more dramatic language: "metal striking metal" and "thud." If the trial lawyer is listening these new descriptive words can be used against the witness.

All of the techniques highlight the first opportunity that undermines the credibility of the witness. Some of the techniques go on the offensive and highlight the additional witness language. Look for the new opportunities when the witness adds to the answer. Do this by listening.

§ 9.16 Ask, Repeat, Repeat

The lawyer has asked a fair, clear question, in its simplest form, using commonly understood words. The answer can only be "yes." In order to avoid giving the cross-examiner an answer, the witness has sidestepped with a non-answer.

Without taking our eyes from the witness, we simply ask the question again, in exactly the same words and tone of voice and articulating each word. The pace of the question is slightly slower. If the witness is foolish as to again ignore the obvious "yes," we may slowly lean slightly forward without taking our eyes off the witness. The next step is to repeat the identical brief, simply constructed question, but even more slowly.

The successively slower repetition of the *identical words and tone* emphasizes to the witness, the court and — most importantly — the jury that the witness is refusing to answer a short, straightforward, easily answered question. The forward body motion emphasizes that all are waiting for a response. Even the most evasive witness has great difficulty in evading the third posing of the question.

Some lawyers question whether a judge would permit them to ask the same question three times. In fact, this is a technique that maximizes the likelihood that the judge will voluntarily intervene and insist that the witness actually answer the question, in order to "move it along." Furthermore, it is not redundant to ask the same question, if that question has not been answered.

Q: The car was blue? (In a situation where the witness knows the car was blue).

A: The car was traveling down the street, it started to go through the red light, I didn't even see brake lights . . . (babble, babble, babble) . . . and finally it did turn the corner and I still hadn't seen the brake lights.

Q: (Slower) The car was blue?

A: Well, it was going so fast when it went through the red light.

Q: (Slower still) The car was blue?

A: Yes, it was blue.

Q: The car was going south?

This technique is particularly effective with children and expert or professional witnesses. In any case, children are intimately familiar with having a question or a command directed a second time. This is particularly true when the second command is said slower — not louder.

The effect on an expert is just the opposite. He is stunned that anyone would repeat a question. He is an expert witness because he is at the top of his profession. How often is a surgeon asked the same question? How often is a tenured professor in chemistry asked the same question? In each instance, whether child or expert, the desired response is obtained.

It is worth a reminder: There was an offending behavior (an evasive answer) followed by a sanction (a repeat of the question), resulting in an appropriate behavior (a short responsive answer) followed by reinforcing positive stimuli (next question).

§ 9.17 Reversal, or Ask, Repeat, Reverse

This technique of ask, repeat, reverse is a variant of the first technique. We ask the question. We then ask the identical question, but slightly slower and leaning forward. This gives the witness two opportunities to tell the truth before we reverse the question in the third asking.

For example, in a divorce case it is necessary to establish that the defendant-husband signed financial statements indicating a net worth of several hundred thousand dollars. The lawyer knows from prior depositions and interrogatories that the husband now contends that his net worth is really zero. He contends that the financial statements were exaggerated to obtain a bank loan. Undoubtedly, the defendant/witness has been warned by his lawyer that this subject will definitely come up at trial:

> **Q:** Mr. Allen, you signed Plaintiff's Exhibit 10, your financial statement, as of August 1, 2008?
>
> **A:** You have shown me so many documents, I am not sure. I know that I signed some financial statements and others I didn't sign. I was trying to borrow money to keep my family afloat for so long, I just wasn't sure what I was signing many times. They really don't mean anything.
>
> **Q:** Mr. Allen, you signed Plaintiff's Exhibit 10, your financial statement, as of August 1, 2008?
>
> **A:** She knew why I wrote that. Who signed it is beside the point.
>
> **Q:** Mr. Allen, you did <u>not</u> sign Plaintiff's Exhibit 10?
>
> **A:** (Mumble, mumble, mumble) I didn't say that. I signed it.

The third asking could also be phrased: "Mr. Allen, you did *not* sign Plaintiff's in Exhibit 10, your financial statement, as of August 1, 2008?"

It is a question of style and personality as to whether to truncate the reverse question or to emphasize the word "not" and restate the entire question on the reverse.

The technique of ask, repeat, reverse is one of the most effective methods of controlling an expert witness. This is particularly true when the expert has reports, operative notes, letters, or any other type of documents. Because the document or fact, whatever it may be, will not go away, this technique is particularly effective.

§ 9.18 An Obvious and Indisputable Truth

The technique of ask, repeat, reverse is best used when the witness will not confirm even the most obvious and indisputable truth. When used early in the cross-examination during confrontations with the witness over simple questions, it dramatically sets the scene for repeating the technique.

Ask, repeat, reverse is often used in establishing foundational answers that will be used on numerous occasions during the remaining cross-examination. A witness who has experience testifying recognizes the sound of a foundational question and knows he faces an upcoming potential problem. The witness is then more likely to resist the foundation. An example from a criminal case:

Q: Detective Brown, you signed the report of July 1, 2007?

An experienced criminal detective (a professional witness) hearing this question realizes that it is prefatory to an attempt to impeach the witness. In fact, experienced detectives will correctly predict that the cross-examiner intends to point out something that is "missing" from the report.

A: I sign many reports. I don't know if I signed this report. In fact, this report was done very hurriedly. You would have to understand that we are under such tremendous strain because of crime in the street and in America today, and the paperwork comes last.

First note that the question has not been answered. Instead, the witness has injected into the trial for the jury's benefit that (1) he is overworked; (2) that he must combat crime every day; (3) that he fears crime in the street, as do the members of the jury; and (4) that paperwork is not fun. No one would disagree with that.

All of these devices or dodges are offered in the hope that the cross-examiner will take the bait and never establish the foundation question. In the alternative, it invites the cross-examiner to abandon a slow meticulous foundation and jump ahead with the witness. (If this is done, the witness will best the cross-examiner later because no effective foundation has been set.)

The next question (identical to the first):

Q: Detective Brown, you signed the report of July 1, 2007?

A: Can I see the report? As I said, I have been very busy. I am also recovering from a hospitalization caused by another defendant on crack cocaine who attacked me while I was trying to make an arrest. It is very hard to keep up with all of the paperwork.

Again the officer attempts to steer the cross-examiner away from the foundation question and inject emotional or sympathetic issues into the trial.

Q: Detective Brown, you did *not* sign the report of July 1, 2007?

A: I *signed* the report. Yes, I signed it. (Customarily this last admission is given with some exasperation. The exasperation stems from the realization that all efforts to steer the cross-examiner away from the focus of this question have failed.)

§ 9.19 Medical Malpractice Usage

In a medical malpractice case, the defense lawyer for the doctor has told the doctor that much of the case comes down to the defendant's failure to include in his operative notes and his discharge summary reference to certain critical diagnostic procedures.

The defendant doctor knows that the expert witness for the plaintiff will specifically attack and criticize the defendant as falling below the standard of responsible care on the basis that those critical procedures did not occur because they were not referenced in the doctor's operative notes and discharge notes. It is fair to predict that the verdict hangs on the jury's belief in the accuracy of these notes:

Q: Dr. Torch, you dictated operative notes of June 24, 2007?

A: I am in the business of taking care of sick people. I am required to make certain notes about what I have done. I dictate them quickly after surgery. They are transcribed several days later. By the way, the hospital is terrible with this, and it sometimes takes three or four weeks to have my notes returned to me. Sometimes I sign them, sometimes I initial them, and sometimes I review them, but don't sign them. In comparison with all my other important duties I just don't know. (By not taking the bait to other areas, the trial lawyer preserves this question and now highlights it for the jury.)

Q: You dictated operative notes of June 24, 2007?

A: As I said . . . (babble)

Q: You did not dictate those notes, Doctor?

A: No, no, I didn't say that. I just said that, well, I don't know. Do you have my notes there? Do I have my notes here? Oh, I see my notes. No, I didn't say that I didn't dictate it.

Q: In fact, Dr. Torch, you did dictate operative notes of June 24, 2007?

A: Yes, of course, I dictated them.

§ 9.20 Full Formal Name

A previously compliant witness has for the first time run away with an answer. This witness has thus far appeared to be trying to answer fairly. Jurors can sense the witness's apparent candor, so the lawyer has to rein in the witness without provoking the jury's hostility. Anything that changes the customary tone of questioning serves as a mild rebuke to the witness. We need not use a harsh tone or angry gesture to remind a witness of his obligation to answer the question. The use of the witness's full formal name represents a change in the style of the questioning and thereby provides a sanction:

Q: You failed to review the x-ray of her neck?

A: Well, any person this old, with bones so soft, x-rays can be difficult to interpret.

Q: Doctor Franklin Jeremiah Toth, you failed to review the x-ray of her neck?

A: Correct.

This technique depends on a childhood reflex. When someone calls out a full name in a public place — whether an airport, theater, or ballpark — that person does not just look up; he snaps to attention. The witness's eyes snap to connect with the cross-examiner's. Years of human experience have taught that when authority figures use full names to address someone, the person is in trouble. The ingrained drive to avoid trouble with authority figures will ordinarily make the non-malicious runaway witness resume safe "yes" and "no" answers. In reality, the full formal name makes the witness focus. That is all that is necessary with this type of witness.

§ 9.21 Embarrassment or Humiliation

[1] Use of Formal Names

[a] Application to Expert Witnesses

Always keep in mind that no witness wants to be embarrassed or humiliated. By calling the witness by his or her formal name and title, if there is a title (such as Doctor, Professor, Captain, etc.), the witness senses that humiliation is not far away.

There is no down-side risk with this technique. There is no objection possible. There is no connotation or suggestion that the cross-examiner is in any way denigrating the witness. The cross-examiner is merely making the question more formal. That added formality subtly changes the tone in the courtroom. The witness can be expected to be aware of that change of tone and desire that the tone return to a more conversational mode. The cross-examiner should meet the short and honest answer of the witness with a return to the less formal tone of questioning so that the witness has fully experienced both the negative sanction and the positive reward.

Experts are accustomed to being called by their titles, e.g. Doctor, Professor, etc., but they are unaccustomed to hearing their entire name with their title attached. Example: Evelyn P. Brown, III, M.D. FACS, you saw the blue car? Experts are very much like trial lawyers. Neither wants to be embarrassed.

[b] Child Witness

Since this technique is based on responses learned in childhood, it is extremely useful in stopping a child witness. The full formal name need not be spoken harshly or in an authoritative tone. In fact, it is better used in a quiet but firm voice.

§ 9.22 "Sir" or "Ma'am"

[1] Use

[a] Younger Witnesses

Once the formal name has been used, it is seldom necessary to use it again, even if the examination is a quite lengthy one. Simply starting the question with "sir" or "ma'am," as the case may be, will immediately bring back in line the unresponsive but non-malicious witness. Just as there is no down side risk for using the "full formal name" technique, there is no down-side risk of objection or proper interruption to this technique. What would the objection be? "Objection, the cross-examiner is being polite." Use the "sir" or ma'am" at the beginning of the question for maximum effect.

This is also a very effective technique when dealing with young people (not children), who are not used to being addressed as "sir" or "ma'am." By promoting them to the more formal and adult status of "sir" or "ma'am," we remind them of the seriousness of the task at hand; they will then resort to more serious (i.e., more responsive) answers.

[b] Evolution of Politeness

It is an interesting geographic phenomenon that in the South where "sir" and "ma'am" are customarily and commonly used, even when addressing young people, that a frequently used "sir" or "ma'am" still works and highlights the need to respond directly to the question in the courtroom. In other sections of the country where "sir" and "ma'am" are not used as commonly the effect is multiplied. The world has not gotten more polite. Consequently, the technique works better and better.

§ 9.23 Shorten the Question

Even when we are properly implementing the three rules of cross-examination (see chapter 4, *The Only Three Rules of Cross-Examination*), questions can be shortened to highlight the malicious, non-responsive nature of the witness. We are using a leading question. We only have one fact in the question and the question is in logical order. Nonetheless, the witness refuses to responsively answer the question. In this circumstance, continue to eliminate words from the question until the witness is left with only the key word of the question.

Example:

Q: The car was blue?

A: The sun was in my eyes . . . I really wasn't paying that much attention. I was looking for my ride. . .

Q: Car . . . blue?

A: As I said, I was distracted. I wasn't paying as close attention as you might think. I am just not really sure.

Q: Blue?

A: Blue . . . yes, blue.

This technique isolates the essence of the question. It provides a substantial negative consequence to the unresponsive demeanor of the witness. It should be reserved for those witnesses who maliciously refuse to answer obvious questions. This technique highlights for the judge and jury that the witness is intentionally being obstructive. There is no need to use a loud or harsh voice. The technique is so powerful a soft tone produces a bountiful effect. In fact, this is one of those techniques harmed by use of a loud or harsh tone of voice. The power of the technique lies in the simplicity of the question. Any addition to the technique tends to make the questioning sound degrading.

§ 9.24 Ethical Note for Use of Techniques That Interrupt

It would be unethical for the cross-examiner to interrupt the answer of a witness. This consideration is over and above the evidentiary objection most likely to be heard. However, if the interruption is followed by the identical previously asked question, the ethical objection is eliminated. A different question is not asked. The same question is asked.

§ 9.25 Polite Interruption

The question is put to the witness. The witness becomes unresponsive. The witness's unresponsive answer would lead to a mistrial.

While ordinarily the lawyer should never verbally interrupt a witness, this is the exception to the rule. The advocate must weigh the damage of a possible mistrial against an objection by the opponent.

Once the cross-examiner has decided that a polite interruption is required, the interruption must be made quickly and before the harm that would result in a mistrial can be stated by the witness. We then immediately address the court (preferably before the objection is even made) and ask to approach the bench with opposing counsel to explain the reason for the interruption.

Example:

Witness: . . . And then after the fall, the adjuster from the . . .

Cross-Examiner: I'm sorry. You must not have understood my question. Your Honor, may we approach the bench with opposing counsel to discuss a matter immediately?

Opposing Counsel: Objection. He is interrupting the witness.

Court: Approach the bench.

Note that the cross-examiner appears to put the onus on herself as she indicates there is a problem with her question. Normally the problem is not with the question, but with the unresponsive answer. Being polite is more important than being right in this instance.

§ 9.26 Objection: Non-Responsive Answer

The cross-examining lawyer has only one legal objection that can be used as a technique to control the runaway witness. The objection is stated as follows: "Objection, non-responsive answer." The objection that the witness is being non-responsive in his answer calls upon the court to enforce the rules of witness examination.

It is, in a sense, inviting the court to assist in controlling the witness. Therefore, the cross-examiner should use this objection only when many other techniques have been used but have not succeeded in controlling the witness.

It is particularly helpful to use this objection when the court has given non-verbal indications of impatience with a non-responsive witness. The cross-examiner then takes the non-verbal cue and gives the court an opportunity to volunteer to control the witness. The more malicious the rambling answer is, the more likely the trial court will accept the invitation to help control, and the more likely that that intervention will be harsh and critical of the witness's behavior.

There are two substantial risks to this technique. First, once invited to participate in the cross-examination, the court may continue to intrude in the cross-examination. This is never good. Too often the judge may see this objection as an invitation to referee the cross-examination on a question-by-question basis. The risk is that all continuity will be lost. This risk is substantial and must be weighed carefully by the cross-examiner when considering this technique.

The second down-side risk that the trial lawyer must weigh before using this technique is the likely response by the court. For this technique to work, the judge: (a) must be listening; (b) must know the rule of evidence; (c) must know that the objection belongs to the cross-examiner; and, (d) must be willing to enforce the rule. Weigh these factors carefully.

When the technique is properly deployed and the objection sustained, the result is dramatic and lasting:

Cross-Examiner: Objection, non-responsive answer.

Court: Sustained.

Cross-Examiner: I ask that the non-responsive answer be stricken from the record.

Court:	The answer will be stricken.
Cross-Examiner:	I ask that the jury be admonished to disregard the answer.
Court:	Jury is instructed to disregard the last answer.

In this interchange, the court has delivered a sharp rebuke to the witness. Even the strongest expert witness will wish to avoid a repeat of this scenario. Shorter, more honest answers will follow.

§ 9.27 The Court Reporter

While the judge is certainly the highest-ranking member of the courtroom staff, the jury views all court personnel as holding power. All members of the judge's staff are seen as "official" and treated by the jury with respect. Most importantly, the courtroom staff is seen as neutral. It is significant when it is perceived by the jury that they are using their power to aid one side or the other.

The technique: Having asked the witness a leading question and having received a rambling monologue, the lawyer may turn to the court reporter and ask, "Please may I have my question read back to the witness?" All action in the courtroom will halt as the reporter slowly articulates each word of the stenographic record.

Having the question repeated word for word by a court official and read back with great clarity intimidates the runaway witness and immediately brings a short, responsive answer.

If the lawyer has the misfortune to be working in a system in which tape recorders have replaced court reporters, some forewarning to the court clerk is required.

Judges also view this technique as employing official powers of the court. The judge believes the court reporter is an extension of the court. When using the court reporter technique, the judge seems to listen more intently to the read-back and often visually, if not verbally, directs the witness to answer the question as read back. This is a very subtle way of having the judge volunteer to get involved by directing the witness to answer the question.

§ 9.28 Use at Depositions

The use of this technique at deposition has had a remarkable and dramatic effect on expert witnesses who are always prepared to give long, unresponsive answers to questions at the deposition. When the deposition is videotaped and the video camera continues to record while the court reporter reads back the question, the effect on the witness is profound. Witnesses not only respond to the question from the court reporter, but also respond better to questions that follow that recitation by the court reporter.

§ 9.29 Use of a Blackboard

Quite often the courtroom is equipped with a blackboard, whiteboard, or other large writing surface. The blackboard can serve in much the same way as having the court reporter read the question back. If a witness is consistently unresponsive, and the question is short and to the point (see chapter 4, *The Only Three Rules of Cross-Examination*), the cross-examiner may simply write the question on the board during or after hearing the unresponsive answer. When faced with the written question, the witness often will stop the unresponsive answer. Even if the witness does not stop the unresponsive answer, he will recognize that he must eventually respond to the question.

If the cross-examiner is fortunate, the witness will see the question being written and respond to it. The lawyer can then highlight the answer by asking the witness if he is responding to the question she has written on the board. Inevitably the answer is "yes."

If the cross-examiner is fortunate, the witness will ignore the question written on the board and finish his answer. This permits the questioner, while pointing at the words on the blackboard, to repeat the question. The graphic simplicity of the question on the blackboard requires the witness to provide a short, plain answer. Furthermore, because it is time-consuming, the judge will often follow up the blackboard's use with a request that everyone "move it along." The witness gets the point of this indirect scolding, as does the jury.

§ 9.30 The Long-Term Effect of Using the Blackboard Technique

Once the blackboard technique has been used, the witness is sensitive to its reuse. If the trial lawyer desires to signal to the witness that the blackboard technique will be used again, we need only pick up the chalk and take one or two steps in the direction of the blackboard. The witness will stop the unresponsive answer he is currently voicing. The mere threat that the lawyer will return to the blackboard technique is enough to stop the witness.

§ 9.31 Use of a Poster

If a blackboard is effective, the poster is not only effective but also intimidating to the witness and opponent. The poster further demonstrates to the jury and the judge the cross-examiner's thorough preparation for the trial.

We all know the heart of our cross-examination. We are often quite able to predict at which point in cross-examinations certain witnesses will rebel or try to evade the critical questions. This is particularly true when dealing with expert witnesses. If the big question can be predicted, and the non-responsive answer is foreshadowed through discovery or pre-trial hearings, then an appropriate poster can be developed before trial. If there is no discovery, careful listening to direct examination questions can develop the material for the poster. The poster can be drawn during a recess. Then, when the critical question provokes the predicted evasion, cross-examining counsel can prop the poster on the desk. The critical leading question is already written on the poster in the identical language. This becomes a written form of the repeat technique.

An example comes from a typical personal injury case. The cross-examining attorney has questioned this witness at deposition. The witness has attempted not to answer a critical question at the deposition, but finally — and after lengthy questioning — has admitted that she suffered from lower back pain before the date of the collision. That pain was caused by an unrelated, on-the-job, lifting injury:

Q: You had injured your back four years before this collision?

A: My back really hurts now. It has hurt so long and it has hurt so much since your client hit me. I wasn't doing anything wrong. I was sitting there stopped at the red light.

Q: (The cross-examining attorney pulls out a poster prepared before the trial, with the identical question printed on the poster.)

There is a long pause. The cross-examiner points to the poster but does not repeat the question. (Whether to repeat the question verbally or only by body language is a question of style.) The witness spontaneously answers:

A: Yes, my back was hurt before the collision.

The witness also must think that the cross-examiner is psychic to know ahead of time that the identical question would be asked and that the witness would be unresponsive. This sanction stays with the witness for a long time. The witness can be expected to want to avoid a repeat of this sanction. The likely consequence is a more responsive witness.

§ 9.32 "That Didn't Answer My Question, Did It?"

First Scenario

Q: The car was blue?

A: (Babble, babble, babble)

Q: That didn't answer my question, did it?

A: What was your question?

Q: The question is: The car was blue?

A: Yes.

Second Scenario

Q: The car was blue?

A: (Babble, babble, babble)

Q: That did not answer my question, did it?

A: Yes, I think it did.

Q: Repeat my question?

A: (If the lawyer is not lucky) I don't know it.

Or

A: (If the lawyer is lucky) . . . (long pause) I don't know it.

Or

A: (If the lawyer is very lucky) . . . I know it was something about a car. What was it?

This technique is confrontational. It is best reserved for use against an expert or professional witness. The jury must sanction this confrontation before it is used. The witness must have repeatedly refused, deliberately and maliciously, to answer straightforward questions.

Under any of the scenarios, the witness is taught to respond to the precise question asked.

§ 9.33 "My Question Was . . ."

This manner of controlling is less confrontational than the preceding technique. It has the same effect, particularly when used after the prior technique that is so confrontational.

The jury is reminded that the question was not answered. They are reminded of the specific wording of your question. In that sense, this technique is much like a verbal blackboard and to the same effect. If analyzed, this technique is the "repeat" technique with a point on it. It is not as aggressive as "that does not answer my question, does it?" technique, but more aggressive than the simple "repeat" technique.

An additional benefit of this technique is that it points out to the jury the precise question that the witness is evading. Because of this, it is best to use this technique in situations where the cross-examiner draws additional attention to the factual assertion contained within the question. The jury receives a better understanding of the importance of the fact at issue, while the witness is sanctioned for the non-responsive or runaway answer.

§ 9.34 "Then Your Answer Is Yes"

This technique is easily understood by jurors. It can be used with any witness, whether that witness is a willfully non-responsive witness or just cannot help answering at length. The cross-examiner's tone can be adjusted depending on circumstances. At the heart of this technique is the cross-examiner's ability to hear what amounts to "yes" hidden within a longer answer.

Quite often an expert witness will respond with a long and involved recitation rather than concede an important point to the cross-examiner. Because the expert knows that a straight denial will not hold up to further cross-examination, the witness seeks to camouflage the admission so that the cross-examiner will be deprived of its value.

Cross-Examiner: The securities and exchange commission has no jurisdiction over fixed annuities?

Witness: The securities and exchange commission has jurisdiction over instruments carrying a market risk. We have jurisdiction over many forms of annuities. In fact, we have jurisdiction over every type of annuity that involves market risk. While fixed annuities do not involve a market risk, per se, they have similarities with investment contracts that carry market risk. Indeed, we have jurisdiction over investment instruments that are essentially the same as fixed annuities.

Cross-Examiner: Then your answer is "yes," the securities exchange commission does not have jurisdiction over fixed annuities?

Witness: Yes.

Or

Cross-Examiner: You had the report that showed toxic levels of mercury in the dirt?

Witness: Well, while there was a report that showed those levels, there was no reason to believe them accurate, and in fact all the evidence to us indicated otherwise.

Cross-Examiner: So your answer is yes. You had the report that showed toxic levels.

Witness: Yes, I had the report.

This is best delivered after a long answer, without moving or taking your eyes from the witness's eyes and with a slight, helpful smile. Usually the affirmative response is quickly forthcoming.

The Nuremberg Trial

This technique has long been used by cross-examiners. An example can be found in Sir David Maxwell-Fyfe's cross-examination of Hermann Goering during the Nuremberg Trials:

Maxwell-Fyfe: This order would be dealt with by your prisoner of war department in your ministry, wouldn't it?

Goering: This department, according to the procedure adopted for these orders, received the order, but no other department received it.

Maxwell-Fyfe: I think the answer to my question must be "yes." (Technique: Then your answer is yes?) It would be dealt with by the prisoner of war department, your ministry, isn't that true?

(Technique: Repeat.)

Goering: I would say yes.

§ 9.35 Story Times Three

Some witnesses seem unstoppable. They have been coached to tell a story and they are going to tell that tale — usually a dramatic story calculated to destroy the advocate's case. This sort of witness will tell this story as often as possible and seems to have the uncanny ability to recognize the worst possible moments. Only in these dire circumstances is the following technique appropriate. Try multiple techniques first before reverting to this technique.

This technique is best used at deposition. There is no jury to be poisoned. No judge to interrupt. By requesting repeated recitations of the "story," all the emotion of the witness and the "story" is drained away. Control for individual questions that follow become better.

Three quick scenarios will illustrate the devastating effect of "the story."

Criminal case: The criminal co-defendant who has agreed to testify against your client says at every opportunity, "Jones (your client) made me do it. He placed the gun to the officer's head and pulled the trigger. Then he laughed."

Civil case: An eyewitness to an intersection collision says whenever he can, "That may be true, but I saw your client's car go right through the red light."

Divorce case: The opposing spouse takes every opportunity to say, "She walked out on my sick child and me. She called from a bar and didn't even ask about the child. She asked me if I knew Fred B., who was with her."

The witness has repeatedly volunteered this story at critical times during the cross-examination. No matter what questions have been asked, the same story finds its way into the answer.

To defuse this situation, ask the witness: "You want to tell your story, don't you?" The answer will be "yes." Instruct the witness to tell it to the jury. Then instruct the witness to repeat it. After the retelling, instruct the witness to repeat it again. (Judges have been known to interrupt at this point with "I have heard enough of that story, now let's ask questions and give answers." Counsel can live with that.)

When the witness is finished with the third (progressively less dramatic) telling of the story, ask, "Have you told us your story? Do you want to tell us all one more time? No? Okay, let's go on." The witness will surely refrain from telling the story again. This is painful in the execution, but effective in stopping the long-term, chronic damage to the case. It remains an effective technique for emotional witnesses at deposition.

§ 9.36 Elimination: Use of This Technique at Trial

This technique is particularly valuable to teach the witness before trial that it is painful and even humiliating to be a runaway witness. It signals the axiom: "We can do this the easy way or the hard way, but we will do it." The technique comes in two forms. When used at a deposition the technique of elimination is longer and more time-consuming. When used in trial, the technique requires questioning that is more to the point. After experiencing the form at a deposition, few witnesses look forward to the trial form.

The question is asked, and the witness gives a non-responsive answer. We begin eliminating other possible factual variations. At some point during the process, the witness will offer to give the "yes" that was warranted by the original question asked. Do not let the witness off the hook. Continue with this technique until the witness insists on giving the response that you first requested.

Q: The car was blue?

A: Well, I only saw it for a moment . . . . (Minutes later the answer concludes without ever giving the color of the car.)

Q: The car was black?

A: No.

Q: The car was green?

A: No.

Q: The car was purple?

A: No.

Q: The car was yellow-green?

A: No, it was blue. It was blue.

Q: Thank you.

The more willfully non-responsive the answer, the more outrageous the process of elimination:

Q: The car was blue?

A: Well, I only saw it for a moment and when I looked over . . . (Minutes later the answer concludes without ever giving the color of the car.)

Q: The car was black?

A: No.

Q: The car was green?

A: No.

Q: The car was purple?

A: No.

Q: The car was yellow-green?

A: No.

Q: The car was puce?

A: No.

Q: The car was burnt sienna?

A: No, no. Blue, blue, blue.

The more willful and undesirable the witness, the more persistent the cross-examiner can be with the technique of elimination.

Deposition Training

This is an excellent technique to train the witness in depositions (where objections do not stop the technique) to be responsive. With the latitude given at depositions, the painful technique of elimination can be used to its full extent, and the witness recognizes that it is an unpleasant experience to be avoided in front of twelve strangers at a jury trial.

Q: The car was blue?

A: Well, I really wouldn't say blue, it was more of a . . . (Minutes later the answer concludes without ever giving the color of the car.)

Q: The car was black?

A: No.

Q: The car was green?

A: No.

Q: The car was purple?

A: No.

Q: The car was puce?

A: No, the car was blue.

Q: The car was burnt sienna?

A: No. No. Blue. Blue.

Q: Well, you weren't sure before, let's make sure that we are absolutely concrete on this. The car wasn't hot pink?

A: No, I said blue. It was blue.

Q: But you were not sure before. Let's make sure that it was blue.

A: It was blue. It was blue. It will always be blue. It will never change from blue.

There is a trial form of the "elimination" technique. It involves a much shorter version, a much quicker rendition.

Example:

Q: That then was a lie?

A: I am not sure that I would call it a lie.

Q: It wasn't the pure truth?

A: No.

Q: It wasn't the whole truth?

A: No.

Q: It wasn't even partially the truth?

A: I guess not.

Q: It was a lie?

A: Yes.

It is the same technique truncated for trial.

§ 9.37 Spontaneous Loops

A loop is the repetition of a key phrase. A spontaneous loop is a repetition of all or part of an unexpectedly good but unresponsive answer. This type of loop is called spontaneous because it happened without the trial lawyer expecting it. More often than not the cross-examiner will use a simple word or phrase from a long answer that the witness has volunteered.

Words of warning: First, to fashion effective spontaneous loops, the lawyer must *listen closely* to the witness's answers. The cross-examiner should use quoted language to get her point across. Second, the cross-examiner should only spontaneously loop quoted words or phrases that are *helpful* to her case. It dramatically undermines the case if the trial lawyer begins looping words or phrases that have no particular value to the theory of the case or words that may be harmful.

In a case about a covenant not to compete employment contract, the cross-examiner is representing the employee attempting to invalidate the contract and the covenant not to compete, based on the over-breadth of the terminology of the contract. It is purely a technical legal argument.

Judges and juries dislike people who sign contracts but do not live by them. In the cross-examination of the employer, the cross-examiner was seen looping the wrong phrase, which was destined to impale his client, the employee, on the basic common-sense concept, "If you sign a contract, you should keep your word and live by that contract."

Here is an example of how *not* to loop, and words that don't help:

A: We negotiated the contract for a long time. We both agreed verbally to it. We shook on it. We gave our word. Then it was reduced to writing. He had his lawyer look at it. I had my lawyer look at it when his lawyer had made some changes, but it was still the same contract. It is the contract to which we agreed.

Q: You gave your word?

A: Yes.

Q: My client gave his word?

A: Yes.

Q: You both gave your word?

A: Yes.

Q: As gentlemen?

A: Yes.

Q: As people who would keep their word?

A: Yes.

This is a classic example of what *not* to loop from the employee's point of view. The employer's attorney could smile and realize that his point was being driven home successfully by his opponent and would ultimately win the case at the trial level. Why was this done? Because the lawyer heard a dramatic phrase in the unresponsive answer. Dramatic phrases tantalize the cross-examiner to spontaneously loop them. Only loop those phrases that help the cross-examiner's theory of the case or hurt the opponent's theory.

Here is an example of the appropriate way to loop:

A: . . . and after the shooting we got into the car and drove away like any normal family would . . . (babble, babble, babble)

Q: Sir, you said that you were like any normal family. (Spontaneous loop of the phrase.)

A: Yes.

Q: Like any normal family you left town in the dead of the night?

A: Yes.

Q: Like any normal family you gave aliases to each normal family member, including the five-year-old?

A: Yes.

Q: Like any normal family, you stole license plates every other day, as the five-year-old watched?

A: Yes.

Spontaneous loops work to silence witnesses because they fear that their own words will return to haunt him. No person is so articulate, careful, or controlled that he doesn't use certain words and phrases that he later wished he could take back.

Whether the witness is a college professor with a doctorate in microbiology or a ruthless government informant trained in the art of lying, her non-responsive answer is likely to include words or phrases that the cross-examiner can use to discredit her. This is why we must listen to the entire answer carefully. Within it are often nuggets of golden opportunity.

§ 9.38 Combinations of Techniques

[1] The Relationship of "Ask, Repeat, Repeat" to "Ask, Repeat, Reverse"

By using the "ask, repeat, repeat," the cross-examiner sets up the "ask, repeat, reverse" technique. The converse is also true. By using the "ask, repeat, reverse" first, the "ask, repeat, repeat" is also in a better position to train the witness. Experience has taught that "ask, repeat, reverse" with expert or professional witnesses is the more dramatic technique and should be used first to set up the "ask, repeat, repeat" thereafter.

[2] The Relationship of Full Formal Name to "Sir" or "Ma'am"

Once the full formal name technique has been used, the "sir" or "ma'am" technique can be used thereafter with good effect. The full formal name technique enhances the use of "sir" or "ma'am" thereafter.

[3] The Relationship of Shortened Technique to Blackboard Technique

We can effectively use the "shortened" technique for dramatic effect individually. But when used as a preceding technique to the blackboard technique — when we know that we will be using the blackboard technique later in the examination of this same witness — the shortened technique dramatically increases the effectiveness of the blackboard technique. Save the blackboard for theory-essential questions.

Once the blackboard technique has then been issued, the return to the "shortened" technique is equally effective.

[4] The Relationship of Court Reporter to the Blackboard or Poster

When we have used the court reporter technique, the witness is extremely sensitive to us moving to the blackboard or the use of the poster technique. It is logical that the silent delay in setting up each of these three techniques creates fearful anticipation in the witness. The common denominator is silence.

[5] The Relationship of "That Didn't Answer My Question, Did It?" to "My Question Was . . ."

Once the very aggressive technique of "that doesn't answer my question, does it" technique has been used, oftentimes with an expert or professional witness, the less dramatic technique of "my question was . . ." is effective. The latter technique does not appear to be overly aggressive, but when used after the very aggressive former technique, it appears to the witness to be more aggressive than when used alone. It receives a prompt response from the witness.

[6] The Relationship of "Then Your Answer Is Yes" to "Ask, Repeat, Repeat"

As so eloquently illustrated by Sir David Maxwell-Fyfe's cross-examination of Hermann Goering, once the witness has been prompted with "so your answer is yes" technique, that technique is significantly enhanced by following it with a repeat of the original question.

§ 9.39 Summary

No one welcomes non-responsive witnesses. But with these techniques in the cross-examiner's arsenal, the trial lawyer will no longer fear them. Through these techniques, such a witness can be controlled. The trial lawyer can also use a non-responsive answer as an opportunity to punish the witness, weaken his credibility, and teach him the virtue of a straight "yes" or "no" answer.

An effective cross-examiner can control a witness artistically and subtly by using these techniques. There is no need to raise one's voice or become ugly or unprofessional. The fear in the stomach may remain, but it will appear to our opponents, to the court, and, most importantly, to the jury that it is the cross-examiner and not the witness who is in control. Some unobservant lawyers will say that the cross went well because "the witness never fought her." This is naive. In many cases the witness is up for the fight, until he is trained that the only easy course through the trial is to give simple "yes" and "no" answers.

A cross-examiner who can control the runaway witness through these techniques experiences positive feedback. Because more control is exerted, the witness fights less. Because the witness fights less, we can concentrate on the three basic rules and experiment with the more advanced techniques.

Chapter 10

LOOPS, DOUBLE LOOPS, AND SPONTANEOUS LOOPS

§ 10.01 Loops as a Flag-Planting Device

The cross-examiner needs a variety of techniques that ethically and appropriately enable the advocate to call the jury's attention to a particular fact. While we hope that jurors will hear all the answers, the reality is that some answers matter more than others. There are those facts of such importance that they deserve highlighting. In essence, the lawyer wishes to "plant a flag" on that fact. Any trial technique designed to highlight a particular fact — whether the technique involves voice, movement, demonstrative aid, or oratorical device — plants a prominent flag. The techniques of looping, in various forms, unfurl flags designed to call additional attention to a fact of importance.

§ 10.02 Three Looping Techniques

In trial, certain facts, phrases, and descriptions deserve to be emphasized. Lawyers on each side of the case want to stress their strong points and their opponent's weaknesses. Looping techniques emphasize facts and phrases in a subtle, but dramatic, ethical, and unobjectionable manner. There are several types of loops including: the simple loop, the double loop, and the spontaneous loop. Each loop technique emphasizes selected words and phrases. However, each type of loop can be used most effectively in certain circumstances. Each is designed to add emphasis by permissible repetition, avoiding objections, and lowering the risk of bad answers.

§ 10.03 The Problems with Merely Repeating an Answer

Unaided by looping, lawyers often attempt to emphasize words and phrases by re-asking the question or by repeating the answer:

Q: You saw that the company's financial rating was downgraded?

A: Yes.

Q: There really is no question, you saw the company's financial rating was downgraded?

A: Well, now that I think about it, I got the whole report but I cannot recall if I actually read the part about the company being downgraded.

This technique of re-asking the question is akin to blunt force. It is flawed, both tactically and legally. The second question in the example is objectionable as being "asked and answered" or "redundant, repetitive." Worse, the hostile witness is offered an easy opportunity to immediately retreat from his previous answer. The witness is alerted to the fact that the cross-examiner is happy with the admission concerning reading about the downgrade. Having been signaled by the cross-examiner's second question that it is an important fact, and having been offered an immediate opportunity to soften the answer, the witness often does so. Understandably the cross-examiner becomes frustrated. The witness now sees where the cross-examiner is going and knows what additional excuses must be offered to avoid giving the information desired by the cross-examiner.

Some lawyers engage in an equally dangerous but more amateurish technique. They pretend not to have heard the favorable answer. They will attempt to use their lack of comprehension as an excuse to repeat the question:

> **Q:** You knew for months that Northwest intended to cancel their order?
>
> **A:** Yes.
>
> **Q:** I am sorry, I didn't hear that. Did you say that you knew for months that Northwest intended to cancel their order?

At best this technique may work once in a trial. At worst, it offers the witness a chance to withdraw or modify the answer that so clearly helped the cross-examiner. This technique undermines the cross-examiner's personal credibility (lawyer pretends to be deaf) and still permits the witness to soften or withdraw the answer.

The cross-examiner needs a method of reinforcing a favorable fact while minimizing the ability of the witness to withdraw or modify the already given favorable answer. Looping provides a subtle method of adding emphasis without encountering either of the drawbacks inherent in the old "re-asking" method. It does so by capturing the answer from the witness and reinforcing it rather than questioning it. The voice and phraseology of the cross-examiner will give no clue that the answer is extraordinarily helpful. It is the repetition of the fact that provides the emphasis.

§ 10.04 Simple Loop Formula

Looping is a method by which an important or favorable fact is re-emphasized by repeating the information to be highlighted in the body of the next question. At its most basic form it works like this.

Definition:

1) Through a leading question establish the desired fact or phrase;
2) Use the fact or phrase established within the body of the next question, but without re-asking the fact; and
3) Connect the looped fact or phrase with a question that contains an undisputed fact. Attach the looped fact to a safe fact in the second question.

§ 10.05 Analysis of the Formula

This is one of those very effective techniques that looks simple on paper and is simple in practice. By repeating the helpful fact or phrase within the body of the next question or questions, the lawyer re-establishes the importance of that fact. Remember that more time spent on a fact in the courtroom attaches more importance to that fact. In trial, time is a measure of importance. Because the lawyer has precisely quoted the phrase used earlier by the witness within later questions, the jury is reminded that it was the witness who established the critical fact or agreed with the critical fact. The lawyer has neither misstated nor overstated the fact established. Furthermore, by reusing the critical fact within the body of next question, the lawyer does not take the risks that come with re-asking the fact.

Once the cross-examiner has learned to loop, the three-step technique becomes automatic. The steps do not need to be memorized. In fact, they won't even be remembered. Instead, the technique of repeating a very favorable fact within the succeeding question will become a natural process in the courtroom.

The fact or phrase to be looped should be easily understood, not vague or unduly complex. The fact to be looped must be clear and concise. The looped fact must be inserted as a predicate, or a given, into a new question that contains an undisputed fact. By connecting the looped fact or phrase with a fact not in dispute, the lawyer leaves the witness no basis upon which to deny the succeeding leading question. The fact asked in the new question is selected because it is beyond dispute. It is an "easy" question. Since the witness has already admitted in the prior question the "looped" fact or phrase, the witness cannot refuse to answer the question on that basis, either. Therefore, the witness cannot refuse an affirmative answer to the succeeding question or questions.

§ 10.06 Simple Loop Example

In a personal injury case where the plaintiff was ejected from the vehicle, the cross-examiner's goal was to use this fact to show the severity of the impact. However, the facts can objectively be interpreted as the plaintiff was thrown or fell with much less force from the car. Plaintiff's counsel needs to create a vivid picture, inasmuch as the plaintiff miraculously avoided permanent or disfiguring injuries. Damages (more precisely, the extent of damages) — not liability — are the critical issues that remain in the case:

Step 1:	**Q:**	The man was *hurled* from the car?
	A:	Yes.
Step 2:	**Q:**	After he was *hurled* from the car,
Step 3:		he landed on the highway?
	A:	Yes.

In Step 1, plaintiff's counsel uses a leading question to establish her desired fact that the plaintiff was "hurled" from the vehicle.

In Step 2, having induced the witness to adopt this descriptive fact, plaintiff's counsel inserts the fact (loops it) into a "safe" (Step 3) second question.

In this example, there is no question that the man was lying on the highway after he exited the vehicle.

Therefore, Step 3, attachment to an undisputed fact, was satisfied. The cross-examiner had previously established that the collision had occurred and that the man had been in the car involved in the collision. The only issue in the preceding question was how the man left the vehicle. The cross-examiner, through careful pre-trial analysis, had chosen the word "hurled," which the cross-examiner felt best illustrated the force of the collision. The lawyer chose a vivid but fair word.

§ 10.07 Looping Emotional Words

The goal is to loop powerful words and images tied directly to the cross-examiner's theory of the case.

An example from a domestic relations case: At issue was the cause of the separation. The defendant husband testified that the plaintiff wife was not upset by the separation and was not emotional when told. He testified that she might have had tears in her eyes, but that she certainly hadn't cried. An independent witness is called and examined by the wife's attorney on various other issues, but is cross-examined on the emotional impact to the wife on hearing that the husband was leaving, with a specific chapter goal to emphasize the emotional impact on the wife:

Q: Helen was *crying*?

A: Yes.

Q: She was crying when she turned to the defendant, Harry, and asked: "Why, Harry?"

§ 10.08 Looping Is a Learned Skill — Adjectives Are Easiest

Like most techniques in trial work, looping is a learned skill. The easiest words to loop are descriptive words, such as adjectives. They are easier for emphasizing concepts. An example of an adjective loop:

Q: The car was speeding?

A: Yes.

Q: The speeding car crossed the intersection?

A: Yes.

This is not to say that nouns, verbs, and other forms of words should not be looped. They are all fit subjects for looping after the cross-examiner has become comfortable with the technique of looping. For instance, "hurled" was looped, and it is a verb in that question.

The cross-examiner may loop phrases as well:

Q: This was undeniably a bad development?

A: Yes.

Q: After you learned of this *undeniably bad development*, you called your boss?

A: Yes.

§ 10.09 Multiple Simple Loops

The cross-examiner may use the loop technique repeatedly to build a consistent picture with the repetition of certain powerful or thematic words. In a previous example, the cross-examiner emphasized the fact that the wife was crying while she asked the defendant about the cause of the separation. The word "crying" can be looped repeatedly by the cross-examiner to emphasize the severity of the emotional impact.

An example from an identification case: The defendant is charged with armed robbery of a fast-food operation. The manager was face-to-face with the robber and has identified the defendant. The manager is five feet eleven inches tall; the defendant is five feet nine. A goal of the cross-examination is to challenge the current testimony of the eyewitness that the defendant was the robber. As part of this challenge the cross-examiner wishes to show that on a prior occasion the witness described the robber as being a tall man. The lawyer begins by taking facts from the discovery and putting into context the factual situation in which the manager saw the robber:

Q: You were at work behind the counter?

A: Yes.

Q: And you looked up from work and saw the robber?

A: Yes.

Q: You judged him to be a tall man?

A: Yes.

Q: In fact that is how you described the robber to the police: "he was a tall man"?

A: That's what I told them.

Q: The tall man (loop) was no more than three feet away?

A: Yes.

Q: You looked the tall man (loop) up and down?

A: Yes.

Q: And you noticed you had to look up (loop) at him?

A: Yes.

Q: He was tall?

A: Yes.

Q: Taller (loop) than you?

A: Yes.

Q: And you're pretty tall (loop) yourself?

A: Yes.

Q: You're five foot eleven?

A: Yes.

The lawyer established the phrase "tall man," then integrated the phrase into the body of a subsequent question. The lawyer does not re-ask the witness whether the robber was "tall." That fact is simply put in as a given. It is a fact already established.

The simple loop highlights a fact of importance. This use of a simple loop is to emphasize that a product was failing:

Q: There was a marketing plan for the product?

Q: The marketing plan for this product called for sales of 600,000 units in the first quarter of 2003?

Q: Sales of this product barely made 200,000 units in the first quarter?

Q: The product was failing to even approach what you needed?

Q: He tried to put even more advertising dollars behind this failing (loop) product?

Q: You thought the failing (loop) product needed a brand overhaul?

Q: Eventually you brought together an entire team to discuss what to do about this failing (loop) product?

The simple loop of the term "failing product" cannot help but emphasize to the jury this fact of importance.

§ 10.10 Simple Loops for the Purpose of Labeling

By the time of trial, the lawyers are quite familiar with the names of all the witnesses. Jurors are requested to immediately memorize the names of the parties, witnesses, and lawyers. If this was not difficult enough, they are then expected to listen to questions about what one witness, whose name they can barely recall, heard another witness say to perhaps even a third witness. Questions refer to exhibit numbers or the names of important exhibits. Keeping up with the flow of new names may prove overwhelming. When jurors cannot follow the questioning they mentally shut down. If jurors become frustrated at their inability to link the testimony with the names or exhibit numbers being used, they are likely to stop listening. No theory can get through to a juror who has tuned out.

We can attach labels to important witnesses and even to important exhibits. We can label a person "the best friend" or "the defendant's closest adviser" or "the man who warned **the defendant."**

§ 10.11 The Technique of Looping to Label

The technique of looping to label is a simple and natural way of assisting people's memory in the courtroom environment. Looping labels can be used in any case, any cross-examination, and any questioning. Looping assists the memory anytime there is a need to label a fact, a witness, or a particular exhibit. The technique is simple: Find a descriptive but fair label that is consistent with the cross-examiner's theory. Use that label in place of the name of the witness, or the number of the exhibit, or the date of the event. Use the label consistently throughout trial so that both jurors and witnesses can easily equate the label with the person, event, or exhibit. In a self-defense case:

Q: You looked out the door and saw several boys?

Q: One of the boys had a stick in his hand?

Q: The boy was quivering? (establish)

Q: The quivering (loop to label) boy said, "Where's John? I want to see John."

Q: You looked through the screen and said to the *quivering* boy (reloop), "If you're looking for trouble, you found it."

Q: And the quivering boy (reloop) looked back at you, but said nothing?

This is a simple loop used multiple times. The phrase "quivering boy" is looped both for the purpose of labeling and for the purpose of imparting information. The repetition of the phrase is essential in creating within the juror's minds a vivid picture of the quivering boy. When the key phrase "quivering boy" is used in closing argument, the picture is revived and becomes more vivid. The previous testimony is more easily recalled by the jury. The label used ("quivering") is more memorable and consistent with the lawyer's theory than "defendant," "murderer," or even his name. When the jury deliberates, it is essential that the jury equate the phrase "quivering boy" with the defendant, not the fact that the defendant shot the witness five times.

§ 10.12 Loops to Label Exhibits

Trials can become complicated. Particularly in commercial litigation, the exhibits frequently number in the hundreds. The most conscientious judge or jury cannot keep the exhibits straight. The lawyers who have dealt with the case for months and years before trial have a most difficult time keeping up with exhibits. Why is there a reasonable expectation that judges or juries could do so?

Looping helps to label exhibits and eliminates the need for the judge or jury to memorize the exhibit number. We can label a key exhibit "the cease and desist request" or "the crisis memo" or "the executive sign-off." In this way we simplify the job of jury and judge. Looping is the technique that lends itself to this labeling process. Everyone begins to refer to the exhibit by the label loop. It is chosen to be consistent with the cross-examiner's theory.

In a commercial case a critical memo read: "I believe the brokers should contact their clients." After a meeting with his boss, the author of the memo changed the memo to read: "I believe the brokers should <u>not</u> contact their clients." Understandably this memo was one of the most critical documents in the lawsuit brought on behalf of clients who were not contacted about a failing investment. Of course the memo had an exhibit number — out of hundreds of exhibit numbers. The memo had a date with no particular significance. Instead, plaintiffs' counsel referred to the memo as the "<u>Not</u> memo." The label stuck because the label was fair and because it was natural shorthand for the exhibit.

This "smoking gun" exhibit was marked sequentially as plaintiff's exhibit no. 136. It clearly was the brilliant nova of the plaintiff's theory of the case, but it was buried in the exhibits as exhibit no. 136.

Whenever the exhibit was referenced, it was called "the not memorandum." Whether on direct examination, cross-examination, or in closing argument, it was consistently called "the not memorandum." Not only was the label descriptive and vivid, but it was also consistent with the cross-examiner's theory of the case. Soon everyone in trial used the same description:

Q: The original version of the "not memo" was not distributed to the clients?

A: No.

Q: The original version of the "not memo" was not sent to the brokers?

A: No.

Questions to a separate witness should reinforce this label:

A: You did not keep your copy of the "not memo"?

Q: No need to.

A: In fact you made it a point to destroy your copy of the "not memo"?

A: I tossed it.

The label is so much more effective than an exhibit number or a date where neither the number nor the date had any special significance.

§ 10.13 Loops to Label Events

If the date of a particular event is important to the theory of the case, then a way to productively label and loop the label is to refer to the event by its date:

> **Q:** At the September 28th meeting . . .

Or more vividly:

> **Q:** After the merger the entire sales department was fired?
>
> **Q:** They got the word by group e-mail?
>
> **Q:** The e-mail was sent out on Saturday, May 26?
>
> **Q:** You have heard that e-mail referred to as "the Saturday night massacre"?
>
> **Q:** As a result of the Saturday night massacre . . .
>
> **Q:** Within days of the Saturday night massacre . . .

§ 10.14 Loops of Undisputed Facts Critical to Theory

While the purpose of simple loops is always to accentuate a fact or phrase, the fact or phrase is not always the subject of dispute. Instead, the fact or phrase may represent a concept so central to the theory of the case, and so important to the cross-examination, that its mere establishment and repetition adds weight to the thrust of the cross-examination. They are words to remember, i.e., word choices that the cross-examiner believes will support the theory of the case in the most meaningful way possible (see chapter 2, *Developing a Theory of the Case* and chapter 4, *The Only Three Rules of Cross-Examination*).

What follows is an example of the establishment of the key adjective that will be used in the cross-examination of an expert witness:

> **Q:** You told us in direct examination that you consider yourself an expert in accident investigation?
>
> **Q:** You have taken classes at the Colorado Law Enforcement Training Academy on traffic accident investigation?
>
> **Q:** But those courses were basic?
>
> **Q:** The real training took place at the Institute of Police Traffic Management?
>
> **Q:** There you took a two-week course called Technical Accident Investigation?
>
> **Q:** The book they used primarily in their teaching was "The Northwestern University Book on Technical Accident Investigation"?
>
> **Q:** It is considered to be the leading book in the field?

Q: You were taught out of it, you respect it, and in fact, it is *the bible* of the industry?

Q: It is *the bible* (loop) of accident investigation?

Q: One of the critical measurements in determining speed is from a skid coefficient to friction on the roadway?

Q: This is called the "drag measurement"?

Q: To determine the drag measurement, you use a drag sled?

(Chapter on drag sled usage and its importance in determining speed is measured from skid marks.)

Q: Now let's talk about what the Northwestern University Book, *the bible* of accident investigation, says you ought to do?

Q: *The bible* says multiple measurements are to be taken along the path of the skid mark?

Q: *The bible* says that multiple measurements must be taken in order to show a range of drag factors?

Q: *The bible* says that it is critical to show a range of drag factors as different parts of the roadway have completely different coefficients to friction?

Q: Now that's what *the bible* says?

Q: Let's compare how you did it to *the bible*?

Q: You pulled the drag sled across the skid marks near the south end of the north median?

Q: That's not the way *the bible* says to do it?

Q: You did not perform multiple drag tests over points along the skid?

Q: That's not the way *the bible* says to do it?

Q: You did not run multiple tests at any point?

Q: Your calculations are based on a single drag test?

Q: That's not the way *the bible* says to do it?

A: No, sir.

During cross-examination when the witness felt safe, the witness was happy to admit that the Northwestern University book is "the bible" of accident investigation. The selected phrase, "the bible," can then be repeatedly looped as a label in impeachment to show a string of comparisons between the work done and the dictates of "the bible." Having earlier accepted this characterization or label, it is now too late for the witness to deny or hedge on that key label.

§ 10.15 Using Loops in the Cross-Examination of Experts

Experts are always difficult to cross-examine. They are intelligent. They generally know their field of expertise. Most importantly, they are experienced in testifying. The looping technique is just as valuable in the cross-examination of the expert as it is in the cross-examination of a lay witness. Any time an affirmative answer is provided to a leading question, the fact proved in that leading question is capable of forming the basis for a loop. Neither the technique nor its usefulness is affected by the fact that the witness happens to be experienced at testifying:

Q: In 2001 he lost more than $2 million on his stock investments?

Q: A $2 million loss was an enormous loss in comparison to his net worth?

Q: This enormous loss resulted in . . .?

Q: As a result of this enormous loss . . .?

Q: On his financial statement, this enormous loss is reflected in a decrease . . .?

A separate technique is to loop a conclusion used by the opposing expert and pair it with other facts that contradict the conclusion. In the cross-examination of an independent medical examination expert who has testified dozens of time, the cross-examiner used simple loops:

Q: You needed to do a thorough physical examination?

Q: You needed to do a complete physical examination?

Q: You needed to do an unbiased physical examination?

Q: Your thorough, complete, and unbiased physical examination took less than twenty-five minutes?

The expert initially believed that admitting to "thorough," "complete," and "unbiased" was a trivial matter. The expert may well have thought it would help his posture in the eyes of the jury. But when those words were juxtaposed with the fact of "less than twenty-five minutes," the effect was terrible.

§ 10.16 Looping to Lock in Disputed Subjective Facts

The most difficult words to force on a witness are nebulous, vague, or subjective words. Often, this is in the area of description: "pretty dark" versus "dark" versus "very dark"; "pretty quick" versus "almost immediately" versus "instantly." Because all such words convey multiple meanings, they allow the witness a broad range of responses. Using a conclusion to describe a scene can also be disputed. Calling a meeting a "crisis meeting," referring to an accident as "horrific," asking the witness if an event "shocked" gives the witness ample room to both dispute our suggested description and provide his own. If such a subjective term is the goal of the cross-examiner, she should first build a factual chapter that provides a context or picture that infers the desired conclusion and then use a leading question to insert the desired conclusion. This will minimize the risk, but the risk remains substantial. In addition, when asking for the conclusion, the cross-examiner must avoid the tendency to emphasize the conclusion. Extra emphasis, even a change of tone, forewarns the witness that the conclusion will be a great aid for the cross-examiner. However, once the witness has answered "yes" to the desired conclusion, he becomes more comfortable with the term if it is then used in relation to any other facts in the case. We can use the loop technique to emphasize the conclusion in succeeding questions.

There is a technique by which the cross-examiner can increase the odds of getting the witness to accept the cross-examiner's characterization of the subjective fact. This technique requires the cross-examiner to reverse the ordinary loop process. By inserting the hoped-for fact or phrase in a leading question that contains a second, unarguable fact, the witness is more inclined to quickly affirm — without fully considering the implications of the vague, subjective, or arguable phrase. Once rewarded with an affirmative response to this most desired fact or phrase (see chapter 4, *The Only Three Rules of Cross-Examination*; and chapter 5, *The Chapter Method of Cross-Examination*), it is helpful to loop the response at least once, so as to permanently establish it and make backtracking by the witness more difficult later in the cross-examination or redirect examination. In the example below, the desired term is "instantly." The cross-examiner should first establish an easy (undisputable) fact:

Q: You heard the shot?

Q: You were standing outside the drug store when you heard the first shot?

Q: The first shot was followed instantly (instantly is very subjective) by shots two and three? (No question there were three shots?)

Q: Three shots instantly (looped) following each other caused you to run?

§ 10.17 Looping Subjective Emotional States

Whether it is a domestic relations case, a personal injury case, or even a victim's testimony in a criminal case, the emotional state of a person is often at issue. Even in the "white-collar prosecution" of Martha Stewart, a witness's emotional state was an issue. In a previous domestic relations example, the defendant husband testified that the wife was not particularly emotional. The wife testified that she was close to hysteria. The truth may lie somewhere in between, but the cross-examiner's job on behalf of the wife is to emphasize to the jury just how emotional this woman was at the time of the separation. One technique is to first try to gain an affirmative answer to the desired description of the emotional state. If the witness declines to adopt that description, the cross-examiner can follow up with some physical manifestations of the emotional state that will cause the jurors to mentally accept the subjective description that the lawyer first suggested:

Q: Your wife was close to hysteria when you asked for the separation?

A: She was somewhat upset.

Q: She was trembling?

A: Yes.

Q: She was weeping?

A: She was.

Q: As she was weeping and trembling, she asked you, "Why, Harry?"

A: Yes.

Q: You said to your trembling, weeping wife that you felt you needed to "move on"?

A: Yes.

Q: And as your wife stood there weeping and trembling you asked her how soon she thought she could go back to work?

A: Yes.

The cross-examiner has not gotten the witness to adopt the subject of description "close to hysteria." But the factually based descriptions of a weeping, trembling wife, shows the phrase "somewhat upset" to be understated. Another example:

Q: The man who robbed you was tall?

Q: Taller than you?

Q: You are five eleven? *key fact*

Q: You could see he was a very tall man? *Establish phrase*

Q: The very tall man was wearing a blue jean jacket? *loop*

§ 10.18 Building a Chain of Looped Facts

If the cross-examiner wishes to move a witness from point A to point Z in the story — where point Z is the sought-after testimony — it is often possible to move the witness along the path to admission of the key point by a series of loops. In this technique, the lawyer establishes a fact, loops that fact to the next fact, loops the second fact to the next fact, and continues to loop answers until the lawyer gets to the most desired answer.

Looping in this manner is really an extension of logic: If A, then B; if B, then C, and so on. The mass of facts connected with newly introduced fact drives and accelerates the momentum for the witness and the jury. The series of loops is a desirable method in such cases, as it very quickly moves the witness from A to Z while offering less room for the witness to evade. A civil example:

Q: You picked up a salad at McDonald's?

A: Yes.

Q: You were eating your salad as you drove?

A: Yes.

Q: As you drove, you changed the radio station?

A: Yes.

Q: As you changed the radio station, you looked down?

A: Yes.

Q: While looking down, you failed to see the stop sign?

A: Yes.

Q: Not seeing the stop sign, you drove straight into the intersection?

A: Yes.

Q: You drove into the intersection at about 25 miles per hour?

A: Yes.

Q: And at 25 miles per hour, you slammed broadside into Randy Garman's car?

Another example:

Q: You filled out a *bank loan application* at First National?

A: Yes.

Q: In the *application*, you told the bank that you *owned a house*?

A: Yes.

Q: You told them the *house you owned* was worth *$85,000*?

A: Yes.

Q: You told them that this *$85,000* house had a *$40,000 mortgage*?

A: Yes.

Q: The *$40,000 mortgage* never existed?

A: No.

Q: The *$85,000* value never existed?

A: No.

Q: You never owned that house?

A: No, sir.

Q: You lied to the bank about owning that house?

A: Yes.

Q: The *value*, the *mortgage*, the *house* were all lies?

A: Yes.

Q: They were lies you put into a *bank loan application*?

A: Yes, sir, they were.

Q: The bank loan application was a con?

A: Yes, sir, it was.

Q: To complete the *con*, you had to tell several *lies*?

A: Yes, sir.

Q: You needed to *lie* to complete the con?

A: Yes, sir.

Q: You needed the *con* to get the *money*?

A: Yes, sir.

Q: You were willing to take the *money* if somebody was foolish enough to believe the *con*?

A: I guess you could say that.

§ 10.19 Looping Impeaching Facts

When the witness makes an admission, looping the admission in succeeding sentences plants a flag on the helpful admission. Attempting to require the witness to simply repeat the answer exposes the lawyer to objections (redundant, repetitive). It also drains the answer of its vitality. By using a loop, however, the lawyer can sustain interest and avoid objection:

Q: When you told the police that you had borrowed the money from loan sharks and were paying them 5% interest a week, that was not the truth?

A: No, it was not.

Q: You put that story together out of thin air?

A: Yes, sir.

Q: *Out of thin air*, you invented facts?

A: Yes, sir.

Q: *Out of thin air*, you invented people?

A: Yes, sir.

Q: *Out of thin air*, you invented conversations?

A: Yes, sir.

The lawyer is the one who chooses the phrase "out of thin air" to equate with "not the truth." Certain phrases lend themselves to greater memory by the jury. Certain word choices or selections (see chapter 4, *The Only Three Rules of Cross-Examination*) lend themselves to physical expression when verbalizing them.

We can easily envision the lawyer repeatedly using this phrase "out of thin air" in closing argument. We can see the lawyer gesturing with her arms when using the phrase "out of thin air" each time that she uses it in closing arguments. Who doubts that the jury will remember the phrase "out of thin air" and the physical gesture when deliberating the veracity of this witness?

§ 10.20 Double Loops Technique

Simple loops can be quickly mastered. Once they are, it takes only minimal additional effort to learn the double loop technique. Double looping is a technique that can be used for two distinct purposes. The first and the most frequently employed purpose is its use to juxtapose two inconsistent concepts. We juxtapose two dissimilar or inconsistent facts in a single question in order to promote a desired jury reaction. We push two facts together to show the lack of logic inherent in a witness trying to verify both facts.

The second common purpose of the double loop technique is to use two or more looped facts in combinations to heighten an image and produce a result that will be more memorable and closely linked than the two facts alone.

§ 10.21 Double Loop Formula

1) Establish first desired significant fact.
2) Establish second desired significant fact.
3) Loop both facts together in a third question and later questions.
4) Always tie the double loop to a "safe" undisputed fact.

§ 10.22 Double Loop for Contrast

In the following example, the cross-examiner contrasts the size difference between the two combatants:

(Establish fact one.)

Q: Eddie is six one?

A: Yes.

(Establish fact two.)

Q: George is five seven?

A: Yes.

(Loop both established facts.)

Q: You saw six-foot, one-inch Eddie hit five-foot, seven-inch George?

A: Yes.

(Loop both again.)

Q: Six-foot, one-inch Eddie beat on five-foot, seven-inch George with his fists?

A: Yes.

The first two questions establish a great disparity in size. The double loop contrasts this disparity in the third question. Please note that the cross-examiner could have chosen not to double-loop both facts in a fourth question. The cross-examiner chose to use the double loop in a succeeding question to emphasize the size disparity. This double loop may now be used repeatedly.

§ 10.23 Building the Double Loop

Example in a criminal snitch case:

Q: When you said, "I didn't do it!" to the police, you lied?

Q: You lied because the lie was better than the truth? (loop)

Q: You lied because the lie was more likely to help than the truth? (reloop)

Q: You lied because you hoped the lie would get you out of trouble?

Q: And when you lied to get out of trouble, you made up details? (double loop)

Q: And when you lied to get out of trouble, you made up events? (double loop)

Q: And when you lied to get out of trouble, you made up conversations? (double loop)

The cross-examiner loops the word "lied" as a simple loop several times and then ties that simple loop with another loop of "get you out of trouble." Once this second fact has been established, the cross-examiner double-loops the word "lied" with the phrase "get out of trouble," and uses it several times to heighten the effect of the double loop. The double loop is intended to tie "lie" and "get out of trouble." In closing argument the lawyer can argue that the snitch is in trouble, and the snitch lies to "get out of trouble."

It is obvious from this example how much emphasis can be placed on simple words or phrases that if used separately would escape the attention of the jury. When used repetitively, without running the risk of an objection, the key facts and phrases are emphasized to the jury.

§ 10.24 Use of the Double Loop to Juxtapose Inconsistent Facts

In an impeaching cross-examination, assume the witness has said something that the jury may accept as true. However, if we introduce other facts that do not make sense if the first assertion were true, the story casts doubt upon the original assertion. The witness has told a story or fact, often in direct examination, which in isolation appears reasonable. The technique is to use a series of leading questions to cause the witness to admit other facts that, when examined in context with other testimony of the witness, causes the original assertion to be exposed as untruthful or illogical. In such cases, it is likely that the witness will have testified to the illogical fact during direct examination. If the witness first mentions the illogical fact in cross-examination, the technique remains the same; in cross-examination we set the illogical fact against other facts using a double loop that juxtaposes the first assertion and shows it to be implausible.

The double loop technique to juxtapose inconsistent facts is at the heart of the following example from a commercial case:

Q: You have told us that you were unaware of any facts that caused you any concerns about the financial health of this company?

Q: You knew the company had twice been downgraded by the rating services?

Q: You know the company had lost money for three consecutive years?

Q: This double-downgraded, money-losing company caused you no concern?

Another example is drawn from a criminal case. The purpose is to cast doubt upon the credibility of a witness by allowing the jurors to see the inherent inconsistency between established facts and the position taken by the witness.

In the homicide case discussed, an eyewitness claims she was forced to prostitute herself to get money to feed her starving baby. The starving baby story is central to her version of events. She has testified to that on direct examination. There is no reason to believe that the witness is going to abandon such a central feature of her story. Hence, the lawyer should not be afraid to ask the phrase: "Your baby was at home starving?" Having established that phrase, perhaps at a very early stage of the cross-examination and having received a defiant "yes," the lawyer may later double-loop it in juxtaposition to other inconsistent known facts of the case.

In reviewing the chronology of events the lawyer finds that, after committing the first act of prostitution, the witness went to a local fast food chain to eat a hamburger. Consider a double loop of the phrase, "Your baby was at home starving," in juxtaposition with this new fact in an attempt to make the previous story of the starving baby appear unlikely: "Your baby was at home starving, and you sat down to eat a hamburger?"

The lawyer has double-looped an answer from a previous chapter (Your baby was at home starving") in juxtaposition to a newly established fact ("You sat down to eat a hamburger"), which has the effect of making less credible one of the two assertions by the witness. Since the two facts cannot logically exist simultaneously, and since one of the facts is uncontested (ate the hamburger), the jury is led to reject the double-looped fact (baby at home starving).

§ 10.25 The Cross-Examiner Chooses Which Fact to Validate and Which Fact to Discredit

If a particular area of testimony of a witness will become less credible because of some other testimony of the witness, then a loop of the original testimony and a loop of the subsequent testimony (hence, a double loop), juxtaposing two irreconcilable sets of facts, will leave the jury to reflect upon which one is untruthful. The cross-examiner can elect which fact to strengthen and thereby tilt the scales as to which fact will be rejected. Contrast the fact to be discredited with an undisputed fact. It is a matter of selection by the cross-examiner.

Left to their own devices, some jurors might notice the two assertions and come to the opinion that they are in logical opposition. The science and techniques of cross-examination are used to make this possibility a certainty. The double loop of concepts in opposition accomplishes this goal.

There is one situation where it is entirely predictable which of the two assertions the jurors will accept. When a witness is confronted with facts that he admits to be true, and the witness gives an opinion (lay or expert), expresses a subjective point of view, or otherwise offers a nonfactual expression inconsistent with the admitted facts, the facts will prevail over the subjective assertion of the witness. Similarly, when a witness swears to a fact or an event or an emotion, but we can cause the witness to admit facts (not emotions or conclusions) that are logically inconsistent with the fact we doubt or wish to discredit, the result will be that the jurors will recognize and reject the illogical version of the facts or the illogical conclusion.

The prepared cross-examiner juxtaposes these inconsistent facts and phrases from various parts of the witness's testimony and places them in one sentence, so that the jury can reach the desired conclusion as to the absurdity in the juxtaposition of both phrases. Often the witness notices that her story is inconsistent and begins to offer new excuses and more unbelievable testimony to attempt to reconcile these positions. The more unbelievable excuse creates more opportunities for juxtaposed double loops.

§ 10.26 Use of the Double Loop to Highlight Contrasting Theories

The double loop is not only used to contrast inconsistent or irreconcilable facts, but it can be used effectively to show the jury the contrasting positions of the parties.

In a personal injury suit, where part of the insurance company's defense is that the collision just wasn't a big deal, the plaintiff's lawyer can use double loops to her advantage. In the cross-examination of the defendant driver:

Q: The man was unconscious?

A: Yes.

Q: The unconscious man was lying in the front seat bleeding?

A: Yes.

Q: The unconscious man that we are talking about is the plaintiff?

A: Yes.

Q: But you walked away from your car?

A: Yes.

Q: You weren't lying in the front seat bleeding; you walked away?

A: That's right.

Q: You ran the light?

A: Yes.

Q: And after you ran the light, it was you who walked away from your car, and it was the plaintiff who lay unconscious, bleeding in his car?

A jury may understand why the defendant believes the collision to be no big thing; the jury will also understand why the plaintiff considers the collision a major event. It is the plaintiff who benefits from the contrasts of the facts that the defendant walked away from the collision without a scratch while the plaintiff was rendered unconscious and bleeding. To accentuate that contrast, the cross-examiner may well add the phrase "without a scratch" to the description of the defendant walking away from the collision. Now that phrase, "without a scratch," can be used in a double-loop contrast later in the cross-examination.

In a civil case involving police brutality, plaintiff's counsel knows the officer will resort to the phrase "just trying to get the situation under control" from pre-trial testimony. Hence, the cross-examiner establishes it, loops it, and then ties it to loops of earlier testimony concerning the injuries to the plaintiff forming a double loop:

Q: You were just trying to get the situation under control?

Q: You used your 5-cell flashlight to help you get it under control?

Q: Specifically, you used your 5-cell flashlight to get Mr. Johnson under control?

Q: And after you got him under control you needed to call an ambulance?

Q: You needed to call an ambulance to look after his head injuries?

Q: His head injuries occurred when you were trying to get the situation under control?

§ 10.27 Use of Double Loops in Combinations

One fact, one adjective, or one description may not convince the listener of the severity of an event, but that multiple descriptions combined may well have such an effect.

One of Johnny Carson's favorite comedy routines with Ed McMahon is an example:

Carson: It was really a big event.

McMahon: How big was it?

Carson: (Smiling shyly at the audience) It was so big that . . . . (The routine continues with multiple examples of how big the event was, beginning with gross distortions and ending with absolute, but hilarious, absurdity.)

The cross-examiner can double-loop to place together multiple descriptions in one question or in a series of questions. This leads the jury to conclude that the event was significant. This is not to say that the witness will ever agree that the event was significant, but only that the witness will be required to agree to a list of facts that will ultimately lead the jury to conclude the event was tremendously significant.

In a personal injury case, the defendant has denied that the plaintiff was severely injured by the collision:

Q: The other driver was unconscious? (fact one)

A: Yes.

Q: He was unconscious and lying on the front seat of his car? (loop)

A: Yes.

Q: You walked over after the collision and looked in his window?

A: Yes.

Q: You saw that he was unconscious? (relooped)

A: Yes.

Q: You also saw that his shirt was soaked in blood? (fact two)

A: Yes.

Q: As you stood there looking through the window, you realized that this unconscious, blood-soaked man might die? (double loop)

A: I didn't know one way or the other.

§ 10.28 Expert Witnesses and Double Loops

Expert witnesses often testify in jargon, conclusions, and subjective interpretations. The rules of evidence permit expert witnesses to give their opinions in these forms, but the rules also permit the cross-examiner to attack those statements in multiple ways. Undermining the factual basis of the opinion is a time-honored method. The double loop lends itself to this attack.

Q: Doctor, you said on direct testimony that Ray is doing "as well as can be expected"?

A: Yes.

Q: Ray has a shattered tibia?

A: Yes.

Q: Ray is doing "as well as can be expected" for a teenager with a shattered tibia?

A: Yes.

Q: Ray is doing "as well as can be expected" for a teenager with a shattered tibia who can never walk on uneven ground again?

A: Yes.

Q: Ray is doing "as well as can be expected" for a teenager with a shattered tibia who can never play football again?

A: Yes.

Q: Ray is going "as well as can be expected" for a teenager with a shattered tibia who will always walk with a limp?

A: Yes.

When the expert is confronted with the double loop showing the incongruity of the conclusion "as well as can be expected" against hard-edged facts, the expert becomes uncomfortable on the stand. The opponent is placed in a position of not wanting to talk about "as well as can be expected" in his closing argument. The double loop comparison of the conclusion of the expert to the hard-edged facts changes the psychodynamic of the courtroom. That phrase has been poisoned for the opponent for the balance of the trial. When double loops are used in combination, the purpose is to irretrievably connect the two facts in the mind of the jury.

Q: The child was bleeding? (fact one)

A: Yes.

Q: Her mother was crying? (fact two)

A: Yes.

Q: The crying mother was holding her bleeding child? (double loop)

A: Yes.

§ 10.29 Creating the Double Loop for Use Against the Expert

Every expert must admit certain facts in order to be considered by the court an expert. Every expert must admit certain facts to be believed by the jury.

Those same facts that the expert admits, and in most cases embraces, can be compared to individual hard-edged facts that dramatically undermine the expert. The cross-examiner need not find the basic facts or admissions that the expert must show to be considered an expert. Those facts are obvious; they need not be sought out. Example:

Q: Doctor, you have assured us that you used "all of your professional skills" in operating on Ms. Babb?

A: Yes.

Q: You sliced into Ms. Babb's bowel with your scalpel?

A: Yes.

Q: Now, you were using "all of your professional skills" when you sliced into her bowel with your scalpel? (double loop)

A: Yes.

Q: You were using "all of your professional skills" when you completely overlooked the fact that you had sliced into her bowel with your scalpel?

A: Yes.

Q: You were using "all of your professional skills" when you overlooked the fact that you had sliced into her bowel with your scalpel and fecal material was leaking into her abdomen?

A: Yes.

§ 10.30 Spontaneous Loops

All of the loops shown thus far have been written and executed according to the cross-examiner's script. They were prepared pre-trial and may even be found within prepared chapters. There is nothing spontaneous about them, although simple and double loops sound spontaneous to the witness and the jury. These loops were planned; the lawyer carefully selected the words.

However, one of the most effective uses of looping occurs when a witness gives an unexpected answer which has in it a wonderfully helpful fact that substantially advances the lawyer's theory of the case. The critical difference between spontaneous loops and simple or double loops is that the spontaneous loop builds on words chosen by the witness.

In a pure spontaneous loop, it is the witness who has made that word choice during his direct or cross-examination. Having personally selected those words in front of this jury and judge, the witness will find it very difficult to disown that word choice, no matter how ill conceived or regrettable. The planned loop is based on a leading question containing a fact to which the witness agrees. In contrast the spontaneous loop is based on the phrase that has escaped the lips of the witness. Forever in this trial, the witness will be charged with the responsibility of uttering it.

§ 10.31 Word Selection and Simple Loops Lead to Spontaneous Loop Opportunities

In the setting of a commercial litigation case involving two professionals dividing a practice, the more senior partner who maintained all of the books of the practice reacts to the well-thought-out word selection by the cross-examiner and offers a more dramatic opportunity for a spontaneous loop:

Q: You had an extremely profitable practice?

A: Well, it was only the appearance of a profitable practice.

Q: It was the "appearance of a profitable practice," but it was a fake?

A: Yes.

Q: It was the "appearance of a profitable practice," but it was intended to deceive?

A: Yes.

Q: It was the "appearance of a profitable practice," but it was a believable lie?

A: True, I guess.

Whatever softening of the phrase "profitable practice" that the witness believed he could achieve by suggesting "it was only the appearance of" was dramatically reversed by the destruction of the witness's overall credibility. The witness ran from the planned loop and created the opportunity for the spontaneous loop.

§ 10.32 Why Spontaneous Loops Happen

> The shaft of the arrow had been feathered with one of the eagle's own plumes. We often give our enemies the means of our own destruction.
>
> – *Aesop*

The Eagle and the Arrow

The witness who volunteers answers too often will eventually volunteer a truly bad answer. Out of his mouth will come the fact that we could never have gotten through a leading question.

Two events must occur for a spontaneous loop to happen. First, the witness must say something that helps the cross-examiner's theory of the case or uses a powerful word that may dramatize the cross-examiner's theory of the case. Why does this happen? Some witnesses are simply trying to tell the truth. Their answer is both truthful and harmful. We use the spontaneous loop not to contradict the answer but to highlight the answer. Some witnesses are not trying to describe the events in a way helpful to the cross-examiner's theory of the case. But the courtroom is a difficult stage on which to improvise. Witnesses who fence with the cross-examiner often blurt out a foolish response.

The second event that must occur is that the cross-examiner must be listening. Listening is one of the most difficult skills for a cross-examiner. In the heart-thumping drama of a cross-examination, where goals must be accomplished and distractions avoided, it is difficult for the cross-examiner to listen. When the cross-examiner does listen and the witness offers that powerful phrase, there's the opportunity for a spontaneous loop.

§ 10.33 Definition of Spontaneous Loop Technique

1) Listen. Any answer other than a "yes" or "no" may offer an opportunity for the cross-examiner. Listen with the cross-examiner's theory of the case in mind.
2) Lift. Extract any useful word or phrase from the answer.
3) Loop. Use the helpful factor phrase in the body of the next question.
4) Tie the spontaneous loop to a safe, undisputed fact.

Compare the definition for spontaneous loop with the definition of a simple loop. There is but one difference. The cross-examiner must listen for the spontaneous loop. All other steps to the spontaneous loop are identical to the simple loop.

§ 10.34 Examples of Spontaneous Loops

The plaintiff is thrown from the vehicle after a collision. A portion of the cross-examination of the defendant is shown:

Q: The impact hurled him (the plaintiff) from the car?

A: I wouldn't say hurled, more like tossed.

Q: It "tossed" him about 30 feet? (spontaneous loop)

A: Well, yeah.

Q: In fact, it tossed him up against a light pole?

A: True.

This example can be analyzed as follows: The lawyer intentionally selected the word "hurled" in order to create an answer to loop. The question's goal was to illustrate the tremendous impact of the collision. "Hurled" was to be looped throughout the cross-examination. It was used in place of a word such as "thrown," which was taken from the investigative officer's police report.

The defendant chose to disagree with that word choice. But even fast-thinking witnesses are caught off guard when confronted with well-thought-out word choices designed to jar the jury. The defendant, in hindsight, made a worse choice when he selected the word "tossed." Unquestionably, the defendant was thinking that "tossed" was a less violent type of throw when compared with "hurled." Unfortunately for the witness, the lawyer coupled the word "tossed" with the very frightening facts in the case. She gained the benefit of the picture of a man tossed from his vehicle and the bonus of a defendant who unfairly tried to minimize those facts in front of the jury.

§ 10.35 Spontaneous Loop Opportunities Come from Witnesses Who Are Unresponsive

The following is an example of looping from a spontaneous answer by a government informant. The questioning comes at the end of a series of chapters on the informant's prior felony convictions. This chapter summarizes previous chapters:

Q: Three times in ten years you have been convicted of felonies?

A: Yes, but they were never violent crimes, they were just "cons" (a phrase to loop spontaneously).

Q: You "con" people?

A: I didn't hurt people, I just deceived them (two phrases to loop spontaneously).

Q: And when you didn't hurt people, but you just deceived them, you did it to get their money?

A: Yes, I guess so.

Q: And when you didn't hurt people, but you just deceived them, you did it to get what you wanted?

A: Yeah.

Q: And when you didn't hurt people, but you deceived them, you did it to get what you needed?

A: Yeah. (Witness looks at prosecutor.)

In this example, the witness volunteers the word "cons." "Cons" is immediately looped. This in turn leads to an additional phrase to loop spontaneously.

Spontaneous loops at first taunt the witness to volunteer again. Then they punish the witness for volunteering. Silence from the witness soon follows.

§ 10.36 Spontaneous Loops to Silence the Witness

Spontaneous loops silence the unresponsive or out-of-control witness (see chapter 9, *Controlling the Runaway Witness*). Spontaneous loops eventually threaten the witness so much that the witness will refuse to volunteer in any matter. Through spontaneous loops, the cross-examiner exercises control over the witness by punishing the non-responsive answer.

In the preceding examples, note how each time the cross-examiner effectively uses the spontaneous loop, the witness's answers become shorter and shorter until they are monosyllables. An example from a commercial case:

A: Counselor, you have to understand that net worth means "real worth."

Q: Sir, you said that net worth was "real worth," but what you call the "real worth" did not include the hidden bonds?

A: Well, yes.

Q: What you called the "real worth" was understated by $56,000?

A: Yes.

Q: What you have called "real worth" wasn't real?

A: Yes.

Q: It was unreal?

A: Yes.

Q: It was fantasy real?

A: . . . Yes.

§ 10.37 Spontaneous Loops — Selecting Power Words

Spontaneous loops are a method of planting a flag on a fact or phrase. Therefore the technique must be used only with the most helpful facts volunteered by the witness. Do not loop power words that are detrimental to the cross-examiner's theory of the case, themes, or theme phrases. As seemingly obvious as this may appear, in the heat of the battle, we often seize on a powerful description without analyzing whether the word or phrase helps our case. The cross-examiner cannot simply listen for a power word and then spontaneously loop it. She must listen to the entire answer and compare any extra information beyond Yes or No with the competing theories of the case.

In a self-defense case, the cross-examiner asked a witness who did not participate in the fight, but who was clearly a friend of the victim, the following:

Q: When Barry (the "victim") came through the door fast, he didn't say a word?

A: No, he just came barreling through the door and drilled the guy.

Q: The guy he drilled was Brian? (spontaneous loop)

A: Yeah.

Q: When Barry barreled through the door and drilled Brian, Brian didn't even have his hands raised? (spontaneous loop)

A: No, he didn't.

In the first question, the cross-examiner only wants the witness to agree that the "victim" came through the door fast. Instead the cross-examiner is rewarded with the dramatic phrasing and power words of "barreling through" and "drilled." The cross-examiner wisely chooses to loop "drilled" first and "barreled through" second. Why is this the wise selection? It is more important to the cross-examiner's theory of the case that the "victim" drilled (hit) the eventual defendant in a homicide case, than it is that the victim came through the door fast or "barreled through." When given a variety of power words, take the most critical to the theory of the case first. Then follow up with the other less critical words.

In a personal injury case, in attempting to set up a loop of the word "smashed," the plaintiff's lawyer asked the defendant:

Q: You smashed into Tony on his motorcycle?

A: I don't know what I hit. I just heard a thud and the sound of metal smashing metal.

Q: When you heard the thud, followed by the sound of metal smashing metal, you knew you had hit something? (spontaneous loop)

A: Well, yes.

Q: And when you looked up from the thud and the sound of metal smashing metal, you saw you had hit a man? (reloop)

A: I thought so.

Q: A man on a motorcycle?

A: Yes, apparently so.

Q: It was apparent because the man was lying in the street? (spontaneous loop)

A: Yes.

The cross-examiner was only looking for a "yes" to the word "smashed." "Smashed" was a pre-planned loop. The defendant, in an effort to avoid that word, offered a far more chilling description of the collision. Clearly, the thud and the sound of metal smashing metal is a much more graphic description than the single word "smashed." It deserves to be spontaneously looped immediately.

§ 10.38 Spontaneous Looping of Theme Phrases

We use cross-examination to develop not only our best facts, but also our theme phrases, which express our theory of the case.

The following example is taken from a commercial case. The plaintiff sold his business but kept a right of first refusal, which he claims allows him to buy back any portion of the business that the buyer might intend to sell to a third party. The plaintiff alleges that the right of first refusal is so broad that transfers for no consideration from the buyer to his brother and sister trigger the right of first refusal. The defendant and his expert term such a transfer as a "convenience transfer." The defendant argues that this transfer for tax considerations falls outside of an arm's-length transfer contemplated by the contract. Plaintiff has endorsed an expert witness on contract law. During the cross-examination of the plaintiff's expert he is asked the following questions:

Q: You have been involved in "convenience transfers"?

A: I have been involved in such brother/sister transactions.

Q: A brother/sister transaction is not the same as the sale of an asset?

A: There would be differences.

Q: There is nothing illegal about brother/sister transactions?

A: No, they are common.

Q: Brother/sister transactions are a common and perfectly valid way to move an asset between family members?

In this example the cross-examiner is given two opportunities to spontaneously loop answers from the expert in such a way as to stress the theme of the defendant's case. Defendant's theory is heavily dependent on stressing that transactions among family members that do not involve arm's-length bargaining are common and do not trigger a right of first refusal such as that included in this contract. The volunteered statements by the expert assist in establishing that theory of the case. Though the expert had no intention of offering such an opinion, the cross-examiner can use his answers.

A short example follows from a domestic relations case, in which the entire theory of the plaintiff wife was that she was "a good and loving mother." The lawyer for the plaintiff wife cannot really emphasize that the woman was particularly loving or supportive of the husband. Good wife — no. Great mom — yes.

The jury trial for assets and alimony commenced after a non-jury trial in which the court awarded the wife custody of the minor children. Custody was no longer the issue — only money. The cross-examiner had managed to cross-examine the defendant at length concerning the fact that the plaintiff wife was a "good mother." It was effective and it obviously stayed in the mind of the defendant husband. In front of the jury, the following occurred:

Q: She was a good mother?

A: A great mother.

It was obvious from the look of the witness that he had hoped to cut short the line of cross-examination that would establish for the jury all of the wonderful things that the woman had done for the children during the marriage. The cross-examiner does not take the bait, but spontaneously loops the phrase "great mother," using it in connection with individual facts.

Q: As a great mother, she did her best for the kids when times were tough?

A: Yes.

Q: As a great mother, she did her best to get the kids to study and to go to school?

A: Yes.

Q: As a great mother, she nursed her kids when they were sick?

A: Yes.

§ 10.39 Delayed Spontaneous Loops from Direct Examination and Discovery

Sometimes the witness has given an answer on direct examination that is either better than expected or phrased in such a way as to be of great use to the cross-examiner. Remember: What sets spontaneous loops apart from other loops is that the word choice is generated by the witness. The witness makes that choice, not the lawyer. In order to spontaneously loop the phrase or word in cross-examination, the lawyer must refresh it in the juror's minds by immediately bringing it forward in the cross-examination.

Return to the personal injury case earlier discussed. The insurance company calls an independent medical examiner whose job it is to minimize the plaintiff's pain and suffering claim. While trying to minimize the damages, the doctor says on direct examination, "He's doing absolutely as well as could be expected." Plaintiff's counsel, in cross, spontaneously loops this phrase:

Q: Doctor, you mentioned that Ray is doing "absolutely as well as could be expected"?

A: Yes, I did.

Q: He's doing absolutely as well as could be expected for a person whose tibia was shattered?

A: Yes.

Q: He's doing absolutely as well as could be expected for a person whose fibula has a metal rod in it?

A: Yes.

Q: He's doing absolutely as well as could be expected for a person who's got metal screws holding parts of his leg together?

A: Yes.

Q: He's doing absolutely as well as could be expected for a person who has gone through four separate surgeries?

Here the cross-examiner uses a delayed spontaneous loop from direct examination concerning the phrase "absolutely as well as could be expected." Note that a spontaneous loop does not have to be a dramatic or powerful phrase each time. It can be helpful or it can be in the theory of the cross-examiner's case. In this example, it is both helpful and in the theory of the cross-examiner's case. That spontaneous loop is then tied to facts already in evidence. The facts are so powerful that they recast the implications of the phrase "absolutely as well as could be expected" and make more vivid to the jury the tough job the plaintiff has ahead in his recovery.

The delayed spontaneous loop does not have to be taken just from the direct testimony of the witness at this trial. It can be taken from any statement made by the witness, even statements made pre-trial. In the example that follows, the government informant had described himself in an early statement to the police as an "honest man":

Q: You have told us that you are an "honest man"?

A: Yes.

Q: You told Mr. Smith if he would just co-sign a loan for you, you would pay him back right away?

A: Yes.

Q: That's the same "con" you had run on Bob Isaacs?

A: Might have, yes.

Q: It's a con you've run before?

A: I've said those words before, yes.

Q: But you are an "honest man"?

A: In those particular instances, no, I was not, sir.

§ 10.40 Relationship to Other Techniques

Loops incorporate the art of word selection that is a feature of leading questions. Once a loop or double loop has been introduced into the cross-examination, opportunities for spontaneous loops increase as witnesses try to flee from the descriptive words used by the cross-examiner. By looping theme phrases, the cross-examiner repeatedly emphasizes her theory of the case. Simple loops and double loops are set up by her use of the only three rules of cross-examination. Spontaneous loops are set up by an appropriate leading question to which the witness answers with more than a yes or no answer. Because we are armed with prepared pages of cross-examination, the volunteered answer does not divert the cross-examiner. She can listen and use it, if she chooses, or simply continue with her prepared chapter.

Chapter 11

CROSS-EXAMINATION WITHOUT DISCOVERY

§ 11.01 The Scenario of the "No-Discovery" Witness

The trial lawyer sits at counsel table, confident because she has prepared chapters of cross-examination for each anticipated witness. And then it happens.

The opponent calls the next witness. The cross-examiner does not know the witness. Maybe she does not know why this witness is called. Perhaps she does not recognize the name. Or perhaps she does know this witness but does not know why he is being called. The one thing she does know is: She has no formal pre-trial discovery from or about this witness. Her stomach is in knots. Her confidence is evaporating. Anger, fear, and frustration engulf her.

This situation has intentionally been painted to be "as bad as it can be." The lawyer must now assemble a useful cross-examination and deliver it in just minutes. It can be done. It is not a test of willpower or spontaneity, but of science and technique and, indeed, there are useful techniques for these situations.

There are certainly easier cross-examination scenarios, but there are tougher ones as well. Every lawyer has to confront the witness who is destructive to her case by being well prepared and capable of delivering testimony without a trace of bias. In these cases, the presence of discovery would not matter much. The absence of discovery is not the greatest obstacle to the trial lawyer's ability to successfully handle a witness. A witness is a package of pluses and minuses. With or without discovery, the lawyer is called upon to quickly assess the witness's credibility with the jury, his testimony, and the consistency of his testimony with other testimony or evidence, among other factors. Discovery is simply one factor that provides or limits the immediate availability of certain techniques at the onset (and at the onset only) of cross-examination.

So the cross-examiner must put herself in the necessary mindset. The lawyer has no discovery on this witness. This means there are no reports of interviews and no depositions. The trial lawyer must quickly prepare to cross-examine. The trial lawyer must therefore listen very attentively to the testimony.

§ 11.02 Control Your Emotions

First, the trial lawyer must recognize that she is angry and frustrated. To do a competent job, she must get rid of that distraction. She is in trial. She must postpone pondering questions such as: "Why did this happen?" or "What did I do wrong to let this happen or not be able to fix it?" Now is the time to focus on handling this problem.

Anger, frustration, or self-doubt will betray the trial lawyer in many ways. If the lawyer concentrates on the wrong done to her, it will distract her from listening to the witness. During cross-examination, the lawyer's unusually hostile demeanor will portray her as either frustrated or angry. This will distract the listener (be it a judge or jury) from listening to the substance of the cross-examination and may give the impression to the fact finder that the direct examination was extremely damaging, even if it wasn't.

Negative emotions may cause the lawyer to show anger or uncertainty in the tone of her questions. The listeners — judge, jury and witness — will hear the cross-examiner using a less confident tone. Sensing weakness, the witness may be emboldened to fight back. Feeling ill at ease with the facts, the cross-examiner will often resort to questions that center on generalities, opinions, legalisms, and conclusions. ("You were negligent, weren't you?" or "You looked after your own interests rather than the interests of your client?" or "You really didn't get a good look at the collision, did you?") The use of global language or conclusory questioning contrasts with the most effective methods of cross-examining (see chapter 4, *The Only Three Rules of Cross-Examination*). When the cross-examiner is frustrated or angry and lacks facts learned prior to trial, it is common to revert to non-fact-based questioning.

In such circumstances, the lawyer must rely on the familiar techniques she has learned — short questions (Only Three Rules), grouped by subject matter (Chapters), and built upon logic. All are designed to cast doubt on the opponent's theory of the case, or support her theory. The one good emotional aspect that flows from the "no-discovery" witness is the inevitable rush of adrenaline. It will make the cross-examiner quicker and better able to accomplish the task: Analyze what the witness presents in a systematic way in order to find cross-examination areas likely to be productive.

§ 11.03 Logic Provides Safe Questions

A big reason the cross-examiner feels overwhelmed by the "no-discovery" witness is that she has heard the axiom: "Ask no question to which you do not know the answer." This misunderstood axiom leads to an absurd mindset: "Lacking discovery, I cannot guarantee what this witness will say to any of my questions; therefore I cannot safely ask any questions."

This reasoning is false. There are more ways to "know" the answer than by reading facts in discovery. Even if the lawyer has no discovery about this witness, she may already possess discovery about much of the subject matter of the testimony. She may be aided by the testimony of previous witnesses and her interviews of her own witnesses and client. And undoubtedly, the cross-examiner is aided by logic and common sense. The trial lawyer may not be equipped to impeach the witness with a prior inconsistent statement, but she knows the logical facts that flow from the testimony. She also knows the facts that logically led to the information recited in direct examination.

The cross-examiner can add to her potential cross-examination all the questions to which answers are dictated by common sense. That is, the direct testimony of the witness should have been in accord with common sense, and the answers received in cross-examination should comport with sense. The risk of an answer defying common sense is borne by the witness, not by the cross-examiner. Certainly, the witness can say anything by way of an answer, but that does not mean it will be believed. The cross-examiner may, therefore, safely ask leading questions containing facts that logically flow from the facts recited by the witness. If the witness denies the truthfulness of these assertions, the cross-examiner may have to live with the "no" answer, but the witness will have to live with the lack of credibility from giving an illogical answer. In this scenario, the cross-examiner wins.

§ 11.04 The Cross-Examiner's Advantage: The Witness Does Not Know the Cross-Examiner

Often, if the cross-examiner does not know anything about the witness, the witness does not know anything about the cross-examiner. The witness does not know the cross-examiner's style or degree of preparation. Pre-trial questioning of a witness educates both the lawyer and the witness. Witnesses learn about the trial lawyer as they observe the trial lawyer depose them, take testimony from other witnesses, or do other courtroom work. Witnesses perform discovery on the lawyer, too. With the "no-discovery" witness, the trial lawyer is an unknown factor. To the extent that the cross-examiner observes the witness during direct testimony, the ability of the lawyer to observe and mentally prepare for the coming cross-examination far outweighs the ability of the witness to observe the lawyer and prepare for cross-examination.

If the cross-examiner is anxious about the witness's answers, think how anxious the witness feels, having no idea of what the questions might be. If the witness does not understand enough to be anxious about that lack of knowledge, so much the better. A witness unaware of the likely scope of cross-examination has precious little time to game-plan what might be good and bad answers. At the end of each chapter of cross-examination (see chapter 5, *The Chapter Method of Cross-Examination*), the cross-examiner will be mentally saying "no more questions (on that subject)" just before she turns the page and starts her next chapter. The witness can never say "no more answers" to a particular area of inquiry. The witness is seldom a courtroom veteran, and most witnesses do not enjoy the trial experience. In truth, the witness feels more anxiety than the cross-examiner, especially when the witness has no prior experience with the cross-examining lawyer.

The cross-examiner has a repertoire of techniques that the witness has not seen. In the critical area of observation of the "opponent," the advantage lies with the cross-examiner. Through observation of direct examination, the cross-examiner has a fix on the style, confidence, and emotional pitch of the witness, while the witness has little or no idea of the cross-examiner's approach.

§ 11.05 The Cross-Examiner's Advantage: The Witness Does Not See the Full Scope of the Case

A witness may understand his limited role in the overall case, but rarely knows the roles played by other witnesses on the opponent's side. Rarer still is the witness who fully understands the opponent's theory of the case. No witness understands all nuances of the competing theories of the case, but the prepared cross-examiner does. No witness can understand the strategic importance of the array of facts, but the prepared cross-examiner can. As a result, the witness cannot easily identify how a particular answer will aid the cross-examiner's theory or weaken the opponent's theory; but the prepared cross-examiner can recognize such an answer.

The cross-examiner has dissected the case. No matter how little time the cross-examiner has had to prepare for the trial, that is more global than the witness's preparation. The cross-examiner understands the likely strengths and weaknesses of both sides. The cross-examiner understands the competing theories. The witness does not. This knowledge of the contrasting theories provides a monumental advantage for the cross-examiner.

Knowing the contrasting theories means the cross-examiner possesses a broader knowledge of the important facts and, just as importantly, which facts are the most important to each theory of the case. The cross-examiner can quickly seize on a seemingly innocuous answer and understand how it affects the competing theories. The "theory of the case" advantage goes to the cross-examiner. Since there are two theories of the case, the cross-examiner's advantage is doubled.

§ 11.06 Cross-Examiner's Advantage: Witnesses Cannot Know How Their Testimony Fits

Cases are built on facts. The cross-examiner knows far better than the witness what has been said and what will likely be said by other witnesses. The cross-examiner also knows the demonstrative evidence and the exhibits. Because of that knowledge, the cross-examiner can easily recognize how the testimony of this witness may contradict another witness called by the opponent, or how it may support a witness who has been called or who will be called by the cross-examiner. There may be times when the witness testifies in opposition to an exhibit and does so confidently because the witness has not seen or does not recall all exhibits. But the cross-examiner knows the exhibits and can see how to use the witness's testimony. Likewise, the cross-examiner can make educated decisions on strategies to integrate the testimony available from this witness into the balance of the trial. A witness simply cannot have all of this detailed case knowledge. As a result, the trial lawyer enjoys a decided factual advantage over the witness in the ability to integrate the witness's answers into the case.

§ 11.07 "No Discovery" Seldom Means "No Information": Witness's Name Allows Database Discovery

In crafting a cross-examination we begin by taking stock of what we know (or reasonably believe) about the witness and his anticipated testimony. Even in the absence of formal discovery, the cross-examiner enjoys several strategic advantages over the witness. Often she has or can find some "discovery" to help her cross-examine the witness. She may not have formal discovery, but that does not mean she has no knowledge about the witness's role.

Once she knows the witness's name, the lawyer can run database searches and potentially find much useful information. She may investigate the witness using conventional techniques. The lawyer can simply ask her client: "Where does this person fit?" Anything that she already knows before the witness takes the stand assists in forming her potential cross-examination chapters.

The opponent may identify witnesses by name in the opening statement. Take this opportunity to begin discovery on potential witnesses. With the ready availability of computer databases, such as LexisNexis or other Internet search engines, the time between hearing a witness's name in opening statement and the cross-examination affords the cross-examiner additional methods of investigation. While databases cannot tell the lawyer what the witness will say, they may reveal powerful facts useful in attacking credibility. Such information could include unpaid judgments, tax liens, name changes, divorces, lawsuits by and against the witness, news articles mentioning the witness, articles written by the witness, and other facts from public records. The witness seldom expects the cross-examiner to know these details, so the early and appropriate use of such information often causes a witness to believe that the lawyer knows even more. This causes the witness to be more forthright in cross-examination.

Example: The plaintiff sues his former employer. At trial the plaintiff calls a former stockbroker of the employer to support plaintiff's theory. The credibility of this "no-discovery" witness interests the cross-examiner. A quick database search by witness name brings up the following facts: The witness has several unpaid tax liens, and two unsatisfied judgments. None of these matters are disclosed in the U-4 form required to be filled out and updated by the witness/stockbroker. Armed with this knowledge, the cross-examiner could prepare several chapters demonstrating that the witness obtained his brokerage job with the defendant by omitting required information; that the witness has obtained a new brokerage job without advising his new employer or the government of the required information; and that in spite of earning an ample income, the witness has failed to file tax returns or pay taxes owed. Such chapters are only a beginning. Undoubtedly there will be more cross-examination on the details of the direct testimony. But, armed with only the name and an inexpensive database search, the cross-examiner now has more cross-examination material available.

§ 11.08 "No Discovery" Seldom Means "No Information": Testimony of a Witness Can Often Be Anticipated

While it is reassuring to know who the witness is as a person, if the lawyer does not, there are still many avenues into a successful cross-examination. The most important information is knowledge of what testimony will be offered. Knowledge beyond "absolutely nothing" is some knowledge, a starting point for the development of cross-examination. It is possible that if the cross-examiner knows who is to be called, even with no formal discovery, she will know enough to perform several useful chapters of cross-examination. Perhaps there will be chapters (see chapter 5, *The Chapter Method of Cross-Examination*) relating to motive, interest or bias, based solely on the cross-examiner's knowledge of the need of this witness to support the opponent's side of the case. Does the witness have some business relationship with the defendant? Does the witness have something to gain if the contract is unenforceable? Is this witness engaging in the same conduct that has caused the brokerage firm to sue its former stockbroker? If the answer is yes, these are fertile areas for preliminary chapters demonstrating a motive, interest, or bias of the witness.

There are many trial situations in which the lawyer lacks discovery but still knows a great deal about the witness. There are temporary restraining order hearings in commercial and family law contexts. There are criminal cases where the victim and defendant know each other, or certainly have a good idea about what the "no-discovery" witness is going to say. There are temporary order hearings in divorces where the parties may not yet have been deposed but know an enormous amount about what the other party is likely to say.

If the lawyer does not know the person but knows the subject matter of testimony, she can assemble chapters based on what the client or others have told her about the issues. Only where there is absolutely nothing known about that witness — not the name, not profession, not connection to the case, not connection to the other party, not connection to the opposing counsel — is the trial lawyer truly starting from zero. That is rare. But even then there are techniques that will assist in formulating useful chapters of cross-examination.

§ 11.09 The Opponent's Opening Statement Must Reveal the Opponent's Theory of the Case

The opponent will almost certainly give an opening statement. Remember, if the opponent declines to open, they hide their evidence from both you and the fact finder. Because you have studied the case, you are still in a position to know where the opponent must go and how they intend to get there. The fact finder knows precious little. The opponent who hides his case from the fact finder has crippled himself. In any event, give your opening statement. Two can play this game, but none should.

The more detailed the opponent's opening statement, the more the cross-examiner will be alerted to important details of the opponent's theory and the prospective witnesses who will build upon that theory (see chapter 7, *The Relationship of Opening Statement to Cross-Examination*). Even if no witness is named, the opponent has revealed the facts underlying the theory of the case.

There are opponents who deny the cross-examiner the opportunity to comprehend his theory of the case by limiting or waiving the opening statement. Perhaps the opponent rationalizes that he does not want to "give away" his best facts. Perhaps he doesn't have a fully formed theory. In either event, if the cross-examiner cannot comprehend the strength of the opponent's theory of the case, with the facts and witnesses that will support it — neither can the fact finder. This is good news for the cross-examiner.

The opponent may have denied the cross-examiner discovery of his theory and witnesses, but he has paid too high a price. The case is not won by confusing the opponent. The correct technique is to use the opening statement to teach the fact finder. If an opponent makes a useful opening statement, he must simultaneously provide the cross-examiner with an excellent opportunity to "discover" what is coming. Similarly, trial counsel is not tempted to hide her theory of the case, witnesses, and the facts that support her theory. The opening statement is a vital component in teaching the case. It must not be abandoned or truncated. Let the opponent cope with how well she teaches, not how effectively she hides her theory.

§ 11.10 Listen Carefully to the "No-Discovery" Witness

Prepare for the "no-discovery" witness by listening carefully to the opponent's opening statement for the themes of the case. A good opening statement may reveal several themes upon which the opponent will depend.

Example:

In a civil case alleging copyright infringement, plaintiff's opening statement revealed the following themes:

- We devised a computer program.
- It was very advanced.
- It had great market potential.
- The market for our program collapsed.
- As a result we lost millions in likely sales (damages).

None of these themes should surprise the defendant. However, in articulating these themes, the opening statement will likely reveal much factual support. Furthermore, within each broad theme, there are sub-themes that the skillful opponent will advance. Sub-themes may be thought of as groups of factual chapters that the opponent will develop to prove his themes and thereby his theory of the case. These sub-themes are likely to become evident in the opening statement. As a result, the necessary and available cross-examinations will also become evident.

Opponent's Theme:

- Our computer program had great market potential.

Sub-Themes:

- The 20 largest insurance companies were a prime market for our software.
- Four large insurance companies had already expressed an interest in our software.
- One large insurance company was already testing our software and preliminary results were favorable.
- Hundreds of individual copies of our software had already been sold to individual insurance agents.

When we listen to the opponent's opening statement, the themes and sub-themes are easily identified and the testimony of prospective witnesses is better understood and prepared for. The cross-examiner may not know which witness will be called to support these sub-themes. Nonetheless, as the topics can be anticipated, the necessary cross-examination chapters can be prepared.

§ 11.11 The Opponent's Opening Statement Must Reveal Information About the Opponent's Witnesses

The opponent's opening statement is an enormous opportunity for the cross-examiner to "discover" more information about the opponent's witnesses and the facts she seeks from her witnesses. By paying close attention to the opponent's opening statement we can learn of the hidden witness or unanticipated testimony. A good opening statement tells the jury what the opponent intends to prove and how. His opening statement tells the cross-examiner no less. She should compare what the opponent promises to prove to her knowledge of the opponent's witnesses. When she hears a fact or event she cannot identify with a known witness, she is either hearing about a previously unknown witness or learning about an extension of testimony from a known witness. She does not need the name of the witness to assess her need to cross-examine on the issues raised by that promised testimony. When preparing for the "no-discovery" witness any preparation time is precious.

§ 11.12 Take Notes on the Opponent's Opening Statement in the Chapter Method

We begin our preparation for the no-discovery witness, indeed for any case, by taking notes on the opponent's opening statement. The manner in which we take our notes can be either an aid or a hindrance to our preparation for the testimony to come. We take notes using the chapter method. We will use quite a bit of paper, so come prepared. Start with a full legal pad, preferably in a different color from the pad you used to create your prepared pages of cross-examination. (Yes, this is a bit anal retentive, but then successful trial work benefits from such habits. Besides, you are anal retentive anyway.) We do this so that we can quickly identify the source of these notes. The opponent will have settled on some method of organizing the discussion of his case. Often the presentation will be chronological. Sometimes the opponent will proceed witness by witness, a less advantageous method of teaching a case, but equally easy for us to follow. As the opponent reveals his anticipated evidence, we write at the top of a sheet of paper the name we give that chapter. Perhaps it is "How the plaintiff met the defendant" or "The plaintiff's investment goals" or "the meeting of October 6." What matters is that we are imposing our method of organization on his case. We are immediately putting his case into a system that matches up well with our methods of page preparation. As a result, our notes are already broken down into our system that allows us to see areas of cross-examination. Happily, we almost always see that we have prepared chapters for these areas. When we recognize chapters we have prepared, we are simultaneously recognizing the pairing of testimony to witness. What is of equal importance is that we can now spot the new areas. When the opponent talks about facts or events of which we were unaware, we have identified the areas of the "no-discovery" witness. Although we may lack a name, we have identified the subject matter of the testimony and can begin our preparation for the cross-examination.

A good opening statement introduces key witnesses to the jury. Both sides attempt to build the credibility of their important witnesses and, where possible, damage the credibility of the opponent's key witnesses. As a result both sides often identify by name the witness who will provide the promised facts. We should track on our pages of opening statement the name of the witness who will give that testimony. When we hear a name we do not recognize, we may not be hearing about a "no-discovery" situation. We may find that we were prepared on that issue or event but that our chapters were written with another witness in mind. In that event, we are well prepared and have only to consider whether there are chapters not yet written that are specific to this witness. Such chapters are ordinarily motive, interest, or bias chapters or other forms of credibility attacks.

Having heard the opponent's opening statement, we should be able to identify the opponent's theory of the case, theme, what the opponent considers his strongest points, and methods to attack the trial lawyer's theory. Be mindful of facts or testimony the opponent promised to the jury that the lawyer believes will not be proved or are overstated. Then seek opportunities on cross-examination to use the opponent's witness to disagree with or fail to support the assertions made by opposing counsel in opening statement. Using this technique, the opponent's witness unknowingly attacks the credibility of opposing counsel's case.

Example: Plaintiff sues for breach of contract. Plaintiff has identified an important defense witness. Plaintiff had a romantic relationship with this witness. Part of defense counsel's theory of the case is that the acrimonious breakup is part of the motivation for this lawsuit. Defense counsel intends to cross-examine plaintiff on this issue.

Plaintiff's counsel, seeking to minimize the relationship, asserts in opening statement that plaintiff's mother witnessed the relationship and will tell the jury that it was just a "brief flirtation." Defense counsel neither deposed plaintiff's mother nor anticipated this testimony. Nonetheless, defense counsel need not wait until this witness is on the stand to challenge plaintiff's characterization of the relationship. Other witnesses called by the plaintiff may be unaware of this description. There may be no discovery as to these witnesses. In fact, defense counsel may not know which people will be called to support the plaintiff. Nonetheless, defense counsel may draft chapters for the cross-examinations designed to show how close and durable the relationship was. Now, when the plaintiff calls a business associate or friend in support of some other proposition in the case, that witness may well be an excellent witness to the close relationship between the plaintiff and the anticipated defense witness. Furthermore, it is unlikely that this witness has been prepared by plaintiff to discuss that relationship.

Through these chapters, used with witnesses who likely do not understand the implications of their testimony, it will be possible to paint the picture of a close relationship. It will become apparent to the fact finder that opponent's phrase "brief flirtation" is untrue. While these chapters would have been worthwhile to support the credibility of defense counsel's witness, their value is increased by the fact that they demonstrate that opposing counsel was not honest in this aspect of his opening statement. We can build on the opponent's promises in the opening statement to add chapters to cross-examinations to come.

§ 11.13 Determine Why the "No-Discovery" Witness Is Being Called

When the opponent calls a witness who, by name and relevance, is unknown to the cross-examiner, the first objective is to identify the goal of the direct examination. Obviously the opponent believes the witness will support his side of the case. No witness should be called to support the abstract notion that she is a "good witness." Each witness should be called to add a specific set of facts to the case. The cross-examiner need not fear witnesses who are called for appearance's sake but know little or nothing that advances the opponent's theory. In fact, it is dangerous to call witnesses merely to get a good face before the jury. Such witnesses have little or no functional goal, and therefore no anchor to cling to during cross-examination. They are prepared on so few facts that they are far more vulnerable on cross-examination than the witness called to nail down a factual goal. The "look-good" witness does not know what to protect against and can be led into areas where she cannot foresee how a particular answer affects the opponent's theory.

A witness takes the stand either to build the opponent's theory of the case or to weaken the cross-examiner's theory. The direct examination will reveal the purpose. The cross-examiner's job is to identify the purpose, analyze what has to be done to further that purpose, and analyze whether the witness can be taken into different areas to assist her theory.

The lawyer may discover that a witness's principal purpose is to bolster a fact she had already concluded she could not successfully counter or did not need to counter. The witness is new, but the information is old and may not be in dispute. No cross-examination is needed. To cross-examine on that issue is to fight an unnecessary battle that the lawyer cannot or need not win.

§ 11.14 The "Me Too" Witness: Do They Really Add Anything to the Case?

There is a slightly different situation when an opponent calls a "no-discovery" witness to testify to a matter identified as deserving of cross-examination but thought to be offered by a different witness. The opponent had one officer testify to the confession; now they have two. They had one executive testify that the company cares about its shareholders and would never deceive them. Now they have two executives saying the same thing. If the lawyer was prepared to cross-examine the first witness, the extra witness adds little or nothing new to the opponent's case. In fact, multiple people testifying about the same set of facts are likely to produce inconsistent testimony. To the extent that the cross-examiner has chapters that worked on the previous witness testifying to the same area, those chapters may safely be used again. To the extent that multiple witnesses provide inconsistent testimony, chapters pointing out that inconsistency can be drafted quickly.

Many witnesses offer "me too" testimony. Yes, his testimony hurts, but the judge and jury have heard most of it before. The cross-examiner is not going to need many notes,. Those chapters prepared for the other witnesses that preceded or will follow the "me too" witness are applicable to this witness. The cross-examiner actually has a greater advantage. The cross-examiner knows better than the witness how the other witnesses have or will testify to the same events. While listening to the direct testimony of this "no-discovery" witness, the cross-examiner will be mentally comparing the rendition from this witness against the testimony of the other witnesses and documents that the cross-examiner intends to use with other witnesses for contradiction and consistency.

To this extent, the cross-examination of this "no-discovery" witness gives the cross-examiner an extra opportunity to contrast inconsistencies among witnesses. There is also a greater opportunity to highlight word selection and phrasing used by this witness that may be more favorable to the cross-examiner's theory than that of the other witnesses.

§ 11.15 Prepare for Likely Topics of Cross-Examination

Assume the worst: The lawyer knows nothing about this witness. The cross-examiner recognizes neither the name nor the reason this witness is called. The initial "discovery" must come from the direct examination. What is the opponent's purpose for putting this particular witness on the stand? Once the lawyer identifies this purpose, she may well discover that she already has prepared chapters (see chapter 5, *The Chapter Method of Cross-Examination*) on those topics, believing them to be useful for a different witness.

In other words, she is prepared for a witness in these chapters, although with a different name attached to the anticipated testimony. Many times a lawyer is prepared to cross-examine a relative of the opposing party in a domestic relations case, but the opponent puts on a different relative who has been neither deposed nor interviewed. Similarly, in a commercial case, the lawyer may be prepared to cross-examine an attendee from a meeting, but the opponent decides to put up a different attendee who has not been deposed.

In the criminal context, the prosecutor often calls a detective who is not as prominently mentioned in reports rather than the detective who has previously testified in a preliminary hearing or motion to suppress hearing. Because the cross-examiner was prepared for many of the same topics, the chapters prepared for one detective will generally work for another.

Lawyers are confronted daily with relatives or friends who "support" the party. They have not been interviewed or subjected to pre-trial cross-examination. As an example, in the simple street crime case, where the criminal episode is relatively confined (a fight, a drug deal, a theft), the prosecutor knows what she is looking for in cross-examination, though she may not know whom the defendant will call. In larger cases, such as white-collar crimes and conspiracies, it is likely that the prosecutor has background on the key events, though she may have nothing directly from this witness. The topics are known; what is not known is this witness's precise statement. Using whatever she knows about the likely topic, she can write chapters of cross-examination to cover the likelihood that the opponent will call a witness in these areas.

The same concept applies to a defendant cloaked with a Fifth Amendment right. The prosecutor may have no discovery but well knows the case from the viewpoint of other witnesses. Cross-examination chapters can be written for the potential testimony of the defendant. The prepared cross-examination for the defendant will often serve as chapters for other defense witnesses as well.

In these circumstances, the cross-examiner is prepared to cross-examine the type of witness and often can prepare cross-examination chapters for the important topics. The cross-examiner is not going to be able to cross-examine the individual witness she envisioned. But the cross-examiner is largely prepared. The names of the witness may change, but the cross-examination does not.

When the "no-discovery" witness is called, those chapters prepared for this kind of witness should be at the forefront of the lawyer's mind. Although they may not be a precise fit, they are useful. They form the basis upon which to listen actively to the direct examination and perhaps modify chapters of cross-examination for this witness. Each witness brings unique personality traits to the stand. However, by preparing for this type of witness (eyewitness, investigating detective, attendee at a meeting, relatives/friends of a party, recipient of a memo), the cross-examiner has the best potential to overcome the lack of discovery.

§ 11.16 Evaluating the Pre-Testimony Behavior of the Witness; First Impressions

Additional "discovery" occurs as soon as the witness's name is called. Because the cross-examiner has no pre-trial information about this witness, she needs to be more focused than usual on available "in-trial" discovery. She begins learning when the witness is called. A trial lawyer observing the witness walk to the stand can immediately learn about sex, age, race, confidence level, how the witness walks, dresses, and any other characteristics she can detect. Does the witness demonstrate that he knows the opposing party? Does he know the opposing lawyer? Is he carrying a book or a file? The cross-examiner has started her investigation before the witness starts talking. Now her task is to hear the witness's story, read character traits, and recognize what is available for cross-examination.

Once the witness takes the stand, we can evaluate the character traits. Even before testimony, the confidence displayed by the witness and the comfort that the witness shows as the oath is administered tell us additional stories about this witness and his emotional state. Some witnesses appear calm and ready to testify. Most look uncomfortable and hesitant even during a prepared direct examination. The witness stand is not a user-friendly place, and few people seek the role as trial witness. By following the witness's eyes, the trial lawyer can often determine if the witness is uncertain, knows anyone in the courtroom, or truly wants to cooperate with opposing counsel. While these observations do not guide the lawyer to the chapters of the cross-examination, they can lead to an informed opinion as to the experience, confidence, and emotion of the witness. These factors, in turn, help the lawyer decide what tone to adopt in the first moments of cross-examination.

The moment the witness begins talking, we can begin to assess the "type" of witness. This begins with the swearing-in process. Every trial lawyer in her career has seen a witness raise his left hand rather than his right hand to take the oath. Acts like this, and more importantly the witness's reaction to this embarrassment, tell the cross-examiner more about the witness. Is the voice loud and strong on "I do"? Does the witness seem proud to testify? Does the witness appear eager to be here? If so, the cross-examiner is likely seeing evidence of a committed witness. The witness is not neutral. The witness is involved in the case and wants to help the side that called him. This witness will fight back at every opportunity. The cross-examination needs to be fact intensive and precise, as the witness can be expected to quarrel with conclusions or loose questions that use imprecise facts.

If, on the other hand, the witness seems uncomfortable or has the look of someone who would rather be elsewhere, that is telling. In this latter case it is less likely the witness is attached to the side that called him. Therefore, it is likely that the witness will be more malleable in answers he will give on cross-examination. This type of witness may be more flexible, less willing to fight, more willing to accept the lawyer's leading questions. Compared to the calm, confident witness, the lawyer is more able to push her cross-examination into areas where she lacks discovery but believes she knows the truth. This type of witness is more likely to make admissions that are logically true but thus far only provable by inference.

§ 11.17 Note Taking During Direct Examination: Three Elements

[1] Focused Listening

When the cross-examining lawyer lacks discovery and the direct examination testimony is previously unknown, the trial lawyer often tries to compensate by writing down as much of the direct examination as possible. This is a natural reaction. Since the lawyer had no prepared chapters, she compensates by taking more notes. The theory being: more notes = more discovery = more preparation for cross-examination. But the trial lawyer cannot effectively listen, observe, absorb new material, and consider the impact of this witness on the fact finder — all while writing copious notes. The value of copious notes is almost always less than the value of focused listening accompanied by selective note taking.

[2] Selective Note Taking

The cross-examiner does not need to "learn" the entire direct examination. In almost all circumstances, the trial lawyer is concerned with only parts. Only selective notes are needed. The guiding questions are: (1) which areas are worthy of note taking; and (2) how to take those notes. When faced with the task of cross-examining the witness without aid of pre-trial discovery, the advocate takes selective notes solely to assist in the cross-examination of this or other witnesses or, occasionally, the closing argument.

The cross-examiner will not want to repeat the full scope of the direct examination. Furthermore, the cross-examiner has the ability to select the areas to be covered in cross-examination. The trial lawyer has the right to cross-examine only on parts of direct examination that interest her. She has the right to cross-examine on details never brought up by the witness. That is, the cross-examiner may question "in the gaps." In fact, there may be limited circumstances in which the cross-examiner declines to cross-examine at all and proceeds to other chapters.

[3] Identifying What Areas Are Worthy of Note Taking

Lawyering and court reporting are different professions. Trial lawyers and witnesses make a record. Court reporters preserve the record. But even an accurate record of what was said is often misleading, as the impact of what was said is vital and wholly absent from the transcript. There are no sounds, movements, tones, or mannerisms in a transcript.

It is not unusual for a transcript of a cross-examination that went particularly well to read as if the witness was getting the better of the lawyer. The words on the page show what was said, not what was believed. The cross-examiner must concentrate on the vital information while hearing the tone and hesitations, and while witnessing the faces, mannerisms, and nuances of testimony that tip off areas where the witness was evasive, confused, or confident. If required to choose, the cross-examiner is better served by actively listening and taking fewer notes than by taking complete notes and missing the opportunity to absorb non-verbal signals.

Freedom from the legal pad also affords the lawyer the opportunity to track the impact of the witness on the trier of fact. The reaction of the listeners is more important than the trial lawyer's own reaction. To judge the impact on the fact finder, the cross-examiner must observe the fact finder. When the cross-examiner does not have pre-trial discovery, listening and observing the reaction of the judge and jury to the direct is of greater help in deciding on the course of her cross-examination.

§ 11.18 Taking Notes on Direct Examination in a Chapter Format: One Chapter per Page

A pivotal issue for the cross-examiner is how to effectively take notes during the "no-discovery" direct examination. (For the layout of the trial notebook page, and a discussion of how to take notes during trial, see chapter 6, *Page Preparation of Cross-Examination*.) There are several useful systems. Any note-taking system must be efficient, meaning it must produce notes of immediate use in forming cross-examination chapters without inordinate time or effort.

Ironically, note-taking techniques honed over years as a student are incompatible with the role of a trial lawyer. When a student is confronted with new information in a classroom, she takes extensive notes and later studies those notes in preparation for a final exam, in which the lecturer asks questions based on what the lecturer said in class. In other words, the task is, "Can you repeat what the lecturer said?" In contrast, trial lawyers seldom have the luxury of even an overnight recess to study for the cross-examination, and it will certainly not succeed if it merely repeats the direct examination. Furthermore, much of what is said in direct examination is neither new nor worthy of notes. She needs only those notes that will help with the cross-examination to come.

One system for efficiently tracking the direct examination is to take notes in a chapter form. (For the structure, makeup, and content of chapters of cross-examination, see chapter 5, *The Chapter Method of Cross-Examination*.)

Most direct examinations are chronological. Opposing counsel can be expected to take the witness chronologically through whatever topics the witness is expected to support. The opponent may not realize it, but this pattern is similar to chapter method of presentation. As a result, the cross-examiner can follow and organize the direct examination for note-taking purposes.

Effective note taking of a direct examination is a paper-intensive process. The cross-examiner is going to need many sheets of paper, but she is not necessarily going to take a lot of notes. For some ill-conceived reason, trial lawyers try to put notes on as many topics as possible on one sheet. The result is a hodge-podge of note-crammed pages on every topic raised on direct examination. This is not a system. It is a recipe for frustration. Encyclopedic notes on all issues raised on direct examination are not in a form to be immediately useful in preparing a cross-examination.

Once again we turn to a familiar technique: the chapter method. In utilizing the chapter method of cross-examination preparation, the lawyer has learned that every chapter deserves a separate page. No chapter will exceed a single page. Each chapter will be contained on the front side only of the page (see chapter 6, *Page Preparation of Cross-Examination*). There are good reasons to utilize the same system for note taking during direct examination, especially for a witness for whom there is no discovery. For starters, one system is better than two systems. Immersed in the trial, a single familiar system reduces our stress and is easier to employ.

Preparation is similar to that for the opponent's opening statement. When faced with any witness — especially the "no-discovery" witness — the cross-examiner needs a blank legal pad. As the direct examination proceeds, the cross-examiner can identify where the chapters break. In turn, the cross-examiner breaks down her notes of the direct examination into chapters. All notes on one chapter of the direct examination are on one page. On that page the cross-examiner notes potential issues for cross-examination. Through this process the cross-examiner is breaking the direct examination into component chapters. Some chapters will lead to cross-examinations. Some will be omitted from the cross-examination. By taking notes in this chapter method, the lawyer is better equipped to identify likely areas of cross-examination, to take notes of what those questions might be, and even to order the pages of potential cross-examination in a sequence helpful to the lawyer.

The cross-examiner does not need a full rendering of the direct examination, but only the key testimony on which to cross-examine and the lawyer's thoughts on what to do. Undoubtedly, the cross-examiner's notes on a single chapter will not fill the entire page. But each chapter will be on a separate page. Leave the partially filled page as is. Lawyers should prepare their chapters of cross-examination one chapter per page to avoid confusion and simplify sequencing of chapters.

Remember, the opponent probably will not understand the chapter method, so he will tend to cover areas at the issue and event level rather than at the more instructive and detailed chapter level. As a result, during the direct examination, the cross-examiner must be attuned to shifts in chapters within the issues. An issue may be large, but the chapters of cross-examination expose the helpful facts at a finer level. The opponent may be asking about a meeting (event) while the cross-examiner understands that several important things (chapters) occurred at the meeting. As each chapter is identified she should take notes on a new sheet. At the top of each page, she will note the title of that chapter, just as she would have done had she the opportunity to write out chapters in advance (see chapter 6, *Page Preparation of Cross-Examination*).

Another advantage of one chapter per page is that at the end of the direct examination, the cross-examiner can quickly discard unproductive material, add other chapters previously developed for other witnesses, and reorganize these pages into a persuasive order. Then she can effectively begin cross-examination. This reorganizing of the newly noted, admittedly truncated, chapters takes just seconds. This time is well spent for the effect on the witness and opponent. Had the cross-examiner chosen to work from the non-system of pages of notes taken on the direct examination as it was unfolding, she would have had little opportunity to enhance chapters, eliminate chapters, or persuasively organize chapters.

Why only one chapter on a page? Why label the chapter name at the top of the page? Remember, some notes may prove useful in cross-examination of other witnesses who are hours or days away from being called.

The problem with noting more than one chapter to a page is that the cross-examiner is led into cross-examining from a page of notes that relate to many chapters. That will inevitably cause the cross-examiner to follow the chronological order used by the opponent in the direct examination. Chronological order almost always is a mistake on cross-examination. A big risk of following a strict chronological approach crowded on a page of notes taken during direct examination is that the cross-examiner will inadvertently wander into areas on which she never intended to cross-examine. Cross-examining from a crammed page of notes also leads the cross-examiner into a series of one- or two-question chapters. In other words, when the cross-examiner is looking at the one or two points she had time to write down during direct, she is led to think these are the only points worth making. In reality, if the cross-examiner has one or two points already outlined on a chapter, by logically considering the topic, and recalling previous testimony and anticipated testimony on the same chapter, the cross-examiner is likely able to add facts that support the chapter goal. The lesson: one chapter = one page = one system = less confusion = more control of the cross-examination.

§ 11.19 The Concept of "Filtered Listening" — What to Take Notes On

As a first step to note taking during direct examination, active listening is more beneficial than extensive note taking. This is especially true when confronted with the no-discovery direct examination. The cross-examiner must mentally filter the information that she is hearing and seeing. The filter sifts only the direct examination testimony that may be useful for possible cross-examination chapters.

This sifting comes through a dual filter process. The cross-examiner should listen with a critical ear, searching for material that may be employed in the coming cross-examination. As always, useful material tends to strengthen the cross-examiner's theory of the case or tends to weaken the opponent's theory. Material that can be used to attack the credibility of that witness or any other witness of the opponent should be categorized as material that tends to weaken the opponent's theory. Anything that fails this dual screening should be eliminated from consideration for the immediate cross-examination.

(1) The filters must operate in real time so that the trial lawyer can apply them as the witness is testifying. An overabundance of notes hinders the speedy organization of an effective cross-examination. If this were a deposition, pre-trial hearing, or any other occasion when a transcript might be available, the lawyer might well spend time studying the answers to ferret out useful cross-examination material. But in trial, there is little time to contemplate all nuances of direct testimony. In preparing the no-discovery

cross-examination, the cross-examiner must make decisions rapidly. Studied reflection is a luxury not available.

(2) The filters must be easy to apply. Since there is little time to consider all ramifications, the filters must extract evidence that the cross-examiner already understands and can immediately employ.

(3) Finally, and most importantly, the cross-examiner must trust the filtering process. Otherwise she will not use the filters with confidence.

§ 11.20 The "Dual Filters" Method of Note Taking

(a) The most important filter is the cross-examiner's own theory of the case. Testimony, or the gaps in the direct testimony that affect the cross-examiner's theory, are worthy of consideration for immediate cross-examination. Does this testimony or gap in testimony help the cross-examiner's theory? This is the most important and timely question for the cross-examiner to ask herself. If so, conducting a no-discovery cross is an acceptable calculated risk.

(b) The second filter is expressed by this question: "Does this testimony contain material that can weaken the opponent's theory of the case?" Testimony that hurts the opponent's theory is worthy of consideration.

With these two filters, the cross-examiner comes away from the direct examination with useful notes that suggest cross-examination chapters. Not all notes are of equal value. How can these notes be quickly prioritized? One useful starting point for organization is to employ the resulting notes to create chapters that will be used in the following order: (a) chapters that support the cross-examiner's; and (b) chapters that can damage the opponent's theory.

There are several reasons for this technique of prioritization. We have only two types of information to listen for during direct examination. Witnesses called by an opponent have almost certainly been prepared by the opponent. The opponent can be counted on to do a better job preparing the witness to defend the opponent's theory of the case than to cope with the cross-examiner's theory of the case. Furthermore, the witness ordinarily has a factual grounding in the opponent's theory and is better able to understand how his testimony bolsters the opponent's theory. In contrast, the witness has less understanding and almost certainly has received less preparation in the cross-examiner's theory. By concentrating on making the witness a positive witness for the cross-examiner's theory, we enter areas in which the witness is less prepared. In addition, the cross-examiner knows her theory better than she knows the opponent's theory. The witness, in all likelihood, has not been prepared for a cross-examination that supports the cross-examiner's theory. Instead, the witness has been prepared to withstand an attacking cross-examination designed to hurt the opponent's theory — the side of the case that the witness is prepared to support. Many cross-examiners instinctively think their first obligation is to "attack" the credibility or the testimony of the witness. Antiquated notions cause the lawyer to view attack as the principal focus of cross-examination. It is especially unwise to rely on attack as the principal goal for the cross-examination of the "no-discovery" witness.

The witness is less prepared for that area of cross-examination and valuable information assisting the cross-examiner's theory that can be extracted without fight from the witness. Confrontational chapters are ordinarily more difficult to successfully accomplish. It is therefore better for the cross-examiner to accomplish what can be gained without a battle before wading into confrontational chapters. Difficult cross-examinations tend to exhaust the cross-examiner. Under the strain of a difficult cross-examination, there is an understandable tendency to "get out" of the cross-examination. This is particularly true of the "no-discovery" scenario. The cross-examiner leaves behind useful chapters that could have been accomplished with less effort.

§ 11.21 First Example: A Domestic Relations Case

In a domestic relations case, the cross-examiner is confronted with the elderly mother of the 50-year-old male defendant. The mother, while known to the plaintiff, was neither deposed nor interviewed. Why? Because the defendant had listed so many relatives, there was neither enough time nor money in the plaintiff's arsenal to depose every relative. It is also true that unconsciously the plaintiff's attorney thought that she could conduct a "you love your son" cross-examination if, in fact, the mother was put on the stand.

Opposing counsel put the defendant's mother on the stand to testify about personal property that was "inherited or gifted" to the son only (not the son and wife) from his family. The antiques involved were valued at several hundred thousand dollars.

Instead of giving in to the temptation to conduct a confrontational "you love your son" type of cross-examination, the lawyer actively listened to the direct testimony in which the defendant's mother testified that she was in the home of the plaintiff and defendant many times per week. The witness testified that she observed the location of the antiques and the manner in which the parties utilized them.

The lawyer began the cross-examination with a chapter that was consistent with her theory. The plaintiff's mother-in-law admitted that when she visited the home of the plaintiff, she was always treated with respect, offered coffee, and shown the achievements of her grandchildren. The house was always clean.

Each chapter was developed in length. All were consistent with the wife's theory of the case. The mother-in-law did not feel confronted. The mother-in-law felt like a proud grandmother, not her son's advocate.

The cross-examiner was also performing chapters on the willingness of the daughter-in-law to share meals (when the mother-in-law had stopped in at lunch or dinnertime); that the meals were well prepared (but not as good as the mother-in-law's); and that the daughter-in-law often sent with the elderly, widowed mother plates of food for later consumption. The mother-in-law readily admitted all of the pertinent facts in these chapters. All were consistent with the wife's theory of the case.

What the witness did not understand is that the defendant/husband had already complained in his direct examination to various facts:

- that the plaintiff/wife was seldom at home;
- that she did not cook;
- when she did cook, the results were poor, of the "fast food" variety; and
- that she did not keep the house in a clean manner that he had been accustomed to growing up in his mother's home.

Without confrontation, the cross-examiner turned this "no-discovery" witness into a formidable witness who supported the cross-examiner's theory and contradicted the defendant's previous testimony. This form of cross-examination is quite common. The witness comes most prepared to defend her anticipated direct testimony. Successful cross-examination on areas outside of her preparation zone is far easier. Once one witness for the opponent gives the answers the cross-examiner needs in her selected areas, it becomes problematic for the opponent to call other witnesses who will disagree with his first witness. Good testimony in cross-examination has the effect of not only making its points but also in eliminating other witnesses that the opponent might have intended to call. The opponent sheds witnesses to avoid a conflict among his own witnesses. Even if the opponent calls those additional witnesses, they will usually be careful to avoid areas already conceded in the advocate's cross-examination of the earlier witness. The opponent can ill afford to begin impeaching a witness he adopted as his own.

§ 11.22 Another Example: A Published Slander

In a slander case, the plaintiff called a witness who was a neighbor of the plaintiff at the time the slander was published. The court permitted this witness to testify in substance that upon hearing the published slander about the plaintiff, the neighbor witness had thought less of the plaintiff. The witness admitted that she had socialized less with the plaintiff and his family until the plaintiff and his family moved from the neighborhood some months after the published slander. Despite objection, the neighbor witness also testified that the slander continued to bother her. She testified that it had stayed in her mind despite the passage of several years. She stated that when she had last seen the plaintiff at a social gathering, she had asked the plaintiff about the comments that constituted the slander. She said the plaintiff appeared uneasy and distracted, which she had presumed was caused by the plaintiff's uneasiness in seeing his former neighbor and being asked about the slanderous statement.

The neighbor witness had been offered on direct testimony for the purposes of establishing a massive amount of damages for the plaintiff. It was part of the direct examiner's theory that the plaintiff had been had been ostracized and continued to be ostracized by the community because of the slanderous remarks.

The cross-examiner began her first chapter consistent with her theory — the plaintiff had no damages:

(Establish the witness saw the plaintiff often.)

Q: From what you said on your direct examination, I understand the plaintiff, Mr. McLeod, moved from your neighborhood some months after July '99 (the date of the publication of the slander)?

A: Yes, I don't remember the exact date, but several months later.

Q: Before they moved, they lived across the street from you?

A: Yes.

Q: Because they lived across the street from you, you literally saw them every day of the week?

A: Almost every day.

Q: You all lived so close that seeing them was an easy thing to do?

A: Yes.

Q: In fact, many times there was no plan to it — they either saw you or you saw them?

A: Often.

Q: You saw them when you both lived in the same neighborhood in passing but also at planned social gatherings?

A: True.

Q: In passing you may just say hello or you may stop and talk about the weather, the children, or things affecting the neighborhood?

A: Yes, we talked about many things.

New Chapter:

(Witness continued to socialize with the plaintiff after the "slander.")

Q: Socially, you would visit with them for barbecues or drinks or such as that?

A: Yes.

Q: You would host some of these gatherings?

A: Actually we did very little in hosting. Mr. McLeod often hosted gatherings, as did several of the other neighbors.

Q: You were invited to these gatherings by the plaintiff?

A: Yes.

Q: You went to those?

A: Yes.

Q: You chose to go to those?

A: Yes.

Q: You were invited by other neighbors to gatherings?

A: Yes.

Q: You knew the plaintiff would be present as well, in all likelihood?

A: Well, I didn't really know that.

Q: Well once you got to the gathering, you would see the plaintiff?

A: Yes.

Q: You would know that he was there?

A: Yes.

Q: You chose to stay?

A: Yes.

Q: You never left just because the plaintiff was there?

A: No.

New Chapter:

(After the plaintiff moved, continued socializing.)

Q: After the plaintiff moved away from your neighborhood, you continued on occasion to see the plaintiff socially?

A: Yes, but not as much.

Q: That's right, "not as much" because you just didn't live as close to each other in the same neighborhood?

A: Well yes, that is true.

Q: The plaintiff still invited you to social gatherings?

A: From time to time.

Q: You attended?

A: Yes.

Q: You obviously knew the plaintiff was going to be there?

A: Yes.

Q: You attended even though you knew the plaintiff was going to be there?

A: Yes.

Q: You made a special effort to get there because it wasn't just in the neighborhood anymore?

A: I suppose that is true.

Q: You had to drive further and you had to make more arrangements?

A: Yes, I suppose that is right. I just did it. Didn't really think about it.

Q: You not only attended these events, but you spoke with the plaintiff?

A: Yes.

Q: You shared a drink, whether it was alcohol or not?

A: I don't drink alcohol.

Q: Well, you shared a nonalcoholic drink or whatever was being eaten?

A: Yes, I suppose we did.

New Chapter:

(Exposed family to the plaintiff.)

Q: You took your family?

A: Yes.

Q: Your spouse and your children?

A: We only took the children when kids of their age were invited.

Q: I understand. But on those occasions, you did take your children?

A: Yes.

Q: You took your children and your spouse knowing that you were not exposing them to bad influences?

A: No, I wouldn't do that.

Notice that the cross-examiner did not confront the witness on areas that seemed ripe for confrontation (i.e. "you are a friend of the plaintiff, therefore . . ."). Rather, she started the cross-examination on more informational chapters, guaranteed to undermine the opposing plaintiff's theory of the case concerning damages. She also strengthened her theory that there was slander, it was published, but there was no damage. She successfully cross-examined the witness where there was no discovery. The witness never showed an appreciation that he was supporting the defendant's theory of the case nor that he was undermining the plaintiff's theory of the case on damages.

§ 11.23 Cross-Examining Outside the Tunnel Vision of the Witness

In these examples, it could be asked why the witness would volunteer a fact that was helpful to the cross-examiner's theory of the case or hurtful to the proponent of the witness's theory. Witnesses see their role with tunnel vision. They want to present the facts that they have prepared with the other lawyer, which help that lawyer's side of the case. But they don't understand in depth the theory of the cross-examiner's case or the direct examiner's case. The lack of in-depth appreciation of the two opposing theories relegates the witness to answer with truthful unprepared responses.

Some lawyers ask, "Why should I try to develop with an opponent's witness chapters that will help my theory or hurt the opponent's theory when I have my own witnesses who will testify to those facts?" Assuming the cross-examiner has the material with which to score the points, the answer is that the fact finder — judge or jury — will more easily accredit statements and facts given by the opponent's witnesses. Admissions by the opponent's witnesses are more valuable than those same facts and statements made by witnesses on the cross-examiner's side. No matter how articulate or erudite the cross-examiner's own witness, his testimony sounds self-serving. There is always an advantage to using the opponent's witnesses to establish or bolster chapters in the cross-examiner's case. Think of these facts and statements as verbal requests for admissions. When the witness says "yes," that is proof beyond a doubt. In this way much of the burden is removed from the cross-examiner's own witnesses.

The tone of these types of cross-examination often is not hostile. The witness does not fight the cross-examiner as she establishes a chapter. The witness has already testified on direct examination in a manner congruent with that chapter. The cross-examination actually more fully builds upon the direct testimony. As long as the cross-examiner by tone, word selection, or body language does not use attack, the witness is not encouraged to fight the cross-examiner. Often the cross-examination sounds conversational. It is more of a tone of "let's talk a little more about the things that you have already talked about" as opposed to "isn't it true . . .?," or "you love your son, so (you will lie)," or "the plaintiff is your friend, so (you will lie)."

§ 11.24 Turning Notes into Potential Areas of Cross-Examination

Note taking is only a preliminary step in creating cross-examination chapters. The notes tell what was said, but the advocate is left to plan how to use this information. She needs techniques that move beyond the direct examination into the possibilities for cross-examination. She must recall that cross-examination is not limited by the exact chapters covered by direct examination — she is free to cross-examine on any area raised by the direct examination and on credibility. It is entirely conceivable that cross-examination will cover facts never discussed anywhere in the direct testimony. After all, the direct examination was designed to tell the opponent's best story — not the entire story. The direct examination was designed to leave out entire sections of the case and omit harmful material even in covered areas. It is the cross-examiner's job to bring out new areas deserving of consideration and weaken, where possible, points made by the opponent in direct-examination.

In addition, the motive or bias of a witness is always a fair subject for cross-examination. As the cross-examiner listens to the "no-discovery" direct examination, she can add notes on motive, interest, and bias. The trial lawyer may not have known who was to be called or what they would say, but she may spot their motive and bias. Every witness's credibility is fair game for cross-examination. The witness may have testified to things he could not know, or things that are both incredibly helpful to the opponent — and incredibly unlikely. Testimony that defies logic, the physical laws of nature, or common sense deserves to be cross-examined. In short, notes of direct examination do not mark the boundaries of potential cross-examination.

The cross-examiner's page layout must accommodate a separate set of notes — counsel's notes to herself containing observations about the direct examination and possible questions for cross-examination. These notes evolve from what the lawyer is hearing. During direct examination, she recognizes facts she wishes to accentuate in cross-examination. She hears gaps in the testimony to exploit, contradictions between this witness and another witness called by the opponent. The lawyer needs notes to herself on how to approach these chapters. When the notes relate to those she is making during direct examination, those notes can be put opposite her question notes. These "thought" notes are tactical thinking, placed in the column for tactics (see chapter 6, *Page Preparation of Cross-Examination*).

The cross-examiner's notes of the direct examination were taken in chapters. So the notes on the lawyer's thoughts belong on the same page as the direct examination that spurred the lawyer's thoughts. Almost immediately after writing the notes, it will be her turn to cross-examine the witness. So what does the cross-examiner write in her cross-examination column?

(1) Note chapters that can safely be emphasized.

(2) Note chapters left out of the story that counsel can have the witness admit.

(3) Note entire chapters that witness will logically admit, even if not part of the witness's direct examination.

(4) Note logical inferences; since witness said x, he must admit y and z.

(5) Note contradictions with the facts, circumstances, witnesses, exhibits.

(6) Note facts relating to motive, interest or bias.

§ 11.25 The Testimony Begins: Keying in on Voice Tone

[1] Tone Offers Clues

A critical clue to the certainty and vulnerability of a witness is the tone of his answers. Whether or not there is discovery, the lawyer must always be aware of the witness's tone of voice. Tone gives insight into the mind and character of the witness. When there is no discovery, the advocate needs all the clues she can get. Tone often schools the trial lawyer on the confidence of the witness. Is the tone objective? Is the tone laced with emotion? Is the tone uncertain? Tone helps the lawyer understand the degree that this witness feels tied to the opponent or his own story. The lawyer can thereby better judge the flexibility the witness is likely to demonstrate. The advocate begins to learn why the witness is here. She can now better understand the role the opponent expects the witness to play.

The witness's tone can be a crucial clue. Listen for tone changes as direct examination proceeds. Some parts of the direct will sound rehearsed. The lawyer may detect areas where there is an assuredness in tone. The cross-examiner learns where the witness is within his testimonial zone of comfort.

[2] The Less Confident Tone as a Guide to Cross-Examination

A starting place is where the witness's tone betrays the witness's lack of confidence. Almost every witness changes his tone when he becomes less confident about the subject matter of the questioning. This tone change often occurs when the witness is led or strays into areas in which he does not want to. When the cross-examiner hears this change of tone, it is a signal that this may be a fertile area for cross-examination. Wherever the lawyer picks up on a change of voice, it is vital to focus on the witness, not on our note pad. Whenever a witness betrays a lack of confidence in his testimony, we should be especially observant of word choices, hesitation, and mannerisms. When the witness lacks confidence in an area, we are most likely to hear the "oops" testimony — the admission of confusion, the nonsensical assertion, the fact that does not logically fit. Perhaps the witness is in an area he does not want to discuss in detail. Perhaps his own uncomfortable role in the case is about to be revealed.

[3] The Confident Tone as a Guide to Cross-Examination

A confident witness tone in a particular area of testimony gives equally valuable information. How can confident testimony in an area be a guide to successful cross-examination? The answer lies in the analysis of how that particular testimony impacts the two competing theories of the case. A witness may offer information (whether sought by the direct examiner) that either directly aids the cross-examination theory or weakens the opponent's theory. The cross-examiner, recognizing the witness's tone of certainty, may on cross-examination guide the witness first into a repetition of the useful material and then into an elaboration of the topic. This cross-examiner's technique can be done in relative safety, even without benefit of pre-trial discovery. The confident tone ensures cooperation on cross-examination in this area. The witness will not back off this area of confidence. Instead, the witness is positioned to both repeat and support the version he has given in direct examination. The cross-examiner's job is to help him express his certainty.

[4] Taking Cues from Opposing Counsel's Tone

The cross-examiner can also receive important clues from the tone of the opponent conducting the direct examination. When the tone betrays a lack of preparation or confidence, it is a sign for the cross-examiner that the script of the direct examination is uncertain, not being followed, or fraught with hazards for the direct examiner. This change of tone is often a signal that the direct examiner knows there is danger in asking questions in this area because the witness may be unsupportive or go too far. Alternatively, the direct examiner may not know what details the witness will supply in areas where only the general answer is known. Once again, this is agreeable ground for possible cross-examination. The cross-examiner must listen carefully for nuances in the tone of the lawyer conducting the direct examination.

§ 11.26 Does the Testimony Conflict with Testimony of Other Witnesses?

The witness who is called to do nothing more than bolster another witness may well provide opportunities for effective cross-examination. First, has the witness said anything at variance with another witness called by the opponent?

It is the rare witness who can testify about the entire case. Rarer still are "no-discovery" witnesses who can testify about the entire case. Almost every witness is a niche witness. That is, he can testify about single events or issues. His testimony will not encompass the case. Most witnesses assume that if their testimony "sounds good" for "their side," it must be assisting their side. The flaw in this reasoning is that testimony can sound good but actually be supportive of a concept important to the cross-examiner's theory of the case. This occurs because cases are almost always more complex than any one witness can envision. The testimony that protects one issue may simultaneously assist the cross-examiner on another issue.

In a trademark infringement action, let us assume the defense calls a "no-discovery" corporate executive to testify to the lengths his company routinely goes to make sure they do not transgress on the copyrights of others. However, the more the witness testifies on how seriously his company treated trademark protection issues, the more vulnerable he becomes on the importance of any trademark holder protecting their trademark. He opens up many chapters on how seriously his company fights to protect its many trademarks and how harmful it is when other companies try to mark their products in ways similar to trademarks of his company. He becomes an unknowing expert on damages for his opponent. In addition, the more this witness describes the care his company takes, the more vulnerable he becomes to a cross-examination on steps his company did not take to discover the plaintiff's trademark, any warning his company ignored, any marketing actions his company took even after learning of the plaintiff's trademark. The better he tries to make his company appear, the higher he sets the bar for their expected behavior. Predictably the advocate can make the opponent's witness into a supporter of portions of the cross-examiner's theory. Predictably both the witness and the opponent will ask themselves how this happened. It happens all the time. Witnesses protect their themes without recognizing how portions can work to the other side's advantage.

The niche witness will instinctually protect his niche, his testimony. At the same time, he may testify to facts destructive or contradictory to other niche witnesses, without realizing that he has damaged the case of the lawyer who called him on direct examination. There is a technique to spot and exploit this weakness: Listen for areas in which the witness is at odds with another witness called by the opponent. In cross-examination take this witness back into that chapter and cross-examine him so that he repeats and expands the portions of testimony that are at odds with testimony by another of the opponent's witnesses. This technique effectively attacks the credibility of both witnesses, each without notice as to why their testimony is being reinforced by the cross-examination.

§ 11.27 Keying Off of the Overly Precise Question

We should listen not only to what is being asked, but equally to what is not being asked. Is opposing counsel asking a precisely worded question? This is often a signal that this lawyer and witness have agreed that he can truthfully and safely answer the question if, but only if, the wording is precise and narrow. What is not being said may be apparent to the cross-examiner, who may reveal the misleading nature of the direct testimony by pointing out the narrow scope of the opponent's question and using a series of leading questions to flush out the hidden facts. Look for this most often with expert witnesses. With the expert, listen for what is *not* added to foundation questions or hypothetical questions on direct examination. It is often the precise question that leaves out a fact or qualifies a fact dramatically where the lawyer can attack on cross-examination.

§ 11.28 Fact Fumbles

The cross-examiner is, of course, listening for the fumbles. Where is the answer that surprises the direct examiner? When the cross-examiner hears or sees the surprise, she concentrates on the precise question and the precise answer it produced. The opponent is now in trouble. The advocate must silently observe what facts can assist the cross-examination.

Most direct examinations, by nature, appear less goal-directed than cross-examination. Direct examination must be conducted using open-ended questions. As a result, direct examinations can more easily meander because of miscommunication between counsel and his witness. Facts that support the cross-examiner's theory of the case or hurt the opponent's theory fall out and the listening cross-examiner must pick up on them and build chapters based on these fumbles. When we listen using the dual filter, the fumbles are more easily heard.

§ 11.29 Keying Off of Answers that Veer Off Course

A direct examination can suddenly veer off on a tangent. This usually happens either because the examining lawyer has taken the witness into unrehearsed territory or the witness has answered a direct examination question unresponsively. The direct examination may also go off the script when the witness continues to testify after the initial question has been answered. These are some of the most revealing times of the direct examination. The cross-examiner may recognize this by the words, the tone, or facial expressions of the witness or the direct examiner.

The unexpected tangential information and the proffered details of a witness may well open up areas of cross-examination. These new areas of cross-examination can undermine the impact of the direct examination just concluded. The jury has witnessed the direct examination go astray. They realize there was a slip or something did not fit. When the cross-examiner takes advantage of the slip-up by pulling out more information in that area, the jury values this information highly. In essence, the testimony becomes more important because it leaked out. Listen for the volunteered details.

Example: The plaintiff has sued the defendant for damages arising out of personal injuries in a car accident. The defendant's vehicle hit the back of the plaintiff's vehicle at a stoplight on a road with a moderate slope. From the plaintiff's point of view, she was "slammed into" as she sat at the stoplight. From the defendant's point of view, she "drifted into" the plaintiff at "idle speed." Defense counsel seeks to minimize the impact. Because the slope of the road would affect the speed of the "drift," the plaintiff's lawyer had conducted an on-scene investigation that included the exact degree of slope of the road.

The defendant calls an eyewitness in an attempt to show that this was a low-speed collision. The plaintiff had not deposed this witness because of the expense relative to the size of the likely damages. The effort to interview the witness had been unsuccessful. When called by the defendant the witness testifies that the collision was not a substantial collision. On direct examination, the opponent asked the witness about the speed of the defendant's vehicle when it collided with the rear end of the plaintiff's vehicle:

Q: How fast was Mrs. Rupert's car (the defendant) traveling?

A: Not too fast. The road is pretty much flat there at the light and she really just drifted into the plaintiff's car.

At this point, defendant's counsel has received the answer he was seeking — defendant's car "drifted" into the rear of plaintiff's car. But the witness has added an unasked fact: the slope of the road. The witness has testified erroneously concerning the slope of the road. Her tone was more hurried, but not dramatically so. Some damage has been done, but the misstep should be further exploited on cross-examination.

The cross-examiner heard the words concerning the slope of the road and also noted the abrupt shift of subject matter, the change in tone and pace of the direct examiner's words. She realized that the chapter concerning the slope of the road would be productive on cross-examination. This "no-discovery" witness can be safely asked now about "the road is almost flat there . . . ." One way to spot the miscommunication: The testimony is not tied up by the opponent. Instead the matter is dropped.

§ 11.30 A Cross-Examination Clue: Opposing Counsel Interrupts His Own Witness

When opposing counsel interrupts his own witness, we are seeing a direct examination off its tracks. Interruptions by the examining attorney are attempts to steer the witness back into safe or rehearsed territory. When the cross-examiner knows the opposing counsel is uncomfortable in an area, she needs to give the witness more room to deliver damaging material. She may object to the interruption. By allowing the witness to continue, the lawyer potentially opens up further areas for cross-examination.

Regardless of whether the lawyer offers an objection, there are at least two lessons when the direct examiner interrupts his own witness. First, the witness had either intentionally or unintentionally wandered into an area that the direct examiner did not want to pursue in direct examination. This is an area that should be considered for cross-examination.

The second and less obvious lesson is to use this opportunity to observe how the witness reacts to an interruption. Does the witness talk over the interruption? Is the witness submissive to the interruption? Is the witness frustrated? Is the witness embarrassed that he has gone into an area into which the lawyer did not want him to go? These factors tell the cross-examiner which of many methods available to control the runaway witness would be most effective(See chapter 9, *Controlling the Runaway Witness*).

This is often an overlooked lesson. Direct examination allows the cross-examiner to "go to school" on how best to control this witness. Assess the witness to determine which methods available to control the runaway witness will work best if these are needed in cross-examination. Assess whether this witness is someone who is determined to say what he came to say regardless of what is asked. Or, to the contrary, is this a witness comfortable with confinement in an area selected by the examiner. Does this witness allow himself to be herded back into areas that the lawyer wants to explore? The advocate's understanding of the tenacity and personality of the witness better arms her for cross-examination.

§ 11.31 Spotting and Exploiting Gaps in the Direct Testimony

Most direct examinations are conducted chronologically. Most trial lawyers do this because it is easier to convey the information, for the witness and the fact finder who is unfamiliar with the story.

By moving through chapters of direct examination chronologically, opposing counsel has also made it easier for the cross-examiner to analyze the direct examination. The cross-examiner is better able to spot gaps in the story. Is the witness skipping over information? Is the direct examination lawyer encouraging the witness to quickly move over part of the story? Are the questions skipping an event that logically should be raised? These are questions that the actively listening cross-examiner should be asking herself.

There are at least six types of gaps. As the direct examination progresses, the cross-examiner should be attuned to listening for each.

§ 11.32 Gap 1: The Conspicuously Missing Event

The most obvious gap is a skip in the chronological presentation by the direct examination. As an example, assume a prosecutor is conducting the direct examination of a state trooper involved in the stopping, questioning, and testing of a suspect for driving under the influence. Methodically, the prosecutor takes the trooper through the reasons that the officer had activated his blue lights and stopped the vehicle. Methodically, the prosecutor takes the officer through the initial contact with the defendant. Then, in one question, the direct examiner focuses the officer on scenes beyond the tests:

Q: What did you do after the defendant exited his vehicle?

A: I had him perform a series of field sobriety tests.

Q: After the field sobriety tests, what did you do?

The prosecutor might then develop the handcuffing and arrest procedure. He covers the reading of certain rights. He takes the officer chronologically through the balance of his contact with the defendant.

The gap concerning the field sobriety tests suggests an opportunity for the cross-examiner. There was a reason the opponent left a gap in the direct examination. If the opponent thought there was good news in the field sobriety exam, the cross-examiner likely would have heard detailed testimony.

§ 11.33 Gap 2: Lack of Details Gap

Similar to the "complete gap" is the "lack of details" gap.

In a medical malpractice case, an operating room nurse testified in detail, to the tenth of a milligram, about the administration of certain medicines to a hip replacement patient. She testified to the exact size of the orthopedic reamer/drill, to the exact millimeter. However, when she was questioned on direct examination, she testified that a "small amount" of synthetic bone was placed in the hip. As to this part of the surgery the witness was asked nothing and offered no details. No exact measures. In fact, no discussion. The plaintiff contended that this "small amount" of synthetic bone is a reason that there was no in-grow of the hipbone into the orthopedic device.

The witness omitted the details for a reason.

§ 11.34 Gap 3: Gaps in Timing of Questions

When preparing to cross-examine, the lawyer should be alert to the cadence of questions and answers in direct examination. An acceleration in the pace of the direct questioning may well be designed to camouflage a testimony gap. The direct examining lawyer is signaling to the witness to hasten through this area. This is frequently a tip-off that this direct examiner has concerns about this area of testimony. Look at this material closely for cross-examination.

Conversely, when the direct examiner slows the questions, it may be for tactical reasons. The direct examiner may be trying to emphasize this set of answers by building in additional time for the jury to process the answers. Another reason the direct examiner may consciously slow the pace of questioning is to make sure the witness hears the precise phrasing of the questions. In either case, the lawyer performing the direct examination is giving off clues that this is the meat of the direct examination.

We gain additional information by observing the reaction of the witness to the slowed cadence. If the reduced speed of questioning causes the witness to testify in greater detail, the cross-examiner has likely discovered the strength of the witness and the primary reason he was called to testify. This also signals to the cross-examiner that this is where the witness is most prepared.

However, if the tempo slows and the tone of the direct examination lawyer becomes less confident, that may signal to the cross-examiner that the direct examination attorney is unsure of or concerned about the responses of the witness in that area. In each case, the cross-examiner must scrutinize the cadence of questions for its implications on cross-examination of those chapters.

§ 11.35 Gap 4: Stories Told Out of Order

The cross-examiner should be conscious of where the direct examination begins chronologically. The direct examination, after introduction of the witness to the fact finder, should start where it is easy for the fact finder to follow the testimony. When the direct examination attorney attempts to ignore facts or events that happened before the point where the direct examination begins, it is an effort by the direct examination attorney to steer the witness away from those earlier facts and events. The cross-examiner must ponder the previous testimony of the witness, the testimony of other witnesses on this point, and events for potential chapters on cross-examination.

§ 11.36 Gap 5: An Illogical Stopping Point

The cross-examiner also must listen for the chronology of when the witness stops testifying but the story keeps going. Does the testimony stop abruptly? Does the testimony stop before the logical end of the story? These breaks signal to the cross-examiner that there may be potentially successful cross-examination chapters that post-date the testimony on direct examination.

§ 11.37 Gap 6: Covering the Entire Time, But Not the Entire Story

Perhaps the subtlest gap on direct examination occurs when the witness or the direct examination lawyer intentionally omits issues or events that occur simultaneously with events to which the witness is testifying. An example: A witness gives direct testimony about a workplace confrontation in a hostile work environment case. The witness is able to reconstruct that he heard the defendant yelling at the plaintiff (Bobby). The witness testifies in some detail as to the words, tone, and volume of the defendant's voice during this confrontation.

The cross-examiner noted that the witness was never asked nor did the witness volunteer about what the plaintiff, Bobby, had said. There was no testimony about the words, tone, or volume Bobby used, nor the responses Bobby made. There was no testimony about Bobby's utterances at all. The cross-examiner took a brief note on this gap for prospective use on cross-examination.

Whenever there is a gap in testimony on direct examination, that gap is normally one that may produce favorable cross-examination material. Listen for the gaps. The witness creates some gaps. The direct examiner creates others.

§ 11.38 Sourcing the Direct Examination

Just as was true for pre-written chapters (see chapter 6, *Page Preparation of Cross-Examination*), the lawyer needs a column on the page for cross-examination that she creates during direct where she would ordinarily have her "source" information. There may be no pre-trial source when there is no discovery on this witness. Even the "no-discovery" witness may testify about an exhibit, and the lawyer may discover the exhibit is the source of the witness's testimony on a particular point. The cross-examiner must make a note of the exhibit number in the source column (see chapter 6, *Page Preparation of Cross-Examination*).

There is also another source for the cross-examination. That source for prior statements to be used in the cross-examination is the direct examination. If the cross-examiner attempts to impeach using testimony from the direct examination, it is not exact enough just to refer the witness to "your direct examination." It is better to have a more specific source.

If counsel were impeaching from a deposition, she would speak more specifically than "didn't you say in your deposition . . . ." She would refer to the page number and line number. Similarly, she may refer to the exact time that the statement was made on direct examination. It takes less than a second to note the time that a witness has made a statement that will be used in cross-examination. If the noted material is too voluminous and there is no opportunity to note the time, don't bother. Just as the cross-examiner would be better actively listening and observing than taking the first note, it is better to forgo noting the time if that is a distraction to active listening.

§ 11.39 Get the Transcript: Tiny Transcripts Can Have Big Impacts

Occasionally during direct examination, a witness may say something so helpful or impeachable that the cross-examiner wishes she had a transcript of exact words. This can be done in time for cross-examination. The technique is to note, as closely as possible, the exact wording of the question, the answer and the exact time. Then, at the first recess, counsel should ask the court reporter for a transcript of just that small block of testimony. The cross-examiner's ability to supply some of the exact words and/or the time will allow the court reporter to quickly search the transcript, find and type the needed passages. The cross-examiner is now armed with the witness's exact words and can impeach or elaborate on them. The jury and judge love this technique. The cross-examiner must make sure the passage was worth the effort as this device makes the most highlighted chapter of the cross-examination.

§ 11.40 Sequencing the Cross-Examination: Safety and Control

The most important guideline with the "no-discovery" witness is to control the witness on cross-examination. Of course, the absence of pre-trial discovery tends to lessen counsel's ability here. The beginning of the cross-examination is more important than usual in that a lawyer's cross-examination of "no-discovery" witnesses will tend to be shorter, and the witness will have more room for evasion. Consequently, with the "no-discovery" witness it is crucial that counsel begin the cross-examination with a "control" chapter. If the cross-examiner has solid chapters on motive, interest, or bias, she should lean toward using them at the start of the cross-examination. There is a safe sequence for the "no-discovery," based primarily on control of the witness and safety for the cross-examiner. Because this is the focus of the sequencing, counsel's confidence will build as the cross-examination goes on. The confidence of the witness will recede for the same reasons that the cross-examiner's confidence goes up. There is always an inverse ratio between the confidence level of the cross-examiner and that of the witness.

We must start our cross-examination with safe material. We prioritize what chapters will help our theory of the case and what will hurt the opponent's theory. It may well be that by doing these safe and productive chapters, the witness will offer up answers that help in other targeted areas: bias, assistance to the cross-examiner's theory, harm to the opponent's theory, marginalization, or credibility. So much the better. The hastily planned and safe cross-examination has yielded more safe material — only now it is the opponent witness who is forced to work without discovery.

Let us assume no such impeaching chapters are available. Perhaps this is a disinterested witness or the lawyer knows too little about the witness to prepare an attack built on bias. In such cases counsel can turn to another effective method of control: informational chapters. More often than not, this type of control chapter will also be a non-confrontational chapter designed to enhance the cross-examiner's theory of the case. The cross-examiner may pick up one or more statements made by the witness that support the cross-examiner's theory of the case. Counsel then elaborates on those statements. In that sense, the cross-examiner is not confronting the witness on what was said on direct examination. Instead this first chapter of cross-examination is an extension of what the witness has said in his direct testimony. Since the witness was mentally there already, taking him deeper into that chapter will be less dangerous.

If no motive or credibility chapters are available to the cross-examiner (or after these chapters are exhausted), the cross-examiner can turn to chapters that build upon aspects of the direct examination that hurt the opponent's theory of the case. Counsel has used the available motive and bias material, developed that which helps her theory or bolsters her witnesses, and exploited the testimony that hurts the opponent's theory. Now the cross-examiner can consider chapters that marginalize the witness. Finally, the lawyer can use general credibility attacks that show inconsistencies between this witness and every other witness, inconsistencies with common sense or with documents, or internal inconsistencies in the testimony.

§ 11.41 Logic-Based Cross-Examination

The cross-examiner is never restricted to those questions to which she knows the answer. We may ask with confidence and with safety all leading questions (facts) that logically flow from testimony. As an example, the witness has testified on direct examination that he saw the defendant at the scene of the crime. Then the cross-examiner can logically infer that the witness saw the crime scene. Note: This is different from seeing the crime. The cross-examiner can infer that the witness had the ability to see the details surrounding the crime scene. Undeniably, the witness can testify that he did not see other things, but the less the witness recalls of the scene, the less the jury will credit the original testimony. But what if the witness denies the leading questions that logically flow from facts stated on direct examination? In that event, the cross-examiner will still have a good cross-examination chapter. Imagine a witness who says he saw only one fact but none of the related facts. Such testimony is inherently weak. Testimony that can be shown to be illogical loses its credibility and, as a bonus, the witness loses personal credibility.

Just as admitted facts flow to other facts that should be admitted, certain emotions logically flow from facts. Where the admitted facts logically would produce a particular emotional, physical, or behavioral reaction in most people, the witness can safely be asked a leading question that suggests he experienced that reaction. Show the witness facts that would ordinarily produce surprise and the witness should admit being surprised. Show the witness a factual setting in which the normal person would inform their supervisor, and the witness can safely be asked the leading question, "You told your supervisor?" Certainly, the witness can deny the leading question, but in so doing loses credibility. The witness comes off to the fact finder as "not normal." The technique of cross-examining from the known fact to the logical but unsourced or undiscovered fact is useful, easy, and safe. It is one of the foundations of cross-examination of the "no-discovery" witness.

This opens broad factual areas in which to cross-examine logically, and consistently with the cross-examiner's theory, based on fleeting direct-testimony references. A note of caution: Emotions are subjective; therefore, asking a witness to admit an emotion is far more likely to produce disagreement than asking a witness to admit a fact. What shocks one witness does not shock another. Going down this path, the proper technique to lower risk is to ask through leading questions the many facts that set up the emotional situation. It must appear plain to both jurors and the witness that the logical answer is to admit the emotion suggested by the cross-examiner. Even then, we should ask ourselves whether we need ask about the emotion. Will an admission to that emotion gain us anything we have not already gained through our fact-based presentation?

Example: The "no-discovery" witness (police officer) has testified on direct examination that he arrived at the scene moments after the cars had collided. The collision resulted in a vehicular homicide prosecution. The witness has testified that the defendant, as he was taken out of his vehicle, was unsteady on his feet, nearly hysterical, and that other on-scene persons had to insist that the defendant not walk away from the scene of the collision.

Because the witness made the observations concerning the defendant, the witness can be cross-examined successfully and safely on areas that are consistent with the defense theory of the case. The following chapters suggest themselves. The witness should acknowledge that:

(1) It was dark;

(2) It was raining;

(3) There was no lighting at this particular intersection;

(4) The cars were mangled;

(5) There was tremendous damage to the deceased's vehicle;

(6) He would be able to identify the tremendous damage to the deceased's vehicle;

(7) The defendant was also in that same collision and his car was also "totaled";

(8) The windshield of defendant's car was shattered;

(9) It appeared as if defendant had hit his head against the windshield;

(10) A head injury to the defendant was completely consistent with the amount of damage done to his vehicle;

(11) Defendant's hysterical behavior was consistent with head injuries;

(12) Defendant's loud boisterous conduct was consistent with head injuries;

(13) Defendant's being "unsteady" on his feet was consistent with head injuries; and

(14) Defendant's disorientation was consistent with head injuries.

All of these facts are consistent with the defendant's theory of the case. It is true that the witness could refuse to acknowledge any or all conduct resulting from head injuries by saying: "I don't know." Is that really a down-side risk to the cross-examiner? The fact finder could accept these responses as illogical or untruthful. On the other hand, the cross-examiner could become more aggressive. She could attack the illogical lack of information more aggressively. The cross-examiner's choice is a courtroom judgment. Because of the rule of logic, the material available to the cross-examiner is expanded.

§ 11.42 Direct Examination Chapters Can Be Used for Cross-Examination

If we have prepared chapters for the direct examination of our witnesses, those same chapters can be pressed into service as cross-examination materials. When analyzing the direct testimony of this "no-discovery" witness, the cross-examiner has at her disposal those chapters prepared for her direct examination of her own witnesses. Those chapters can be utilized to take the witness on with chapters consistent or at least congruent with the cross-examiner's theory of the case. The technique is to listen for testimony that bolsters testimony she will advance. She can then use her chapters to show that, in several respects, the opponent's witness supports her theory.

What the cross-examiner has prepared for one witness (even her own on direct examination) helps her cross-examination. Those chapters designed to be effective with the type of witness, whether on direct or cross-examination, serve as a starting point from which to listen to the direct examination. The cross-examiner is gauging which of her chapters will work and which can be quickly adapted.

§ 11.43 Building Cross-Examination on Consistencies, Inconsistencies, and Contradictions

Whether the witness is a discovery or "no-discovery" witness, immediately upon hearing the direct testimony, the cross-examiner customarily recognizes how the direct examination fits into the context of testimony of other witnesses. We will also be able to recognize how the testimony fits with the documents and demonstrative evidence. The fact that this witness was unexpected does not deter us from utilizing those same factors to our advantage with this "no-discovery" witness.

A witness may also offer direct examination testimony that is internally inconsistent with some other portion of his own testimony. This is always a worthy subject for cross-examination. Counsel must avoid the temptation to ask the witness to explain the reasons for the internal inconsistency. Instead, separately and independently establish each fact and allow the fact finder to hear the contradiction. Of the two points in contradiction, the better technique is to firmly establish the weaker or more changeable testimony first, then follow up with the stronger or less changeable but contradicting testimony. In this way, the witness is less able to alter or amend his testimony when confronted with the inconsistencies. In other words, lock in the testimony the witness is most capable of changing, then reintroduce the testimony that was already completely established. Leave to the opponent the risky business of explaining the inconsistency on redirect examination.

§ 11.44 Using the Witness to Bolster the Cross-Examiner's Witnesses or Theory

The cross-examiner can use the opponent's witness to bolster the credibility of her own witnesses. The technique is to show that the opponent's witness is consistent with her witness on testimony that the cross-examiner intends to elicit during her direct examination. This has the natural consequence of aligning this witness with the cross-examiner's theory of the case. The technique is to find items of importance within the direct testimony or within the logical cross-examinations that tie them to the cross-examiner's case. Inasmuch as the jury or judge has had the benefit of the lawyer's opening statement, the leading question will communicate that this testimony is a helpful admission by the witness. As the cross-examiner spots these helpful areas, she can cross-examine at greater length, confident in a safe area.

Showing this type of testimony of the opponent's witnesses favorably influences the fact finder, while simultaneously discouraging the opposing lawyer from calling more surprise witnesses.

Recall that the witness has gone through no discovery process and thus is less able to appreciate the subtleties of the case. The witness is likely to testify with as much certainty on facts that help the cross-examiner's theory as on facts that help the opponent. The witness simply does not recognize the danger. The cross-examiner can often find in the direct examination some testimony that contradicts other witnesses called by the opponent. Counsel has only to put the two witnesses' versions in opposition. As the witness discusses the fact in detail, the witness simultaneously damages the other witness, often with no recognition.

The opposing lawyer knows this witness has been pulled out of the "no-discovery" bag. If the cross-examiner can handle this witness effectively, a warning shot has been fired across the opponent's bow. A few good chapters performed on an opponent's "no-discovery" witness can deter the opponent from calling more such witnesses.

§ 11.45 Comparison of Values to Conduct

A useful technique is to take a witness into areas in which he is likely to want to answer in a particular way, and then craft logically linking questions that cause the witness to adopt positions that seem helpful to the direct examiner's theory but are actually helpful to the cross-examiner's theory. Often this technique is built on a witness who wants to testify to abstract values rather than facts. Once called to testify about certain values or principles, the witness cannot easily limit the testimony in that area. Thus, the witness can be made to embrace the logical extension of such values, even when to do so will help the cross-examiner's theory of the case.

Example: A brokerage firm is accused of hiding negative financial information on a particular investment from investors. The defendant calls an executive to testify generally about the high-principled corporate culture. The executive testifies about the brokerage firm's philosophy about sharing information with clients. This executive is called to say that the firm strives to be completely candid and helpful to its clients and that the company has no reason to deceive clients. The direct is all very helpful. But the technique of comparing values to conduct will lead to an easy and effective cross-examination.

During that direct testimony, the executive is given the opportunity to tell the jury that A.B.C. is a conscientious and candid stock brokerage firm. "Our brokerage firm is the best" seems like a perfectly safe area of testimony. The witness perceives no danger in this niche and believes that presenting this testimony can do nothing but help defendant A.B.C.'s side of the case. His thinking is that the better the corporation looks generally, the better for the corporation's side. It is very difficult for a witness testifying to abstract values to see the danger that comes from the comparison of these abstractions to the specific, factual corporate conduct.

In this situation, the cross-examiner is faced with a "no-discovery" witness called to offer new information. After identifying this information, the lawyer can see that it is not necessary to take on the witness in cross-examination by attacking the testimony. Instead, the motivation of the witness to protect his limited role of praising the corporation can be used by the cross-examiner to construct one or more chapters that help the plaintiff's theory. When the cross-examiner's theory of the case involves the failure of the corporation to communicate with the plaintiff about serious financial matters, the cross-examiner gains value by encouraging the witness to embellish on the ability and willingness of the brokerage firm to communicate accurate financial information to clients. The executive is set up on cross-examination to assist the advocate's theory of the case without realizing the destructive nature of the questions:

Q: Sir, you are senior vice president of A.B.C. Brokerage Firm?

A: Yes.

Q: You are proud of A.B.C. Brokerage Firm?

A: Indeed I am.

Q: You have told them that A.B.C. does not try to live up to minimum standards of integrity and service, but instead A.B.C. intends to live up to the highest standards of integrity and service?

A: Yes.

Q: In fact, that's what you advertise to your clients: "count on A.B.C. for superior financial advice"?

A: Yes.

Q: As senior vice president with 28 years at A.B.C., your company exhibits fundamental, good character values, such as trustworthiness?

A: Yes.

Q: Your clients can count on, in fact should count on, A.B.C. for accurate information concerning their investments?

A: Yes, they should.

Q: A.B.C.'s clients should depend on A.B.C. to have superior research on their investments?

A: Yes, we pride ourselves on our excellent research department.

Q: And your clients can count on your research department?

A: What do you mean?

Q: Well, if your research department came across bad financial news on a company your clients were heavily invested in, your research department wouldn't ignore the bad news?

A: No.

Q: They wouldn't hide the bad news?

A: Of course not.

Q: In fact, it would be completely foreign to A.B.C.'s culture and advertising to fail to disclose bad financial news?

A: It would be contrary to our culture.

Q: It would be wrong?

A: It would be wrong.

Q: Because full and fair disclosure of investment facts is the job of A.B.C.?

A: It's certainly part of the job.

Q: A.B.C.'s clients can count on A.B.C. to truthfully communicate the financial — whether it is good news or bad news?

A: Yes, we have been accused of giving too much information.

Q: You would err on communicating too much rather than too little?

A: Yes.

Q: That is what A.B.C. is supposed to do?

A: Yes.

Q: That is what A.B.C. does?

A: Yes.

Q: And if A.B.C. didn't do that, didn't tell investors the facts for better or worse, that conduct would be beneath the level you have set for A.B.C.?

A: Yes.

Q: That conduct would be beneath the level A.B.C. has set for itself?

A: Yes.

Q: That conduct would be beneath the level that your investors should reasonably expect from A.B.C.?

A: I would agree.

Q: Timely, accurate and candid communication is one of the corporate character traits that you say makes A.B.C. Brokerage special?

A: Just one of them, but yes.

Q: And to be accurate and candid, your communication should not add what is untrue, or omit what is true?

A: I would agree.

This "no-discovery" witness unwittingly benefits the cross-examiner's theory of the case. The proud corporate executive has now established a high standard for the disclosure of financial information. He has cemented the "duty" issues. He has told the jury that investor reliance on A.B.C. for information is reasonable. He has even said that a failure to fully disclose the financial facts is a breach of duty. This bright, high-ranking executive has bragged his firm into liability problems, all the while believing he was doing nothing more than what he had done on direct examination — convincing the jurors that A.B.C. Brokerage Firm is a fair and honest company adhering to the highest standards, a company to be trusted to know and tell the truth.

§ 11.46 Impeachment by Inconsistent Statement

When the lawyer has pre-trial discovery of inconsistent statements, she can plan her impeachment as part of a scripted cross-examination. That planned impeachment cannot exist at the time that the "no-discovery" witness begins testifying. With no discovery, there is no pre-trial prior inconsistent statement. But even this limitation may evaporate once the witness testifies. The witness may say something on direct examination and later contradict himself, either within his direct examination or in the course of cross-examination. In this way, even the technique of impeachment through use of prior inconsistent statements may arise during the cross-examination of a witness where no pre-trial discovery exists.

When a witness says something on cross-examination inconsistent with what he has said on direct, there is an understandable tendency to impeach using the former statement. Often the impeachment begins with a phrase such as "didn't you say on direct examination . . . ?" Before taking this approach, the cross-examiner should examine which statement is more helpful — the statement made on direct examination or the purportedly inconsistent statement made on cross-examination. It is the more helpful version that the cross-examiner needs to bolster, and the less helpful version should be weakened by further cross-examination.

If the better version of the facts is the statement made on cross-examination, the cross-examiner may well choose to bolster that answer by providing the witness with other facts that logically support the new answer. As usual, cross-examination should feature leading questions. The tone is important. The cross-examiner should display by her tone and attitude that this chapter is so clearly correct that there can be no question as to the accuracy of the answers. In other words, by the form of the question and the cross-examiner's attitude, the witness must be reassured in the answer that most aids the cross-examiner. The "impeachment" of the less useful answer given on direct examination or on cross occurs through the gentle and detailed verification of the more useful answer, rather than through the more abrupt confrontation concerning why two different answers have been given.

§ 11.47 Credibility Cross-Examination

Certainly general credibility attacks that the cross-examiner may use on any witness may be applied to the "no-discovery" witness as well. However, because this witness is "no discovery," the lawyer has the same problem: how to find the credibility attacks within the direct examination. To some extent, because the cross-examiner does not have a prepared script for this witness, counsel's creativity is not restricted. Counsel should concentrate on the basics of the general credibility attacks: bias, interest, and motive.

Example: The plaintiff alleged that the defendant had committed domestic violence upon her more than four and one-half years before the separation of the parties. The court permitted the opponent to call the wife's sister, despite the fact that she was not listed as a potential witness. The sister testified that on the night of this domestic violence, she had driven the wife to the hospital. Once there, the wife feared that her husband's military career would be damaged if she entered the emergency room. She and the children would be financially punished. She refused to go into the medical facility to be seen by the doctor.

This undiscovered witness (sister of the plaintiff) was offered to verify that she had in fact taken the wife to the hospital, and that the wife in fact had numerous bruises, red marks, and a blackened eye. She was called to bolster the testimony of the plaintiff who had been rather successfully cross-examined earlier in the trial as to the severity of this domestic violence, the fact that the wife had not seen a doctor, and the fact that this had gone unreported to anyone for years.

The plaintiff had also been cross-examined consistent with the lawyer's theory of the case, that she had been plotting for years to sue the defendant as soon as he had retired from the military and his military retirement had begun to pay out. Rather than attack this sister/witness directly about the veracity of the details to which she testified, the cross-examiner attacked the witness's motive, which was consistent with the cross-examiner's theory of the case:

Q: Mrs. Schubert, you testified that you carried your sister to the medical facility but she refused to go in?

A: Yes.

Q: You testified that you begged her to go in?

A: Yes.

Q: You testified that you told her that as time passed that she would forget how badly brutalized she was?

A: Yes.

Q: You testified that, in fact, you sat there with your sister in the car that night and wrote down details about what you testified today?

A: Yes.

Q: Your sister knew that you were writing those details down?

A: Yes.

Q: Your sister agreed that you would keep those notes?

A: Yes.

Q: In fact, you still have those notes, but your explanation is that you just didn't bring them to trial today?

A: Yes.

Q: Your sister always knew that you had those notes hidden in your home?

A: Yes.

Q: She always knew that you would be available to her with those notes?

A: Yes.

Q: When your sister filed this lawsuit, she discussed with you that you still had those notes?

A: Well, I don't know that she actually discussed that with me.

Q: But she knew that you still had the notes?

A: Yes, I am sure that she did.

Q: She knew that you were prepared to testify about what was on those notes?

A: Yes.

Q: Every night since those notes were made that your sister went home to her husband, she knew that you had those notes ready to use in a divorce trial against her husband?

A: I guess she did.

Q: Well the fact is, ma'am, that she knew that?

A: Yes.

Q: She knew and you knew that those notes would be used if she ever filed this divorce action?

A: Yes.

Q: She knew that those notes were there available for her with great detail?

A: Yes.

Q: The details were to be used to convince a jury that this had occurred?

A: Yes.

Q: That was a secret that you and your sister shared?

A: Yes.

Q: You never shared that secret with her husband?

A: No.

Q: You never shared that secret with counselors?

A: No.

Q: You never shared that secret with ministers?

A: No.

Q: You never shared that secret with law enforcement?

A: No.

Q: You never shared that secret with the husband's military supervisors?

A: No.

Q: It was never shared with anyone?

A: No.

Q: Instead, you kept these notes for one purpose — waiting to be used when your sister asked for alimony and property division?

A: Yes.

§ 11.48 Marginalizing the Witness

The technique of marginalizing a witness applies to the "no-discovery" witness. As discussed, most witnesses are niche witnesses. They can testify to a rather small number of facts. If this "no-discovery" witness cannot support the cross-examiner's theory of this case, or hurt the opponent's theory, and cannot be attacked safely on the facts, then the cross-examiner may consider marginalizing the witness by asking a series of chapters to illustrate that this witness knows precious little about the case.

In a case about a driver who had something to drink on the afternoon before a collision, whether it is a criminal case or personal injury case, where the opposing lawyer has newly "discovered" this witness who observed the cross-examiner's client consuming alcohol earlier in the day, the cross-examiner marginalized a witness by utilizing a series of chapters to highlight the lack of knowledge. Each numbered paragraph is the name of a chapter, not individual questions. There are many more detailed and supporting questions for each chapter.

(1) You saw Mr. Jones (the cross-examiner's party) for less than thirty-five minutes?

(2) That observation period was before 2:00 p.m.?

(3) You did not see Mr. Jones after that time, including and up to the time of the collision after 10:00 p.m.?

(4) You did not see what Mr. Jones had to eat in that eight-hour period?

(5) You did not see what physical activity Mr. Jones did in that eight-hour period?

(6) You did not see what liquids, including non-alcoholic beverages, Mr. Jones consumed in that eight-hour period?

(7) You did not see whether Mr. Jones napped in that eight-hour period?

(8) You did not see how Mr. Jones conducted himself in that eight-hour period?

(9) You did not see how Mr. Jones drove his vehicle in that eight-hour period?

These are but nine of the chapters used to marginalize the witness.

Often in commercial litigation, the corporate party will call an executive as a spokesman for the corporation. This executive is often selected because he has the right look and sound and is articulate. It can even be the president or CEO, who makes a great appearance but had little or nothing to do with the matter at issue. Such a witness can be marginalized by a series of leading questions designed to show that he was not at the key meetings, often because the decisions were made below his level. He did not write or receive the key memos at issue. This witness was not involved in giving the orders. He was not involved in performing the due diligence or testing the product.

It may well be that it wasn't the witness's job to do these things. That is certainly a helpful answer to the cross-examiner as it helps to further marginalize the witness. The point of marginalizing the cross-examination is not to blame the witness for anything, but rather to take the witness out of the case. This form of cross-examination tends to be short and punchy. It is characterized by questions such as: "You were not assigned . . . ," "It wasn't your job . . . ," and "You were not aware . . . ."

§ 11.49 Avoiding Unnecessary Risk in Cross-Examination of the "No-Discovery" Witness

The most useful analysis identifies those chapters upon which the cross-examiner may productively examine the "no-discovery" witness. To be thorough, an analysis must include what points to avoid. Cross-examination provokes anxiety. Cross-examination without benefit of pre-trial discovery produces greater anxiety principally because the lawyer intuitively and logically recognizes there is a greater risk. The cross-examiner understands the damage done on direct examination, but fears even more the damaging testimony that an ill-conceived cross-examination may reveal.

The single most important technique to use in minimizing additional damage on cross-examination of the "no-discovery" witness is to realize that the opponent has almost certainly directed his witness on direct examination into areas in which the witness can do the most damage to the cross-examiner's theory or the most good for the opponent's theory. Accordingly, before the cross-examination begins, the cross-examiner has probably heard the worst the witness has to offer.

Consequently, to minimize the risk of cross-examination of "no-discovery" witnesses, avoid asking for a repetition or elaboration on the most damaging aspects of the direct examination. A frontal assault upon those damaging areas often produces greater damage to the cross-examiner. The witness repeats and makes worse the worse parts of direct. The cross-examiner becomes frustrated. Lacking details that are useful and could have been verified in discovery, the cross-examiner begins using more global terms, which, of course, are easily deniable by the witness (see chapter 4, *The Only Three Rules of Cross-Examination*). The damage is enhanced, and the foundation level rises.

Examples:

WEAK

Q: Your conduct was negligent?

A: I wouldn't agree.

BETTER

Q: The speed limit was 60 mph?

A: Yes.

Q: On a normal weather day 60 mph was as fast as you could drive?

A: I guess so.

Q: But this wasn't a normal weather day?

A: Not really.

Q: On this day it was snowing?

A: Yes. It was.

Q: In fact, it was snowing hard?

A: Yes.

Q: The road was icy?

A: In spots.

Another example: First, the cross-examiner tries to eat the entire subject in one gulp by putting before the witness an entirely conclusory statement.

WEAK

Q: Your software was never accepted in the marketplace?

A: I disagree.

BETTER

Q: You had been trying to sell your software for 3 years?

A: We weren't trying, we were doing it.

Q: Your biggest sale was 200 copies to one company?

A: Yes, but we hoped to sell more.

Q: In 1999 you sold less than 3,500 copies?

A: Yes.

Q: In 2000 you sold less than 3,500 copies?

A: Yes.

It is better to indirectly attack the witness (logic, motive or bias) if an attack must be made. It is better still to take the witness into chapters designed to support the cross-examiner's theory of the case or hurt the opponent's theory without a direct attack upon the witness. Only after control of the witness has been established are direct attacks advisable.

§ 11.50 Conclusion

The "no-discovery" witness presents the cross-examiner with additional challenges and stress. However, techniques exist for dealing with this situation — techniques that the cross-examiner already knows.

The cross-examiner has the advantage of being well prepared for the case as a whole. Moreover, "discovery" is available in the opening statement and the direct examination. The cross-examiner must listen carefully for the opponent's theme in the opening statement and for statements representing what the witnesses will prove. With focused listening and selective note taking during the direct examination of the "no-discovery" witness, the cross-examiner can plan the scope and content of the cross-examination.

Using her knowledge of the facts of the case, the opponent's theme, and the testimony of other witnesses, the lawyer can successfully handle cross-examination of the surprise witness with familiar tactics: the chapter method, (see chapter 5, *The Chapter Method of Cross-Examination*) sequencing, and logic-based questions. Rarely is a "no-questions" cross-examination the best solution. Normally, the witness is valuable to the cross-examiner's theory of the case and should be used for that purpose.

Chapter 12

COPING WITH OBJECTIONS

§ 12.01 The Problem: Objections

The more experience a lawyer has, the better she understands that the standard of admissibility is a very flexible one. Relevance is almost always a discretionary call and very much depends on the parties' theories of the case and the court's appreciation of those theories (see chapter 2, *Developing a Theory of the Case*). What is collateral to the case versus what is plainly relevant often depends on the ability of the court to understand the significance of the evidence. In other words, the more the advocate can give context to a chapter, the better the trial court can recognize the relevance of facts to the case being tried. Objections often stem from the fact that the opponent neither recognizes nor wishes to recognize the context of a chapter of material.

A second area of likely objection is the purely technical: Does the evidence offered comply with the applicable Rules of Evidence? As a brief example, most trial lawyers believe they know hearsay when they hear it. However, most trial lawyers are not as well studied as they might be with regards to the exceptions to the rule against hearsay. For instance, the Federal Rules of

Evidence give the lawyer twenty-two reasons to except the evidence from the hearsay rule to get the evidence in front of the ears and eyes of the jury. But if those are not good enough, a twenty-third exception, the discretionary "other" exception used in the discretion of the court, gives even more latitude.

At times when the cross-examiner is working in a chapter the context of which the opponent does not understand, the opponent may mistakenly believe or harbor a hope that the cross-examiner is working in an area that the court will rule out of bounds. The opponent's objection may be based on relevance or based on the cross-examiner's alleged failure to comply with some applicable Rule of Evidence. Sometimes a judge, caught off guard, can fail to understand why a chapter may be relevant and therefore can mistakenly rule with the opponent. Alternatively, the judge may need further factual development within a chapter in order to understand that the Rules of Evidence permit the line of inquiry. In any event, the risk is that the cross-examiner could be cut off from a fruitful line of inquiry. It would be unfortunate and unprofessional for the cross-examiner to allow this to happen.

This book does not deal specifically with the subjects of the Rules of Evidence or the foundations necessary to introduce evidence. These subjects are a part of the techniques of cross-examination to lay evidence before a fact finder in a way that minimizes objections and maximizes the admissibility and understanding of the facts in the chapters. It is therefore critical for the cross-examiner to find ethical, professional ways to follow desired lines of cross-examination. This chapter discusses techniques that allow a cross-examiner to avoid unnecessary objections, and fairly meet objections — all with the purpose of allowing the lawyer to continue cross-examining in areas relevant to the theory of the case. More importantly, these techniques permit the lawyer to go on the offensive when an objection is made and expand the depth and breadth of cross-examination.

§ 12.02 Objections Represent Distractions to Teaching

All objections are distractions to the cross-examiner's efforts to teach her theory of the case. They also distract efforts to expose the defects in the opponent's theory of the case. Each of the techniques discussed is designed to minimize the distraction of the objection and, where possible, discourage further objections. In the rare instance when the cross-examiner is baiting an objection, her purpose is to eliminate objections that might occur later in the cross-examination when she develops more significant chapters. However, she must never lose sight of the fact that the purpose of cross-examination is to teach the judge and jury. The purpose is not to show the opponent that she knows the rules of evidence better, has quicker wits, or is more skilled in handling objections. The true purpose of trial is to obtain the best possible outcome, not to win a game of one-upmanship with the opponent or witness.

Distractions are not helpful to the teaching process. However, when the listener becomes irritated by the distraction, the person causing the distraction (the opponent) becomes the object of the negative emotion. These are times to take advantage of the opponent's overuse or misuse of objections.

§ 12.03 Following the Only Three Rules of Cross-Examination Eliminates Many Objections

If we are adhering to The Only Three Rules of Cross-Examination, fewer questions will need to be rephrased due to the opponent's objections. By following these rules of leading questions and cross-examining in a logical progression to reach a specific goal, we leave few "form" objections for the opponent to make. Compound questions have been eliminated. Every question is leading. About all the cross-examiner needs to worry about is argumentative, hearsay, relevancy, or foundation objections. Each of these objections is easily handled.

§ 12.04 Objections Based on "Argumentative"

"Argumentative" objections are made in several instances. The most common circumstance giving rise to this type of objection is the lawyer's body language, tone, and volume during cross-examination. The best "teaching" cross-examinations do not rely on a loud voice, aggressive body language, or a sarcastic tone. Each of these techniques, in its own way, is a distraction to the learning potential of the fact finder. The words that the cross-examiner selects — *not* these artificial devices — bring the power to the question. The techniques described in this chapter and book are designed to work better with a calm demeanor, businesslike tone, and less aggressive volume. While there are places for a change of tone, an appropriate gesture — even a sarcastic tone — such places are few and far between. Such techniques are best used sparingly.

The second most common reason for an "argumentative" objection is the word selection of the cross-examiner. The advocate should view an "argumentative" objection to the word selection not as a sanction but as a positive response acknowledging the power of her word selection.

With this said, she should willingly rephrase the question, not by eliminating the vivid word description but by breaking the word selection down so that it is more clear to the fact finder that the original, vivid word selection was appropriate. The goal is to achieve understanding, create the picture, and communicate the information. Seldom is the precise word chosen by the cross-examiner the only word that can accomplish those goals. Example:

Q: She had suffered a massive amount of blood loss at the scene?

Opp: Objection, argumentative as to the word "massive."

Q: Your honor, I will rephrase.

Judge: Fine, do so.

Q: When you arrived at the scene, you saw blood on the carpeted floor?

A: Yes.

Q: The blood was surrounding Ms. Magic?

A: Yes.

Q: The blood was matted in her hair?

A: Yes.

Q: The blood was still coming out of her shoulder area?

A: Yes.

Q: As a trained EMT, you attempted to stop the blood loss?

A: Yes.

Q: You did that by direct pressure?

A: Yes.

Q: It was not easy to do so?

A: No.

Q: It was not easy because everything was slippery with blood already pumping out of her shoulder?

A: Yes.

Q: It was arterial blood?

A: Yes . . . .

Whether the cross-examiner returns to the word "massive," originally thought offensive, is now immaterial. We have slid off the objection and have expanded the admissibility and the factual detail of the cross-examination based on the objection made by the opponent.

Whenever the cross-examiner hears an objection made on the grounds of "argumentative," she should hear that as an opportunity to be more factually descriptive, detailed, and precise. It is an advantage given to the cross-examiner.

Another form of the "argumentative" objection is lodged against the cross-examiner's supposedly non-factual conclusion obtained within a chapter. In other words, the cross-examiner requests that the witness adopt her conclusion. For instance, having factually demonstrated that the plaintiff used the defendant's product in a way never intended or in a clearly dangerous manner, defense counsel might try to add, "That was a pretty stupid thing to do, wasn't it?" While the jury may well be thinking the same thing, the objection "argumentative" is likely to be sustained. Defense counsel should have left well enough alone. The facts of the chapter were sufficient; the conclusion is for the jury to determine. Again, the cross-examiner's adherence to the only three rules of cross-examination makes such a nonfactual, conclusory statement unnecessary and counterproductive.

§ 12.05 Objections Based on "Hearsay"

The Rules of Evidence are beyond the parameters of this book, but suffice it to say that an objection based on "hearsay" also gives us opportunities to get into more rich, precise detail in explaining one of the twenty-three exceptions to the hearsay rule. It is not difficult for us to spot where one of our chapters will likely draw a hearsay objection. Having foreseen the objection, the correct technique is to determine in advance the likely hearsay objection and establish the facts needed to overcome that objection before asking the leading question likely to produce the objection. To do so eliminates the distraction made by the objection.

In other words, part of the chapter must be the facts that establish the exception to the hearsay rule. The question sequencing to fit an exception is critical to avoiding the objection or overcoming the objection, if it is made. If done in the wrong order, the judge hears what sounds like a request for hearsay, followed by the appropriate hearsay objection. In this scenario the court is likely to sustain the objection. In response, the cross-examiner will often try to establish the exception that permits the answer. But at this point, the cross-examiner is swimming upstream. Judges do not like reversing their positions. An objection once sustained is more likely to be renewed and again sustained. It is far more productive for the cross-examiner to anticipate the objection, then carefully lay a factual groundwork for the exception so that the opponent must weigh whether to lodge the objection. In this order, the judge will have already heard the best argument for admissibility available to the cross-examiner before ruling on the objection.

§ 12.06 Objections Based on "Relevance"

There are chapters or questions whose relevance cannot be doubted, regardless of the opponent's objection. When cross-examining counsel is completely confident of the relevance of a line of questioning, she should press ahead with the response and anticipate a correct ruling that permits the lawyer to continue with her line of questioning.

However, there are chapters or questions whose may not be immediately apparent. The better technique is to establish context for the evidence in light of our theory of the case. By far the most scientific approach is to give an opening statement that clarifies the theory of the case. Once the court understands the theory, the judge is equipped to immediately compare a chapter to that theory. Seeing a logical relationship will allow the court to deny the objection based on relevance. In fact, many relevance objections are really disguised objections for an opponent who is saying, "I don't see how this chapter matters." When the opponent can recognize the relationship of the chapter to the matters in dispute, fewer relevance objections are made.

By way of example, if the lawsuit is about the act of a corporation taken in the year 2004, then, in the abstract, a conversation or event that took place several years before appears to lack relevance. The time separation of a few years alone works against the cross-examiner. However if the conversation or event is foreshadowed in the opening statement so that its relationship to the case can be explained, the court knows why this evidence is introduced. Once again there is a heavy price paid by lawyers who want to keep secrets from the opponent in opening statement. A secret kept from the opponent is a secret kept from the judge. A surprised judge cannot be counted on to make an informed decision on a disputed item of evidence. It is far better to make clear through the opening statement, or through other chapters, why a particular chapter has relevance to the theory of the case. Then, if the opponent lodges a relevance objection, the court is in a far better position to appreciate the significance of the material.

§ 12.07 Rule 1: Be Willing to Rephrase Objectionable Questions

There are those questions in cross-examination for which the ruling is much more in doubt. The lawyer may have phrased a question poorly in a way that invites objection. Rather than pitch the relevance fight at the sound of the first objection, the cross-examiner may be better off "sliding off" the objection by use of the technique of voluntarily rephrasing the question. To reiterate, relevance is often a discretionary call for a judge. Thus, the willingness to rephrase places the judge in the position of wanting to permit the testimony into evidence, so long as the question's phrasing may be more proper.

Judges always allow lawyers to rephrase questions. It eliminates the need to rule. Experienced judges prefer not to rule if no ruling is necessary. They have learned that the fewer the number of evidentiary issues available for appeal, the fewer the evidentiary grounds for appeal.

For example, the opponent may object, claiming irrelevance, and the cross-examiner may believe additional facts will assist in establishing relevance. It is a far better technique to ask to rephrase rather than to attempt to make a speaking response to the objection that tries to place before the judge the facts that supposedly establish relevance. In such a situation, the cross-examiner might say, "Mrs. Jones, let me rephrase that question." Alternatively, the advocate might address the problem in this way: "Your honor, I wish to withdraw that question and lay a better factual foundation." Now the judge has even less reason to become involved in the cross-examination or rule on the objection.

What is the judge going to do when the cross-examiner voluntarily and quickly offers to rephrase or lay better foundation? The court is unlikely to say: "No, you cannot rephrase the question," or "No, I will not allow any further foundation."

By offering to rephrase the question or establish additional factual points that will moot the objection, the cross-examiner has made it clear that she is lowering the emotional level of the courtroom by assuring the judge that she is minding the rules, attempting to do only what is permissible. The primary thrust of this technique is to remove the necessity for the court to rule. The cross-examiner should rephrase the question or withdraw that question until additional supportive facts have been introduced. Often the rephrasing of the question discourages the opponent from renewing his objection.

In these gray areas, it is often most helpful to use the rephrase technique before resorting to providing the court with a clear-cut answer to admissibility. If the opponent renews the relevance objection, the subject area is still open for debate on the relevance issue. In effect, the advocate has created a second opportunity to offer the testimony into evidence. If there is no objection after our rephrases, then the evidence is in. If a second objection is made, the cross-examiner may now argue the admissibility of this area of facts.

There is a pleasant by-product to this technique. The judge normally will smile at the lawyer who quickly and voluntarily agrees to rephrase the question. Judges who smile at a lawyer seldom hurt that lawyer's case.

§ 12.08 Rule 2: Acknowledge the Correct Use of the Objection

Occasionally, the cross-examiner must privately admit that the opponent has objected appropriately. She should be willing to act on that private admission; it is the professional thing to do. Juries like it and so do judges. It shocks the opponent. Maybe it will cause the opponent to think he should concede points when he has done something objectionable.

There are many ways to gracefully concede a valid objection. If the objection is to a question that could be better phrased or in any other way is objectionable, but can be made not objectionable, accept the ruling or make the ruling unnecessary by withdrawing the question and beginning again.

If, on the other hand, the objection is valid because the question in its current form is inadmissible, counsel may elect to discontinue trying to put into evidence that particular testimony but continue to press a similar, but admissible, line of questioning. The cross-examiner should return to this similar line of questioning and highlight its difference with some changes of wording or sentence structure.

Example:

Q: Dr. Moffitt, looking at Exhibit 17, the letter from Dr. Bloom to Dr. Hutt, would you agree that it warns Dr. Hutt of the patient's deteriorating condition?

Opp.: Objection, your honor — calls for speculation, and the document speaks for itself.

Q: That's correct — it may call for speculation. Let me ask you this, Dr. Moffitt: Isn't it true that your state of mind when you read Exhibit 17 was . . . .

It may be argued that it is the same question just worded differently. However, now it is not objectionable.

When continuing the line of questioning in this manner, question the witness in a matter-of-fact voice. Do not be grandiose with gestures, voice, or attitude. The idea is to do it quickly, concisely, and in a business-like demeanor. The opponent is put back because the cross-examiner has placed her opponent in the jury's eyes as someone who has "interrupted." Every trial lawyer is sensitive to that characterization. By moving along in a matter-of-fact voice and doing so without hesitation, the point is made. The similar line of questioning has continued. The jury will now become irritated if the witness is further interrupted or not permitted to answer.

Remember, there may be multiple ways to prove a fact. If a single question within any chapter draws a sustained objection, the chapter should not be abandoned. The advocate should work around the problem and continue with the chapter. If an entire chapter is ruled inadmissible (likely on relevance grounds), the cross-examiner should endeavor to determine whether there is another chapter available or a chapter which could be quickly assembled that establishes many of the same facts, or leads to the important inferences that the cross-examiner hoped to accomplish with the inadmissible chapter. The advocate is reminded that objections are sustained to particular questions, seldom to entire areas of questioning. It is unwise and unnecessary to assume that a sustained objection as to a particular question means that the court will not permit any questioning in that area. Of course, if a judge has ruled in limine, or has ruled in trial that a particular area, event, or conversation is inadmissible, it is the duty of counsel to obey that ruling. Chapters that seek to get into forbidden areas by subterfuge must be avoided.

§ 12.09 Rule 3: Baiting the "Foundation" Objection

The technique of baiting the foundation objection should be used in the event we have a feisty opponent who attempts to object whenever possible. The cross-examiner must be sensitive to the fact that objections are a matter of tactics. A trial is not a law school examination in which spotting an objectionable question earns a point for the objecting party. Offering an opponent the opportunity to make an unnecessary "foundation" objection is also useful in a cross-examination that will contain numerous "gray areas" that must be developed later in the cross-examination.

Early in the cross-examination, ask at least one or two questions that require a foundation. As to each of these questions lay the foundation meticulously. Preferably, it should be done in such a way that the jury vaguely understands the ritualistic nature of foundation questions. Soon thereafter, pose leading questions to which the answer will be "yes." Deliberately remove all foundation questions to this line of questions. Go right for the jugular.

Do not set up the foundation at all, despite the only three rules and chapter method.

When the objection comes, say a silent prayer of thanks and acknowledge it gracefully. Then use this response: "Your honor, I did shorten my questions. I will more fully establish the foundation."

Now slowly, meticulously, inch by inch, small fact by small fact, establish the foundation. Do not leave out any possible foundation material. Discomfort your opponent by questioning in meticulous detail. Once the opponent has been punished with this intentionally meticulous foundation material, the opponent will be less likely to object on foundation grounds in the future. This then gives the cross-examiner tactical choices and advantages as to when and in how much detail to lay future foundations. No doubt the attention of the judge and the jury have been captured by this interaction. Both recognize, because of the earlier full foundation questions, that cross-examining counsel knows how to perform the ritual. Because counsel has now completely and accurately laid the foundation for this question, judge and jury know that no deception was involved in this statement. And because the eventual leading question was answered "yes," they know that the cross-examiner was being impeded in route to a goal she could easily establish.

Under these circumstances, the perception is that it is the cross-examining counsel who is trying to "move it along," and the objecting counsel who is throwing up unnecessary roadblocks to the establishment of the truth. Having established the necessary foundation, move to the precise "bottom line" question to which your opponent objected. The opponent can no longer object.

We just taught the opponent that it is not wise to object when we are cross-examining. As gray areas are developed, the opponent is gun-shy of further objections, even if the objections are not as to foundation.

§ 12.10 Rule 4: Moving It Along

Opponent: Objection, this is cumulative.

Examiner: Your honor, I think I can move this along fairly rapidly.

When was the last time that a judge resented a lawyer trying to "move it along?" If the lawyer is in a gray area and the cross-examiner perceives that it permits the court to make a discretionary call, a pitched battle is probably undesirable. It is better to offer to pursue it briefly. Keep the promise. Move it along. Cut to the bottom line and then leave the area entirely. Once the court becomes acquainted with the idea that we know that the trial must be moved along, the court is more likely to permit brief forays into possibly tangential areas. Because the matter is handled briefly, the judge often views the call as having gone both ways. The cross-examiner cannot complain that she was not permitted to delve into the area, yet the opponent's objection was recognized by limiting the cross-examiner on this issue. There is something for everybody — be satisfied with it. Make the point. *Do not* try to go back and fill in the rest of the chapter. Move on into an area whose admissibility cannot be questioned. The court sustains objections much less often with this method. This is a fact of life. Lawyers who police themselves best are least policed by others.

§ 12.11 Rule 5: "Your Honor, I'll Tie It Up"

Opponent: This is a collateral matter and should not be inquired into on cross-examination.

Examiner: Your Honor, I am about to tie it up.

Judges permit lawyers to "tie up evidence." Lawyers who are skilled in tying up evidence get far more borderline evidence before the jury. Further, the lawyer who has been conducting goal-oriented cross-examinations has built up her credibility with the judge. One of the first added benefits of the chapter method of cross-examination (see chapter 5, *The Chapter Method of Cross-Examination*) is that it produces a series of questions that move toward resolution or clarification of a definable fact issue. A judge who understands that counsel consistently questions toward a goal is far more likely to permit questioning in a hazy area on the assumption that she knows where we are going and have a plan on how to get there. Since she has always tied matters up in the past, she will be permitted more latitude in "gray" areas of inquiry. Of course, the cross-examiner must always tie it up. Never promise without clearly delivering on the promise.

If the cross-examiner has given a theory-driven, fact-intensive opening statement, this response is needed less often. That opening statement occurred because the advocate understood that the chapter's fact would be performed in order to support the theory of the case. Now the cross-examination is occurring through the chapter method. There are no one-question chapters. Every chapter establishes the factual context in which a leading question is asked. As a result, there are fewer occasions when counsel needs to reassure the court that she can "tie it up." More often the court understands how the desired testimony is tied to the theory of the case and the chapter in which it is being asked.

§ 12.12 Rule 6: Tie It Up, Then Go Back

Opponent: This is a collateral matter and should not be inquired into on cross-examination.

Examiner: Your Honor, I am about to tie it up.

When confronted with this objection, do not meander toward the goal and do not speak in parenthetical points. If there is a reasonable risk that the court has lost patience with this line of inquiry or is on the fence concerning its admissibility, sacrifice greater context for admissibility. Everything but the essence should be eliminated. Cut to the bottom line and establish the goal-fact.

This is not to say that the lawyer must overlook forever the remainder of the prepared chapter and fail to give the jury the unabridged cross-examination of this line of questioning in due time. What this means is that the cross-examiner must incisively cut to the bottom question that will tie it up. Once the court has been shown that the subject can be tied up, the cross-examiner can properly return to that interrupted line of questioning. By establishing a bottom-line point for the court, the lawyer has satisfied herself and the court that the evidence is subject to being tied up. She can now safely return to her line of questioning, to the question that was first objected to by the opponent, and pick up where the objection interrupted the chapter.

When the cross-examiner uses this technique, the judge knows that she has returned to where she was interrupted. More importantly, the jury knows. Perhaps most importantly, the opponent now understands that objections such as this will not distract the cross-examiner. Establish the point quickly and then return to where the objection began. By giving the jury the entire unabridged line of questioning of that matter and continuing through a re-establishment of the goal point, the advocate teaches the opponent a painful lesson. The opponent has permitted the examiner to give the abridged version and then the unabridged version of that line of questioning. The point has been made not once, but twice. The opponent now realizes that the point can be made quickly or slowly, once or twice, depending on whether the objection is made. Once performed, this technique discourages further objection.

This technique works best when a judge is impatient and wants the trial to "move along."

§ 12.13 Rule 7: Speaking Responses -- Miniature Closing Arguments

Opponent: Objection, this is entirely collateral and should not be gone into on cross-examination.

Examiner: Your Honor, our theory of the case is premised in part on the fact that this witness has on multiple occasions misled or lied to the plaintiff. To have a "thorough and sifting" cross-examination, permit me to present to the jury each of those instances. This instance is about misrepresentation of this witness's ability to the plaintiff.

If a speaking response to an objection is permitted by the court, the cross-examiner has the right to tell the judge where the cross-examiner is going with the line of questioning. If a speaking response is not permitted, seek permission before replying. For example, "May I reply, your honor?" Or, "May I be heard, your honor?" If the matter is of great importance and the court frowns on speaking objections or speaking replies, respect the rules of the court but protect the ability to reply in this way: "May I be heard on this at the bench, your honor?" Always tie the response to the theory of the case. When countering the objection that a fact or line of facts is collateral or irrelevant, it is important that the court understands the relationship of that chapter to the theory of the case.

If the objection, whether stated directly, is that the cross-examination has gone on too long or with too much detail, the cross-examiner's response should also include a key phrase known to the court as being the standard for cross-examination in that jurisdiction. For instance, in Alabama, the standard is "a thorough and sifting cross-examination." When this well-known phrase is included in the response, it encourages the court to rule using another well-known, if not well-worn, phrase, "Well, all right, this is cross-examination."

More importantly, where permitted, the speaking response is designed to acquaint the jury with this area of inquiry (a miniature closing argument). Do not make a speaking response until permitted by the court. Stop if the judge indicates enough has been said. The more liberal the judge on speaking responses, the more specific the speaking responses can be.

Opponent: Objection, this is entirely collateral.

Examiner: Your honor, this line of questioning goes directly to our theory of the case. That theory is that the plaintiff breached this contract by making it impossible for my client to be able to perform it. This line of questioning is designed to show that the plaintiff is a man of manipulative means and bent of mind who would have the audacity to manipulate this contract in such a way as to make it impossible for my client to perform. Then he sues my client.

Argumentative, you say? Yes, it is. This is the time to argue. Remember, it is a miniature closing argument. If the court permits speaking responses, push your speaking response as far as accuracy, ethics, and professionalism permit.

A word of caution: Never push the speaking response further than the cross-examination can establish. In other words, if the cross-examiner is going to use words such as "manipulative," the cross-examination had better show that the plaintiff is "manipulative." Remember the judge and jury are always weighing the lawyer's credibility. The advocate's passion and enthusiasm cannot be permitted to interfere with the advocate's credibility.

§ 12.14 Rule 8: Dealing with Objections Designed to Assist the Witness on Cross-Examination

[1] Talking Objection That Suggests Answers to Witness

There are lawyers who, having exposed their witnesses to penetrating, effective cross-examination, feel the call to come to their aid (much in the sense of an ill-timed cavalry charge). They often do so by voicing an objection that is designed not to engender a ruling, but to coach the witness. These objections, like trick-or-treaters, come in many costumes. Underneath, all are based on childish motivations.

There are many forms of this objection designed to assist a witness, but all have the same basis. The opponent is attempting to tell the witness how to safely answer (or evade) the question. The by-product of this objection is that it interrupts the cross-examiner's flow. Don't let it happen. Slide off the objection. Make the interruption a part of the cross-examination. The objection may suggest the witness "doesn't know" or "doesn't remember," or it may actually suggest lines of testimony. Each type of objection can be turned to the advantage of the cross-examiner.

The cross-examiner, in control, must expose these objections for what they are. By our doing so, the jury is taught that the objection should not have been made. The cross-examiner stays calm. She knows the objection was improper and distracting, but she also knows techniques to punish the interruption and reward her theory of the case. Simultaneously, the cross-examiner's appropriate response warns the opponent against further frivolous or "coaching" objections. The witness is taught not to look for help from his lawyer. The witness is all alone.

[2] The Favorite Suggestion: "Only If the Witness Knows"

A frequent suggestion offered by way of objection is that the witness shall only answer "if he knows." This hint may be dealt with in a number of ways.

Technique 1:

Q: You recognize Dr. Clark as an expert in the field of pediatrics?

Opp.: Objection, your honor; only if she knows.

Q: Dr. Shaw, I have been asking you questions for more than forty-five minutes.

A: Yes, though it seemed longer.

Q: And before that my opponent asked you questions for about ninety minutes?

A: Yes.

Q: All this time you understood that we were both asking you what you knew?

A: Well, I suppose so.

Q: In fact, you never once thought that if you didn't know something, you should fake the answer.

A: Of course not.

Q: So, in fact, every question asked by both sides asks for you to answer using only what you know?

A: Yes, I suppose so.

Q: Now let's return to my question — What you knew about Dr. Clark was . . . .

The objection was designed to give the witness an "out" before answering. The cross-examiner shows that it is much too late for the witness to avoid answering. The witness will answer rather than appear illogical and foolish.

[3] The Evading Witness: "I Don't Know"

When a cross-examination is successful, there are certain times when the witness will know the answer but not want to give it. This is particularly true with theme-related questions. This is absolutely true with important concluding questions.

For example, in a divorce case, after the cross-examiner had taken the defendant wife through multiple instances of spending what would appear to the jury to be frivolous and rather outrageous amounts of money on clothing and jewelry, the cross-examiner brought the questioning to a conclusion by asking the witness the effect these purchases had on the marriage:

Q: When you spent $3,300 on shoes during the summer of 2002, you knew that your husband was struggling to make ends meet?

A: (A lengthy pause.)

Opp.: That question calls for my client to speculate. She has no way of knowing that answer.

Judge: The witness is instructed not to speculate. If you don't know, say you don't know.

A: I don't know.

Q: You don't know?

A: I don't know.

Q: You do know that you spent $3,300 on shoes in the summer of 2002?

A: Yes.

Q: You do know that your husband was managing the money?

A: Yes.

Q: You do know that he was working very long hours?

A: Yes.

Q: You do know that he told you that summer that he was having trouble making ends meet?

A: Well . . . he might have said that.

Q: Then, Mrs. Grey, you know that your spending $3,300 on shoes that summer was affecting his ability to make ends meet?

A: I'm not sure.

Opp.: She has already testified that she didn't know.

Q: I am cross-examining on the truthfulness of that very response. Your husband had complained to you that there just was not enough money to pay the bills?

A: Yes, he said something like that.

Q: Then, Mrs. Grey, if I understand it correctly, you knew that you had spent $3,300 on shoes the summer of 2002, and you knew your husband was complaining there wasn't enough money in the family budget?

A: Yes.

Q: What you didn't know was that spending $3,300 on shoes was making it hard to make ends meet?

A: Yes, I just don't know.

The point to be made is: Don't let the witness off the hook just because her lawyer has suggested the witness doesn't know the answer. Often, claiming not to know the answer is worse for the witness than any answer the witness could give. More importantly, when the witness says she doesn't know the answer, often the jury knows that the witness does know the answer but just doesn't want to answer it. The dodge of "I don't know" is exposed by carefully building up the known facts to show the obviousness of the desired, but evaded, answer to the original question.

We must avoid permitting the line of questioning to be stopped by the "I don't know" suggested by the opponent's objection. Following the technique described above, the objection actually permits us to re-establish the line of questioning and go through the line of questioning a second time. The jury hears the bad facts concerning the witness's conduct multiple times. Using this technique, the evidence is highlighted rather than suppressed. Whether the concluding answer is, "I don't know," or the answer that the cross-examiner wants is immaterial, the jury understands the "I don't know" to be evasive. The jury hears the evidence and sees the evasive character of the witness.

[4] Coping with the Objection: "If He Remembers"

The same technique applies when the opponent suggests to the witness that the witness cannot (read: should not) remember. The phrase makes no sense in any event. Witnesses tell the facts they do remember. Implicit in every question is a request to relate what is remembered. Putting aside the gamesmanship of the suggestive objection, through appropriate cross-examination this response can be a strong comment to the jury that the witness doesn't care to remember. That it is, in fact, an open and obvious deception.

In a medical malpractice case:

Q: Doctor, when the child was brought to the emergency room, both parents were there?

A: Yes.

Q: They both told you how terribly hard the child had struck her head on the concrete?

A: How hard? (pause)

Opp.: The doctor previously testified on direct examination and on this cross-examination that he doesn't remember those types of details.

Q: Your honor, let me approach it a different way.

Judge: Proceed.

Q: You do remember the child coming into the emergency room?

A: Yes.

Q: You do remember the parents being there?

A: Yes.

Q: You do remember the fact that the child had struck her head?

A: Yes.

Q: You do remember she had a closed head injury?

A: Yes.

Q: You do remember from medical school training that the severity of the blow to the head is important?

A: Yes.

Q: You do remember from medical school that taking a history is important?

A: Yes.

Q: You do remember that if the patient is not conscious or cannot verbalize the history that you take that history from whatever reliable source is available?

A: Yes.

Q: You do remember that the parents gave a portion of the history?

A: Yes.

Q: You do remember they gave you the child's name?

A: Yes.

Q: You do remember they gave you her name because you asked for that information?

A: Yes.

Q: You do remember they gave you her age because it was important to your diagnosis and treatment?

A: Yes.

Q: You do remember they gave you her prior medical history because it was important to your diagnosis and treatment?

A: Yes.

Q: You do remember they told you how hard she hit her head because it was important to your diagnosis and treatment?

A: I guess so.

Q: Doctor, you do remember that the parents told you that the child struck her head very hard?

A: I guess so.

In this context, the tag phrase "you do remember" is used to highlight or loop the phrase "doesn't remember" used by the opponent in his objection. It simultaneously points out the absurdity of the witness not remembering the big fact when he remembers less important facts.

The opponent has made this objection to distract the jury from the cross-examination and educate the witness "not to remember" certain critical admissions needed by the cross-examiner. Instead, the contrary occurred. The cross-examiner shall look forward to this type of objection in the future. It can be used to intimidate the witness thoroughly and to force the admission. It can be used to educate the jury that the witness and the objecting lawyer are both trying not to be helpful and intentionally not recall critical evidence. It silences objections.

The technique is to slide off the objection. Immediately revert to a series of questions, each containing one fact, and each requiring a "yes" answer.

We may use the phrase, "You do remember," in each of these questions. Work slowly and methodically up through the facts remembered, taking them either in chronological order or order of importance to the case, leading up to the critical issue that the witness claims he can't remember. Along the way, punish the witness and your opponent with the phrase, "You do remember." We are spontaneously looping the phrase from the objection and all the time making a bigger point of the fact that the witness claims he can't remember. The objection permits greater cross-examination, not less. However, keep in mind that use of the phrase "you do remember" can become as repetitive and boring a habit as any other tagline. The phrase should be used in this scenario as part of this specific technique and then discontinued.

[5] Coping with the Objection: "The Witness Already Said . . ."

In its most sophisticated form, this type of objection is designed by the opponent to educate the witness under cross-examination as to what story to give. The opponent attempts this either by repeating some portion of direct testimony or some portion of the answers given on cross-examination.

While the objecting lawyer understands that he is now testifying rather than the witness, the jury will hear it as an objection. Further, the witness is educated to repeat the litany delivered by the lawyer.

This is a *speaking* objection. In response, we might argue that was not what was said on direct examination or earlier in cross-examination. In the alternative, we might argue that the lawyer is improperly making speaking objections.

A third method is to handle it by sliding off the objection. For example, in a criminal case, the prosecutor attempts to save the witness by a speaking objection. The girlfriend/informant is now testifying against the former boyfriend/drug dealer. The girlfriend testified on direct that she was afraid of the boyfriend to explain why she did not talk with the police until weeks after her arrest and weeks after the defendant boyfriend's arrest. The defendant's theory of the case is that the girlfriend agreed to speak to the prosecutor only after her lawyer arranged for immunity for her testimony. Substantially into the cross-examination and as a concluding question to a chapter of questions on her failure to talk with the police, the following occurred:

Q: The fact of the matter is you waited two full weeks after the arrest to tell the police that your boyfriend was the drug dealer?

A: Yes, but, but . . . .

Opp.: Your honor, she has already testified that she was afraid of the defendant and that was why she did not notify the police right away.

The defense lawyer is trying to misrepresent to the jury.

Q: Your honor, I am not misrepresenting anything to the jury. I am cross-examining the witness on that point. I will be glad to rephrase so that there will be no question of exactly what I am asking this witness.

Judge: Why don't you do that?

Q: Your lawyer said in his objection that you were afraid of your boyfriend?

A: Yes.

Q: And you are now telling us that you were afraid of your boyfriend and that was the reason you didn't tell the police about his drug activity?

A: Yes.

Q: And you are now telling us that you were afraid of your boyfriend from the time before the arrest until you finally went and talked with the police?

A: Yes.

There are two chapter paths to follow for the cross-examiner.

The First Chapter Path:

Q: Your lawyer was with you when you went to talk to the police?

A: Yes.

Q: You heard your lawyer discuss the fact that all charges against you would be dropped?

A: Yes.

Q: Your lawyer told the police that once the charges were to be dropped, you were willing to talk with them.

A: Yes.

Q: Your lawyer said that in front of you?

A: Yes.

Q: Your lawyer said now that the charges were dropped you were willing to tell that the cocaine was your boyfriend's (the defendant)?

A: Yes.

Q: You were present when your lawyer said that to the police?

A: Yes.

Now the point is "the lawyer" is a witness with a vested interest. His objections will not be listened to in the same light. It now appears to the jury that the opponent was misrepresenting facts to them. The issue is "your lawyer" now. The opponent has suffered substantial blemishes to his credibility.

The Second Chapter Path:

Q: Your lawyer didn't say in his objection that after your arrest, you and the defendant went home together?

A: No, he didn't say that.

Q: Your lawyer didn't say that you then moved home to your parents for two weeks?

A: No, he didn't say that.

Q: Your lawyer didn't say that you were away from the defendant for fourteen days with your daddy before you went to talk to the police?

A: No.

Q: Your lawyer didn't say that your parents have money and immediately got you to a lawyer?

A: No.

Q: Your lawyer didn't say that your parents kept you away from the defendant?

A: No.

Q: Your lawyer didn't say your parents wouldn't let you talk to him or him to you during that two weeks?

A: No, he didn't.

Q: Your lawyer didn't say that in spite of your parents' feelings, that you snuck out to see Billy Bob, the defendant?

A: No.

Q: Your lawyer only said in the objection that you were afraid of Billy Bob, the defendant.

A: Yes.

Q: And you are now telling us that two weeks away from him and the three separate times that you were intimate with him, you were afraid of the defendant?

A: Well . . . I don't know.

The witness stares at her lawyer at the prosecution table with the message, "Help me, help me," in her eyes for the jury to see. The opponent will not help. His credibility has been tarnished.

The objection of the opponent can be used to open up a new line of chapters highlighted by the phrase, "your lawyer." The lines of distinction between her defense lawyer and the prosecuting lawyer fade during this line of questioning.

To those lawyers who believe that there would be objections to the phrase, "Your lawyer didn't say in his objection . . .," there are three responses. First, the objection may well hurt the prosecution more than no objection at all. Second, the judge is now in a position to have to comment on a previous objection by the opponent. Most judges would prefer not to be put in that position. Most judges would look at your opponent as having opened up this can of worms. Most judges would decline to require a rephrase. If the judge does so, rephrase it. Only use that phrase in the concluding question. If the prosecutor wants to object then, again the objection may hurt more than not objecting. Third, if necessary, replace the phrase "your lawyer" with "the prosecutor."

Now the objection has been removed, but the tie between the witness and the lawyer remains.

[6] Spontaneous Looping Off of the Objection

A preferred technique of dealing with the objection that coaches an answer is to spontaneously loop off of the objection itself. This example comes from a lawsuit between a real estate developer and his architect. The developer sues for malpractice in design. The developer's project manager is being cross-examined about trying to assign fault that certain change orders were not incorporated in the field drawings.

Q: You never called Mr. Greenberg's architectural office to see if there were any change orders in the brickwork?

Opp.: Objection, your honor; the witness has already testified that he had been told by the brick mason that he was working from the newest plans.

Q: You talked to the brick mason?

A: Yes.

Q: The brick mason said he was up to date?

A: Yes.

Q: Not Mr. Greenberg, the architect?

A: No.

Q: Because you never talked to Mr. Greenberg, the architect?

A: No.

Q: You never talked to Mr. Greenberg's wife and partner, Mrs. Greenberg, also an architect?

A: No.

Q: You never talked to any of his staff?

A: No.

Q: The brick mason was not with the architect's staff?

A: No.

Q: You never called the architect?

A: Not on the bricks.

Q: You never relied on their word?

A: Not on theirs.

Q: You relied on the brick mason?

A: Yes.

Or

Q: You relied on the brick mason?

A: Yes.

Q: The brick mason does not work for the architect?

A: No.

Q: The architect did not select the brick mason?

A: No.

Q: The developer selected the brick mason?

A: Yes.

Q: The brick mason got paid by the developer?

A: Yes.

Q: The brick mason does not draw the plans?

A: No.

Q: The architect draws the plans?

A: Yes.

Q: But you called the brick mason?

A: Yes.

Q: Never the architect?

By spontaneously looping the phrase "the brick mason" from the objection and contrasting it to "the architect," the cross-examiner expands her admissible scope of examination.

§ 12.15 Dealing with the Interventionist Judge

The techniques within this chapter are helpful with the variable that judges differ on the degrees to which they will permit lawyers to ply their craft. Some judges no longer respect the value of cross-examination nor appreciate the subtle application of technique. These judges are not disposed to permit counsel to have input into any objections by opponents. In the courtroom, where these objections will result in an argument with the judge in front of the jury, cross-examining counsel must tailor the use of these techniques to the style and level permitted by the judge. But the lawyer must try them first. No one knows how a judge will react to these techniques until they have been tried. No one knows how the judge will respond with this witness in this trial. Always try the techniques first. Always adhere to the ruling of the court. If the judge insists that these types of techniques to respond to objections not be used, then desist.

Show the court and your opponent that going back to the old-fashioned way of responding to objections is easy. Show the ethical and professional fortitude to abide by the ruling.

Chapter 13

PRE-TRIAL APPLICATION: USE AT DEPOSITIONS AND PRE-TRIAL HEARINGS

§ 13.01 Practicing the Skills

Practice does *not* make perfect. Perfection is not possible in trial work. Fortunately, perfection is not necessary. But practice is necessary. When we rehearse a technique outside of trial, we become comfortable with it. That technique then feels natural in trial. Trial is the last place to learn a technique. We all need to practice trial skills and techniques. It is better to practice when a client's fate does not hang in the balance. Since cross-examination skills need to be practiced outside of trial, where can they be practiced? They are easily practiced in all manner of pre-trial settings, including depositions, preliminary hearings, motion practice, and any other setting in which a witness can be examined by leading questions. But just as importantly, trial techniques need to be rehearsed in one's head. We can listen to a conversation and silently loop a key word or phrase. We can hear ourselves ask leading questions, and we can think about in what order the facts ought to be revealed. We should spend a great deal of time thinking about our cross-examinations so that when we get to the courtroom, we feel as if we have done this cross-examination before.

§ 13.02 Breaking Out of Learned Behaviors; Applying Conscious Decisions

"The unexamined life is not worth living."

Socrates

Cross-examination techniques work best when they flow naturally. The more energy the advocate must spend on remembering the steps of a technique, the less effective the technique. This is the reason to avoid any complex trial technique. Trial work is tough enough without adding complex techniques we have a difficult time remembering or performing. The techniques of cross-examination are meant to be solutions. They should not create new problems. If a lawyer practices cross-examination techniques in an inconsistent way, there may be some short-term benefit in an individual cross-examination. But the advocate will not have gained the long-term benefits that come from applying techniques in the everyday cross-examination of witnesses.

These cross-examination techniques are not meant to be saved up for the tough cross-examinations. They should be used in every cross-examination so that the tough cross-examinations will feel easier. The lawyer cannot afford to have two sets of techniques: one for practice and one for courtroom work. Or loose techniques for easy witnesses and tight control for tough witnesses. Recall that the object of this book is not to equip the lawyer with techniques capable of occasionally producing a wonderful cross-examination, but to equip the lawyer with those techniques necessary to regularly produce predictably strong cross-examinations. In the pursuit of powerful cross-examinations, a single technique that is used occasionally is inefficient. However, a scientific method dramatically raises the level of cross-examination for the remainder of the advocate's career.

To put this in the trial setting: No client wants his lawyer to develop new skills during his trial. Undoubtedly we all learn from each trial, but the good news is that advocates do not have to wait for trials in order to master cross-examination techniques. The classical view that cross-examination skills could be developed only during trial led to lawyers using old, comfortable techniques. The techniques were used even if they were incomplete or outmoded. The development of new and better cross-examination skills was sacrificed daily in an attempt to work with the techniques the lawyer had long used — whether or not they had proven successful. This criticism extends beyond the legal profession. Each person falls into familiar patterns. Once behavioral patterns have been developed, it feels safer to repeat them than to learn new ones. All lawyers recognize that learning and practicing new cross-examination skills during trials is difficult.

The use of poor practices in actual trial settings makes for permanent imprinting of techniques *regardless of their value*. Through practice, the lawyer essentially learns how to execute bad habits and unsuitable styles of cross-examination.

Sometimes lawyers find themselves relying on undeveloped or misunderstood techniques. Many experienced trial lawyers, when asked how they perform good cross-examinations, respond that they don't know because they do only what has worked over the years. Once a trial lawyer understands why a technique works, she can consciously select the appropriate one, and with practice instinctively, reflexively, and appropriately apply the technique. The goal of pre-trial practice is to allow the practitioner to become comfortable with the technique before it is needed in trial. The lawyer can learn to perform the essential techniques of successful cross-examination so that they become ingrained responses at trial.

§ 13.03 Practicing the Chapter Method of Cross-Examination

Every cross-examination breaks into chapters. This is true in the shoplifting trial and the homicide trial. It is true in a contract case focused on furniture and the contract case focused on a telecommunications satellite. If the lawyer is working on her own small case, it is imperative that she prepare the entire case in the chapter method. Even if she is an associate in a larger firm or the second chair to a more experienced lawyer, the lawyer can help the team while still improving her own skills. The lawyer need only accept the responsibility to outline all of the chapters for one witness or some chapters for an important witness. The act of creating chapters of cross-examination for another lawyer's use is substantially the same as preparing those chapters for her own use.

Similarly, if a lawyer must comb the discovery to build the chapters, the lawyer learns how to assemble facts to build logical progressions to specific goals. Preparation is the most underrated of cross-examination techniques. It is the least appreciated but most valuable skill a cross-examiner can acquire. The more quickly a lawyer learns how to pull together facts to create chapters, the more natural it will become. It will be easier to form chapters under the time pressures that eventually plague every lawyer. Preparation of cross-examination chapters, the amalgamation of facts, the spotting of facts beyond change, and development of theories of the case are decidedly not the grunt work of the trial profession.

§ 13.04 Trials Require Real Time Decisions

Some valuable learning can be accomplished by watching an experienced trial lawyer exercise her skills. Unfortunately, watching is no substitute for the highly interactive process of cross-examination. A person may carefully watch someone drive a car, but it won't teach her how to drive or at least how to drive safely. When a driver must make a split-second evasive maneuver, all the watching is no substitute for practical experience.

Studying books, listening to lectures, and observing demonstrations of skills are all helpful, but they are not sufficient to educate a trial lawyer. They should all be practiced. Once inexperienced lawyers have been exposed to the teaching of trial skills, they are obligated to practice and reaffirm those skills time after time. Trial skills are *not* like bicycle riding. A lawyer cannot get back on years later and be as good as new. Unused trial skills atrophy. To retain their condition, they must be regularly exercised. In an era where trials occur less frequently, a trial lawyer cannot count on a regular flow of trials in which to practice her skills. The solution is to employ trial cross-examination techniques in non-trial settings.

For lawyers who have a tremendous amount of courtroom experience, the techniques discussed here are equally applicable. All lawyers have developed certain bad habits that must be broken. Once a bad habit is established, it is more difficult it. Beyond that, trial work has become a much more complex vehicle than it was even five years ago. It is now recognized that trial work is a specialty. Fewer non-trial lawyers go through the periodic charade of being a trial lawyer. Consequently, the opponents are better. They are more skilled and more experienced.

Another layer of complexity has been added with the advent of the professional expert witness. Courts are demanding greater expertise for witnesses who testify on expert issues. Witnesses are better prepared. They are more skilled in evading questions on cross-examination.

There may well have been a time in American history when courts were not clogged, disputes remained small, and criminal sentencing acts were less draconian. In general, trials were frequent, less expensive for the litigants, and the preferred method of dispute resolution. In that era, it may well have been possible to hone one's trial skills by trying many cases. It is no longer the case. Trial lawyers must find places other than trial to practice and perfect their craft.

§ 13.05 Other Solutions

This is not to say that the legal profession has ignored this predicament. Clinical trial practice courses are now standard offerings in law schools in the United States. There is increased recognition of the need for trial skill teaching in law school.

The difficulty with trial skills clinics in law schools are that they terminate for the young professional after graduation and before the prospective trial lawyer ever has a chance to suffer through the rigors of a full blown trial.

State bar organizations and numerous other bar-related organizations offer trial skill programs (e.g., National Institute of Trial Advocacy, National Criminal Defense College). These after-graduation clinical programs are built on the recognition that the only way trial lawyers (whether inexperienced or experienced) can better their trial skills is by actually performing them.

A major drawback, no matter how effective these learn-by-doing techniques have become, is that they are by definition of short duration and usually of great expense. Young lawyers can seldom afford the tuition or the time away from their office. Experienced lawyers cannot imagine being away from their office for one or more weeks at a time. In fact, few professionals can afford the luxury of even two weeks away from their practice to attempt mastery of these necessary skills. Even if a lawyer could break away to go to a trial institute for two weeks, this is not enough time to firmly acquire and practice the cross-examination techniques that are fundamental to a controlled, planned cross-examination. The solution is to acknowledge that cross-examinations skills are best acquired and polished by regular use rather than by cramming for the final examination that trial represents.

This is not to say that every examination in a pre-trial setting must follow the only three rules of cross-examination, that every chapter must be prepared, or that every question must be sourced. Pre-trial is not trial. It is not mandatory that every question be leading. Especially in the deposition context, it would probably be erroneous to make every question leading. Nonetheless, there certainly will be times in every deposition, preliminary hearing, or *Daubert* hearing, in which it is profitable to employ leading questions.

§ 13.06 Cross-Examination Rehearsals Must Build in a Lack of Cooperation

The people who do not have to try the case will bravely announce, "I'd try that case." The people who do not have to do the cross-examination are the people who will tell you how much fun this examination will be. It always looks easy to the outsider — or at least easier. Trial in general, and cross-examination in particular, is almost never easy. There is the central fact that the opponent's witnesses will not be cooperating with the cross-examiner. Every witness has an agenda. As a result, it is virtually impossible to accurately replicate the trial cross-examination experience. But it is possible to mentally replicate the lack of cooperation that is likely in trial.

In preparing for trial, the veteran trial lawyer as much as the beginner benefits from envisioning where the conflicts are likely. When the cross-examiner has sourced a fact (see chapter 6, *Page Preparation of Cross-Examination*), she has no fear of the possibility of denial. If denial occurs, it is followed promptly by impeachment. Where the cross-examiner must be most attentive in preparation is in those chapters, or those parts of chapters, where the facts are critical but independent proof does not exist. She must carefully construct these chapters. As part of that preparation the cross-examiner should envision the likely methods any witness may use to deny the leading question. What excuses will the witness give? What alternative facts might the witness insert? If the witness says "no," are there methods of incorporating that answer rather then fighting it?

In other words, the practice of cross-examination requires the expectation of things gone wrong. Things gone right take care of themselves. Once the trial lawyer is accustomed to scenario planning for the problem areas and answers, those answers in trial no longer take the lawyer by surprise. The lawyer would be delighted with the "yes" answer, but has conceived of how to deal with alternatives. Often the result of this exercise is the crafting of additional chapters that establish what seemed to be minor facts, all with the intention of blocking the escapes or excuses likely to be offered by the hostile witness. Before the deposition, the advocate should concentrate on how the witness is likely to evade questions in particularly important chapters. She can then can ask more questions in those chapters and establish more facts so as to either block the likely excuse or evasion or appreciate exactly how the evasion will occur at trial.

To be forewarned is to be forearmed. The advocate must constantly keep in mind that it is impossible to form a bulletproof cross-examination of any duration. One of the objects of pre-trial preparation is to weed out chapters that will not work. Identifying the battles that cannot be won allows the cross-examiner to find the theory of the case so as to accommodate those weaknesses.

A tremendous amount of trial skill can be acquired by the acts of cross-examination preparation. Yes, the full interaction between the advocate and the witness can occur only when a witness is under oath and facing cross-examination. But everything that allows a lawyer to create control of that cross-examination can be practiced and implemented before trial.

§ 13.07 Traditional Deposition Methods Employing Open-Ended Questions Do Not Produce the Most Usable Results

Civil firms have long depended on the taking of depositions as a method of enabling the inexperienced advocate to learn cross-examination skills outside the courtroom. Properly used, depositions are an excellent method of acquiring cross-examination skills. However, in order to get the best value out of a deposition, both as a training and trial preparation tool, it is necessary to abandon the notion that depositions are purely discovery devices. This is especially important in a case where many witnesses live in faraway locations and cannot be compelled to attend trial. In those cases, depositions are often the trial, or at least the trial testimony of that witness. Asking exclusively open-ended questions at depositions automatically puts the witness in control of the flow of facts. Practicing how to ask open-ended questions does not produce aggressive and accurate cross-examiners.

Furthermore, the Rules of Evidence at a deposition are phenomenally different from the Rules of Evidence at trial. The lawyer can easily be lulled into bad habits such as poor question formation, inadequate evidentiary foundations, and conclusory questioning. It is customary in civil practice to reserve objections other than the form of the questions until the time of trial. Further, most depositions are conducted in a discovery fashion of open-ended, direct examination-type questions. This lack of structure may be fine for discovery, but it is clearly a sin in trial.

While it is beyond the parameters of this book to discuss the myriad tactics of deposition practice, it must be stated forcefully that there is ample room in depositions for the use of leading questions, posing one new fact per question, with the facts organized in logical progressions to specific goals. Clearly the deposition cannot be properly conducted until the advocate has developed a theory of the case. A deposition unaided by a theory is not trial-focused discovery.

Where possible in depositions, the advocate is advised to establish through leading questions the facts she wishes to deploy at trial. Those facts should be established in short questions, not through an invitation for an answer that might contain desired facts. Where possible, the lawyer ought to refrain from taking the most important depositions until document discovery has taken place. In this way the lawyer may appear at the deposition armed with the documents that can be used to gain admissions, impeach where necessary, and allow the lawyer to engage in detailed cross-examinations on critical aspects of the case.

§ 13.08 Pre-trial Experience Using the Techniques of Cross-Examination Develops Confidence

The techniques set out in this book are designed to develop the abilities of the trial lawyer. The techniques set out in this chapter are designed to instill confidence in the trial lawyer. Confidence is the intangible factor that marks not the experienced trial lawyer — but the capable trial lawyer. The advocate who has practiced the techniques of cross-examination instinctively feels more comfortable using those techniques at trial. That comfort level shows. Strangely enough, it shows by a lack of unusual mannerisms rather than by the ostentatious display of ego or technique. In other words, confidence breeds a focused attitude in the trial lawyer. The most noticeable aspect about a trial lawyer comfortable with her techniques and her abilities is her lack of wasted energy.

The confident lawyer unconsciously but continuously exhibits her confidence to the jury in many forms. The jury is more inclined and almost compelled to believe and trust that lawyer. Self-confidence motivates others. Use of the leading question technique alone displays great confidence. It tells everyone in the courtroom that the lawyer views herself as a master of the facts. By assuming the role of a teacher rather than a student of the facts, the lawyer expresses her confidence that the facts of the case fairly lead to a verdict in favor of her client.

How does a trial lawyer master the techniques to build confidence? The following sections discuss several methods in learning and polishing cross-examination techniques in all pre-trial stages in which witnesses can be examined under oath.

§ 13.09 A Real Witness Deserves a Real Cross-Examination

The science and techniques appropriate for trial are likewise largely appropriate for pre-trial hearings. While there may be tactical reasons to use open-ended questions in certain pre-trial proceedings, the general theories of teaching do not change. In fact, much of the ability to successfully cross-examine at trial is dependent on the advocate's pre-trial adherence to the only three rules of cross-examination and the chapter method (see chapter 5, *The Chapter Method of Cross-Examination*).

If at a pre-trial hearing, deposition, interrogatory, or other discovery procedure, cross-examining counsel asks a compound question, the value of the resulting answer is markedly decreased value for impeachment at trial:

Q: Did you see the car coming down the highway at a high rate of speed, try to avoid hitting the truck, but then crash into the rear of the truck?

A: Yes.

Analysis: Yes to what fact? Because the questioning counsel has violated the rule of one fact per question, the resulting answer is ambiguous. If the witness apparently changes his answer to any *one* of the above facts during trial, the witness can explain that the pre-trial answer applied only to one or some but not all of the facts contained in the question.

By adhering to the one-fact-per-question format, questioning counsel produces a usable transcript. Regardless of the content of the answer, counsel must require the witness to give a clear answer.

While trials have become less frequent, the questioning of witnesses in some pre-trial proceedings is more frequent. Criminal law has preliminary hearings. Civil law has pre-trial challenges to experts and numerous depositions. These forums, as well as any other pre-trial forum in which advocates confront witnesses, are ideal opportunities to practice the science and techniques of cross-examination.

There is not a skill in this book that cannot be applied in a pre-trial setting. While it is true there will be no jury to hear the spontaneous loop or pick up on the theme, there is still a witness who is trying to dodge and deny. There is still a cross-examiner who needs to clarify, amplify, and impeach. Often, there is still a fact finder present who is learning facts and gauging credibility. For tactical reasons, a trial lawyer may elect not to try a particular technique at a pre-trial hearing (perhaps in order to save an impeachment for trial or gain more discovery through open-ended questions). The fact remains that when the lawyer elects to use a technique, the method of presentation in a pre-trial hearing need not be different than that which would be used in trial.

As a result, this description of the practice and techniques in pre-trial settings is relatively short: *That which the cross-examiner would want to do in trial should be practiced in pre-trial settings.* The DEA agent on the stand at a motion to suppress statements can be led, looped, and impeached in the same manner as if a jury were present. In fact, a fact finder is present. While judges are fond of saying, "Counsel, this isn't trial," the fact is they comprise a jury of one. The elements of persuasion do not change. The trial lawyer hoping to better her skills as a cross-examiner is best advised to press ahead in the same meticulous manner, using the appropriate voice tones and movements, and applying the same techniques as if a jury were present.

§ 13.10 Cross-Examining at Depositions

Civil lawyers are both blessed and cursed with a potentially large deposition practice. Too often, these affairs become tedious and unending: "And what happened next?" While these questions have their place, and the use of a deposition to gain discovery is understood, there are almost always large parts of a deposition that should be conducted in leading questions performed one fact at a time, building toward establishment of a goal.

Whether the deposition is going to be used in lieu of testimony at trial or whether it is for discovery purposes and to prepare the lawyer for the trial cross-examination, it is critical that the cross-examining lawyer apply lessons found in chapter 4, *The Only Three Rules of Cross-Examination*, and question along the goal-oriented lines discussed in chapter 5, *The Chapter Method of Cross-Examination*. The lawyer should use loops, spontaneous loops, establishment of theme, and other techniques. These techniques are all designed to establish control of the witness, and witness control is as critical to success at a deposition as in a trial setting. Furthermore, if the lawyer's goal is to create a transcript that can be used later for impeachment, precise answers to single-fact questions are a requirement. A witness who can successfully evade at a pre-trial hearing or churns out damaging information in the form of non-responsive answers must be sanctioned at the preliminary proceeding, lest he learn bad habits and devices that he can use against the lawyer at trial.

Far better that the witness should learn to answer the question put to him truthfully the first time. It is better if the lawyer emerges from the deposition with particular, dependable answers, rather than with a mushy transcript worthless for impeachment purposes. It is far better to know the witness's answer than to know that the witness prefers not to answer. For all these reasons, the cross-examiner is advised to practice the techniques of cross-examination at every occasion in which cross-examination is called for, including depositions.

§ 13.11 Pre-trial Presentation Equals Trial Presentation

There is yet another reason to continually practice trial techniques in non-trial settings. The pre-trial use of appropriate cross-examination techniques mentally trains and conditions the lawyer to rely upon those techniques as the foundation of trial cross-examination. At the time of trial, there is much confusion, anxiety, and interruption. There is less time for the cross-examiner to concentrate on how to do a task. Certain techniques — such as one new fact per question, building toward a specific goal, use of loops and spontaneous loops — must become such a practiced part of the cross-examiner's repertoire that they can be effortlessly formed in the trial setting. The easiest way to condition a mind to do these complex tasks successfully is to practice them at every opportunity.

The same is true with tone of voice, movement, impeachment, and other skills designed to have a particular impact on a jury. First, tone, timing, and emphasis work best when applied naturally to the questions the lawyer is asking. The advocate needs to concentrate on the facts and allow her moods and voice to flow in conjunction with the leading questions. As she practices the techniques of short, one-new-fact-per-question leading questions, she is simultaneously preparing herself to behave naturally in the courtroom. Cross-examination is a teaching opportunity, not an acting opportunity.

The harsh tone of voice that becomes offensive in front of a jury is equally offensive in a deposition or preliminary hearing. Better to practice more moderate tones of voice and changing tones of voice in a non-trial setting. Practice in a pre-trial setting gives the lawyer the comfort to perform the technique automatically and confidently in front of the jury.

§ 13.12 Use of Pre-trial Cross-Examinations to Train the Witness

Just as trial lawyers pattern their minds to the practice of techniques in pre-trial settings, so do witnesses. A witness learns what is expected, what he can get away with, what is safe, and what responses will be punished. It is dangerous to allow the witness to be in control at a pre-trial setting, since it encourages him to seek control during trial. The trial lawyer has a variety of techniques for bringing the witness back under control at trial (see chapter 9, *Controlling the Runaway Witness*), but the cross-examiner would be better off if these techniques were not needed because she had already taught the witness to respond honestly and directly to leading questions. Hence, the use of the only three rules of cross-examination at a pre-trial setting trains the witness to respond to that form of questioning when trial occurs. The closed-ended, one-fact-per-question method of building toward a goal programs a witness to deliver the short, responsive answer required of them at trial.

Again, it must be acknowledged that some pre-trial matters, whether motions to suppress, hearings challenging the admissibility of an expert's opinion, deposition practice, or preliminary hearings, are engaged for purposes not limited to discovery. In such an instance, it may be that many open-ended questions are asked. However, the answer, when favorable to the position of the lawyer, can be looped and re-established in multiple closed-ended questions. The fact can be cemented in place and put in context. Finally, a transcript can be built with such clarity that any changes by the witness at trial can be impeached.

Lawyers are fond of saying that they are taking a "discovery" deposition. The jargon is well understood, but the translation may be inappropriate. Depositions need not be a wholesale fishing expedition in an attempt to see what the witness will answer about the case. It should be, in pertinent part, the establishment of answers already known to the cross-examiner that she will depend upon at trial. Some part of what the witness says may be new. Much should be responses to leading questions.

Whether the deponent is an eyewitness to an auto accident, a doctor performing an independent medical examination of the plaintiff, or an accident reconstructionist hired by the defense, he can be handled through leading questions. In each instance, matters that can impeach witnesses at trial can impeach them at pre-trial hearings or even at depositions. If the witness is going to falter at the pre-trial hearing or deposition, it is better to find out now than at trial. The tests performed, the results obtained, things seen and not seen, all can be established through leading questions that rein in and pin down the witness. A well-choreographed cross-examination done in a chapter format establishing these facts through hostile witnesses at pre-trial hearings and depositions may be the single greatest way to prevail in the case without the necessity of the trial. In that regard, the pre-trial hearing or deposition is nothing but an extension of the trial — it is part of the advocacy designed to prevail in the case. It should be given the same attention, sophisticated preparation, and execution of technique called upon at trial.

§ 13.13 Pre-trial Cross-Examination Preparation

It is ironic that lawyers will stay up nights and work weekends preparing for a trial but seem less willing to put in an hour or two of preparation for a pre-trial hearing or deposition that could obviate the necessity of trial. The well-honed cross-examination that results in suppression of a statement or evidence in the criminal case may take a fraction of the time of a trial. Damaging admissions made by the opponent's expert witness at a deposition can frequently lead to a favorable settlement. The facts established in a deposition may well cripple the opponent's theory of the case. In fact, it is easier to obtain useful admissions in a deposition of any trial because opponents ordinarily spend less time preparing the witness for deposition than for a trial. If the cross-examiner's goal is to prevail on behalf of her client, then pre-trial hearings and depositions must be accorded their just place as major events in the case. They are worthy of preparation and application of technique so as to arm the cross-examiner should trial occur.

In this light, time spent scientifically preparing and executing cross-examinations prior to trial is a better use of time than performing pre-trial matters in a cursory way. Lawyers who hear themselves doing trial-level cross-examinations at pre-trial hearings are hearing the sounds of success. When the lawyer hears herself spontaneously loop an answer, create a trilogy, establish a theme, control a witness, build a chapter, or establish a goal, she is hearing superb advocacy. Superb advocacy is always rewarded. The trial is not the primary showcase for the lawyer's talent. It is never a waste of talent and time to diligently cross-examine in pre-trial settings.

§ 13.14 Preparation and Practice Are Their Own Rewards

It has already been pointed out that such diligent preparation and presentation may obviate the necessity of trial. Good advocacy is its own reward. The cross-examiner becomes accustomed to applying techniques under difficult circumstances. The techniques of effective cross-examination can become matters of rote. The cross-examiner gains confidence in the use of leading questions, looping, impeachment by inconsistent statement, voice, tone and movement, and a host of other techniques. Her practice of techniques in non-trial settings results in added courtroom confidence. As a result of the confident employment of the fundamental techniques of cross-examination, counsel is rewarded by better control of opposing witnesses. In addition, her practice of the only three rules of cross-examination enables the advocate to better teach her case to jurors who are then more in tune with the facts that support her theory of the case.

As the cross-examiner's ability to teach complex facts to the jury grows, better verdicts are obtained. The lawyer's sense of integrity grows. As the courts learn that the lawyer is willing to depend on preparation and the application of ethical and understated techniques rather then trickery and overly emotional or abusive cross-examination styles, the courts grant more latitude to the lawyer in trial. The judge's respect for the lawyer's ability to ferret out facts and establish goals leads to broader parameters of cross-examination. For all of these reasons, the best method for perfecting the science and techniques of cross-examination is to practice them at *all* pre-trial opportunities, regardless of the audience or format. The trial lawyer should learn a single system of preparation.

Chapter 14

HOW TO MASTER THE TECHNIQUES WITHOUT TRIAL EXPERIENCE

§ 14.01 Innovative Training Exercises

It is exciting to be a trial lawyer. There is a mystique. But how can trial lawyers learn to do the job more effectively? Clients and employers are hesitant to give newer lawyers the opportunities we need to learn, refine, and polish cross-examination techniques.

Happily, the techniques of cross-examination can be learned and practiced outside of trial. Available are additional innovative teaching devices that allow lawyers to practice the fundamental skills of cross-examination. It is possible to learn to be a good cross-examiner adept at the techniques of cross-examination even if the lawyer has little access to witnesses in a trial setting. These same exercises permit more experienced lawyers to identify and correct poor habits.

§ 14.02 Cross-Examining Inanimate Objects

Future surgeons practice on cadavers. Future dentists practice carving chalk. Trial lawyers can take a lesson from these practices. Trial lawyers need to search out alternatives to practicing on live witnesses.

The ultimate objective of any cross-examination should be for the jury to visualize and otherwise understand the specific goal of the cross-examiner in such a way as to make the objective unforgettable to the jury during deliberations. The jury must be on such intimate terms with the objective of the cross-examiner.

The cross-examination of inanimate objects is a training technique that can be practiced anywhere, at anytime. There is no need for another participant. Therefore the cross-examiner can practice this technique much like the swimmer who practices laps for hours and the golfer who practices a swing repeatedly.

There are levels of difficulty in this training technique and, therefore, it is suggested that the participant begin with the simplest of inanimate objects, such as a bar of Ivory soap. There is something pure with this type of start.

Remove the soap wrapper. By using strictly leading questions, developing one fact per question and progressing from the most general to the most specific, direct questions to the bar of soap. Assuming the bar of soap could speak, it would have to utter the response "yes" to every question:

(1) You are an inanimate object?

(2) You are a three-dimensional figure?

(3) You are rectangular in shape?

(4) You are approximately four inches long?

(5) You are approximately two-and-a-half inches wide?

(6) You are approximately one-and-a-half inches deep?

(7) You are white in color?

(8) The edges of your sides are rounded?

(9) There is the word "Ivory" pressed into you?

(10) There is the word "Ivory" on two of your sides?

(11) The word "Ivory" is on the sides with the dimensions four by two and a half?

The lawyer has to develop further the line of inquiry in regard to the other senses, with the final question being: "You are a bath-size bar of Ivory soap?" If the soap actually answers, stop — you've been speaking too long with inanimate objects.

This example produces an idea of what can be done with any simple inanimate object. What at first blush seems a useless exercise is, in reality, a superb method of ingraining the three rules of cross-examination: (1) leading questions only; (2) one new fact at a time; and (3) leading toward a definable goal. These rules are short, simple and straightforward. However, non-courtroom practice is necessary to ingrain the techniques.

§ 14.03 Cross-Examining in the Office

The inanimate object technique can be turned into a game involving two people. Time in the office can be used to practice cross-examination techniques. This practice method does not require a second lawyer. Any person with an interest in the questioning process is fair game. This second person will play the devil's advocate and will assess whether the lawyer has put too many facts into a question, whether the lawyer is proceeding from the general to a specific goal in a logical progression, and whether the lawyer has correctly formed the question in a leading manner. This person takes on the voice of the inanimate object — looking for an opportunity to say "no," claim a lack of understanding of the question, and otherwise voice the accurate responses of the inanimate object. Why bother? Because the greatest strength of the cross-examiner is derived from the cross-examiner's ability to command an absolutely unbroken string of "yes" answers to a series of tightly controlled factual inquiries. When the game becomes boring, the lawyer has internalized the basic techniques of witness control.

Any of the non-lawyers can be given a script of facts to follow. Take it from a case, a former trial advocacy course, a factual pattern that has been experienced in the practice, or simply make up the facts. But reduce them to writing so that all players are following the same script.

First step: Practice short chapters of leading questions.

In much the same way that the lawyer cross-examined the inanimate object, the lawyer can cross-examine these living, willing witnesses. Of course, the cross-examiner wants to start as simply as possible with short chapters of cross-examination (see chapter 5, *The Chapter Method of Cross-Examination*) with short intermediate goals. Remember, the object is to make the fundamental rules of cross-examination instinctual. As these skills develop, the cross-examiner will progress to more difficult scenarios and use more advanced techniques. This exercise is one of the best for working on advanced techniques, such as loops or spontaneous loops.

While this practice method can be used by a single lawyer cross-examining a witness, the addition of a second opposing lawyer substantially toughens the exercise. First, an adversary keeps the cross-examiner honest.

Not only would your adversary object to questions soliciting clearly impermissible evidence (hearsay as an example), but the opponent is also charged with the responsibility of objecting to violations of the three rules of cross-examination, i.e., objecting to non-leading questions, sequences of questions that do not progress logically from a general topic to a more specific goal, and questions that contain too many facts per question within them.

Second step: Practice techniques that block redirect examinations.

In the second step of this cross-examination exercise, at the conclusion of the cross-examination, the lawyer who has cross-examined the witness must endure the redirect examination from the opponent. This will assist in teaching the lawyer how to foresee dangerous redirect examinations and apply techniques that close doors to render redirect examinations more difficult.

Third step: Play the role of a witness.

The final step in this three-step process within the law office is for the lawyer to become the witness and the witness to become the lawyer. It does not matter if the witness who becomes the lawyer is not trained in the law. The importance of the exercise is that the lawyer will experience the cross-examination from the receiving end. Through this exercise, the lawyer will be able to watch from the witness chair the frustration of an examiner when the questions are not formed carefully enough, when the questions contain too many facts, and when the questions do not proceed from a general to specific goal. The lawyer, as witness, will be able to test methods of derailing a cross-examination. As a result, the lawyer will better understand the pitfalls that await the disorganized or inattentive cross-examiner.

§ 14.04 Training as a Witness Helps Prepare for the Witness

It does not take long for the lawyer who assumes the role of the witness to understand how a witness thinks and what evasions a witness will use to avoid the question. The lawyer will be surprised, however, at how quickly the lawyer in this exercise develops the basic skills of cross-examination. The process has three steps. The first lawyer conducts a cross-examination. The second lawyer conducts redirect examination. The first lawyer then plays the witness on cross-examination. For each lawyer working in the process, the procedure is completed.

§ 14.05 Group Cross-Examination (The Exercise of Cluster Cross)

Just as in the cross-examination in the office training exercise, the exercise of cluster cross-training sequence regards the lawyer as a participant in a group setting. That is, in the law office setting the lawyer plays both the role of the lawyer and the role of a witness to experience the emotions felt by the witness, i.e., to look at the courtroom from "the other side."

In this exercise, the lawyer is teamed with other lawyers who ask questions one at a time in rotation. The true learning concept of this exercise is based on the fact that no lawyer criticizes herself well enough to understand that she is her own worst enemy on cross-examination.

Often, the lawyer feels frustration and, at times, humiliation when the lawyer's twentieth question results in an answer that destroys the preceding nineteen questions. The lawyer is unwilling to search those questions for the fatal error, which often occurred at the tenth or eleventh question in that cross-examination.

Because one lawyer follows another lawyer in this sequence, and the goal is to eliminate all other lawyers from the game or exercise, each lawyer can "hear" the errors of other participants that she would not "hear" from her own mouth.

§ 14.06 Official Rules of Cluster Cross

The purpose of the exercise is to reinforce the basic rules of cross-examination. It will refine and highlight the need for a detailed analysis of the progression of a particular cross-examination for the more advanced cross-examiner.

Obviously required are closed-ended questions, one fact per question, and questions that proceed from the general to the specific. Knowing when to sit down is also required.

The exercise requires each participant to listen and be patient with questioning so as not to become too aggressive.

§ 14.07 How the Exercise Is Conducted

A participant asks one question. Then the rotation begins. All all other participants ask one question before returning to the first participant to ask a second question.

§ 14.08 Objections and Disqualifications

The instructor (if there is one) and all participants may object. If an objection is sustained, the participant who asked the question is removed from the exercise, and may not participate further unless the removed participant makes an objection that is sustained. If that participant makes an objection that is sustained, that participant re-enters the exercise.

The instructor, if there is one, rules on all objections. If there is no instructor, one participant is selected to make the rulings. There are no appeals. Some types of objections include:

(1) Failure to ask a leading question;

(2) Failure to have only one fact per question;

(3) Failure to proceed logically from point A (general point) to point B (specific point), the goal.

(4) Greed — when a participant does not logically follow the sequence of the preceding questions and takes too large a jump toward the objective (results with the next participant having no ability to ask a question that will receive a "yes" answer).

(5) Backsliding — when a participant is unsure of where to proceed, that participant often backslides. Instead of going to point B, the participant backslides towards point A.

(6) Delay of Exercise — when participants are unsure of the direction in which to proceed, they stammer, shift feet, and otherwise wiggle. It is in the discretion of the participants before the exercise begins as to what time limit will be placed on each question.

(7) Breaking Character — too often when frustrated, a participant will attempt to break character and discuss some point, either with other participants or the instructor. This is more clever than delay of exercise but equally objectionable.

(8) Couch Potato Objection — when a poor objection is made from one of the participants, that participant suffers disqualification if the objection has no reasonable good faith basis.

(9) Lame — when the progression is so slow and so minuscule as to alienate the jury, the objection of "lame" is made. This objection should not be sustained normally, as it is much safer to proceed very slowly towards the objective rather than becoming too aggressive and skipping ahead.

§ 14.09 Goal

It is essential that everyone agree on the well-defined goal before the exercise begins. If the goal is not clearly defined, there will inevitably be arguments over whether a question leads to the established goal.

§ 14.10 End of Exercise

When a participant feels that more questions are unnecessary and potentially counterproductive, the participant may state "no more questions." If it is felt that this is appropriate, the goal has been reached, and the remaining participants in the exercise have won. However, in the event that additional questions need to be asked, that participant who states "no more questions" is eliminated and the questioning continues in rotation with the remaining participants.

Conversely, if a participant should say "no more questions" and does not, that is subject to an objection and, if sustained, that participant who asks the "one question too many" is eliminated.

§ 14.11 Timing

The cluster cross-exercise should be used periodically throughout the teaching of cross-examination. A limited, relatively straightforward, factual situation is recommended so that there can be clearly established goals.

§ 14.12 A Brief Example of a Cluster Cross

Instructor: The goal that we are to reach is to ask this witness to admit that she could not see the defendant at a bus stop on First Avenue as she walked up Main Street, an intersecting street. There was a building between her line of travel and the bus stop. It did not have any windows or doors through which to see the defendant. The witness did eventually see a man walking away from her on First Avenue when she reached the intersection of Main Street and First Avenue, but his back was to her. On direct examination, she testified that she saw the defendant and described his face and other features.

For purposes of this exercise, it is imperative that the witness be controlled so she will not be able to testify that she saw him standing at the bus stop before he turned his back and started to walk away from her. Example:

Participant 1: You were walking on Main Street?

Answer: Yes.

Participant 2: You were walking on Main Street towards the intersection of First Avenue?

Answer: Yes.

Participant 3: You never saw the defendant while you were on Main Street?

Participant 4: Objection. Greed.

Instructor: Sustained. Participant 3 is out of the exercise.

Participant 4: As you walked towards that intersection you were on the sidewalk on the left-hand side of the street?

Participant 3: Objection.

Instructor: On what grounds?

Participant 3: There is only supposed to be one fact in the question. He asked two. Both the fact that there was a sidewalk and that the person was on the left-hand side of the street.

Instructor: That is true, but that is very close to "lame." Participant 4, you are now out of the exercise. Participant 3, you are back in.

Participant 5: You were walking on the sidewalk?

Answer: Yes.

Participant 6: The sidewalk that you were walking on was on the left-hand side of the street?

Answer: Yes.

Participant 7: . . .

Participant 6: Objection. Delay of exercise.

Instructor: She only waited eight seconds to start her question. Overruled. Participant 6, you are out of the exercise.

Participant 6: I cannot believe that was only eight seconds; it seemed like more than an hour.

Instructor: I am sure that it would feel that way to a jury as well.

Participant 7: You were walking towards the intersection of First Avenue?

Participant 6: Objection. Backsliding.

Instructor: Sustained. Participant 7, you are out of the exercise. Participant 6, you are back in.

Participant 8: There was a building to your left?

Answer: Yes.

Participant 1: That building has no windows on the bottom floor?

Answer: That is correct.

Participant 2: That building has no doors with windows in them on the bottom floor?

Answer: Yes.

Participant 3: That building blocked your view of First Avenue?

Participant 7: Objection. Failure to have only one fact in a question.

Instructor: I am not sure on this one.

Participant 7: The witness could see portions of First Avenue.

Instructor: Oh yeah, that's right. Sustained. Participant 3, you are out of the exercise. Participant 7, you are back in.

Participant 5: The building prevented you from seeing to your left and to the left of the building?

Answer: That is true.

Participant 6: You know there is a bus stop on First Avenue near that intersection?

Answer: Yes.

Participant 7: That bus stop is to the left of the building, to the left of that intersection?

Answer: Yes.

Participant 8: You could not see through the building to see the bus stop as you were walking up Main Street?

Answer: That is true.

The exercise continues.

§ 14.13 Practicing Techniques in Non-Legal Settings

Too often the lawyer views cross-examination as applicable only to the courtroom or courtroom-like settings. Nothing could be further from the truth.

Interviews employ the same skills required as the courtroom setting. Discussion of office procedure with partners and employees often require similar skills. On a more broad-based view, talking with anyone at any time can be used to develop these skills.

For example, a lawyer meets an attractive member of the opposite sex at a holiday cocktail party. The lawyer wants to get to know that person, so she initiates a conversation. After introducing herself, to develop more information about this person, she begins to ask questions. Not only can she ask these questions in a direct examination format eliciting open-ended responses, but she can also develop cross-examination questions that are designed to give the listener as much information about her as she is asking about the listener.

As another example, from time to time, lawyers must purchase something, such as clothes or a gallon of milk on the way home from the office. They can use this opportunity as a quick experiment to practice one or more of the techniques for controlling the runaway witness.

The lawyer might ask why she would use this in buying a retail item. The answer is simple.. Salespeople volunteer continuously. They never answer the question that you ask. They always want to give the customer more information than requested.

The lawyer goes into a store. She is short of time but wants to purchase a pair of jeans. She asks the salesperson for a certain brand. The salesperson does not have it and tries to steer her to another brand. The lawyer utilizes the repeat, repeat, reverse technique:

Customer: Sir, do you have a pair of Bugle Boy jeans?

Salesperson: Well, actually those are not very much in style any more. What we prefer to sell is Jordache. They are much more popular and fit better.

Customer: You have a pair of Bugle Boy jeans?

Salesperson: As I was saying, we prefer Jordache, but if that is not good for you, Calvin Klein is excellent. Much better than Bugle Boy.

Customer: You don't have a pair of Bugle Boy jeans?

Salesperson: Yes, we have them.

In another example, assume that the lawyer is in a grocery checkout line. There must be some rule somewhere that grocery checkout people (except for the express lane) must talk to stay sane. The lawyer may use this opportunity to find out if she can stop a runaway witness by the use of body movements, such as the hand technique, the finger technique, or the head shake technique. For example, the lawyer asks. “Isn't it a shame that the tomatoes are not as large or as firm as they once were?” The cashier responds by saying yes and discusses the weather, the time of the year, and the season. The lawyer simply raises his or her hand in a stop motion. As a result, the cashier stops the conversation and quietly continues to ring up the purchase. The cashier never voluntarily enters into conversation again with the lawyer.

In a final example, the lawyer returns home from work. It has been a long and difficult day. Her child's bicycle is in the driveway. She calls the child in to talk with him. This is a cross-examination that no one does well. She uses it as an opportunity to spontaneously loop the child:

Lawyer: Matthew, you left your bike in the driveway, didn't you?

Matthew: Well, I don't know that it is in the driveway. See, what happened was, Dad called me and told me to come in right now and to stop what I was doing. Dad called me to get in this house right now. Dad called me and that is why I left the bike where it was. Then, I tried to tell him that I was going to get in trouble for where the bike was and he told me that he didn't care about that, that he wanted me in the house right that minute.

Lawyer: Then you realized when you left the bike in the driveway that you would get in trouble?

Matthew: Oh, boy. How much trouble, Mom?

This technique can be very hard on families.

§ 14.14 Use of Digital and Videotape Technology

Videotape and digital recording devices have had a revolutionary effect on the preparation of witnesses for trial. Digital recording and videotape offer equally dramatic opportunities to address the trial lawyer's preparation for trial, as well.

The digital or video camera not only is used to film crime scenes, accident scenes, clients wearing neck braces, children at play in lovely surroundings in custody cases, and numerous other evidentiary matters. This visual technology should be an essential means of preparing the lawyer for trial. How the lawyer uses her body movements, tone of voice, and the integration of these activities with the content of the questions can all be enhanced by the use of digital recordings or videotape.

Too often and for too long, trial lawyers stumbled about blindly thinking that they looked, moved, and spoke in a pleasing manner congruent with the theory of the case. After all, each had graduated from law school and become relatively successful in an intensively competitive profession. In each of the previous training exercises, the video or digital camera can be used so the lawyer may review her body language, movement, tone, and the congruency of those activities with the theory of the case.

Some may ask, "Why would I want to videotape myself asking a bar of Ivory soap what color it is?" While asking those questions, watch the lawyer's face. Are the lawyer's eyes scrunched so tight in concentration that she appears to be in need of vision correction? If so, the expression may be worse when the lawyer is questioning a living, breathing witness under the microscope of the courtroom setting.

When the lawyer asked the bar of Ivory soap a non-leading question and caught herself, did she visually react in such a way that everyone watching her would know that she somehow had made an error? If this were true while the lawyer was cross-examining a bar of Ivory soap, it would be more evident in the courtroom.

If this short discussion has not convinced you of the need for digital or video technology to enhance trial preparation and learn vital trial skills, take ten minutes and record yourself performing a cross-examination. Play the tape back. Within this time, if you do not verify for yourself that a digital recording or videotape is essential to development as a trial lawyer, dispense with it.

§ 14.15 Practice Does Not Make Perfect; Practice Makes Permanent

These exercises may seem sophomoric to experienced trial lawyers. They may seem beneath the lawyer. The fact is that each lawyer wants to become better a cross-examiner. That's why we wrote the book. That's why you purchased it.

Whether we analyze cross-examination minutely or have a visceral feeling for cross-examination, we know that we need to do it better. Each of these exercises is designed to improve the skills of the cross-examiner. Each of these exercises is designed to permit us to cross-examine in a safe and comfortable setting. Pick those exercises that will best enhance the skills you need as a trial lawyer. Practice your techniques before trial. The reward is that you will experience trial as a less stressful experience, supported by familiar techniques.

INDEX

D

E

F

G

H

I

L

M

N

O

P

R

S

T

Notes

Notes

Notes

Notes

Notes

Notes

Notes

Notes

Notes

Notes